MUHAMMAD AND THE
ORIGINS OF ISLAM

SUNY Series in Near Eastern Studies
Said Amir Arjomand, Editor

Ann E. Mayer, ed., *Property, Social Structure, and Law in the Modern Middle East*

I. P. Petrushevsky/trans. Hubert Evans, *Islam in Iran*

Hamied Ansari, *Egypt: The Stalled Society*

S. N. Eisenstadt, *The Origins and Diversity of Axial Age Civilizations*

Said Amir Arjomand, ed., *Authority and Political Culture in Shi'ism*

Sajida Sultana Alvi, trans., *Advice on the Art of Governance (Mau'izahi-i Jahangiri) of Muhammad Baqir Najm-i Sani: An Indo-Islamic Mirror for Princes*

Serif Mardin, *Religion and Social Change in Modern Turkey: The Case of Bediuzzaman Said Nursi*

Emmanuel Sivan and Menachem Friedman, eds., *Religious Radicalism and Politics in the Middle East*

Said Amir Arjomand, ed., *The Political Dimensions of Religion*

F. E. Peters, *Muhammad and the Origins of Islam*

The History of al-Tabari
33 volumes to date, various editors and translators
First volumes published in 1985

MUHAMMAD AND THE ORIGINS OF ISLAM

F. E. PETERS

State University
of New York
Press

Published by
State University of New York Press, Albany

Production by Susan Geraghty
Marketing by Dana Yanulavich

For information, address State University of New York Press,
State University Plaza, Albany, N.Y., 12246

Library of Congress Cataloging-in-Publication Data

Peters, F. E. (Francis E.)
    Muhammad and the origins of Islam / F. E. Peters.
        p.   cm. — (SUNY series in Near Eastern studies)
    Includes bibliographical references and index.
    ISBN 0–7914–1875–8 (alk. paper). — ISBN 0–7914–1876–6 (pbk. :
alk. paper)
    1. Muḥammad, Prophet, d. 632. I. Title. II. Series.
BP75..P4 1994
297'.63—dc20   93–10568
                                                              CIP

10 9 8 7 6 5 4 3 2 1

For Ian and Gina Peters,
a small gift

CONTENTS

PREFACE

Muhammad stands at the Islamic center, of course, as he has from the beginning; and those who have sought to stand beside him, or even perhaps within him, have essayed biographies of the Prophet of Islam.[1] Whatever the value of the individual author's insights, these are not all on the same scale, of course, or of the same critical merit, and undoubtedly Montgomery Watt's two-volume life of Muhammad written at the mid-century has become the standard for students and scholars alike. Works of such magnitude and conviction usually signal a pause, the reshaping of a new *communis opinio*, and such seems to have occurred here: no one has since attempted a like enterprise in English. But if Watt's two volumes closed one large door, they opened many others. From 1960, when M. J. Kister began his remarkable labors in Jerusalem, down to the present, investigation of the life of Muhammad, and particularly the religious environment of his native Mecca, has been one of the most productive and provocative areas in the entire field of Islamic studies.

The present work is biographical, but it is at the same time something broader. It is an inquiry—or perhaps a joint inquiry because the reader will be provided with the same sources available to the historian—into the religious environment of the person Muslims hail as the "Envoy of God" and an attempt to trace his progress along the path from paganism to that distinctive form of monotheism called *Islam*. The Arabic *islam* means "submission," and though we may never come to any firm conviction as to why this man first "submitted" to the Almighty God in Western Arabia in the seventh Christian century, then persistently and persuasively convinced others to do likewise, we do have at hand a large body of evidence to enable us to try, as well as a long tradition of scholarship from Muslims and non-Muslims who have gone before along this way.

However long the search has gone on, the "quest of the historical Muhammad" is still surrounded by enormous difficulties from both the growth and encrustations of centuries of pious regard and the difficulty of the source material. The historian must tackle both. The removal of the first is a painful process to many Muslims, who are not as accustomed as Jews and Christians to the abrasive burr of the so-called "higher criticism." But in the end, it is the latter, the provenance, reliability, and sometimes the sheer intractibility of our sources, that has made the quest so arduous and the results appear at times so exiguous. This is an issue that must be addressed, but it is highly technical, and rather than put such daunting stuff between the reader and the subject of this book, I have placed in an appendix. Readers who may wisely wish to inspect the ground beneath their feet before stepping onto the path before them are invited to turn immediately to the appendix entitled "The Quest of the Historical Muhammad" and begin there.

I started this work a number of years ago, first in a classroom, and not without some trepidation—but with a sense of inevitability. Islam is not my faith, but it is assuredly my profession, and this is where both my professional training and my professional and personal inclination has now at last lead. It is not a work written out of either piety or zeal for polemic, but from a keen interest in one of the liveliest and most important subjects in human history: how did this man come to announce in that place a religious message that hundreds of millions across the face of the planet still regard as the authentic Word of God?

I am not sure that I or anyone else can answer that question in all its enormous complexity, or indeed that any answer offered by a historian would be convincing even to other historians, much less the *mu'minin*, the "believers." My aim is considerably more modest, as will be seen, to cast some additional light on the religious history of Western Arabia and so on the religious past and the contemporary political and religious milieu of the man Muhammad. The light is not my own, assuredly. It comes from others, many others, beginning with Muhammad's own contemporaries and continuing down to the present; and some indeed with those same motives of piety or polemic that I disavowed for myself.

My thanks to my more distant and recent predecessors and contemporaries are in my notes, the acknowledged underpinning of what I have attempted to say. But there is also a kind of *apparatus in pectore* as well, the names of the men and women who have shaped or helped the author and so the work and have no assigned number at the bottom of this page or that. Who is there who has met Mary Peters and would doubt that she should have a superscript number at the bottom of *every* page? Or that E. P. Fitzsimmons should recline across half a column in the index, or that Eamon and Carol Brennan should be prominently displayed, diptych fashion, on the cover flaps? Where is Jill Claster's footnote? Or Eddie Oakes's? Or Ken Zysk's? *In pectore*, gentles, *in pectore*.

ACKNOWLEDGMENTS

Permission is gratefully acknowledged from the publishers to reprint portions of the following copyrighted translations:

Nabih Faris, *Ibn al-Kalbi's Book of Idols,* Princeton: Princeton University Press, 1952.

The Life of Muhammad. A Translation of Ishaq's *Sirat Rasul Allah,* with Introduction and Notes by Alfred Guillaume, Oxford: Oxford University Press, 1955.

The History of al-Tabari, vol. VII, *The Foundations of the Community,* translated by M. V. McDonald, annotated by W. Montgomery Watt, Albany: The State University of New York Press, 1987.

The History of al-Tabari, vol. VI, *Muhammad at Mecca,* translated and annotated by W. Montgomery Watt and M. V. McDonald, Albany: The State University of New York Press, 1988.

The History of al-Tabari, vol. IX, *The Last Years of the Prophet,* translated and annotated by Ismail Poonawala, Albany: The State University of New York Press, 1990.

CHAPTER 1

The Founding Fathers

Such is the celebrity of the later shrine and the growth of the modern city that it is difficult to imagine Mecca in the sixth century of the Christian era, when Muhammad first heard the words of God there. The Quran itself describes it as a place "in a valley without cultivation" (Quran 14: 37), and Ali Bey, a visitor to the city in the early years of the nineteenth century wrote from his own experience the definitive gloss on that verse. Mecca, says Ali Bey, "is situated at the bottom of a sandy valley, surrounded on all sides by naked mountains, without brook, river or any running water; without trees, plants or any species of vegetation" (Ali Bey 1816, vol. 2, p. 112).

For the rest, there was in Muhammad's day only a collection of rude mud huts clustered around a spring and a cubelike house of stone, the dwelling, it was said, of a god. If it was a market town, it was a long way away from the great emporia where a later generation of Arabs imagined their Meccan ancestors traded. At the ordinary pace of a caravan—20 to 25 miles a day, a fairly sprightly pace of 4 miles an hour for six hours a day[1]—Gaza lay thirty-odd days to the north of Mecca, and the Yemeni centers all of that and more to the south.[2]

There were Christians at Gaza and Christians and Jews in the Yemen, but none of either so far as we know at Mecca, where the Quran unfolds in what is unmistakably a pagan milieu. The revelations granted to Muhammad confound and condemn what then passed as divine worship in his native city, to be sure, but their vision is somewhat broader and deeper than the here and now. As the Quran itself makes clear, what was occurring at Mecca in the name of religion was in part the work of a debased paganism, it is true, but it also bore some trace of an earlier tradition, what the Holy Book calls the "religion of Abraham" (2: 130), namely, the practices that God had earlier commanded should be instituted in connection with what is referred to as His "sacred House" (5: 100), or His "ancient House" (22: 29), in that city.

ABRAHAM AND ISHMAEL IN THE HIJAZ

Though the Quran, unlike the Bible, does not begin with Creation—its various revelations address "occasions" rather than develop into a narrative line—it often comments upon it. It knows too about the cosmological Adam, and Noah consistently appears in its enumeration of the prophets sent to humankind; but by the frequency, length and importance of its references to Abraham, it is clear that he is the central figure in the development of God's relations with His human creation, and not merely as a prophet. The Quran is more generous than the Bible in providing details of Abraham's "conversion" to the worship of the One True God (Quran 2: 74–79, 21: 52–71, etc.), but it passes thence directly to Abraham and his son Ishmael in Mecca and God's command to father and son to construct the Ka'ba there.[3]

There is no mention in the Quran of Hagar or Sarah, nor any reference to the Bible's elaborate stories of the early days of Ishmael and Isaac. Their history was left for the later Muslim tradition, and so too was the explanation of how Abraham and Ishmael got from the land of Israel to Mecca. Later writers responded with enthusiasm to the challenge, and there is more than one medieval Muslim version of how it came about. The historian Tabari (d. 923 A.D.) had read a number of them and presented his own conflation of the different traditions on Abraham's transit to the Hijaz of Western Arabia.[4]

> According to . . . al-Suddi: Sarah said to Abraham, "You may take pleasure in Hagar, for I have permitted it." So he had intercourse with Hagar and she gave birth to Ishmael. Then he had intercourse with Sarah and she gave birth to Isaac. When Isaac grew up, he and Ishmael fought. Sarah became angry and jealous of Ishmael's mother. . . . She swore to cut something off her, and said to herself, "I shall cut off her nose, I shall cut off her ear—but no, that would deform her. I will circumcise her instead." So she did that, and Hagar took a piece of cloth to wipe the blood away. For that reason women have been circumcised and have taken pieces of cloth (as sanitary napkins) down to today.

Sarah said, "She will not live in the same town with me." God told Abraham to go to Mecca, where there was no House at that time. He took Hagar and her son to Mecca and put them there. . . .

According to . . . Mujahid and other scholars: When God pointed out to Abraham the place of the House and told him how to build the sanctuary, he set out to do the job and Gabriel went with him. It was said that whenever he passed a town he would ask, "Is this the town which God's command meant, O Gabriel?" And Gabriel would say: "Pass it by." At last they reached Mecca, which at that time was nothing but acacia trees, mimosa, and thorn trees, and there was a people called Amalekites outside Mecca and its surroundings. The House at that time was but a hill of red clay. Abraham said to Gabriel, "Was it here that I was ordered to leave them." Gabriel said, "Yes." Abraham directed Hagar and Ishmael to go to the Hijr,[5] and settled them down there. He commanded Hagar, the mother of Ishmael, to find shelter there. The he said "My Lord, I have settled some of my posterity in an uncultivable valley near Your Holy House . . ." with the quote continuing until " . . . that they may be thankful." (Quran 14: 37) Then he journeyed back to his family in Syria, leaving the two of them at the House.

At his expulsion from Abraham's household, Ishmael must have been about 16-years-old, certainly old enough to assist his father in the construction of the Ka'ba, as described in the Quran and is implicit from the last line of the preceding. Tabari's version of what next occurred is derived from Genesis 21: 15–16, transferred from a Palestinian setting to a Meccan one. Its object is now clearly to provide an "Abrahamic" explanation for some of the features of the Mecca sanctuary and the Islamic *Hajj* or pilgrimage. The helpless Ishmael sounds much younger than 16 in these tales, and some Muslim versions of the story do in fact make him a nursing infant,[6] which means, of course, that Abraham will have to return on a later occasion to build the Ka'ba with his son.[7]

Then Ishmael became very thirsty. His mother looked for water for him, but she could not find any. She listened for sounds to help her find water for him. She heard a sound at al-Safa and went there to look around and found nothing. Then she heard a sound from the direction of al-Marwa. She went there and looked around and saw nothing. Some also say that she stood on al-Safa praying to God for water for Ishmael, and then went to al-Marwa to do the same.

Thus is explained the origin of the pilgrimage ritual of the "running" back and forth between the two hills of Safa and Marwa on the eastern side of the sanctuary.[8] Tabari continues:

> Then she heard the sounds of beasts in the valley where she had left Ishmael. She ran to him and found him scooping the water from a spring which had burst forth from beneath his hand, and drinking from it. Ishmael's mother came to it and made it swampy. Then she drew water from it into her waterskin to keep it for Ishmael. Had she not done that, the waters of Zamzam would have gone on flowing to the surface forever . . . (Tabari, *Annals*, vol. 1, pp. 278–279 = Tabari 1987, pp. 72–74)

The Quran is quite explicit on the subject of Abraham as the builder of God's House, though it describes it with what are to us, at least, some unfamiliar, and so presumably authentic, Meccan cult terms:

> Remember We made the House a place of assembly (*mathaba*) for the people and a secure place; and take the station (*maqam*) of Abraham as a prayer-place (*musalla*); and We have a made a pact with Abraham and Ishmael that they should sanctify My House for those who circumambulate it, those using it as a retreat (*'aqifun*), who bow or prostrate themselves there.
>
> And remember Abraham said: My Lord, make this land a secure one, and feed its people with fruits, those of them who believe in God and the Last Day . . .
>
> And remember Abraham raised the foundations of the House, yes and Ishmael too, (saying) accept (this) from us, for indeed You are All-hearing and All-Knowing. (Quran 2: 125–127)

And again, "Behold, We gave to Abraham the site of the House; do not associate anything with Me (in worship)! And sanctify My House for those who circumambulate, or those who take their stand there (*qa'imin*), who bow (*rukka'*) or prostrate themselves (*sujud*) there"[9] (Quran 22: 26).

What the Muslims were told on divine authority about the ancient cult center at Mecca is summed up in those verses, and it was left to the piety and curiosity of later generations of Muslims to seek out additional information on what was not merely an antiquarian survival but the most sacred building in the world. And many of them did. The authority here is the classical exegete Zamakhshari (d. 1144 A.D.), commenting on Quran 2: 127 with special insistence of the identity of the Abrahamic Ka'ba with its heavenly prototype:

> Then, God commanded Abraham to build it, and Gabriel showed him its location. It is said that God sent a cloud to shade him, and he was told to build on its shadow, not to exceed or diminish (its dimensions). It is said that he built it from five mountains: Mount Sinai, the Mount of Olives, Lebanon, al-Judi, and its foundation is from Hira. Gabriel brought him the Black Stone [that is, the stone embedded in the southeast corner of the Ka'ba] from Heaven.
>
> It is said that Abu Qubays brought it [that is, the Black Stone] forth,[10] and it was drawn from inside it, where it had been hidden during the days of the Flood. It was a white sapphire from the Garden, but when menstruating women touched it during the pre-Islamic period, it turned black.
>
> It is said that Abraham would build it as Ishmael handed him the stones.
>
> *Our Lord* (2:127) means that they both (and not Abraham alone) said "Our Lord," and this activity took place in the location where they erected (the House) in (its) position. Abdullah demonstrated that in his reading, the meaning of which is: "The two of them raised it up, both of them saying, "Our Lord." (Zamakhshari, *Tafsir*, 311)

Zamakhshari's information does not pretend to add historical detail; it simply fleshes out the story at one or another point, as does the commentator Tabarsi (d. 1153) on Quran 2: 125, though by Tabarsi's day most commentators were convinced that the Quran's not entirely self-evident reference to a "station of Abraham" (*maqam Ibrahim*) referred to a specific stone venerated in the Mecca *haram*:

> God made the stone underneath Abraham's feet into something like clay so that his foot sunk into it. That was a miracle. It was transmitted on the authority of Abu Ja'far al-Baqir (may peace be upon him) that he said: Three stones were sent down from the Garden [the heavenly Garden of Eden, that is, Paradise]: the Station of Abraham, the rock of the children of Israel,[11] and the Black Stone, which God entrusted Abraham with as a white stone. It was whiter than paper, but became black from the sins of the children of Adam.
>
> *Abraham raised the foundations of the House* (2:127). That is, the base of the House that was (already there) before that, from Ibn Abbas and Ata who said: Adam was the one who built

it. Then its traces were wiped out. Abraham ploughed it (in the original place to establish the foundations). That is the tradition from our Imams. But Mujahid said: Abraham raised it up (originally) by the command of God. Al-Hasan used to say: The first to make the pilgrimage to the House was Abraham. But according to the traditions of our comrades, the first to make the pilgrimage to the House was Adam. That shows that he was [the one who built it] before Abraham. It was related on the authority of al-Baqir that he said: God placed four columns beneath the Throne. . . . He said: the angels circumambulate it. Then, He sent angels who said, "Build a House like it and with its measurements on the earth". He commanded that whoever is on the earth must circumambulate the House. (Tabarsi, *Tafsir*, vol. 1, pp. 460, 468)

This, then, is how most later Muslims understood the proximate origin of the Ka'ba, alluded to in Quran, to wit, that the Patriarch Abraham, on a visit to his son Ishmael in Mecca, put down, on God's command, the foundation of the House on a site already hallowed by Adam.[12]

Mecca After the Patriarchs

According to the traditional accounts preserved in the historian Tabari and the Meccan chronicler Azraqi,[13] Abraham and Ishmael were the first ones to govern the district of the Ka'ba, then apparently an isolated building in an uninhabited area:

It [that is, the Ka'ba] had not had any custodians since its destruction in the time of Noah. Then God commanded Abraham to settle his son by the Ka'ba, wishing thereby to show a mark of esteem to one whom he later ennobled by means of His Prophet Muhammad. Abraham, the Friend of the Compassionate,[14] and his son Ishmael were custodians of the Ka'ba after the time of Noah. Mecca was then uninhabited, and the surrounding country was inhabited by the Jurhum and the Amaliqa. (Tabari, *Annals*, vol. 1, p. 1131 = Tabari 1988, p. 52)

Ishmael, the biblical scion, had two orders of neighbors. The *Amaliqa* is a transparent reference to the Amalekites, another biblical people, whereas in introducing the tribe of the Jurhum, the Arab accounts have passed over into an entirely different tradition, a native Arabian one. The Quranic commentators, who generally worked verse by verse, had no obligation to produce a continuous historical line between Abraham and Muhammad, but the Muslim historians attempted just that—the standard Life of Muhammad opens in fact with a genealogy that connects Muhammad, as the Gospels do Jesus,[15] with the biblical Patriarch. The material at hand did not easily lend itself to this end, however. The Quran and the Muslim tradition did not have much sense of what had gone on among the Israelites after Ishmael, while their own Arab genealogies, long as they were, led back into the past in a direction that had no apparent connection with the Bible. There was a further complication, as we shall see. Their own history told the Muslims that Muhammad's immediate ancestors at Mecca, the Quraysh, were in the first place relative newcomers to Mecca, that they replaced another Arab people; and second, that they were pagans. Thus the appearance in the story of the Jurhum, an Arab people who replaced the Banu Ishmael at Mecca and who introduced paganism into Abraham's sanctuary.[16]

So, we are told, to coexist peacefully with his powerful new neighbors, the Jurhum and the Amaliqa, Ishmael had eventually to marry a woman of the Jurhum, Sayyida bint Mudad, who bore him twelve sons. It is not entirely certain who the "Amaliqa" actually were, except that in Arabs' eyes both they and the Jurhum were "genuine Arabs" in that Arabic was their native tongue, as contrasted, for example, to the Banu Ishmael, "made Arabs," because "they only spoke these (Arab) peoples' languages after they had settled among them."[17] There are biblical Amalekites, of course, Israel's sworn enemies (Exodus 17: 8–16; 1 Samuel 15), but whoever their Arab counterparts actually were—possibly, it has been guessed, the Nabateans[18]—their presence in the traditional accounts provides yet another opportunity to connect the Mecca-Medina tradition to the earliest biblical narratives, even though the biblical Amalekites have nothing to do with Medina but according to Exodus 17: 8–16 were found in the southern Negev.

The same Amalekites reappear somewhat later in the Bible—this part of the story is ignored in the Muslim tradition—though apparently still in the same general area in the Negev-Sinai, when Saul is commanded to destroy them utterly (1 Samuel 15: 2–3). Contrary to the Lord's specific orders, Saul spared the Amalekite king Agag and the tribe livestock, to his own eventual discomfort, but the Amalekites themselves disappear from the Bible's historical sight.

But not from the Muslims'. To return to the latter's traditional version of Sacred History, Moses did not go to Arabia in person, and when the army despatched by him to the Hijaz in pursuit of the Amalekites returned to Palestine, they discovered that their prophet-leader had perished. They then returned to Arabia, thus establishing a permanent Jewish presence there. Other Muslim versions of the Moses tradition have Moses and Aaron making pilgrimage to Mecca, with Aaron dying near Medina and being buried on Mount Uhud there. Both these accounts serve to explain the later presence of Jews in Western Arabia, but the more general inclination in the Muslim sources is to date the Israelite emigration to Arabia to the sixth century B.C. period of the Babylonian destruction of the Temple.[19]

We return to the era of Abraham and Ishmael:

> At Abraham's death Ishmael became the sole master of the Ka'ba, and when he too died aged 130, his son Nabat succeeded him, apparently without difficulty. The difficulty arose in the next generation: at the death of Nabat, whose mother was a Jurhumite, as we have seen, his sons and grandsons were too few to compete with the powerful Jurhum, who took over the sanctuary. Mudad, the father-in-law of Ishmael, was the first Jurhumite to govern the district of the Ka'ba. Ishmael the son of Abraham begat twelve sons: Nabat, the eldest, Qaydhar, Adhbul, Mabsha, Misma', Mashi, Dimma, Adhr, Tayma, Yatur, Nabish, Qaydhuma. Their mother was Ra'la daughter of Mudad, son of Amr, of the Jurhum. . . . According to report, Ishmael lived 130 years and when he died he was buried in the sacred precinct (hijr) of the Ka'ba next to his mother Hagar.[20]

As has already been noted, the Muslim chroniclers of the early, that is, the pre-Islamic, history of Mecca had two events to reckon with, or rather, a fact and a preconception that had to be accounted for. The fact was that, even though the Quran made it clear (2: 125–127) that Mecca was originally a shrine-settlement in the service of the One True God, the God of Abraham and Ishmael, it was, in the Prophet's own day, a pagan city under the control of a pagan or paganized tribe, Muhammad's own ancestors, the Quraysh. The preconception was that there were two racial strains among the Arabs, the northern "would-be" or "Arabized" Arabs, and the southern or Yemeni "made" or "genuine" Arabs, a distinction based on whether a people were "native speakers" or had acquired the language.[21] The genealogists and the chroniclers, among the latter principally Ibn Ishaq, Tabari, and Azraqi and their sources, assigned the Ishmaelites and Muhammad's Quraysh to the first group, while the southerners like the Jurhum and Khuza'a were responsible for the various interregna that disturbed Mecca between the death of Ishmael and the return to power of one of his descendants, the Qurashite Qusayy.

> The story of Jurhum, of their filling in (the well of) Zamzam, of their leaving Mecca, and of those who ruled Mecca after them until Abd al-Muttalib [that is, the grandfather of Muhammad] dug the Zamzam . . . is that Ishmael the son of Nabat was in charge of the shrine as long as God willed, then it was in charge of Mudad ibn Amr of the Jurhum. The sons of Ishmael and the sons of Nabat were with their grandfather Mudad ibn Amr and their maternal uncles of Jurhum—Jurhum and Qatura who were cousins being at that time the people of Mecca. They had come forth from the Yemen and travelled together, and Mudad was over Jurhum, while Sumayda', one of their men, was over Qatura. . . . When they came to Mecca they saw a town blessed with water and trees and, delighted with it, they settled there. Mudad ibn Amr, with the men of Jurhum, settled in the upper part of Mecca in Qa'ayqi'an and went no farther. Sumayda' with Qatura settled in the lower part of Mecca in Ajyad, the lower part of Mecca, and went no farther. Mudad used to take a tithe from those entered Mecca from above, while Sumayda' did the same to those who entered from below. Each kept to his own people, neither entering the other's territory. (Ibn Ishaq 1955: 45–46)

According to this account, then, the Jurhum lived on the western slopes and heights of the valley, and so controlled the "upper" passage in and out from Jidda and the fertile Batn al-Marr, later the Wadi Fatima, while their allies, and soon rivals, the Qatura, sat on the slopes of Jabal Abu Qubays on the east and monitored the entry and exit toward the Yemen. The two groups were thus in careful separation but in extremely close quarters in the narrow confines of the Meccan valley. Neither seems to have been in control of the shrine itself at that point, but both were apparently attempting to take their sustenance from the same source, a tax on "those who entered Mecca," obviously pilgrims to an already existing shrine, and they soon fell out. Hostilities followed and the Qatura were subjugated by Mudad, and the Jurhum were thus the sole civil and religious authorities—"rulers of the temple and

judges"—in the shrine city, though some at least of their Ishmaelites relatives by marriage—Ishmael, it will be recalled, married a Jurhum woman—were still living there. The final departure
of these latter was apparently under demographic pressure,
though obviously reinforced by political considerations.

> Then God multiplied the offspring of Ishmael in Mecca and
> their uncles from Jurhum were rulers of the temple and judges
> in Mecca. The sons of Ishmael did not dispute their authority
> because of their ties of kindred and their respect for the sanctu-
> ary, lest there should be any quarrelling or fighting therein.
> When Mecca became too confined for the sons of Ishmael they
> spread abroad in the land, and whenever they had to fight a
> people, God gave them the victory through their religion and
> they subdued them. (*Ibid.*, p. 46)

This puts a kind light on the dispersed Ishmaelites, but the
same sources make it clear that it was at their departure from
Mecca that the sons of Ishmael began to turn toward the paganism they would so staunchly defend when they returned to the city
as Quraysh.[22]

The Jurhum, meanwhile, had new neighbors. Tribes were continuously migrating northward from the Yemen, the Azd, for
example, and the Quda'a, some of whom, like the Aws and
Khazraj, settled further north in the Hijaz, notably in the oasis
that would later be called Medina, whereas others, like the Banu
Ghassan, continued their trek into Syria. Finally, there were those
who "split off" and settled in the Tihama or coastal areas of the
Hijaz. "When the Banu Amr ibn Amir dispersed from the Yemen,
the Banu Haritha ibn Amr split off (*inkhaza'a*) from them, settled
in the Tihama and became known as the Khuza'a . . . " (Tabari,
vol. 1, p. 1132 = Tabari 1988, p. 53).

How precisely the southerners called Khuza'a wrested control
of Mecca from the Jurhum was unknown even to the early Arab
experts. Or so we must conclude from the fact there were five
diverse and distinct traditions on the subject.[23] Tabari (*Annals*,
vol. 1, p. 1132) combined the motifs of divine vengeance—"God
sent bleeding of the nose and a plague of ants against the Jurhum
and destroyed them"—with a Khuza'i attack, although Ibn Ishaq
prefers the simpler political explanation.

> Afterwards Jurhum behaved high-handedly in Mecca and made
> lawful that which was taboo. Those who entered the town who

were not of their tribe they treated badly and they appropriated gifts which had been made to the Ka'ba so that their authority weakened. When the Banu Bakr ibn Abd Manat of the (Meccan) Kinana and the Ghubshan of Khuza'a perceived that, they came together to do battle and drive them out of Mecca. War was declared and in the fighting the Banu Bakr and the Ghubshan got the upper hand and expelled the Jurhum from Mecca. (Ibn Ishaq, 1955, pp. 46–47)

Throughout this section Ibn Ishaq or his source invokes events to explain names, chiefly of places. Both he and Tabari. for example, offer an appropriate etymology, and in consequence, a theodicy, for "Bakka," an early and mysterious name of Mecca (cf. Quran 3: 96).

The first of the Jurhum to be custodian of the Ka'ba was Mudad, followed by his descendants, generation after generation. Eventually the Jurhum acted wrongfully in Mecca, held lawful that which was forbidden, misappropriated the wealth which had been presented to the Ka'ba, and oppressed those who came to Mecca. . . . During the Era of Ignorance, any person who acted wrongfully or oppressively in Mecca, or any king who held lawful what was forbidden there, perished on the spot. Mecca was called . . . Bakka because it used to break (*tabukk*) the necks of evil-doers and tyrants when they acted wrongfully there.) Tabari, *Annals*, vol. 1, pp. 1131–1132 = Tabari 1988, pp. 52–53)

The Jurhum era in Mecca appears to have lasted no more than 300 years, from ca. 200 to ca. 400 A.D. in the uncertain chronology of the time, and before he left, the last Jurhumite did something that led directly to the later prominence of Abd al-Muttalib. "Amr ibn Harith ibn Mudad the Jurhumite brought out the two gazelles of the Ka'ba and the corner stone and buried them in the well Zamzam, going away with the men of Jurhum to the Yemen. They were bitterly grieved at losing the kingship of Mecca . . . " (Ibn Ishaq 1955, pp. 46–47).

Once in control of the city and the shrine, the Khuza'a began to make their own dispositions:

The Ka'ba was taken over by the Khuza'a, except that there were three functions which were in the hands of the tribes of (the group called) Mudar. The first of these was the *ijaza*, the giving permission to the pilgrims to leave Arafat. This was in the hands of al-Ghawth ibn Murr, who was (of the clan of) Sufa. . . . The second function was the *ifada*, the permission to the pilgrims to disperse to Mina on the morning of the sacrifice. This was in the hands of the Banu Zayd ibn Adwan. . . . The third function was the *nasi*, the delaying or postponement of the sacred month (by intercalation). The right to decide this was in the hands of al-Qalammas, who was Hudhayfa ibn Fuqaym ibn Adi, of the Banu Malik ibn Kinana. . . . When Islam came, the sacred months had returned to their original times, and God established them firmly and abolished the "postponement" (*nasi*). (Tabari, *Annals*, vol. 1, p. 1134 = Tabari 1988, p. 55).

How Paganism and Idol Worship Came to Mecca

One aspect of the worship of the pre-Islamic Arabs that attracted the attention not only of later Muslim authorities on the "Era of Ignorance" or "Barbarism," as they called pre-Islamic days, but even of the Greek and Latin authors who had come in contact with Arab society, was a widespread cult of stones. From the perspective of both sets of observers it seemed an odd practice to venerate stones, whether these latter were totally unshaped or fashioned into some kind of very rudimentary idol.[24] The practice is testified to both among sedentarized Arabs like the Nabateans of Petra or the priestly Arabs of Emessa in Syria, who had enshrined one such stone within their temple—which their high priest Elagabalus carried off to Rome with him when he became emperor—as well as among the nomads who carried stones enclosed in portable shrines into battle with them.[25]

Later Muslim had some idea of these practices and they traced them back to the earliest history of Mecca, when the sons of Ishmael lapsed into paganism. Ibn al-Kalbi (d. 821), the scholar who made a special study of the pre-Islamic past of Arabia in his *Book of Idols*, connected it directly to the degeneracy of the Banu Ishmael.

> The reason that led them [that is, the descendents of Ishmael] to the worship of images and stones was the following. No one left Mecca without carrying away with him a stone from the stones of the Sacred House as a token of reverence to it, and as a sign of deep affection to Mecca. Wherever he settled he would erect that stone and circumambulate it in the same manner he used to circumambulate the Ka'ba (before his departure from Mecca), seeking thereby its blessing and affirming his deep affection for

the Holy House. In fact, the Arabs still venerate the Ka'ba and Mecca and journey to them in order to perform the pilgrimage and the visitation, conforming thereby to the time-honored custom which they inherited from Abraham and Ishmael.

In time this led them to the worship of whatever took their fancy, and caused them to forget their former worship. They exchanged the religion of Abraham and Ishmael for another. Consequently they took to the worship of images, becoming like nations before them.

At this point Ibn al-Kalbi ties his story to an explanation of Quran 71: 20–24 and incidentally provides the names of some of the gods worshipped in pre-Islamic Arabia: "Noah said: 'O Lord, they rebel against me, and they follow those whose riches and children only aggravate their ruin.' And they plotted a great plot, and they said, 'Forsake not your gods; forsake not Wadd and Suwa', nor Yaghuth and Ya'uq and Nasr.' And they caused many to err . . . "

Ibn al-Kalbi's text continues: "They sought and determined what the people of Noah had worshipped of those images and adopted the worship of those which were still remembered among them."

To a later generation of Muslims it was obviously important, in the light of Muhammad's own adoption of certain of the cult practices current in the Mecca of his day, to maintain some kind of continuous link with the authentic Abrahamic past.

> Among these devotional practices were some which had come down from the time of Abraham and Ishmael, such as the veneration of the House and its circumambulation, the *Hajj*, the *'umra* [or lesser pilgrimage], the "standing" on Arafat and Muzdalifa, sacrificing she-camels, and raising the voice (*tahlil*) (in acclamation of God) at the *Hajj* and *'umra*, but they introduced into the latter things that did not belong to it.

Ibn al-Kalbi then supplies an example of just such an "unorthodox" pre-Islamic acclamation-prayer (*talbiyya*): "Here we are, O Lord! Here we are! Here we are! You have no partner save the one who is yours; you have dominion over him and whatever he possesses."

Ibn al-Kalbi continues his own remarks: "Thus they declared His unity through the *talbiyya* and at the same time associated their gods with Him, placing their [that is, their gods'] affairs in

His hands . . . " (Ibn al-Kalbi, *Book of Idols*, pp. 6–7 = Ibn al-Kalbi 1952, pp. 4–5).

Stone worship is not quite the same thing as idol worship, as even Ibn al-Kalbi understood. According to most authorities, including Ibn al-Kalbi himself, the pagan practices in Mecca took a new turn when the Khuza'a under their leader Amr ibn Luhayy—who had married the daughter of Amr ibn al-Harith, the Jurhum chief—replaced the Jurhum as the paramount tribe in the settlement.

> When Amr ibn Luhayy came (to Mecca) he disputed Amr ibn al-Harith's right to its custody, and with the aid of the Banu Ishmael he fought the Jurhumites, defeated them and cleared them out of the Ka'ba; he then drove them out of Mecca and took over the custody of the House after them.
>
> Amr ibn Luhayy then became very sick and was told: There is a hot spring in Balqa in Syria.[26] If you go there, you will be cured. So he went to the hot spring, bathed therein and was cured. During his stay there he noticed that the inhabitants of the place worshipped idols. So he questioned them: "What are these things?" To which they replied, "To them we pray for rain, and from them we seek victory over the enemy." Thereupon he asked them to give him (some) and they did. He took them back with him to Mecca and erected them around the Ka'ba . . . (*Ibid.*, p. 8 = Ibn al-Kalbi 1952, p. 7)

Later Ibn al-Kalbi turns his attention to the cult of the idols newly introduced into Mecca and its vicinity:

> Every family in Mecca had at home an idol which they worshipped. Whenever one of them purposed to set out on a journey, his last act before leaving the house would be to touch the idol in hope of an auspicious journey; on his return, the first thing he would do was to touch it again in gratitude for a propitious return . . .
>
> The Arabs were passionately fond of worshiping idols. Some of them had a temple around which they centered their worship, while others adopted an idol to which they offered their adoration. The person who was unable to build himself a temple or adopt an idol would erect a stone in front of the Sacred House [that is, the Ka'ba at Mecca] or in front of any other temple they might prefer, and then circumambulate it in the same manner in which they would circumambulate the Sacred House. The Arabs called these stones "betyls" (*ansab*),

but whenever these stones resembled a living form they called them "idols" (*asnam*) and "images" (*awthan*). The act of circumambulating them they called "circumrotation" (*dawar*).

Whenever a traveler stopped at a place or station (to spend the night), he would select for himself four stones, pick out the finest of them and adopt it as his god, and then use the remaining three as supports for his cooking pot. On his departure he would leave them behind, and would do the same at the other stops.

And, like many other Muslims, Ibn al-Kalbi was convinced that Arab paganism was at base simply a degenerate form of rituals of the Ka'ba:

The Arabs were accustomed to offer sacrifices before all these idols, betyls and stones. Nevertheless, they were aware of the excellence and superiority of the Ka'ba, to which they went on pilgrimage and visitation. What they did on their travels was merely a perpetuation of what they did at the Ka'ba, because of their devotion to it. (*Ibid.*, pp. 32–33 = Ibn al-Kalbi 1952, pp. 28–29)

Ibn Ishaq provides a kind of catalog of which tribes worshipped which idols and where. He resumes:

The Quraysh had by a well in the middle of the Ka'ba an idol called Hubal. And they adopted Asaf and Na'ila by the place of Zamzam, sacrificing beside them. They were a man and woman of Jurhum—Asaf ibn Baghy and Na'ila bint Dik—who were guilty of sexual relations in the Ka'ba and so God transformed them into two stones.[27] Abdullah ibn Abu Bakr . . . on the authority of Amra bint Abd al-Rahman . . . that she said, I heard Aisha [one of the wives of Muhammad] say, "We always heard that Asaf and Na'ila were a man and a woman of Jurhum who copulated in the Ka'ba so God transformed them into two stones." But God alone knows the truth . . .

And in a slightly different version of the same detail reproduced by Ibn al-Kalbi:

Every household had an idol in their house which they used to worship. When a man was about to set out on a journey he would rub himself against it as he was about to ride off: indeed that was the last thing that he used to do before his journey. And when he returned from his journey the first thing he did was to rub himself against it before he went into his family . . .

Now along with the Ka'ba the Arabs had adopted *tawaghit*, which were temples which they venerated as they venerated the Ka'ba. They had their guardians and overseers and they used to make offerings to them as they did to the Ka'ba and to circumambulate them and sacrifice at them. Yet they recognized the superiority of the Ka'ba because it was the temple and mosque of Abraham the friend (of God) . . .

Al-Lat (was a goddess who) belonged to the Thaqif in Ta'if, her overseers and guardians being the Banu Mu'attib of the Thaqif. Manat was worshipped by the Aws and the Khazraj, and such of the people of Yathrib who followed their religion, by the sea-shore in the direction of al-Mushallal in Qudayd. (Ibn Ishaq 1955, pp. 38–39)

FATHER QUSAYY AND THE QURAYSH

Eventually the Khuza'a permitted the return to Mecca of the descendants of Ishmael; namely, the Quraysh of the Kinana. The tribal eponym Kinana stands fifteen generations after Ishmael in the line of direct descent, and Qusayy, the chief actor in what follows, is eight generations after Kinana. Thus, according to the traditional reckoning, Ishmael's descendants returned to their father's town some seven centuries after he and Abraham built the Ka'ba there. In the meantime the Ishmaelites, now called Quraysh, had generally lived dispersed in "scattered settlements" throughout the neighborhood.

Ghubshan of Khuza'a controlled the sanctuary instead of the Banu Bakr ibn Abd Manat, the man who was in charge being Amr ibn al-Harith al-Ghubshani. The Quraysh at that time were in scattered settlements and tents [or "houses"] dispersed among their people, the Banu Kinana. So the Khuza'a had possession the shrine, passing it on from son to son until the last of them, Hulayl ibn Habashiyya . . . (Ibn Ishaq 1955, p. 48)

At that point all the sources introduce Qusayy, "the first of the Kinana to achieved the rulership, and who united his tribe, the Quraysh."

When his Qurayshite father Kilab died, the young Qusayy, who must have been born sometime early in the second half of the fourth century A.D., was taken by his mother back to the northern pasturing grounds of her own tribe, the Banu Udhra of the

Quda'a.[28] Qusayy's mother remarried, and as he grew up he had no reason to believe that he was anything but one of the Quda'a. But when he reached young manhood and found that he was not a Quda'ai, Qusayy asked his mother to which tribe he belonged. She told him the entire story: "You are the son of Kilab ibn Murra ibn Ka'b ibn Lu'ayy ibn Ghalib ibn Fihr ibn Malik ibn al-Nadr ibn Kinana al-Qurashi."[29] This revelation awoke in Qusayy a strong desire to return to Mecca and join his own people, the Quraysh.

According to the traditional account, Qusayy's mother advised him that the safest course was to wait for the period of the sacred truce in the pilgrimage season. He followed her advice and eventually arrived in Mecca under the protection of sacred month. Then, when the other Banu Udhra returned to their homes, Qusayy remained behind with his newly discovered Meccan kinsmen. The sources then move rapidly:

> Qusayy was a strong man of good lineage, and when he asked Hulayl ibn Hubshiyya [or Habashiyya] the Khuza'i for the hand of his daughter Hubba, Hulayl, recognizing his lineage and regarding him as a desirable match, gave his consent and married her to him. At that time, it is claimed, Hulayl was in charge of the Ka'ba and ruled in Mecca. According to Ibn Ishaq, Qusayy stayed with him [that is, Hulayl] and Hubba bore him Abd al-Dar, Abd Manaf, Abd Uzza and Abd. His progeny increased, his wealth multiplied and he became greatly honored. (Tabari, *Annals*, vol. 1, pp. 1093–1094 = Tabari 1988, p. 20)

If the report about Hulayl is true, and Tabari may have had some doubts, Qusayy had married very well indeed: his bride was the daughter of the "king" of Mecca, a post identified with control of the Ka'ba. He apparently took up residence in his father-in-law's household, and his four sons all bore the family's traditional theophoric, shrine-tied names: "Servant of the House," "Servant of Manaf," "Servant of Uzza"—the latter two the familiar Meccan goddesses—and finally the somewhat mysterious "Servant" *tout simple*, or perhaps, "Servant of Qusayy."[30] The young man could hardly be blamed if he harbored ambitious dreams.

> When Hulayl al-Hubshiyya died, Qusayy thought he had a better right to the Ka'ba and to rule over Mecca than the Khuza'a and the Banu Bakr, since the Quraysh were noblest and purest of the descendants of Ishmael, the son of Abraham. He spoke to some of the men of the Quraysh and the Banu Kinana and

called upon them to expel the Khuza'a and the Banu Bakr from Mecca. They accepted his proposal and swore an oath of allegiance to him to do this. Then he wrote to his half-brother Riza ibn Rabi'a who was in his tribal lands (northward toward Syria), asking him to come to his assistance and fight along with him. Riza ibn Rabi'a stood up among the Quda'a and called upon them to go to the assistance of his brother and to march with him, and they answered his call. (Tabari, *Annals*, vol. 1, p. 1094 = Tabari 1988, pp. 20–21)

According to this account, which Tabari got from Ibn Ishaq, the critical moment came during the annual pilgrimage. Control of one or more of the rituals of the *Hajj* had remained as an inheritance in the hands of certain clans from the old Jurhum days at Mecca, and particularly the one called Sufa.

The Sufa used to drive the people away from Arafat and give them permission to depart when they dispersed from Mina. On the day of dispersal they went to stone the pillars and a man of the Sufa used to throw stones for the pilgrims, none throwing until he had thrown . . .

And no matter how forcefully he was urged by "those who had matters to attend to," the Sufa custodian stoutly refused to begin the ritual until the sun began to set. Even then, the Sufa stood by their prerogatives:

When they had finished with the stoning and wanted to disperse from Mina, the Sufa would occupy both sides of the pass of al-Aqaba and detain the pilgrims. The pilgrims would say, "Give the permission to depart, Sufa!" Nobody left till the Sufa passed through; when they had dispersed and left, the other pilgrims were free to go, and set out after them. (Tabari, *Annals*, vol. 1, pp. 1095–1096 = Tabari 1988, pp. 22–23)

This is all there is by way of explanation of the precedent and the ritual. Tabari and his sources then return to the nearer present, to Qusayy's day.

This year the Sufa acted as usual. The Arabs recognized their right to do this, since they regarded it as a religious duty during the rule of the Jurhum and the Khuza'a. Qusayy ibn Kilab, accompanied by his followers from his own tribe of Quraysh, from the Kinana and the Quda'a, came to the Sufa at al-Aqaba (near Mina) and said. "We have a better right to this than you." At that they opposed one another and began to fight. A fierce battle broke out, as a result of which the Sufa were put to flight, and Qusayy wrested from them the privileges which had been in their hands . . .

When this happened the Khuza'a and the Banu Bakr drew back from Qusayy ibn Kilab, knowing that he would impose prohibitions upon them as he had upon the Sufa, and that we would exclude them from the Ka'ba and the control of Mecca. When they drew back from them, Qusayy revealed his enmity to them openly and resolved to do battle with them. (*Ibid.*)

Battle they did, and after both sides took heavy casualties, the matter was submitted to arbitration. The arbitrator was from another branch of the Banu Kinana, and his verdict does not seem very surprising, that Qusayy had a better right to the Ka'ba and to rule over Mecca than the Khuza'a. This was not the only version of events that was current, however. Tabari knew and told other, somewhat different stories of the passage of power, how the elderly Hulayl handed over the authority to his daughter, and when she pleaded her incapacity to open and close the door of the Ka'ba, he appointed one Abu Ghubshan as her assistant. Qusayy bought the privilege from Abu Ghubshan for a skinful of wine and a lute, an act that disturbed Hulayl and led to war; or even that a plague struck the Khuza'a and that after they vacated Mecca out of fear, Qusayy simply moved his own people in and took over the Ka'ba.[31] Ibn Ishaq and Tabari each gives his summary of events:

Thus Qusayy gained authority over the temple and Mecca and brought in his people from their dwellings to Mecca. He behaved like a king over his tribe and the people of Mecca and so they made him king. But he had guaranteed the Arabs their customary rights because he felt it was a duty upon himself which he did not have the right to alter. Thus he confirmed the family of Safwan [who were then granting pilgrims the permission to depart from Arafat] and Adwan [who were then granting the permission to depart from Muzdalifa] and the intercalators and Murra ibn Awf in their customary rights which obtained until the coming of Islam when God put and end thereby to them all.

Qusayy was the first of the Banu Ka'b ibn Lu'ayy to assume kingship and be was obeyed by his people as a king. He held the keys to the shrine, the right to water the pilgrims from the well of Zamzam, to feed the pilgrims, to preside at assemblies, and to hand out the war banners. In his hands lay all the dignities of Mecca; he divided the town into quarters among his people and he settled all the Quraysh into their houses in Mecca which they held.

People assert that the Quraysh were afraid to cut down the
trees of the sanctuary in their quarters, but Qusayy cut them
down with his own hand or through his assistants. The Quraysh
called him "the uniter" because he had brought them together
and they drew a happy omen from his rule. So far as the
Quraysh were concerned, no woman was given in marriage, no
man was married, no discussion about public affairs was held
and no banner of war was entrusted to anyone except in his
house, where one of his sons would hand it over. . . . His
authority among the Quraysh during his life and after his death
was like a religious law which could not be infringed. He chose
for himself the council house (dar al-nadwa) and made a door
which led to the mosque of the Ka'ba; in it the Quraysh used to
settle their affairs. (Ibn Ishaq 1955, pp. 52–53)

There follows an account of the offices to which Qusayy succeeded at Mecca.

Qusayy took control of the Ka'ba and rule over Mecca, and
gathered together his tribe from their dwellings and settled them
there. He assumed rule over his tribe and the people of Mecca,
and they accepted him as their king. . . . He held privileges of
being doorkeeper of the Ka'ba, providing the pilgrims with food
and drink, presiding over the assembly, and appointing standard bearers, thus taking all the honors of Mecca for himself.
He also divided Mecca into quarters for his tribe, settling every
clan of the Quraysh into the dwelling places assigned to them in
Mecca . . .
    His authority among his tribe of Quraysh, in his lifetime
and after his death, was like a religion which people followed.
They always acted in accordance with it, regarding it as filled
with good omens and recognizing his superiority and nobility.
He took for himself the council house (dar al-nadwa) and made
the door which (later) led from it to the mosque of the Ka'ba.
The Quraysh used to decide their affairs in that house. (Tabari,
Annals, vol. 1, pp. 1097–1098 = Tabari 1988, p. 24)

Dimly through these lines written by a later staunch monotheist, we can see the faint outlines of the cult in pre-Islamic Mecca.
Qusayy had become not only, or perhaps not even, the political
master of the city, but certainly the holy man of Mecca's sacred
enclosure, a prototype of the same kind of arrangements that
remained current into modern times in South Arabia.[32] But the
impression we are given is that Qusayy was a religious conserva-

tive who was eager for the transfer of authority to his own hands but, like the Khuza'a before him and like his illustrious descendant, was quite unwilling to introduce any radical changes in the cult.

> Qusayy remained in Mecca, held in honor and high esteem by his tribe. . . . As regards the pilgrimage, he confirmed the rights of the Arabs to continue their previous customs. This is because he considered these to be a religious duty which he should not change. The Sufa thus continued as before, (and did so) until they died out, their rights then passing by inheritance to the family of Safwan ibn Harith . . . ; the Adwan also continued as they had, and likewise the intercalator from the Banu Malik ibn Kinana and Murra ibn Awf . . . (Tabari, *Annals*, vol. 1, p. 1098 = Tabari 1988, p. 25)

Another passage in Tabari gives us some ideas of Qusayy's widely ranging powers, most of them, we suspect, already traditional for the master of the Meccan Haram. We have already seen, for example, how he took over the community council hall called the *dar al-nadwa* and made it into his own home.

> People allege that the Quraysh were afraid to cut down the trees of the Haram in their settlements, and that Qusayy thus cut them down with his own hands, and that they then helped him. . . . No woman or man of Quraysh was married anywhere but in the house of Qusayy ibn Kilab, nor did the Quraysh consult together about any matter affecting them anywhere but in his house. When they were about to fight another tribe, banners were tied only in his house, where one of his own sons would hand the banner over . . . (*Ibid.*, p. 1097 = Tabari 1988, p. 24)

Arab historical memory recalled Qusayy as the "unifier," because he was, it was alleged, "the first of the Kinana to achieved the rulership, and who united his tribe, the Quraysh." The later Arabs themselves were perfectly clear who was Quraysh and who was not, but were somewhat uncertain as to where they had come from, chiefly, perhaps, because of the absence of any eponymous "Quraysh" in the tribal genealogy, as Ibn al-Kalbi confesses. The founder of the house's power was generally thought to have been a Qusayy, as we have seen, and his lineage went back through his father Kilab to a certain Fihr ibn Malik, called the *gatherer* of the Quraysh, and in discussing the latter, Tabari reflects on the more general question of who precisely the Quraysh were.

It is said that the Quraysh were so called after Quraysh ibn Badr
... of the al-Nadr branch of the Kinana. This is because when
the caravan of the Banu al-Nadr arrived, the Arabs used to say
"the caravan of Quraysh has arrived." They say that this
"Quraysh" was the guide of the Banu al-Nadr in their travels,
and he was responsible for provisioning them. He had a son
named Badr who dug the well at (the place called) Badr, and the
well called Badr is named after him.

Ibn al-Kalbi (maintains that) Quraysh is a collective name,
and cannot be traced back to a father or mother, or to a male or
female guardian. Others say that the descendants of al-Nadr ibn
Kinana were called Quraysh because al-Nadr ibn Kinana came
out one day to his tribal assembly and they said to one another,
"Look at Nadr, he is like a *quraysh* camel."[33] Others say that
Quraysh were so called after a creature who lives in the sea and
eats other sea creatures, namely, the shark (*qirsh*). The descendants of al-Nadr ibn Kinana were named after the *qirsh* because
it is the most powerful of sea creatures . . .

And so the not very convincing etymologies continue, and at
least one of them suggests that the term *Quraysh* is a more recent
coinage. It is clear that the Arabs, who remembered such things,
had no clear idea of who the Quraysh were or where they had
originally come from.

Mecca Town

The evidence is exceedingly thin, but what seems likely from the
pages of Ibn Ishaq, Tabari and Azraqi is that the establishment of
Mecca as a permanent settlement was the work of the same
Qusayy ibn Kilab, the Qurashite, sometime after 400 A.D.[34] The
tradition is unanimous that there was a shrine there from a very
early date, but the immediate area seems not to have been settled:
witness the fact that the earlier tribes camped on the mountain
slopes above the valley and that Qusayy took the secular initiative
in clearing the immediate shrine area of trees, normally a forbidden act in a *hawta*. He settled his own people, who formerly lived
in "widely scattered settlements," in the newly cleared area, with
a defined territory assigned for the domicile of each tribe. To view
it from a slightly different perspective, at the birth of Muhammad,
Mecca was somewhat over a hundred years old as a genuine settlement and the Quraysh were at that same remove from their earlier lives as nomads.[35]

Close in on the now reduced Haram area Qusayy built—or perhaps simply appropriated—the *dar al-nadwa* to serve as his own residence as well as the council hall for the community, "in which the Quraysh used to decide their affairs."[36] These affairs included all community activities from political acts like declarations of war to religious rituals, circumcision, and marriage rites. In a later generation, no one could enter the *dar al-nadwa* unless he was a direct descendant of Qusayy, and it was forbidden to anyone to take part in the business of the community until he had reached the age of 40.[37] And finally, and significantly, as has already been noted, Qusayy's house gave direct access to the Ka'ba.

The Quraysh, we are told, now moved into Mecca. Perhaps it was Qusayy himself who allotted them two quite distinct quarters of the new settlement. The principal tribes—the Hashim, Umayya, Nawfal, Zuhra, Asad, Taym, Makhzum, Adi, Jumah, and Sahm— lived in the valley bottom in the immediate vicinity of the shrine, while the lesser tribes were settled in the outskirts with what remained of the non-Qurashi inhabitants.[38] Contrary to what convenience or strategy or simple urban common sense might seem to dictate, the choicest part of the city, though the least habitable and least defensible, was exactly what it is today, the wadi bottom, as close in to the shrine as possible. It was perhaps as Qusayy is reported to have said: "If you will live around the sanctuary, people will have fear of you and not permit themselves to fight you or attack you."[39]

Mecca had little save its own holiness to recommend it as a site for settlement. A poet later described it as a place where "winter and summer are equally intolerable. No waters flow . . . not a blade of grass on which to rest the eye; no, nor hunting. Only merchants (dwell there), the most despicable of professions."[40] The Quran itself is willing to concede the point. The speaker here is Abraham addressing his Lord: "O, our Lord, I have made some of my offspring dwell in a valley without cultivation, at Thy sacred House, in order, O Lord, that they may establish regular prayers (*salawat*). So fill the hearts of some among men with love toward them, and feed them with fruits so that they may give thanks" (Quran 14: 37).

The vale of Mecca was not always such perhaps: the prayer of Abraham may be a projection back to the patriarchal age of the perceptions of a later generation who found Mecca situated in a barren and unappealing place. The Arab tradition asserted that when the Jurhum came to Mecca "they saw a town blessed with water and trees, and delighted with it, they settled there."[41] It even recalls the presence of trees in the valley bottom of Mecca in more recent times,[42] trees that, as we have seen, were cut down by Qusayy to make room for his city. But given the unvarying climate of Mecca, it is unlikely that the trees were much more than scrub.

Mecca, it is often said, in an attempt to explain either its prosperity or simply why people chose to settle there in the first place, stood at the nexus of natural trade routes. It in fact does not: the natural route between the Yemen and the north lies well east of Mecca, and caravans going there were obviously making a detour.[43] Many places in the near vicinity of Mecca, Ta'if, for example, had better soil, more water, and a better climate.[44] What Mecca possessed and they did not, though we cannot explain how or why, was an intrinsic holiness. The Quran explained it, and there were no denials from the Quraysh: Mecca was important because it was a holy city, and, it is further explained, that holiness went back to Abraham.

By all accounts, Mecca must have been an extremely modest place in the sixth century A.D., a valley running roughly northeast-southwest, held, or perhaps trapped, between two high ridges of mountains. Did its native son Muhammad claim to be a messenger of God, the Lord of the Worlds? "So ask your Lord who sent you," the Quraysh remarked derisively, "to remove us from these mountains that enclose us. Straighten out our country for us and open up rivers like those of Syria and Iraq."[45] And into this valley was jammed the settled population, close to the Ka'ba and close to each other. The center of town was wrapped in "suffocating heat, deadly wind, clouds of flies," as a geographer later described it, and the so-called outskirts were little more than mud huts clinging to the slopes of the inhospitable mountains.[46]

And in the midst was the small area known as the *shrine,* literally, a "place of prostration" (*masjid*), defined from the beginning only by the fact of its being an open space between the walls of the facing buildings. The "gates of the Haram" were originally nothing more than the alleys between the houses that opened onto that space. On the testimony of Ibn Ishaq and Azraqi, business was conducted in the open courts of houses or in the Haram itself, particularly at the "Station of Abraham," or leaning at ease against the low wall called the *hatim* opposite the northwestern face of the Ka'ba.[47]

The houses of the Quraysh must have been extremely primitive. The Caliph Muʿawiya (r. 661–680) is credited with being the first to build with baked brick in the town, and in the Prophet's own lifetime the inhabitants were incapable of roofing the Kaʿba and had to wait until fortune cast a carpenter into their midst. The Kaʿba, the most important building in the town, was constructed of unmortared stones laid one atop the other, and everything else was built, as far as we can tell, of mud mixed with straw.

Rulers of the Shrine

When they come to speak of the approaching death of Qusayy, the chroniclers of the city's history provide a somewhat more detailed and systematic account of the privileges possessed by the holy man of Mecca and by his holy family after him. As Ibn Ishaq's narrative reveals, there was, or rather, had been, a problem in the succession because the historian was well aware that it was not the offspring of Qusayy's eldest son, Abd al-Dar, who ruled Mecca or were even, as their name, "Servants of the House," openly indicates they should have been, in control of the Kaʿba:

> When Qusayy grew old and feeble, he spoke to Abd al-Dar. He was his first-born but Abd Manaf had become famous during his father's lifetime and done all that had to be done along with Abd al-Uzza and Abd. Qusayy said: "By God, my son, I will put you on a par with the others; though they have a greater reputation than yours, none of them shall enter the Kaʿba until you open it for them; none shall give the Quraysh the war banner but you with your own hand; none shall drink in Mecca except you allow it; and no pilgrim shall eat food unless you provide it; and the Quraysh shall not decide any matter except in your house." He gave him his house, it being the only place where the Quraysh could settle their affairs, and he gave him the formal rights mentioned above.

One of the privileges accorded to Qusayy by reason of his position was the collection of a special tax, the *rifada*, which is here described as supplying the means by which Qusayy provided food and drink to the pilgrims but that was also very likely one of the sources out of which he and his successors funded their commercial ventures. It was still current in Ibn Ishaq's day and so his account has a dual purpose, to explain the tax and to justify its continued practice:

The *rifada* was a tax which the Quraysh used to pay from their property to Qusayy at every festival. With it he used to provide food for the pilgrims who were unable to afford their own provisions. Qusayy had laid this upon the Quraysh, saying: "You are God's neighbors, the people of His temple and sanctuary. The pilgrims are God's guests and the visitors to His temple and have the highest claim on your generosity; so provide food and drink for them during the pilgrimage until they depart out of your territory." Accordingly they used to pay him every year a tax on their flocks and he used to provide food for the people therefrom, while they were at Mina, and his people carried out this order of his during the time of barbarism until Islam came. To this very day it is the food which the sultan provides every year at Mina until the pilgrimage is over. (Ibn Ishaq 1955, pp. 55–56)

These were not only honorable and prestigious positions at Mecca; they were, as we shall see, profitable as well, and they reveal the fundamental outlines of the economy of what was, from Qusayy's day, the shrine-city of Mecca.[48] What emerges from these offices that he either established or laid claim to when he took control of the settlement is clear evidence that in the Qusayy era Mecca was not yet a commercial center. What passes as the "municipal offices" of Mecca have to do only with military operations, which our sources never show us in operation, and with the control of the shrine. In a city that enjoyed a considerable mercantile reputation among later Muslim authorities, there is no sign of the regulation of commerce nor of any municipal institutions governing or encouraging it; indeed, there is a suggestion that at this point the Quraysh may not have traded at all.[49] The principal *functioning* offices, as far as we can tell, were all connected with the shrine and the pilgrimage, and were regarded as religious in character.[50]

Primary among the offices possessed by Qusayy was the wardenship (*hijaba*) of the Ka'ba,[51] including control of access to it, later symbolized by the possession of the keys to the building.[52] As noted, Qusayy also possessed watering and provisioning rights for what the tradition sometimes regarded as needy pilgrims but that was more likely an exclusive franchise—"no man shall eat food in the pilgrimage other than your food"—and one that, in addition to the element of control it implied, was a privilege that could obviously be turned to great profit, as it unquestionably was in later times.[53]

In addition to the profits that might have accrued from buying and selling pilgrimage goods and services, other unmistakable sources of income, whether for Qusayy individually or, as seems more likely, the ruling families of the Quraysh collectively, lie just below the surface. Lammens's investigation of the sources has uncovered a whole range of charges and taxes imposed upon arriving and departing pilgrims and the merchants who took advantage of the "truce of God" surrounding the pilgrimage period to conduct their business at the fairs that followed the rituals.[54] Thus the early Quraysh, who were wardens of the trade at Mecca, though not yet participants in it, must have begun to accumulate from the event of the pilgrimage a small capital stake that not only offered them grounds for subsistence but the foundation for later, more expansive commercial ventures that would lead them out of the narrow confines of the Meccan Haram.

On how these arrangements were organized and administered we have little information; far less, of course, than we possess for Petra, and certainly Palmyra, with its wealth of commercial inscriptions. Qusayy, and after him one or other of his sons, is simply said to be in charge, whereas whatever small pre-Islamic evidence there is seems to point to the fact that the leadership at Mecca was a collective one. Fasi, a later historian of the city, says quite explicitly that "among the chiefs, no one of them exercised authority over the rest of the Quraysh except by a benevolent concession on their part."[55] No mention is made in the sources—the bare list of Qusayy's prerogatives aside—of any actual officials or magistrates, though it is difficult to imagine the collective performance of many of what were doubtless collective responsibilities.

The most concrete example of Mecca's governance in pre-Islamic days is the *dar al-nadwa* or council hall.[56] It was at the same time Qusayy's residence and the administrative center of the city, or if that is too grandiose a notion, it was the place where certain important tribal acts had necessarily to be performed: betrothals, circumcisions, declarations of war; on taxes or commerce in connection with this building in the shadow of the Ka'ba, there is not a word. It was here, certainly, that the shaykhs of the ruling houses of Mecca, the Abd Manaf, Makhzum, and Umayya, met and took common counsel, apparently only as the occasion arose. This would have been the site of the meetings of the *mala'* or Grand Council, the only government body the Quran seems aware of.[57] So the tradition suggests, but it is curious that at no time during Muhammad's career at Mecca, when there were frequent consultations on what to do with this newly declared prophet, were there any meetings of the *dar al-nadwa*, if it was an institution, or even *in* the *dar al-nadwa*, if it was only a place. The early Muslims may in fact have exaggerated the importance of the *dar al-nadwa*,[58] but whatever the case, the rapid political evolution of the Islamic commonwealth, which unfolded, moreover, at Medina rather than Mecca, soon rendered the *dar al-nadwa* otiose. The building was later the private and obviously the secular property of one Hakim ibn Hizam, who eventually sold it to the Caliph Mu'awiya.[59]

THE SONS OF QUSAYY

> After the death of Qusayy his sons assumed his authority over the people and marked out Mecca in quarters, after he had allotted space there for his own tribe. They allotted quarters among their people and among other allies, and sold them. The Quraysh took part in this without discord or dispute. (Ibn Ishaq 1955, p. 56)

At that point, after living space—the "quarters" of the text is obviously anachronistic—had been allocated to the various tribal units of the newly sedentarized Quraysh, the problem anticipated in Ibn Ishaq's account of the Qusayy's disposition of his powers occurred: Abd al-Dar was deprived of his offices by his nephews, Abd Shams, Hashim, Muttalib, and Nawfal, the sons of Abd Manaf, who "considered that they had a better right to them because of their superiority and their position among the people." The move created an even deeper rift among the Quraysh: some of the tribes sided with the Banu Abd Manaf and other with the Banu Abd al-Dar. Both sides collected their allies at the Ka'ba and swore oaths of solidarity and allegiance:

> The Banu Abd Manaf brought out a bowl full of scent (they assert that some women of the tribe brought it out to them) and they put it for their allies in the shrine (*masjid*) next to the Ka'ba; then they dipped their hands into it and they and their allies took a solemn oath. Then they rubbed their hands on the Ka'ba strengthening the solemnity of the oath. For this reason they were called the "Scented Ones." The other side took a similar oath at the Ka'ba and were called the "Confederates." ...

When the people had thus decided upon war, suddenly they demanded peace on the condition that the Banu Abd Manaf should be given the rights of watering the pilgrims and collecting the tax; and that access to the Ka'ba, the standard or war and the *dar al-nadwa* should belong to the Abd al-Dar as before. The arrangement commended itself to both sides and was carried out, and so war was prevented. This was the state of affairs until God brought Islam . . . (*Ibid.*, p. 57)

Mecca, then, was the site of frequent tribal strife in the generations after Qusayy. It was not merely individuals who were struggling for power—the power most often symbolized by control of the religio-economic functions associated with the rituals of the Haram—but extended families, and particularly those associated with Abd al-Dar and Abd Manaf. The Abd al-Dar had been given extended privileges by Qusayy himself, but among his grandsons it was the four chiefs of Abd Manaf—Abd Shams, Hashim, Muttalib, and Nawfal—whose exploits fill the pages of the Arab historians; and one of them, Hashim, is signalled by all the sources as the second founder of the fortunes of the Quraysh.

CHAPTER 2

The Colonial Era in Arabia

The Syrian steppe extends, like some vast bay, between the culti-vated and urbanized lands of Iraq on the east and Syria-Palestine on the west and drops, on its southern side, into the long unfath-omed depths of Arabia. On both fertile sides of the steppe grew up ancient states and empires that reached out to each other, for con-quest or commercial profit, across the Upper Mesopotamian plains that skirted the Syrian steppe along its northern "shore."

From the sixth to the third centuries B.C. Syria, Mesopotamia, and Iraq were all encompassed within single great empires, first the Achaemenids and then, in Alexander's wake, the Seleucids. Thus the Syrian steppe became, in effect, an interior sea, though unlike a true sea, it was neither a convenient means of transporta-tion nor an appreciable source of food. No matter; the Achae-menids and Seleucids could travel around it on the Mesopotamian land bridge to the north or the genuine maritime routes that skirted Arabia from the Persian Gulf to the Gulf of Aqaba and around the peninsula's southern shores. In the third pre-Christian century Seleucid political unity began to be rent by Parthian intruders from the Aral steppes, and by the second century the Seleucids were being thrust back toward the Mediterranean as the Parthians possessed themselves of Iraq and Iran. Somewhere in Mesopotamia a frontier was drawn separating the Hellenic and Hellenized Seleucids on the west and the Iranian Parthians on the east. Above it the two dominant powers struggled to draw Arme-nia to one or other side of that divide; below was still the Syrian steppe, now, however, no longer an inland sea but apparently an immense no-man's land separating first the Seleucids and then the Romans in Syria from the Parthians and their successors, the Sasa-nians, in Iraq and Iran.

The Syrian steppe and Arabia below it was no more a no-man's land than it was a genuine sea. It had, for as long as we can make out, its own inhabitants whose adaptive nomadic life created and

31

guided economic, political, and religious forces as potent and as well-defined as those within the more visible sedentary states. The soldiers, statesmen and historians of the sedentary societies were not so well aware of this as we. Both sides, Roman and Iranian, were tied by their military and communications technology to vehicular roads and supply depots. Their infantrymen could not march the steppe; their heavily armed cataphracts could not ride it; and the cumbersome wheeled carts foundered once they left the leveled and paved roads that were the pride of both empires.[1]

The steppe could not be ignored, however, by the empires of the sown lands. Southward across its spaces lay the lucrative lands of the Yemen and the pearl fisheries of the Persian Gulf. And there were its own inhabitants, the bedouin whose nomadic life carried them, for a few months each year, into the farmlands of Syria, Mesopotamia, and Iraq in search of summer pasturage. There is abundant evidence, particularly from Syria and Mesopotamia, on how destructive those seasonal forays could be. There is evidence too that the waves of summer transhumance left their own human sediment on the arable beaches. Arab bedouin were drawn into the life of the towns and cities that dotted the fringes of the steppe, where they settled and became farmers, landowners, merchants, and soldiers. Sometimes only their names betray whence the had come.[2]

The steppe bedouin were, then, occasionally destructive and possibly useful neighbors of the empires of Rome and Iran. Their depradations had to be controlled, to be sure, but they had the potentially profitable ability to navigate their own environment. The bedouin had long since domesticated the camel., which was naturally adapted to steppe travel, and then, sometime before the first century B.C., they had developed a convenient saddle that enabled a camel to carry a considerable—and profitable—load of goods or serve as a seat for a lethel lancer.[3] Thus the Arab had become, when he chose, a soldier and a caravaneer, and in both habits he was a source of interest and concern to the rulers of the neighboring Great Powers.

We know in some detail how the Romans controlled and profited from the bedouin of the steppe. We know too how the commercial potential of the bedouin could be converted into political power in the form of the Arab "empires" of Petra and Palmyra on the Roman side of the steppe, and at Hatra and Gerrha on the Partho-Sasanian side. But in the first pre-Christian century a maritime "discovery" on the part of Mediterranean-based sailors set a new and profitable course in international trade, that across the high seas.

The ancients generally sailed by coasting, that is, running before the wind in sight of the shore during daylight hours and heaving-to in the nearest port at the approach of dusk. The ancient mariners found neither darkness nor the deep particularly tempting. Under such circumstances a voyage within the Red Sea might be undertaken, or even, with a favorable wind, beyond the straits of the Bab al-Mandab and down the coast of Africa as far as Dar al-Salam. But to sail from Aden to India would be not only a long and tedious and so, for the merchant, a not very rewarding journey, but, as the record suggests, a well-nigh impossible one. Despite the by then fairly detailed exploration of both the Red Sea and the Persian Gulf, no one had yet succeeded in sailing all the way around Arabia. The problem for a coastimg vessel was, it appears, the scarcity of water along the south Arabian coast between Aden and Ras Mussandam.

Rather, it was until the historic voyage to India of Eudoxus, historic because shortly after 120 B.C. the first of a series of inscriptions appears mentioning a "supervising officer of the Red and Indian Seas." Business with India had obviously picked up in some remarkable fashion to justify having such an official, who was probably a customs officer, and so it seems reasonable to look to the voyage of Euxodus as the occasion when, as other sources tells us, a pilot named Hippalus, "by observing the location of the ports and the condition of the sea, first discovered how to lay his course straight across the ocean."[4] What enabled Hippalus to "lay his course straight across the ocean" was a wind blowing seasonally across the Indian Ocean between south Arabia and the delta of the Indus. One had only the choose the right time and the right place, which Hippalus obviously did, and one could sail, *vento secundo adjuvante*, directly, though not necessarily in perfect safety, between Aden and the Indus, and seasonally in both directions.[5]

This first century "turning" of Arabia with the assistance of the southwest monsoon was, in its effects, not unlike the Portuguese turning of Africa in the opening years of the sixteenth century. Thereafter there was direct maritime communication—principally commercial communication, to be sure—between the Roman consumers installed in urban centers around the Mediterranean and the Eastern producers who made markets in the ports of India and Ceylon. In both cases a series of former middlemen were eliminated from the enterprise, most notably in the present case some of the Arab caravan entrepreneurs like the Nabateans of Petra who had once carried Indian or Eastern goods from South Arabian ports to entrepots in the north and grown rich on the trade. Those same goods could now be landed directly onto Egyptian quays.

But Arabia was not simply a strategic resting place between the Eastern producers and Western markets. It was itself a producer—at least South Arabia, the ancients' "Araby the Blest," was—and so the peninsula did not lose its interest to the outside world, as it was to do later. Indeed, increased knowledge of the peninsula led in the first Christian century to a major and ill-conceived expedition deep into Arabia by the Romans under the command of Aelius Gallus. There the matter rested for the Romans, who in the second and third centuries appear to have been far more concerned with the "Saracen" neighbors along their borders in the north of Arabia than with the reputed riches to be found in the south. What rekindled interest in what might lay beyond the near frontiers of Arabia were two fourth century developments: an active and aggressive Iranian involvement in Arabia and the equally aggressive missionary thrust of Roman Christianity across the empire's southern frontiers into Abyssinian and Arabia itself.

ARABIAN CLIENTS AND TRIBUTARIES

The apogee of all the satellite states of the steppe, the caravan cities that were sometimes clients and on occasion rivals of their imperial neighbors in Byzantium and Iran, occurred before the end of the third century A.D. With the fall of the last of them, Palmyra, the nomadic tribes of the steppe slipped into new configurations. There is more than ample documentation to show how the latter-day Christian Romans, called *Byzantines*, eventually adapted to these new circumstances and fashioned from the tribes on their eastern frontiers a protective network of *foederati*.[6] On the other side of the steppe and under similar circumstances—the Sasanians destroyed the caravan city of Hatra in 240 A.D.—the sources are neither so plentiful nor so plain. Nor are they so close to the events: in place of the contemporary Byzantines Procopius and Malalas we must chiefly make do, for the Sasanians' clients, with the later Arab chroniclers Hamza Isfahani, Tha'alibi, and particularly Tabari (d. 923 A.D.).

The well-known account of the Sasanian shahs with which Tabari chose to preface his history of the Islamic Empire is accompanied by a parallel sketch of the Arab kings of al-Hira,[7] an encampment on the edge of the Syrian steppe where it approaches the Euphrates near Kufa. Tabari's intertwining of Sasanians and Arabs was correct: the two were often connected by ties of clientage and occasionally of competition from the time of the first Sasanian shah Ardashir in the third century to the Islamic conquest of Iraq in the seventh. The Arabs also show up frequently in the western sources as allies of the shah: Joshua Stylites, a Syriac chronicler writing in Mesopotamia about 506, and Procopius, the sophisticated court historian of Justinian, both have a great deal to say about the "Arabs of the Persians." Even in the earliest Islamic memories of the Hijaz, which at first glance appears remote from the Euphrates camp city, al-Hira looms large.

What is less discernible in the sources, though scarcely less important to the Sasanians, was the situation of the Arabs on the peninsula side of the Persian Gulf. The earliest focus of that interest was Gerrha, a considerable city on the Arabian mainland near Bahrayn.[8] The place was well known to the Greek sources as a rich emporium down to the second Christian century, when it may have yielded its commercial traffic to the port of Spasinou Charax.[9] And when the Sasanian insurgent Ardashir rose up against his Parthian overlords, one of his first targets of attack was the Arabs around Bahrayn.[10] To secure the territory he refounded Charax as Astarabad Ardashir, colonized Rev Ardashir (Bushire) on the Persian side of the Gulf and Batn Ardashir on the Arabian side.[11] Tabari's text is uncertain about the name of Batn Ardashir, but the historian knew enough about it to identify it with Khatt.[12]

The presence of the Sasanians in eastern Arabia is confirmed by a South Arabian inscription dated to the end of the third century, when the Himyarite king Shammar Yuhar'ish sent one of his commanders to (or against) the king of the Asad and the land of the Tanukh "which belonged to Persia." There follow in apposition two place names, one of which is generally understood as Qatif in eastern Arabia.[13] If the reading and interpretation are correct, it would confirm the Persians' presence in eastern Arabia in the third century.

The Tanukh are best known from the Arab sources as the

dominant tribe at al-Hira.[14] It is difficult to speak of the "found-
ing" of al-Hira. As its name suggests, it was a stopping place, in
Syriac *herta*,[15] for the bedouin tribes who seasonally migrated to
and from the Syrian steppe and the Iraqi Sawad. The Tanukh were
one such group, and at least some of them settled down in their
former camp and so began its passage to a permanent town. But
the Tanukh were not the only Arabs connected with the town.
Hira and its environs were understood by the Arabs to include
both the bedouin Tanukh and another group known as the Ibad, a
mixed body characterized not so much by their tribal identity as
by their Christianity.[16] Hira may have originally been an Arab
encampment, but its religion was Christian and its literary culture,
which came to it with Christianity, was Syro-Aramaic.

The Lakhmids were not Tanukh, nor were they, for a long
time, Christian. But we have some clue as to when the Banu
Lakhm took over the kingship at al-Hira. Tabari notes that some
of the of the Tanukh migrated to Syria,[17] and his observation is
confirmed by the discovery in the southern Hawran of a Greek
and Nabatean inscription commemorating the tutor (*rby/tro-
pheus*) of "Jadhima, king of the Tanukh." It has been plausibly
suggested that this Jadhima, who is connected in Arab legend with
Zenobia, was king of al-Hira and died in the fighting around
Palmyra in the 270s.[18] He was succeeded at al-Hira, under
unknown circumstances, not by a fellow Tanukh but by one of the
Banu Lakhm, Amr ibn Adi, who had a formal alliance with the
Shah Narseh (r. 293–303 A.D.).

Shapur II was declared Shah in 310 A.D., while still in his
mother's womb, a generous gesture on the part of his subjects,
perhaps, but a provocative one to his neighbors. The prospect of a
long minority rule, and possibly the occurrence of drought on the
Arabian side of the Persian Gulf,[19] triggered events that thrust the
Sasanians even deeper into Arabian affairs. It began with an Arab
invasion. "A great number of the Abd al-Qays," Tabari reports,
"came by sea from Bahrain and Kazima until they took a fortress
at Abruvanshahr, on the (Iranian) coast of Ardashir-Khurra [that
is, Firuzabad], and from the cities of Fars they carried away the
provisions of the inhabitants."[20]

Once Shapur reached majority his revenge against the Arab
raiders—it was the first military campaign he led in person—was
exacting and thorough. He collected an army on the coast of Fars,
carried them across the Persian Gulf to Khatt and Bahrayn on the

Arabian side. There was an engagement with the Arabs of Tamim, Bakr ibn Wa'il, and Abd al-Qays, and when the shah had triumphed over them he marched deep into Yamama where he blocked up the tribal wells and waterholes. Finally, he continued across the peninsula to the vicinity of Medina, more than 600 difficult miles from the Gulf coast, and then apparently marched north where the campaign ended "in the region between the Persian kingdom and the Roman guardposts in the land of Syria."[21] In Arab legend Shapur acquired the name of "the shoulder cruncher," because, as Christensen pleasantly explains, "il avait l'habitude de faire transpercer l'articulation scapulaire."[22]

None of this obviously violent intervention in Arabian affairs seems to have affected commercial activity in the Gulf and along its coasts. In the second half of the fourth century the Roman historian Ammianus Marcellinus could still remark that "there are numerous towns and villages on every coast (of the Gulf) and frequent sailings of ships."[23]

In 337 Shapur turned his attention to the Byzantines. In that year he crossed the frontier and besieged the Roman fortress of Nisibis. Additional invasions and sieges took place in 344, 346 and 350. Troubles on his eastern frontier distracted the shah for a few years, but in 359 he was back in Mesopotamia where he took Amida and Singara. Ammianus Marcellinus is our chief authority for these events, as well as for Julian's disastrous counterattack in 363, and his account is filled with references to the Arabs of Beth Arbaye. The Romans accepted the services of the local Arab tribes, and Shapur's motives were presumably the same, because, as Ammianus explains, "they were well suited to guerilla warfare" (*ad furta bella adpositi*). All the Arabs were warriors; their entire life was spent in movement (*vita est illis semper in fuga*).

The shah had his own mercenaries in Mesopotamia in the fourth century, and their function must have been much the same as the Romans' Arab auxiliaries: reconnoitering, skirmishing, and conducting razzias against the rural population. The bedouin were effective at this, as Ammianus noted, but they were also increasingly vulnerable to the evolving modes of warfare in the fourth and fifth centuries. By that time both sides, Byzantines and Sasanians, fought on the plains of Mesopotamia with chain- and plate-mailed *clibanarii*, and even more recently the Hunnic peoples had taught the two contestants the use of the deadly compound bow.[24] When the Arabs were put into set battle formations against such troops, as the Byzantines did at Callinicum in 531, the results were disastrous.[25]

The Romans of Shapur's day had somewhat different concerns in the East. Diocletian at the end of the previous century had been chiefly concerned to shore up Rome's surviving frontier defenses in the East and to that end had concentrated some of the empire's energies into the constructions of those same "Roman guardposts in the land of Syria" that the shah discovered at the end of his Arabian campaign.[26] According to one somewhat later historian, Diocletian "built forts for the frontiers from Egypt as far as the borders of Persia and stationed frontier troops in them."[27]

In addition to fixed fortifications in depth, the Romans began in the late third or early fourth century to experiment with another strategy for the defense of their frontier; namely, to enlist the bedouin themselves. There is evidence that Aurelian had the assistance of the Tanukh, an Arab tribe that later shows up settled on the eastern side of the steppe, in defeating Zenobia's Palmyrene Arabs.[28] We can detect no formality in that, but at the beginning of the present century a revealing inscription came to light at a place called Namara, a Roman watch-station on the eastern side of the Jabal Druse in Southern Syria. It is in Arabic, the first we have in that language, though still written in Nabatean characters.

> This is the tomb of Imr al-Qays, son of Amr, king of all the Arabs, who assumed the crown, who brought to submission both the tribes of Asad and the Nizar and their kings, who scattered the Mahdhij even to this day, who brought success to the siege of Najran, city of Shammar, who brought to submission the tribe of Ma'add, who handed over the tribes to his sons and he appointed them as his deputies to the Persians and the Romans. And no king equalled his glory to this day. He died in prosperity on the 7th of Kislul, in the year 223 [of the era of Bostra, that is, December 7, 328 A.D.].

Very little is certain about the reading, and so the translation, of this famous inscription.[29] Namara was in Roman territory and the inscription itself is dated by the era of Bostra, the nearby capital of the Roman province of Arabia, and we know something of the subject of the memorial apart from the inscription. According to the later Arab historical tradition, this same Imr al-Qays ibn Amr was lord of the Tanukh, the paramount tribe of the Banu Lakhm who were later to play such an important role at al-Hira, their camp city near the Euphrates, far across the Syrian steppe. The Lakhmids will spend most of their history as allies of the Persians, but here early in the fourth century we have one of them, perhaps the greatest of them, since he claimed to be "king of all the Arabs," comfortably entombed on the "wrong" side of the Syrian steppe next to a Roman police station.

We can conclude from both the text of the inscription and its circumstances that Imr al-Qays stood in some sort of client relationship with the Romans and perhaps—this is less certain—with Shapur's Persians as well. We can recall that not long before this Shapur may well have stood before that same "guardpost" with his own army, which may even have included Imr al-Qays. We cannot connect the two events, the Arab shaykh's and the shah's presence in Syria, but it is difficult escaping the conclusion that they are somehow connected, a conclusion that the "Persians" reference in the inscription itself invites us to draw.

Later Muslim authors like Tabari and his sources did not suffer any hesitation. Indeed, they understood Imr al-Qays exclusively in a Sasanian context, and though they do not connect him with Shapur's march to Medina nor credit him with any of the conquests claimed in his own inscription, they do identify him as the "agent" or tax collector for Shapur II's predecessors among the Arabs both in Iraq and the Hijaz.[30]

Imr al-Qays claims to have marched deep into Arabia and to have subjected what appears to us as all the tribes from the frontiers of Syria as far as Najran on the borders of Himyar to his own—or perhaps his distant patrons'—authority. We cannot assess the truth of that claim because there is no confirmation of it in contemporary South Arabian inscriptions or even in the later Arab historians. The event is not implausible, however, particularly if those distant patrons were the Sasanians. There is no sign that the Romans had any influence in Arabia save perhaps in the person of occasional merchants in the Himyarite ports. But the Persians, we have seen, were already capable in the fourth century of intervening directly and in force in both eastern and western Arabia, either directly in the case of Shapur II, or through an agent, as perhaps here with Imr al-Qays. Finally, there is no claim in any source, early or late, that either Shapur or Imr al-Qays reached or subjected what was until then the most advanced and prosperous of the Arabian polities, the kingdom of Himyar in the Yemen.

THE TRIBES OF THE SOUTH

The disappearance of the Arab trading kingdoms of the north, notably Petra and Palmyra, began, as we have seen, a deep-seated change in the life along Rome's eastern frontier and the Romans' thinking about it. The dislocation had equally profound effects in South Arabia. Whether the passage of the Nabateans from traders to agriculturalists was cause or effect, the entire structure of local protection and revictualizing that enabled caravans to make the long journey from the Yemen to the Nabatean emporium of Mada'in Salih in the northern Hijaz began to dissolve. The inhabitants of settlements along the way passed back into nomadism. "Arabs" in the sense of bedouin appear in South Arabian inscriptions for the first time in the third century; they served as auxiliaries to the kings of Himyar on an increasingly disturbed political landscape.[31]

One of those dislocated tribes was the Kinda, a group that had its origins in the south but was forced to leave and migrate northward, where it took up quarters in or close to the territory of the Ma'add and no more than two days march from Mecca. The date in probably sometime around 305–330 A.D.; that is, about the time that Imr al-Qays had marched into Arabia.[32] The tribe continued to have connections with the south, however, and show up in three important South Arabian inscriptions (Ry 535, 506, 508) serving as vassals of the Himyarite kings.[33]

Christianity in Abyssinia and the Yeman

With the conversion of the Roman emperor Constantine to Christianity, the new faith was at last free to pursue, now with imperial approval and support, its aggressive missionary way not only within but far beyond the frontiers of the Roman Empire. One of the earliest of its successes outside the empire took place in Abyssinia, or as it then called, the kingdom of Axum. By the fourth century Axum was already a substantial commercial power in East Africa, and its Red Sea port of Adulis was an important emporium for the Indian trade. Even in our earliest reference to the place, in the mid-first century A.D., when the commercial maritime guide called "Sailing Around the Erythrean Sea" (Periplus Maris Erythraei) was written, there was already a good deal of

Roman commercial interest in Adulis and a perceptible degree of Hellenization in court circles at Axum.

> About 3000 stades (southward) beyond "Ptolemais of the Hunts" [that is, the Ptolemies' elephant-hunting port on the Red Sea] is a legally limited port of trade, Adulis. . . . From Adulis it is a journey of three days to Koloe, an inland city that is the first trading post for ivory, and from there another five days to the metropolis itself, which is called Axumites [Axum]; into it is brought all the ivory from beyond the Nile through what is called Kyeneion, and from there down to Adulis . . . [34]
>
> The ruler of these regions, from the Moschophagoi to the rest of Barbaria, is Zoskales, a stickler for his possessions and always holding out for getting more, but in other respects a fine person and well versed in reading and writing Greek.[35] (*Periplus* 3–5 = Periplus 1989, pp. 51–53)

The *Periplus* then continues (#6) with a long list of imports and exports to and from Adulis and the interior, including "a little Roman money for the resident foreigners," apparently Roman merchants resident in Adulis.

If our first notice of Abyssinia shows it already enjoying a degree of commercial prosperity, a second, more problematic piece of evidence, portrays an aggressively military side of Axum, one that constituted it not merely a trading partner of Rome but perhaps a rival or even a replacement in the Eastern trade.[36] There was a commercial traveler from Alexandria named Cosmas in Adulis in 518 A.D. At the request of the then Abyssinian king he copied down an inscription on a throne there and published it in his *Christian Topography*. Though there is a great deal of debate on the time it refers to or even whether its self-referring king is, as most believe, a ruler of Axum who led an expedition into Arabia or a king of Himyar who led an expedition into Axum,[37] it seems likely that the inscription is Axumite and belongs to the era before the Christianization of Axum. "After this, when I had become strong and commanded those nearest the kingdom to keep the peace, I waged war on the following peoples. . . . " There follows a long list of nations, all apparently inland neighbors to Axum. The inscription continues:

> All these peoples, defended by mighty mountains, I conquered and forced to submit, taking part in the campaign in person, and

I allowed them to keep their land in exchange for tribute. . . . In the same way, after I had sent a fleet an army against the Arabites and the Kinaidokolpites who live across the Red Sea and forced their kings to submit, I commanded them to pay tribute for their land and to keep the peace by land and sea, and I waged war from Leuke Kome to the land of the Sabeans.

. . . And having brought peace to the whole world under my dominion, I have come down to Adulis to offer sacrifices to Zeus and Ares, and also to Poseidon for the safety of those who set sail on the sea . . . (Cosmas, *Christian Topography*, vol. 2, pp. 60–63)

So by the third century, Axum was rich and powerful enough to possess a fleet and even overseas possessions in Arabia.[38] Indeed, the Adulis inscription copied by Cosmas says quite clearly that the king of Axum had conquered and was taking tribute from the entire west coast of Arabia from Leuke Kome in the north to the Yemen in the south, and including the unspecified "bedouin" ("Arabites") of the Hijaz and possibly the Kinana ("Kinaidokolpites"), the larger tribal group from which the Meccan Quraysh would later derive, in Asir and the northern Yemen.

More, Axum was clearly familiar with Roman merchants and their Greco-Roman culture, conditions that proved to be favorable for the introduction of Christianity into the country three centuries later. Our source is now Rufinus, an Italian Christian who in 402 or 403 A.D. translated Eusebius's *Ecclesiastical History* from Greek into Latin, adding some additional material of his own, which included the following:

There was division of the earth effected by the drawing of lots by the Apostles to preach the word of God, and while different regions fell to different Apostles, Parthia, it was said, was allotted to Thomas, Ethiopia to Matthew, and Hither India, which is next to it, to Bartholemew. In the middle, between this latter India and Parthia, but in the center of a vast country, lies Further India, inhabited by numerous and varied peoples speaking different languages. And since it was so far distant, the ploughshare of the Apostolic preaching never turned that soil.

In the reign of Constantine, however, it received the first seeds of the faith in the following manner. It is said that certain philosopher named Metrodorus, who wished to explore that land in detail, had gotten into Further India. Prompted by his example, once more another philosopher of Tyre, Meropius, wished to go to India for similar reasons. He had with him two young boys for whom he was providing a literary education since they were of his family. One, the younger, was called Edesius and the other Frumentius.

Once the philosopher had satisfied himself there with all the information that nourishes the spirit and was on his way back home, the ship on which he was travelling put into a certain port for water or some other necessities. In this region the Barbarians have the custom, if their neighbors tell them that their treaty with the Romans has been broken, to strangle all the Romans who are found in their midst. The philosopher's boat was thus boarded and he and all the others were slaughtered. The children were discovered under a tree studying and preparing their lessons; they were compassionately spared by the Barbarians and taken to the king.

The children were taken into the royal household; Edesius was put into domestic service and Frumentius, the brighter, set to work in the royal chancery, where he served well and faithfully for a number of years. Then at the death of the original king, and the promotion of the queen mother and her minor heir to the throne, Frumentius assumed what appears to be a powerful place in the kingdom of Axum.

. . . Since Frumentius had in his hands the reins of the kingdom, under God's inspiration and prompting he carefully undertook to discover if there were Christians among the Roman merchants. He put all the necessary facilities at their disposal and advised them to set up in their various locations meeting places where they might come together to pray in the Roman manner. He did the same, and more: he exhorted the rest, and he motived them with his appeals and his favors; he gave them whatever they might find useful, land for their churches and whatever else was required. And he did it all with the urgent desire to see the seed of Christianity grow there.

When the royal heir reached his majority the two Romans were then free to leave, which they did, Edesius to his family in Tyre, while Frumentius made his way the episcopal residence in Alexandria.

He told everything that had happened to the bishop, explaining how it had all come about and urged him to find a worthy man who might be sent there as bishop since there were by then a large number of Christians and churches in Barbaria. Then Athanasius—it was he who had recently become bishop—considered carefully and prudently the proposals and accomplishments of Frumentius and then declared before the episcopal assembly: "But what other man could we find equal to yourself or who could fulfill this charge the way you could?"

And he conferred the episcopate on him and ordered him to return, with the grace of God, to the place whence he had come.

When Frumentius arrived in India as bishop, God granted him, it is said, the grace of such great powers that he accomplished the same miracles as the Apostles had and a very large number of the Barbarians were converted to the faith. It was through him that communities of Christians and churches were founded and the episcopate inaugurated in the regions of India.

We have become aware of these happenings not through popular tales but through the account of Edesius himself, first the companion of Frumentius and then later a priest in Tyre. (Rufinus, *Church History*, vol. 1, pp. 9–10)

When and where exactly did this occur? In addition to the usual ancient inconsistency regarding the name *India*,[39] Rufinus is not generous with either the names of peoples and places or the dates of events. It seems nonetheless that we are dealing with ancient Abyssinia—whose coastal regions at least, as well as Eritrea and the entire eastern "Horn of Africa," were often called *Barbaria* by Greek and Roman authors, and that Frumentius was in fact consecrated bishop of Axum, as Athanasius himself testifies. He was still serving as such when Constantius sent a latter to the "lords" of Abyssinia, Ezana, and Saizana, in 356/7 A.D., requesting the return of Frumentius, "bishop of Axum."[40]

We cannot say how deeply the Christian faith penetrated among the people in Frumentius' days "in the time of Constantine," but though there are inscriptions of Ezana, the king to whom Constantius addressed his letter, that still display pagan formulae, one at least has come to light that is unmistakably Christian.[41] Nothing in Rufinus's account suggests that the king was converted, or even the majority of his people, but the evidence is very strong that by the middle of the fourth century—if Constantius's letter and the inscription have to do with the same person—there was a Christian kingdom in Abyssinia.

At about the same time that Constantius sent his letter to Axum, there was another Christian initiative across the straits in the Yemen, though here the source is not Rufinus, who knows nothing of these events, but the fifth century Greek church historian Philostorgios, who is, incidentally, ignorant of Frumentius and his accomplishments.

Constantius [r. 337–361 A.D.] sent ambassadors to the people once called the Sabeans and now named Himyarites. These are

descendents of the people born of Abraham's daughter Ket- ·
thura. The region where they dwell is called Great and Happy
Arabia by the Greeks and touches the Outer Ocean. Its capital is
Saba, whose queen once journeyed to visit Solomon. These are
people of the circumcision and are circumcised on the eighth
day. They sacrifice to the sun and moon and to native gods. A
considerable number of Jews live mixed in among them.

It was to them that Constantius sent an embassy with the
intent of leading them to the true faith. He further thought to
win over the king of that people with rich gifts and persuasive
words and thus to sow the seeds of religion in that place. He
requested that both Romans sailing there and natives of the
region who might wish to convert to Christ should be allowed
to build churches. He gave to the legates a large sum of money
to underwrite the church construction.

The head of this mission was Theophilos the Indian, who
had been sent as a hostage from Divus to the Romans in Constantine's day while he was still a young man. Divus is an island
in that region; the inhabitants are also known as "Indians."
After Theophilos had lived for a long time among the Romans
his manner of life had become extremely virtuous and he had
embraced a true sense of God. He took up the monastic life and
was promoted to the grade of deacon. But all this was earlier.
Later, when he had taken up this mission, he was adorned with
the episcopal dignity by his coreligionists.

For the rest, since he wished the delegation to have a certain
magnificence and charm, Constantius had 200 Cappadocian ·
thoroughbreds put upon ships as well as many other gifts, in
part to provoke admiration, in part to win agreement. Theophilos, then, when he had come to the Sabeans, attempted to win
over their ruler to Christ and draw back from the error of
paganism. And the usual deceit and malice of the Jews was
forced to take refuge in total silence as Theophilos again and
again demonstrated, by his marvelous works, that faith in
Christ was invincible. The embassy had a happy outcome when
the prince of that people sincerely embraced the true faith and
had built three churches in the region, though not with the
money that the embassy had brought from the emperor but
rather from those resources that he generously supplied from his
personal funds, striving to compete with Theophilos' wondrous
works by those of his own. Of those churches one was built in
the nation's capital which they call Zaphar; a second in a market town of the Romans on the Outer Ocean. This place is
called Aden, and there all the Romans are accustomed to make

port. The third was built in another part of the area where there is a a Persian market at the mouth of the Persian Sea. (Philostorgios, *Church History*, vol. 3, p. 4)

The reality of Frumentius can be verified by the independent witness of Athanasius, which in turn points us to Ezana, himself certified by inscriptions, one of which is Christian. In the Yemen, however, there is no trace whatsoever of Christianity in any of the inscriptions recovered there until the sixth century.[42] Philostorgios may be right, but we have no way of confirming it—indeed the pagan inscriptions of the fourth and the following century in South Arabia implicitly deny it—and certainly not from the Arab tradition, which has an entirely different version of how Christianity came to South Arabia. This is how it is put in the eighth century by Muhammad's biographer Ibn Ishaq

> In Najran there were some people who upheld the religion of Jesus son of Mary ["Isa ibn Maryam"], a virtuous and upright people who followed the Gospel. Their head was named Abdullah ibn al-Thamir. The place where that religion took root was in Najran, at that time the center of the Arabs' country; its people, and indeed the rest of the Arabs, were idolaters. A Christian boy by the name of Phemion ["Faymiyun"] had settled there and converted the people to his religion. (Ibn Ishaq 1955, p. 14)

There is another, completely independent account of the "Christening of the people of Najran." It occurs in a Nestorian chronicle, the "Chronicle of Séert," which was compiled about 1036 A.D. but out of palpably older material.

> In the land of Najran of Yemen there was, in the days of (Shah) Yazdigard (r. 399–420 A.D.), a tradesman, well known in his country, whose name was Hayyan. He went to Constantinople on business and returned to his country. Later he planned to go to Persia and passed through al-Hira. There he frequented the society of Christians and learned their religion. So he was baptized there and remained in that place for some time. Finally he returned to his own country and exhorted the people to adopt his faith, and made his family Christians, as well as a number of the people in this part of the country. And certain persons joined him and assisted him in converting to Christianity the people of the Himyarite land and the adjacent tracts of Abyssinia . . . (*Chronicle of Séert* = *Patrologia Orientalis*, vol. 4, p. 218)

There is no necessary contradiction between the two accounts. Theophilos's mission may indeed have had ephemeral results so that Christianity "came to the Yemen" on a number of different occasions.

The Arabs had, as we have just seen, their own version of events. In what follows Ibn Ishaq tells us that he had derived his information from accounts going back to Wahb ibn Munabbih, an early Muslim storyteller about matters both Jewish and Christian:

> The origin of Christianity in Najran was due to a man named Phemion who was a righteous, earnest, ascetic man whose prayers were answered. He used to wander between towns: as soon as he became known in one town he moved to another, eating only what he earned, for he was a builder by trade, using mud bricks. He used to keep Sunday as a day of rest and he would do no work then. He used to go into a desert place and pray there until evening.
>
> While he was following his trade in a Syrian village, withdrawing himself from men, one of the people there called Salih perceived what manner of man he was and felt a violent affection for him, so that unseen by Phemion he used to follow him from place to place, until one Sunday he went as his wont was out into the desert followed by Salih. (Ibn Ishaq 1955, p. 14)

Phemion was apparently threatened by a poisonous snake, and not knowing that the holy man had already disposed of it, Salih cried out and so his hiding place was revealed. He expressed a desire to accompany Phemion. Permission was granted and the two wandered about Syria, Phemion working various miraculous cures.

> They reached the land of the Arabs, who attacked them and a caravan carried them off and sold them in Najran. At this time the people of Najran followed the religion of the Arabs worshiping a great palm tree there. Every year they had a festival when they hung on the tree any fine garment they could find and women's jewels. Then they sallied out and devoted the day to it.
> Phemion was sold to one noble and Salih to another. Now it happened that when Phemion was praying earnestly at night in a house which his master had assigned to him, the whole house was filled with light so that it shone as it were without a lamp. His master was amazed at the sight, and asked him about his religion. Phemion told him and said they were in error: as for the palm tree, it could neither help nor hurt; and if he were to

curse the tree in the name of God, He would destroy it, for He was God Alone, without companion. "Then do so," said his master, "for if you do that we shall embrace your religion and abandon our present faith." After purifying himself and performing two prostrations, he invoked God against the tree and God sent a wind against it which tore it from its roots and cast it to the ground. Then the people of Najran adopted his religion and he instructed them in the law of Jesus son of Mary. . . . This was the origin of Christianity in Najran in the land of the Arabs. Such is the report of Wahb ibn Munabbih on the authority of the people of Najran. (Ibn Ishaq 1955, pp. 15–16)

A Jewish Community

From as far back as there are inscriptions with religious content, the religion of South Arabia was polytheistic; various deities are called upon by name or simply addressed as "all the gods and goddesses." Of those named many are familiar from the larger world of the Semites, Athar, for example, who seems to be the principal god, or at least the one most often mentioned first in lists, whereas others are somewhat more uncertain figures. What does appear to be a consistent trait, however, is that the deity was regarded as the *lord* of a shrine that in turn served as a cult center and was used by a number of different tribes united by their common veneration of the god, an arrangement not very different from what occurred later at the shrine of the lord of Mecca. And, as at Mecca, pilgrimage to one or other of the cult shrines was a normal and popular function of the religious life in South Arabia.

What changes in the portrait of South Arabian religion is the replacement of the normal formulae in the fourth and fifth centuries by inscriptions with a very different and apparently monotheistic terminology.[43] There now appears to be recognized a supreme god, perhaps a unique God, who is generally called by name *the Merciful (Rahmanan)* and who is further characterized as "lord of the heaven" or "lord of heaven and earth."[44] A number of explanations have been offered to explain the appearance of this so-called Rahmanism. One is that "Rahmanism" in South Arabia is identical with what is called *Hanifism* in the Quran and the lives of Muhammad,[45] a kind of homegrown monotheism or henotheism of the type later alleged to have been practiced by certain individuals at Mecca;[46] or that the inscriptions are either Jewish or Judaizing or perhaps even Christian, though they lack the explicit identifying formulae of the unmistakably Jewish or Christian inscriptions.

With the discovery of new material, however, some of the mystery has been removed. Most of these monotheistic inscriptions, particularly the royal ones bearing the name of the king, are in fact Jewish. Further, it is possible to conclude that the royal house of Himyar, and likely most of the nobility, was Jewish from least the time of Malik-karib to that of Shahrbi'l Ya'fur in the mid-fifth century.[47]

If the royal house of the Yemen was Jewish as early as the fifth century, how did this belief arrive in South Arabia? The classical and canonical biography of Muhammad, the *Life* composed by Ibn Ishaq, devotes a good deal of its early attention to the politics and religion of the Yemen. There was once a line there called the Tubba', Ibn Ishaq tells us, and one of its last sixth century members was a certain Tiban As'ad Abu Karib:

> When he [that is, As'ad Abu Karib] came from the east, he had passed by Medina without harming its people; but he left behind there one of his sons who was treacherously slain. Thereupon he returned with the intention of destroying the town and exterminating its people and cutting down its palms. . . . While Tubba was occupied in this fighting there came two Jewish rabbis from the Banu Qurayza . . .

That is, one of the Jewish tribes of Medina. Ibn Ishaq appends a genealogy that traces them directly back through Jacob and Isaac to Abraham.

> . . . learned men well grounded in tradition. They had heard of the king's intention to destroy the town and its people and they said to him, "O king, do not do it, for if you persist in your intention something will happen to prevent your carrying it out and we fear that you will incur speedy retribution." When the king asked the reason for this they told him that Yathrib [as Medina was then called] was the place to which a prophet of the Quraysh would migrate in time to come, and it would be his home and resting place. Seeing that these men had hidden knowledge the king took their words in good part and gave up his design, departed from Medina and embraced the rabbis' religion. (Ibn Ishaq 1955, p. 7)

Thus it was, according to the later Muslim tradition, that the royal line in the Yemen had become Jewish. But the recollection of that event has a somewhat different purpose, to enable the Jews of Medina, in the person of the two rabbis taken from there, to authenticate the shrine at Mecca, as the Medinese Jews contemporary with Muhammad resolutely refused to do.

> ... Now the Tubba and his men were (still at that time) idolaters. He set out (from Medina) for Mecca, which was on his way to the Yemen, and when he was between Usfan and Amaj some men of the Hudhayl came to him saying, "O king, may we not lead you to an ancient treasury which former kings have overlooked? It contains pearls, topaz, rubies, gold and silver." Certainly, said he, and they added it was a temple in Mecca which its people worshiped and where they prayed. But the real intention of the Hudhaylis was to encompass his destruction, for they knew that any king that treated it [that is, the Ka'ba in Mecca] with disrespect was sure to die.
>
> Having agreed to their proposal he sent to the two rabbis (he had taken with him from Medina) and asked their opinion. They told him that the sole object of the tribe was to destroy him and his army. "We know of no other temple in the land which God has chosen for Himself," said they, "and if you do what they suggest, you and all your men will perish." The king asked them what he should do when he got there, and they told him to do what the people of Mecca did: to circumambulate the temple, to venerate and honor it, to shave his head and to behave with all humility until he had left its precincts.
>
> The king asked them why they too should not do likewise. They replied that it was indeed the temple of their father Abraham, but the idols which the inhabitants had set up around it, and the blood which they shed there, presented an insuperable obstacle. They are unclean polytheists, said they, or words to that effect.
>
> Recognizing the soundness and truth of their words, the king summoned the men from Hudhayl and cut off their hands and feet, and continued his journey to Mecca. He went round the Ka'ba, sacrificed and shaved his head, staying there six days, so they say, sacrificing animals which he distributed to the people and giving them honey to drink. (Ibn Ishaq 1955, pp. 8-9)

Then, somewhat unexpectedly, we are instructed on the origin of the *kiswa*, the cloth covering of the Mecca Ka'ba.

> It was revealed to him [that is, the Tubba Abu Karib] in a dream that he should cover the temple, so he covered it with woven palm branches; a later vision showed him that he must do better

so he covered it with Yemeni cloth; a third vision induced him to cover it with fine striped Yemen cloth. He ordered its Jurhum guardians to keep it clean and not to allow blood, dead bodies or menstrual cloths to come near it, and he made a door and a key for it. (Ibn Ishaq 1955, p. 9)

Ibn Ishaq's narrative then picks up its main thread once again.

. . . When the Tubba drew near to the Yemen, the Himyarites blocked his path, refusing to let him pass because he had abandoned their religion. When he incited them to accept his (new) religion on the ground that it was better than theirs, they proposed that the matter should be subject to the ordeal by fire. The Yemenis say that a fire used to settle matters in dispute among them by consuming the guilty and letting the innocent go unscathed. So his people went forth with their idols and sacred objects, and the two rabbis went forth with their sacred books hanging like necklaces from their necks until they halted at the place whence the fire used to blaze out.[48] On this occasion when it came out the Yemenis withdrew in terror, but their followers encouraged them and urged them to stand fast, so they held their ground until the fire covered them and consumed their idols and sacred objects and the men who bore them. But the two rabbis came out with their sacred books, sweating profusely but otherwise unharmed. Thereupon the Himyarites accepted the king's religion. Such was the origins of Judaism in the Yemen. (Ibn Ishaq 1955, p. 10)

Abu Karib was succeeded by his son Hasan, but when this latter attempted to lead an expedition to Iraq, his troops rebelled and the king himself was murdered by his brother Amr. As Ibn Ishaq sums up, "When Amr died, the Himyarite kingdom fell into disorder and the people split up into parties."[49]

After a brief interregnum Hasan's nephew, Dhu Nuwas, was finally put upon the throne of Himyar. "They made him king and all the tribes of Himyar joined him. He was the last of the Yamani kings. . . . He was called Joseph and he reigned for some considerable time" (Ibn Ishaq 1955, p. 14).

THE ABYSSINIANS INVADE

Procopius, the imperial historian of Byzantium in the era of Justianian (527–565 A.D.), was both interested in and informed on the Red Sea region, as was his royal patron. The reason was not very complex: the inauguration of a new commercial strategy against Iran: "At that time [that is, about the time of the battle of Callinicum in 531 A.D.] the idea occurred to the Emperor Justinian to ally himself to the Ethiopians and the Himyarites, in order to injure the Persians" (Procopius, *Wars*, vol. 1, 19.1).

For Procopius the Himyarites were generically the people living in the southwest of the Arabia peninsula, and they had, he explains, close relations with the people on the African shore:

> Roughly across from the Himyarites on the opposite mainland live the Ethiopians who all called Axumites because their king resides in the city of Axum. And the expanse of sea that lies between is crossed in a voyage of five days and nights, with a moderately favorable wind. For here they are accustomed to navigate by night as well since there are no dangerous shoals . . .
> The harbor of the Himyarites from which they are accustomed to sail for the voyage to Ethiopia is called Bulicas; and at the end of the voyage they always put in at the harbor of the people of Adulis. The city of Adulis itself is set back from the harbor at a distance of about twenty stades, and from there to Axum it is (an overland trip of) twelve days. (Procopius, *Wars*, vol. 1, 19.17–22)

The Abyssinians, then, or more precisely, the kingdom of Axum with its port of Adulis on the African shore of the Red Sea, constituted an important part of Byzantine strategy for both Arabia and Persia in the sixth century. The Abyssinians might be able to do what the Byzantines could not, compete with the Persians in the Far Eastern ports.

The Abyssinians were Christians and so could be, and were, manipulated from Constantinople in the name of religion by both Justin (r. 517–527 A.D.) and Justinian (r. 527–565 A.D.). And the occasion was conveniently provided by the Himyarite king Dhu Nuwas. Ibn Ishaq and his sources were aware, as we have seen, that there was a Jewish king named Dhu Nuwas reigning in the Yemen in the first half of the sixth century. He was, as a matter of fact, a rather well-known ruler, and his deeds were recalled not only in his own South Arabian tongue, but in Greek, Syriac and Arabic throughout the Near East.[50] The reason for this widespread notoriety was that Dhu Nuwas instituted a pogrom against the Christians of South Arabia and thus provoked a widespread reaction in Christian communities throughout the Near East and, in the end, an invasion of his territory by the Abyssinians from across the Bab al-Mandab.

This latter was, it appears, the second such incursion in the sixth century. When the first took place we cannot say, though the Byzantine merchant Cosmas, on visit to Adulis ca. 518 A.D., saw preparations for it under way.[51] The expedition was in any event successful, as emerges from another account of the affair, the *Book of the Himyarites,* a Christian work that is a blend of hagiography and history. It claims to have been written sometimes in the 530s and to be based on the accounts of eyewitnesses to the events of some ten years earlier.[52] Chapter V of the work professes to tell of "the first coming of HYWN' and the Abyssinians," and this must have been the expedition Cosmas saw being prepared in Adulis in 518 A.D. When it actually arrived or who "HYWN'" was there is no way of telling, but according to the next chapter of the *Book of the Himyarites,* the expedition was a success, though in what way we are not told, and the troops returned to Abyssinia (Chapter VII).

What seems to have happened thereafter is that after the return home of the invasion army, an Abyssinian viceroy was left behind to rule in South Arabia. At his death, however, he was replaced either by the former king or a new local ruler who was Jewish. This was Dhu Nuwas, the Yusuf al-As'ar of his own inscriptions, who is referred to as *Masruq* and *the crucifier* throughout the Christian *Book of the Himyarites.*

Dhu Nuwas's first target was the Abyssinian "colonists" still resident in Himyar, and specifically in Zafar, after the return of the army. He sent to them "Jewish priests, who were from Tiberias," with a letter swearing "by Adonai and by the Ark and by the Torah" that they would be sent unharmed back to Abyssinia if they surrendered the town.[53]

The king behaved treacherously, according to the *Book of the Himyarites.* He first murdered the Abyssinians who came out of the town in response to his promise of safe-conduct and then proceeded against the undefended town of Zafar itself, where the remaining males, 200 in all, were burned inside the town church. The same rabbis were then dispatched throughout the land of Himyar with orders that all Christians should renounce Christ or be killed.[54]

Dhu Nuwas next turned to Najran, which was inhabited not by Abyssinian colonists but by indigenous Christians. Once again he pledged himself to justice, "swearing by the Merciful One" (*Rahmana*), that those who came out willingly would have only to stand trial on civil grounds of disobedience and might in consequence be subject to fine, but that no other evil would be visited upon them. The Najranites finally decided that their best chance was to go out and submit to Dhu Nuwas, and so 150 of their "notables" presented themselves at the king's camp. There was to be no trial, they learned. They were called upon to deny Christ, and when they refused to do so, were condemned to execution.[55]

There is no doubt that this was a religious persecution, and though hagiographical accounts like the *Book of the Himyarites* and the "Acts" of the various martyrs of Najran pay little attention to it, it is equally clear that a political struggle was going on as well. There was in fact a civil war for power in the land of Himyar, in which one faction, that represented by Dhu Nuwas, happened to be Jews, and the other, in numbers if not in inspiration, Christian. This in turn had escalated into a larger struggle in which the local Christians could count on the support of the Christian kingdom of Axum across the Red Sea and the more distant Christian Roman Empire, whereas Dhu Nuwas and his supporters would naturally be cast into alliance with the Persians.[56]

The news of what had occurred at Najran spread rapidly across the Christian *oikoumene*, to the camp of the Christian Banu Lakhm at al-Hira near the Euphrates,[57] to the Negus or king of Abyssinia across the straits in Axum, and even, according to the later Muslim account, to the Christian emperor at Constantinople:

> A man of Saba'a called Daus Dhu Tha'laban escaped on a horse and taking to the desert, he eluded them [that is, the forces of Dhu Nuwas]. He pressed on till he reached the Byzantine court, where he asked the emperor to aid him against Dhu Nuwas and his troops, telling him what had happened. The latter replied that his country was too distant for him to be able to help by sending troops, but that he would write to the Abyssinian king who was a Christian and whose land was near the Yemen. Accordingly he did write ordering him to help Daus and seek revenge. Daus went to the Negus with the emperor's letter, and he sent with him 70,000 Abyssinians, putting over them a man called Aryat.
>
> With the (Negus's) army there was a man called Abraha al-Ashram [that is, "Split Face"]. Aryat crossed the sea with Daus Dhu Tha'laban and landed in the Yemen. Dhu Nuwas with the

Himyarites and such of the Yemeni tribes as were under his command came out against him, and after an engagement Dhu Nuwas and his force was put to flight. Seeing that his cause was lost Dhu Nuwas turned his horse seawards, beating it till it entered the waves and carried him through the shallows into the deep water. This was last that was seen of him. Aryat entered the Yemen and took possession of it. (Ibn Ishaq 1955, p. 18)

According to the *Book of the Himyarites*, which is poorly preserved in this section, the instigation to action was not a letter from Constantinople but, more plausibly, the arrival at the court of the Negus Kaleb of a refugee from Najran by the name of Umayya.[58] The Negus Kaleb, also known as Ella Asbeha or, as Procopius calls him, "Hellestheaios," despatched the army described by Ibn Ishaq into action across the straits in the Yemen. It was met on the beaches by Dhu Nuwas and his men, all of whom were slain by the Abyssinians.

There is no mention of either Aryat or Abraha in the *Book of the Himyarites*, but Abraha is well known from a variety of sources and the "Aryat" of the Muslims' account of the sequel to the Abyssinian invasion of the Yemen may be the same Himyarite Christian who was delegated by the Negus of Ethiopia to rule the Yemen. He is referred to by the Greek historian Procopius as "Esimiphaios" and called Samu Yafaʿ in the South Arabian inscriptions.[59] Aryat or Esimiphaios, the emperor Justinian had a use for him, as Procopius tells us:

At that time, when Hellestheaios [= Kaleb = Ella Asbeha d. ca. 536] was reigning over the Ethiopians and Esimiphaios [Samuyafaʿ] of the Homeritae, the Emperor Justinian sent an ambassador,[60] Julianus, asking that both should combine with the Romans by reason of their common faith, in making war on the Persians, the object being that the Ethiopians, by buying silk (*metaxa*) from the Indians and re-selling it to the Romans, should possess themselves of great wealth, while profiting the Romans only in that they would no longer be forced to part with their own wealth to the enemy . . . (Procopius, *Wars*, vol. 1, 20.9–10)

The Himyarites were unconvinced by these arguments. Without giving Justinian a direct refusal, they simply took no action, and the emperor had no way of constraining them to do so.

CHAPTER 3

The Arabian Oikoumene

The great Arab trade emporia, enterprises that brought both wealth and power, had their heyday from the first to the third centuries of the Christian era. They were but towns and villages housed in inexplicably monumental ruins—the Quran, for example, has no inkling of the Nabatean commercial prosperity that built the "palaces and castles" (Quran 7: 74) of Mada'in Salih in the northern Hijaz—when there came upon the scene in Arabia the man reputed by the later Arabs to be the founder of the fortunes of the last of the great caravan cities, Hashim ibn Abd Manaf of Mecca.

HASHIM THE TRADER

Lodged somewhere between the Great Powers, though just beyond the direct reach of either of them, was the shrine-settlement of Mecca in Western Arabia. Earlier stories about the place had been confined mostly to struggles about the possession of the shrine, but in the generation of Abd Manaf's sons, the horizons of the Meccan community begin to broaden onto the political and commercial terrain of the Middle East. And the name of one of the sons, Hashim, takes on a particular importance. "The second of Abd Manaf's sons Hashim superintended the feeding (*rifada*) and the watering (*siqaya*) of the pilgrims because (his elder brother) Abd Shams was a great traveller who was seldom to be found in Mecca; moreover, the latter was a poor man with a large family, while Hashim was a well-to-do man . . . " (Ibn Ishaq 1955, p. 58).

Everything the later Arabs knew about Hashim suggested that both his celebrity and his prosperity came from commerce: he was first, foremost, and almost exclusively a trader. We can only guess at his dates. Muhammad was reportedly born in 570 A.D., and according to Ibn Ishaq, he was 8-years-old when his grandfather

Abd al-Muttalib died. Thus Abd al-Muttalib would have passed away sometime about 580 A.D., and if his commonly asserted age of 110 is, like all other such figures, somewhat exaggerated,[1] he must have been born about 500 A.D., shortly after his father Hashim had reportedly concluded commercial treaties in Syria. Hashim, then, lived in the second half of the fifth Christian century, ca. 440–500 A.D.

There follows in the Ibn Ishaq-Ibn Hisham account of Hashim's rise to power another story—this one prefixed with the warning "it is alleged"—of how he levied a tax on the Quraysh to feed the pilgrims and with the selfsame sentiments about the pilgrims' being "God's neighbors" that had previously been attributed to Qusayy. The text continues directly, and Ibn Ishaq expresses yet another reservation concerning his information about Hashim: "It is alleged that Hashim was the first to institute the two caravan journeys of the Quraysh, summer and winter, and the first to provide *tharid* (a broth in which bread is broken up). Actually his name was Amr, but he was called Hashim because he broke up bread in this way for his people in Mecca . . . " (Ibn Ishaq 1955, p. 58).

A parallel account in Ibn Sa'd serves almost as a gloss on this passage, and on the odd and awkward Quranic verses that lie behind it: "For the security arrangements (*ilaf*) of the Quraysh, their agreements of the journey of winter and of summer" (Quran 106: 1–2).

The verses will be put in a larger context in Chapter 4, but here we restrict ourselves to Ibn Sa'd's interpretation, which he derived from Ibn Abbas (d. ca. 687), one of the earliest and most authoritative commentators on the Quran:

> Hashim's name was Amr, and to him is the reference to the *ilaf* of the Quraysh (Quran 106: 1). The *ilaf* of the Quraysh was a custom of the Quraysh, and the person of the Quraysh who introduced the two journeys was he. The first journey during winter was made towards the Yemen and Abyssinia; its ruler, the Negus, honored them and loved him. The (other) journey during the summer was towards Syria and Gaza, and sometimes they reached Anqira [that is, Ankara]. They were admitted before Qaysar [that is, "Caesar"; see later] who honored them and loved him.[2]
>
> Once the Quraysh had to face a famine which lasted for several years, and all they had was exhausted. Then Hashim went to Syria and ordered bread which was baked in large

quantity for him. He loaded it in bags on camels till he reached Mecca, and broke them in smaller pieces and dipped them in a ✓ broth. He slaughtered these camels and then ordered them to be cooked; then he emptied the kettles into plates. The people of Mecca ate to their satisfaction, and then after years of affliction the first showers came upon them. So he received the appellation of Hashim [that is, one who breaks bread and other things into pieces].

[According to another account] . . . Hashim bore that burden which had exhausted the people of high birth and they were unable to bear it. He brought for them bags full of wheat from Syria, which people covet. He entertained the people of Mecca on *hashim* (pieces of bread) and soaked them in the broth of the meat of fat animals. The people began to eat from wooden cups which were brimful, on the verge of overflowing . . . " (Ibn Sa'd, vol. 1, pp. 43–44)

There are two distinct stories here, the first about commercial treaties and the second about bringing provisions from Syria, connected only by the fact that they both have to do with Syria. The account of the commercial treaties is, as we shall see, a rather straightforward *midrash* on Sura 106 of the Quran, but the bread story is somewhat mystifying, with its highly implausible suggestion that bread was carried a month's journey from Syria to feed Mecca. We can well believe that there were occasional food shortages in Mecca and that subsistence provisions had to be brought in from the outside, as they were in even more prosperous Islamic times; but there were much closer sources of grain, even in the Hijaz, and the entire tale has the appearance of being nothing more than a fanciful etymological explanation of "Hashim," ↰ which was obviously understood by that generation, and for long afterward, as a title rather than a name.[3]

Ibn Ishaq's account of Hashim concludes:

Hashim ibn Abd Manaf died in Gaza in the land of Syria while travelling with merchandise, and Abd Manaf's son al-Muttalib assumed the right of feeding and watering the pilgrims. He was younger than Abd Shams and Hashim, but he was held in high esteem among his people, who called him al-Fayd on account of his liberality and high character.

. . . Hashim was the first of the sons (of Abd Manaf) to die at Gaza in Syria, followed by Abd Shams in Mecca, then al-Muttalib in Radman in the Yemen and lastly Nawfal at Salman in Iraq. (Ibn Ishaq 1955, pp. 58–59)

NORTHERN NEIGHBORS

It is above all to the activities of Hashim the trader that the Arab sources look in estimating his role in the evolution of pre-Islamic Mecca.[4] Those activities fall into two distinct but related categories, and both are connected in turn with a brief and highly enigmatic reference in that same early Sura 106 of the Quran. Hashim, we are told, secured a trading permit from the Byzantine *qaysar*. The term is admittedly an elastic one, ranging, improbably, from the emperor himself to a local Byzantine deputy somewhere on the Hijaz frontier. Some of the Arab sources fancy the former, an identification that magnifies the Qurashite Hashim,[5] but Tabari may be much closer to the mark in describing Hashim's contacts as "Byzantine (*rumi*) rulers of Syria and with Ghassan."[6] This too would carry us back to the opening years of the sixth century, when the Banu Ghassan were first emerging as the Byzantine wardens of the steppe in Syria, the Transjordan, and the northern Hijaz.

Ibn Ishaq's detailed information on affairs in South Arabia apart, the Muslim Arab sources, all of them at some remove from the events, give us little sense of the wider political and commercial milieu in which Mecca's economic growth unfolded. But there were other informed witnesses, notably in Constantinople, since in the sixth century the Arab lands had reentered Roman consciousness to a degree unparalleled since the time of Augustus. One reason, as we have seen, was the institution of a new defense system whereby the Byzantines had begun to farm out their security responsibilities to the Arab tribes who dwelt along the frontier. The Arabs received in return both gold and food supplies (*annona*).

By the last quarter of the fifth century the old Roman strategy of defending the frontiers of the empire with regular troops and fixed fortifications had given way, particularly in the east, to other strategies. One of them was the recruitment of frontier militias (*limitanei*) or armed settlers who were subsidized to settle into, and defend, the agricultural areas bordering the steppe. Another was to engage in a formal treaty arrangement with the shaykhs of the bedouin tribes living just outside that sown territory. One such group was the Banu Ghassan who appeared in the Transjordan sometime about 483 A.D. and petitioned the Byzantine authorities for permission to settle on the frontier under the same treaty terms granted to other Arab groups. These conditions are not described, but they almost certainly included conversion to Christianity and, at this early stage, the payment of tribute.

In 473, we are told, the Romans had lost the island of Iotabe at the mouth of the Gulf of Aqaba, and presumably the adjacent coastal territory in the northern Hijaz as well, to a certain Imr al-Qays, "Amorkesos" in the Greek sources. It is not certain who this Arab adventurer was, but for reasons unknown he had come into what was Byzantine territory, expelled the Byzantine customs officials from the island, and begun to carve out an enclave for himself in northern Arabia. In an attempt to regularize his position, Imr al-Qays sent a Christian bishop to Constantinople to speak on his behalf. The Emperor Leo preferred to impress the phylarch himself rather than his deputy, and Imr al-Qays was summoned to the capital and given a royal reception. Not to any great avail, apparently. In the end the emperor was forced to concede to the upstart shaykh his possession of Iotabe, and probably a treaty as drawn up confirming Imr al-Qays's privileges and obligations as a phylarch, a Roman-deputized shaykh, in what can only have been the province the Romans called *Palestina Tertia,* the broad and ill-defined area stretching south of Beersheba into the Negev and there eastward across the Jordan into the northern Hijaz.[7]

Some ten years later, then, the Banu Ghassan concluded a treaty arrangement with the Byzantines and became clients of the emperor in the Transjordan. At some unknown point after that they must have moved into Imr al-Qays's territory and expropriated Iotabe and its commercial revenues for themselves. Thus in the lifetime of the Meccan Hashim the Ghassanids were the paramount tribe and so too the Byzantines' deputies or agents among the bedouin of the northern Hijaz. The course of federation was not always smooth, but between 500 and 528 the Banu Ghassan made their peace with Byzantium, and on that latter date the Ghassanid Harith ibn Jabala performed a valuable service for the empire by taking the field against the rival Arab clients of the Sasanians across the steppe.[8] Harith was rewarded by Rome from the spoils of his Kindite predecessor's holdings; he too was named *phylarch,* which Procopius defines as "any leader of the Saracens federated by treaty to the Romans," with an actual jurisdiction that must have extended from south of Bostra north as far as Damascus and on the east to the vicinity of Palmyra. The Byzantine historian Procopius, a contemporary of Muhammad's grand-father, gives his own sweeping evaluation of the ascendancy of Harith, here called in Greek *Arethas*: "The Emperor Justinian put in command of as many clans as possible Arethas son of Gabalas, who ruled over the Saracens of Arabia, and bestowed upon him the title of king, a thing which among the Romans had not been done before" (Procopius, *Wars*, vol. 1, 17.47).

Harith does not immediately concern us here, but in what was clearly a related move, his brother Abu Karib received his father Jabala's old territory of *Palestina Tertia*, the Negev, and parts of the northern Hijaz. The island of Iotabe that was also included in the deal was, as we shall see, a valuable piece of real estate. According to Procopius, who could scarcely conceal his disdain for the bargain, Justinian was to some extent moved by the fact that Abu Karib had formally ceded to the empire some quite worthless Hijaz real estate called *the Palm Grove*

> ... where absolutely nothing is produced except palms. Abu Karib gave these groves to the emperor Justinian; he was the ruler of the Saracens there and the emperor appointed him phylarch of the Saracens in Palestine. He continually guarded the land from plundering, for Abu Karib always seemed a man to be feared, and exceptionally energetic, both the barbarians over whom he ruled, and to the enemy no less so. Formally, therefore, the emperor holds the Palm Grove, but it is impossible for him to control it in the slightest, for a land completely destitute of human beings, and extremely parched, lies between, extending for a distance of ten days journey. In addition, the groves themselves are completely worthless and Abu Karib gave them only as a nominal gift, and the emperor accepted it as such. So much then for the Palm Grove.[9] (Procopius, *Wars*, vol. 1, 19.9–13)

With Abu Karib we are now in the generation immediately following Hashim, the reputed founder of Mecca's economic prosperity. Procopius, however, knows nothing of Hashim, nor indeed of Mecca, though he was keenly interested in, and informed about, the Red Sea area. In his history of the wars of Justinian (r. 527–565 A.D.) Procopius provides his readers with a survey of the entire coast of western Arabia as it was known in the mid-sixth century:

> The boundaries of Palestine stretch eastward to the sea called Red. This sea begins from the Indian parts and end at that point

of the Roman Empire. And a city lies on its shore called Aila and here the sea comes to an end, as I have said, and becomes a very narrow gulf. As you sail (southward) into the (Red) Sea from there, the mountains of Egypt lie on your right, extending toward the south, while on the other (Arabian) side *a country deserted by men stretches northward for a great distance.*

As you sail on the land on either side (of the Gulf of Aqaba) is visible as far as the island of Iotabe [that is, the present Tirhan Island]. . . . Hebrews had long dwelt there in independence, but under the rule of Justinian, they became Roman subjects. From there onward is a great open sea [that is, the Red Sea]. The land on the right disappears and mariners always anchor along the left [that is, the Arabian] coast when night falls since it is impossible to navigate in the darkness due to the fact that the sea is full of shoals . . .

By this reckoning, the frontier of the Roman Empire stood at the southern end of the Gulf of Aqaba, a notion that smacks far more of the ideal than of the real. Southward from there stretched the political domain of the "Saracens," the common Greco-Roman appellative for Arabs. These latter were so called, the Byzantine authorities claimed, because of their descent from Sarah, "she who was barren" (*kena*).[10]

Procopius continues:

The coast immediately beyond the boundaries of Palestine is held by Saracens who have been settled in the Palm Groves since long ago. The Palm Groves are in the interior, and stretch across a considerable extent of country. . . . Other Saracens, adjoining these, held the coastland. They are called Maddenoi [that is, Ma'add], subjects of the Homeritae. These Homeritae inhabit the land further on, by the sea shore. And beyond them many other nations are said to be settled as far as the man-eating Saracens. Beyond these are the nations of India. But regarding these matters let each speak as he wishes. (Procopius, *Wars*, vol. 1, 19. 8–16)

Procopius had obviously run out of reliable information with the "man-eating Saracens," and though there are uncertainties in the passage—on the basis of the South Arabian inscriptions we do not expect to find the Maddenoi/Ma'add sprawled throughout western Arabia—he has provided a good deal of illumination on region. The defense of Palestine, we are told, the larger Palestine including what had once been the southern frontier of Provincia

Arabia, was from 527 A.D. onward entirely in the hands of the Ghassanid phylarch Abu Karib, brother of the Ghassanid Harith ibn Jabala who performed the same function for the empire further north in the Transjordan and Syria. We can also observe that the empire's control did not extend, even indirectly, south of the Wadi Ramm, and that in Procopius's, and presumably in his contemporaries', knowledge of Arabia, there was a gap that corresponded exactly with the supposed sphere of influence of Mecca. There is no notice by Procopius of the fugitive "Makoraba" sited in Arabia by the Greek geographer Ptolemy,[11] and neither mention nor even space for the Quraysh, who are as invisible as Mecca itself in subsequent Byzantine interest in the region.

Procopius may have been telling us something more, as much by his silence as by his curt dismissal of the Ghassanid appointment. Abu Karib's jurisdiction would have lain directly across what was once a major crossroads in the caravan trade coming up from the south and would later serve the same purpose for the *Hajj* caravans to and from Mecca. And yet there was no mention in Procopius, who was interested in commercial questions, nor in anyone else, of overland trade activity in that region.

It is not as if the bedouin had no interest in trade, though it was not always in their traditional role as carriers. The terms of a peace treaty concluded by the Byzantines with Persia in 561 leave no doubt that the Arabs were also effectively engaged in smuggling all across the Perso-Roman frontier.[12] By this and other treaties the Byzantines tried to force the increasingly aggressive Arabs through the designated customs stations. These stations are all, however, in Mesopotamia: there is no sign or mention in the sixth century of an overland customs station anywhere in South Syria, Palestine, or any other of the southern overland gateways. The Indian maritime trade did go through official stations there, the port of Clysma at the head of the Gulf of Suez and the island of Iotabe at the mouth of the Gulf of Aqaba, and after 530 that latter station was nominally in the hands of Abu Karib. It is impossible to say how much profit, if any, there was in it for the Arab phylarch. Imperial customs duties were 12½ percent *ad valorem* on the import-export trade, but the Arabs of Iotabe may never have imposed it on products passing through there. Silks and spices, the staples of the Indian trade, were sold directly to state agents, *commerciarii*, and at Iotabe it is conceivable that the stuffs were bought right off the boats without benefit of either customs collectors or Arab middlemen.[13] It is, in any event, difficult to imagine the Romans sharing that heavily protected and monopolized trade with their land-bound Arab client in the northern Hijaz.

The activity of Hashim and his brothers was on the other side of this ill-defined, and probably nonexistent, frontier, where they concluded commercial treaties of some sort with the rulers of neighboring territories to the north. It is plausible to think that they may have petitioned, and received, for considerations we cannot even guess, licences to trade in the lands under the sovereignty of others, possibly including the Byzantine-allied Ghassanids in *Palestina Tertia*. But what has complicated the issue is the mingling in the Arab sources of this arrangement with quite another one, the deal struck by Hashim and the Quraysh with nearby bedouin to allow Meccan traders to pass unharmed through tribal lands en route to their commercial destinations and, moreover, the use by those same sources of the identical word to describe both arrangements, *ilaf*, a term understood to mean "a pact guaranteeing safety, safe-conduct, an undertaking to protect."[14]

THE SHAHS AND ARABIA

By the sixth century the Byzantines and the rival Iranian House of Sasan in Iraq and Iran were each using Arab seconds to defend their own borders and threaten the other. Byzantium's Arab clients, first the Kinda and eventually the Ghassanids, appear to have had no permanent center, and their camp was where their chief was. The tribal headquarters of the Tanukh of the Banu Lakhm, on the other hand, who performed the same function for the Sasanians on the eastern side of the Great Syrian steppe, had become fixed, as we have seen, in a settlement called simply "The Camp," in Arabic *al-Hira*, on the edge of the steppe near the Euphrates.

The greatest of the Persians Lakhmid phylarchs was doubtless al-Mundhir, the relentless shaykh who bedeviled the affairs of Byzantium for three decades in the East. Indeed, it was the success of al-Mundhir, Procopius tells us (*Wars*, vol. 1, 17.46), that inspired Justinian to promote his own vassal Harith to an extended bedouin phylarchate. The shah Khusraw was also perfectly aware of the value of a Mundhir, and shortly after 531 A.D. he made him, according to Tabari, king of Oman, Bahrain, the Yamama, and the neighboring parts of Arabia as far as Ta'if in the near vicinity of Mecca.[15] Whatever the truth of this assertion, Mundhir was certainly exercising sovereignty over the Ma'add in Central Arabia toward the middle of the sixth century when Abraha sent out an expedition from the Yemen against him, the same expedition that apparently reached Mecca.[16]

The next notable figure at al-Hira was Nu'man III who was phylarch there from about 580 A.D. His accession to power was engineered by the Christian poet Adi ibn Zayd whose family had long been important at Hira and who was himself in the service of the shah as "Arab secretary." The shah's essential concern in the matter, at least as Tabari tells the story, was whether or not the new phylarch could control the bedouin.[17]

The coming of Christianity to al-Hira is also associated with the reign of the same Nu'man. There was a bishop there in 410,[18] and perhaps even earlier a monastery was founded by Ebedishu', who was consecrated bishop (of the Arabs?) by the Nestorian Catholicos Tumarsa (388–399). Before he came to al-Hira a certain Ebedishu' had worked among the tribes of Bahrain and Yamama, and perhaps here we can see the beginnings of Christianity among the Bakr who dwelled in that region before migrating north behind the Taghlib in the mid-sixth century. There are even stories of Nu'man himself being attracted by the sanctity of Symeon Stylites, the Christian ascetic who dwelled atop his pillar far across the steppe north of Aleppo.[19] Such stories must be no more than legend, however, because the evidence is good and consistent that the Lakhmid princes of al-Hira remained militantly pagan down to the reign of Nu'man III in 580.[20]

The Lakhmids' paganism must have had little effect on their subjects, however. The excavations at al-Hira have not progressed very far,[21] but later Muslim authors give us detailed indications on a great number of churches and monasteries, most of them naturally constructed in pre-Islamic times, at al-Hira and its environs.[22] The town had its own theological school, many of the Nestorian Catholicoi were buried in its churches, and there flourished there a lively literary tradition whose crown was the Christian poet Adi ibn Zayd (d. ca. 604), who appears often in the pages of Tabari and who served as a kind of diplomatic liaison between the shah and his sometimes turbulent allies at al-Hira.[23]

Al-Hira is important to the history of the Hijaz. As is now clear,[24] there was constant coming and going between the Iraqi camptown and settlements like Mecca and Medina in western Arabia. And if Hira was not the closest Christian center to these latter towns—Najran in the Yemen and Axum across the Red Sea were probably more accessible—it was an *Arab* center, and whatever Christian influences were felt in Mecca and Medina were likely to have been brought by Arabs from al-Hira. But if al-Hira was a center of *Arab* Christianity, it was not an *Arabic* Christianity that was in question. There is still no firm evidence of an Arabic translation of the Gospels at this point,[25] and it is almost certain that the Arabs of al-Hira and elsewhere heard and recited their Scriptures and celebrated their liturgies in Syriac, just as most of the unmistakably Christian terms that occur in the Quran are loan words from this same Christian Aramaic dialect.[26]

Nu'man's reign at al-Hira lasted well over twenty years, but the Arab reporters concentrated their notices on how it ended. We do know that Nu'man himself became a Christian, probably around 594, and that in 602 Khusraw II, for reasons variously given, including a suspected Arab coup, had his vassal king put to death. He was not, however, replaced by one of his own line. Khusraw first appointed a bedouin shaykh, Iyas al-Qabisa, to be his "agent" al-Hira, with a Persian supervisor, to be sure, but in 611 that system was abandoned and the Sasanians took over direct control through a *marzban*.[27]

Thus Khusraw II, like his Byzantine contemporaries, replaced a centralized dynastic phylarchate with an "agent" in al-Hira in the person of the new and unknown Iyas ibn Qabisa, while other shaykhs were given fiefs in the border lands.[28] The new system was soon tested. Some years after Nu'man's death, perhaps in 610, about the time Muhammad was receiving his first revelations at Mecca, the steppe tribes revolted against Khusraw II. The shah sent out Iyas to confront them, accompanied by Persian garrison troops from the Sasanian frontier forts. The outcome took place at the famous battle of Dhu Qar, a modest watering-hole whose exact location is unknown, but whose notoriety in the Arab chronicles stems from the fact that it marked the first occasion when the tribes of Arabia met and defeated the forces of the shah, an omen of things to come.[29]

We do not know as much about the shah's dealings with his Arabs as we do of the parallel arrangement on the western or

Byzantine side of the steppe, but it is fairly certain from the Arab traditions that the relationship between the shah, his Lakhmid vassals, the bedouin of the steppe and the settled peoples of the Hijaz and the Tihama was grounded in both profit and force. The shah, as the final sovereign, granted to his Lakhmid "agents" the right to collect taxes from *their* clients, a right that was exercised either by further tax farming or, in the end, by the imposition of force. The troops available to the Lakhmids for these exercises are variously described in the sources, but they were apparently a very mixed bag of Lakhmid family cohorts, levies from the population of al-Hira, hostages, outlaws, and Persian regulars.[30]

The control exercised by the shah through his vassals ranged widely indeed. The Tanukh were settled as far north as Anbar, and south of al-Hira the Lakhmids controlled eastern Arabia as far as Bahrain, and this even after the fall of al-Hira, though then with the shared jurisdiction of a Sasanian *marzban* or military governor.[31] They reached into the Hijaz as well, where for a spell the Jewish tribes at Medina levied taxes for the Lakhmids, who were collecting them, doubtless, in the name of the shah.[32] By the mid-sixth century, then, the Sasanians were in firm control of much of the eastern and central areas of Arabia through the intermediacy of their vassal Lakhmids—the Persians were as little capable as the Byzantines of maintaining a permanent presence in the steppe lands—but a half century later that control was showing signs of disintegration. The Lakhmids were gone, replaced in the Persians' service by less potent and less reliable local shaykhs, and even the Sasanians' new foothold in the prized Yemen turned out, as we shall see in Chapter 4, to be more troublesome, and far less valuable, than had been first imagined.

THE COMMERCE OF MECCA

During the early sixth century lifetime of Hashim, then, the Great Power control of the Arabian hinterlands began to ebb away from Mecca, and particularly to the north, where the direct Byzantine military and administrative presence had receded into the Transjordan, thus providing Meccans the opportunity of becoming frontier traders, though not, as we shall see the international merchantmen of medieval and modern myth.

The Mecca of Qusayy was to all appearances a pilgrimage center, and the Quraysh were its wardens. What Hashim seems to have done was to make them traders as well. Their position as keepers of the holy places gave the Quraysh not only prestige and a modest supply of capital, but even, in the institution of the *Hums,* a degree of political leverage: the *Hums,* as we shall see, was a confederation of tribes pledged to guarantee the security of Mecca, its House, and the holy Quraysh. And because trade on any scale in Arabia was rendered difficult by the presence everywhere of predatory bedouin tribes, the agreements (*ilaf*) negotiated by Hashim with the bedouin provided the final link in the chain of commercial opportunity.

The institution of sacred months, consecutively the last two of the preceding and the first of the following Arab year, when a "truce of God" prevailed, was only a partial remedy. Not all the tribes were bound to this convention, which seems designed in the first instance to protect the trade at the fairs in and around Mecca. Hashim opened broader perspectives by coming to an understanding with hostile bedouin outside the orbit of Quraysh influence, with what one source calls "the wolves of the Arabs." He managed it, according to this same source, by engaging the bedouin in the commerce, using their camels, and taking their goods on consignment in return for a share in the profits.[33] The arrangement had, it seems clear, nothing to do with religion.[34]

The success of the new system may have engendered it own competition. Mecca was not the only shrine center, nor the Quraysh the only entrepreneurs, in western Arabia. The evidence is scanty and suggestive rather than substantial, but there are signs that other places like nearby Ta'if and the more distant Dumat al-Jandal and Hajr were engaged in similar enterprises, though we can read the history of those places only through the eyes of the Meccan tradition.

As later generations of Muslims understood it, the Mecca into which Muhammad was born was a prosperous international trading center, and that understanding derived almost uniquely from the stories told of Hashim. Most Western scholars share that understanding and in fact derive from it a plausible explanation for both the appearance and the success of Islam: the very prosperity of Mecca, with its undermining of traditional moral and social values and its division of the population into the rich and the poor, summoned forth a reformer of the likes of Muhammad.[35]

Whether we accept the conclusion, the premise seems beyond dispute: in the era after Hashim, and due to his economic and polit-

ᴋ ical initiatives, Mecca experienced an increase in trade. How substantial it was, or how in fact it operated, is quite another question.

International Trade in the Sixth Century

What precisely was the international trade in the sixth century?
What goods were being traded and who were its carriers? If
Mecca was part of that trade, the question already begins to
answer itself. Long before the Quraysh—no matter how their
dates are reckoned—an international trade ran north and south
through the Hijaz, and in its transit it must have passed somewhere in the vicinity of Mecca. That trade, which reached its
apogee in the first and second Christian centuries, was in luxury
ʄ items that originated in the Yemen or further east in India or East
Asia and were carried westward, in its last stages by boat from
India and then by camel northward through the Hijaz for eventual
sale for Roman silver in the consumer markets around the
Mediterranean.

It may be doubted whether the Muslim sources who describe
the mercantile activities of the Quraysh knew of that earlier
Roman trade through Arabia, but modern students of the question
certainly do, and it seems to provide the prototype for most current
explanations of the commerce of Mecca in the sixth century:
Mecca, standing at a nexus of trade routes in western Arabia, succeeded to the role of entrepreneurial entrepot earlier played by
ᴋ those other Arab caravan cities, Petra, Palmyra and Hatra.[36]

There is abundant archeological material for those first and
second century caravan cities, and a good deal of literary evidence, much of which has already been reviewed, for the trade
that went on around them. The sixth century has its own evidence, and although it points to what appears to be a revived
prosperity in Syria and Palestine, it seems ill-advised to attribute
that prosperity to the same international trade in luxury goods
that fueled the economy of the eastern provinces of the Roman
Empire four centuries earlier.[37]

The sixth century prosperity of the eastern Roman provinces
is indisputable: its evidence is everywhere in the increased building
activity, notably in refined and expensively decorated churches, in
Byzantine Palestine and Syria. New building means investment
and investment means capital accumulation. But there is no sign
that it came from trade, and particularly from the only interna-

tional trade we know of, that in eastern luxury goods like spices.[38] On the contrary, there is good reason to think that the wealth of the sixth century came from a revival in agriculture. All across the Negev, through the towns that were the links in the Nabateans' commercial empire, there are signs of new building in the sixth century, churches to be sure, and expanded agricultural development as well, while the earlier khans or commercial enterprises lay abandoned.[39]

There can be no doubt that the populations of these eastern towns, and even larger cities like Gaza, Bostra, Damascus, and Aleppo were more and more made up of ethnic Arabs, some of whom were only semi-sedentarized and formed "bedouin suburbs" outside the city walls, as the sixth century advanced.[40] There is no sign that they were there for any but local trade, and all the indices of increased Arab sedentarization within the sown lands during this period point equally certainly to a reciprocal "bedouinization of Arabia," as it has been called. Tribal groups were becoming detached from the disintegrating agricultural societies in the Yemen and the whole steppe population was in motion northward.[41]

The Greeks and the Romans called Arabia *Happy,* as we have seen, principally because of the Yemen, which produced the frankincense and myrrh so dear, and expensive, to the well-off consumers around the Mediterranean basin. Other goods of Thither Asia, which was a mere monsoon stop away, also passed through the Yemen on their way to the same consumers. But there are no indications that the Yemen was either producing or shipping in the middle and late sixth century. The Yemen itself was visited by colonial invasions early in the century, was visited by civil war and lived under the tyrannical control of Abraha and his sons until the Sasanians occupied the land in 575, when Muhammad was small boy. In that same era the Byzantines had lost control of the eastern maritime trade, and while the Quraysh ruled Mecca, Nestorian Christian merchants were carrying Indian goods and only to Sasanian ports. The overland spice trade through Arabia was dead.

International trade through Mecca was even less likely in the lifetime of Muhammad than in that of Hashim. Shortly after the Prophet began receiving his revelations, the final act of centuries of Byzantine-Sasanian hostilities began to unfold in Syria. In 614 the Sasanians overran the Byzantine East, capturing not only

Jerusalem, as Muhammad himself was aware (Quran 30, 1–3), but all of Egypt, Palestine, and Syria. The destruction was considerable, far greater than during the Muslim conquest twenty years later, and both the Jewish population of Syria-Palestine and the local bedouin joined in the looting.[42] Therefore when Muhammad was making his Hijra from Mecca to Medina in 622, both the Yemen and Syria, the producer and the consumer in Mecca's putative international trading operation, were in Sasanian hands. Two years later, the Muslims came down from Medina and sacked a rich homeward-bound Quraysh caravan at the Badr wells. It is difficult to imagine what it was carrying, from where or to whom.[43]

Mecca as a Trading Center

If we look to Mecca itself rather than to the great powers that surrounded it, the picture is not appreciably altered. The Quraysh were rich, we are informed,[44] and their wealth came from the trading patterns initiated by Hashim.[45] In 1924 Henri Lammens painted a vivid picture of the commercial activity and credit capitalism of the pre-Islamic Quraysh in Mecca, a portrait that has been grudgingly conceded by those who should best know, as embodying "a kernel of indubitable facts . . . which are confirmed by non-Arab texts and are, moreover, in accordance with the nature of things."[46] No non-Arab texts reasonably confirm anything about Mecca, including its very existence perhaps, and the *nature of things* suggests the very opposite of the possibility that Mecca was an international trading center. There was, on the evidence, little money in Mecca,[47] and value in specie was the essential ingredient—Meccan merchants had to buy the goods in the Yemen before they could sell them in Syria—for the functioning of a high-value trade in the sixth century. Nor are there any tangible signs, apart from the anecdotes of authors nearly two centuries after the event, of high profits and amassed wealth. The Arab caravan cities like Petra, Palmyra, and Hatra, and even a smaller Arabian example like al-Faw, still bear eloquent testimony to the prosperity of its merchants in the form of capital investment in municipal buildings and monuments. Muhammad's Mecca, on the other hand, boasted one unroofed stone building, the Ka'ba, amidst its mud-brick dwellings. Nowhere is there sign or talk of either commercial or municipal facilities.

Though modern scholars are often seduced by the imagined resemblance between pre-Islamic Mecca and the great caravan cities of the East, Ali Bey, who saw Mecca in 1807, when it was a far more considerable place than its sixth century version, was not deceived:

> Mecca, placed in the middle of a desert, does not resemble Palmyra, which the continual commerce between the East and West elevated to the greatest degree of perfection and splendor, which we even admire in its ruins and which would still have existed but for the discovery of the Cape of Good Hope (route to the Indies). Mecca, on the contrary, is not placed on any direct line of passage. Arabia is surrounded by the Persian Gulf to the east, the Red Sea to the west, the ocean to the south, and the Mediterranean Sea to the north. Its center therefore cannot be in any direct line of communication with the neighboring countries to which access may be had by sea. Its ports at most will only serve as seaport towns to trading vessels, as is the case of Jidda and Mokha upon the Red Sea, and Muscat near the mouth of the Persian Gulf.
>
> Mecca not being situated in the route to any country of consequence, nature has not designed it as a place of commerce, placed as it is in the middle of an extremely barren desert, which prevents its inhabitants from being either husbandmen or shepherds. What resources then remain to them for subsistence? The force of arms, to oblige other countries to give them part of their productions, or religious enthusiasm, to induce strangers to come and bring money to them, with which they can procure the necessities of life.
>
> In the time of the Caliphs these two causes united rendered Mecca an opulent city; but before and since that glorious period, it has no other resource for its support than the enthusiasm of the pilgrims, which unfortunately begins to cool from day to day, through the effects of time, distance of place and revolutions that reduce this place to a mean and precarious existence. Such is its state at the moment, and such it was before the mission of the Prophet.
>
> Mecca has always been the center of religious enthusiasm of different nations. The origin of pilgrimages, and the first foundation of its temple, are lost in the obscurity of ages, since they appear to be anterior to the period of history. The Prophet pulled down the idols which profaned the House of God. The Quran confirmed the pilgrimage, and it is in this manner that the devotion of other nations has been at all times the basis of

the subsistence of the inhabitants of Mecca. But as this could not alone suffice, they were very poor before the coming of the Prophet, and now, after a short reign of glory and riches acquired by arms, it has relapsed into poverty . . .

Thus Mecca is so poor by nature that if the House of God ceased to exist, it would be inevitably deserted in two years, or at least be reduced to a simple *douar* or hamlet; for the inhabitants in general subsist for the rest of the year on what they accumulate during the time of the pilgrimage, at which time the place puts on a lively appearance, commerce is animated, and the half of the people are transformed into hosts, merchants, porters, servants and so forth; and the other, attached entirely to the service of the temple, live upon the alms and gifts of pilgrims . . . (Ali Bey 1816, vol. 2, pp. 101–102)

Mecca's pre-Islamic commercial prosperity is, in fact, a kind of chimera.[48] The town had no port on the Red Sea,[49] and despite repeated assertions to the contrary, it was not on any west Arabian trade route that we know of.[50] The post-Islamic sources may well have been exaggerating the prowess of their ancestors—none of the Greek sources knows anything of this Venice of the Hijaz—and the lack of any material evidence of capital investment at Mecca, which essentially vitiates all comparisons with Petra and Palmyra, indicates that either the riches were exaggerated or so much of the monetary profit had to be returned to the bedouin and the surplus kept for reinvestment at the source, that is, buying new stock, that no money was left for the normal capital investment at Mecca.

If an international trade in spices was impossible at that time and place, and beyond the slender resources of Mecca in any event, must the entire massive tradition of Meccan commerce to be rejected out of hand? That seems far too bold, particularly once it has become clear how and why the tradition developed. It is chiefly modern scholars who have projected the defunct Roman spice and incense trade onto what the Muslims sources say,[51] and most of the latters' speculation occurs in their attempts to explicate the early and, as we shall see, highly problematic Sura 106 of the Quran. Once most of the modern interpretations are stripped away and the sheer exegetical elaborations on Quran 106 are disallowed, something more modest, and plausible, remains.

The Quraysh were, there seems no doubt, traders on some scale: their privileged position as wardens of the Meccan Haram, the traditional fairs that occurred yearly on the occasion of the pilgrimage, and their modest capital stake accruing from *Hajj* dues, all make it appear likely that they were in fact engaged in trade, albeit on a far more modest level than is generally thought. The Arab sources know nothing of incense and spices but they do mention that the Quraysh traded in leather and raisins,[52] both commercial items to which the Meccans had direct and relatively easy access.

If the story of Hashim's initiatives with the bedouin of the Hijaz is true, then Mecca may have indeed begun to construct for itself, out of the matrix of its shrine influence and revenues, and in the face of the rapidly receding economic and political influence of both the Sasanians and the Byzantines, a modest trading zone along the now unpatrolled frontiers of Syria and Iraq. What appears likely is that the Quraysh were involved in an internal trade-barter system in which they sold (or traded) the goods of the oases and bedouin for manufactured items like textiles and oil that were available at Hira, Gaza, Busra and the Yemen.[53]

CHAPTER 4

The Family and City of Muhammad

After Hashim the Arab sources speak no more of commerce at Mecca, not, in any event, in connection with his son and the Prophet's grandfather, Abd al-Muttalib, who was a rather famous man at Mecca, though not as a trader.

A CELEBRATED GRANDFATHER

Abd al-Muttalib's earliest days have an odd cast to them. To begin with, his name was Shayba, and "Abd al-Muttalib," "Slave of al-Muttalib," was his sobriquet. Al-Muttalib was not, however, the name of a deity, as we might expect in such a combination, but the boy's uncle. Ibn Ishaq recounts the curious history of the title as he had heard it.

> Hashim had gone to Medina and married Salma, the daughter of Amr, one of the Banu Adiyy. Before that she had been married to Uhayha ibn al-Julah . . . and bore him a son called Amr. On account of the high position she held among her people she would only marry on condition that she should retain control of her own affairs. If she disliked a man, she left him.
>
> To Hashim she bore Abd al-Muttalib and called his name Shayba. Hashim left him with her while he was still a little boy. Then his uncle [that is, Hashim's younger brother] al-Muttalib came to take him away and bring him up among his people in his town. But Salma declined to let the boy go with him. His uncle argued that his nephew was now old enough to travel and was an exile away from his own tribe, who were the people of the (Meccan) shrine, of great local reputation, and holding much of the government (of Mecca) in their hands. Thus, it was better for the boy that he should be among his own family, and therefore Muttalib refused to depart without him.
>
> It is popularly asserted that Shayba refused to leave his mother without her consent; and this she eventually gave. So his

uncle Muttalib took him away to Mecca, riding behind him on
his camel, and the people cried: "It is al-Muttalib's slave whom
he has bought," and that is how he got the name of Abd al-
Muttalib [or "slave of al-Muttalib]. His uncle cried out: "Rub-
bish! This is my nephew whom I have brought from Medina."
(Ibn Ishaq 1955, p. 59)

We assume that Hashim was dead at this point. With his passing his younger brother al-Muttalib had taken over the traditional
Abd Manaf family right and privilege of supplying food and water
to the pilgrims, but now, with the return of Hashim's son to his
native city, it was this latter, and not al-Muttalib's own sons, who
succeeded to these important and lucrative posts:

Following his uncle al-Muttalib, Hashim's son Abd al-Muttalib
took over the duties of watering and feeding the pilgrims and
carried on the practices of his forefathers with his people. He
attained such eminence as none of his forefathers enjoyed; his
people loved him and his reputation was great among them.
(Ibn Ishaq 1955, pp. 59–61)

One event that contributed to the persistence of Abd al-Muttalib's reputation among the later Quraysh was a political initiative he undertook with some possibly troublesome neighbors, the
Khuza'a, and their use to help solve some of Mecca's own internal
problems. There had been, from the moment of Qusayy's death,
and perhaps even earlier, tension among the Quraysh. They were,
after all, nomads but recently come in from the steppe, all their
rivalries intact and presumably enhanced within the narrow confines of their assigned "quarters" in the hollow of Mecca. We are
told that a treaty made in the generation after Qusayy, when the
two factions of Abd Manaf and Abd al-Dar took their oaths at the
Ka'ba, held until the coming of Islam. That may have been true as
regards that particular social fissure, but there were other problems and other rents in the tribal fabric. It is reported, for example, that Abd al-Muttalib had a falling out with near relatives over
some properties and was on the point of invoking his powerful
mother's relatives from Medina when he was offered an alliance
by a closer source, the same Khuza'ai tribesmen whom Qusayy
had expelled from Mecca and who were still living in the neighborhood. A treaty was drawn up in writing in the council hall and
was then made public in the usual way: it was posted up on the
wall of the Ka'ba.

An alleged version of the agreement is preserved by a later historian.[1] The document is written in the rhymed prose typical of parts of the Quran and the utterances of contemporary soothsayers, but the elevated style is no guarantee of the document. When Muhammad later in his own career was about to come to terms with his Meccan enemies, the Khuza'a entered flourishing a "writing" they had made with Abd al-Muttalib,[2] and the present text, and indeed the entire report, may be a later generation's inventing conditions that they were assured would be fulfilled by events.

The Rediscovery of the Sacred Well of Zamazm

The Zamzam, as we have seen, is the well near the Ka'ba that God had miraculously uncovered for Hagar when her infant Ishmael was near death from thirst. It was known and used, presumably as a sacred source, throughout the era of the Ishmaelites and their successors, the Jurhum. It was the Jurhum, we are told, who filled up the Zamzam and so concealed its exact location from the Khuza'a and the Quraysh. And so it remained until the time of Abd al-Muttalib.

> While Abd al-Muttalib was sleeping in the *hijr*,[3] he was ordered in a vision to dig up the Zamzam. Yazid ibn Abi Habib told me [through a number of intermediaries] that Ali ibn Abi Talib was heard telling the story of the Zamzam. He said that Abd al-Muttalib said: "I was sleeping in the *hijr* when a supernatural visitant came and said, "Dig Tiba." And I said "What is Tiba?" Then he left me. I went to bed again the next day and slept, and he came to me and said "Dig Barra." When I asked what Barra was he left me. The next day he came again and said "Dig al-Madnuna." When I asked him what that was, he went away again. The next day he came while I was sleeping and said "Dig Zamzam." I said, "What is Zamzam?" He said:
>
>> "'Twill never fail and never run dry,
>> 'Twill water the pilgrim company.
>> It lies twixt the dung and the flesh bloody,[4]
>> By the nest where the white-winged ravens fly,
>> By the nest where the ants to and fro ply."

When the exact spot had been indicated to him and he knew that it corresponded with the facts, Abd al-Muttalib took a pick-axe and went with his son al-Harith—for he had none other at that time—and began. When the top of the well appeared he cried "God is Great." Thus the (other) Quraysh knew that he had obtained his object . . .

Immediately a controversy arose as to the ownership of this piece of property that was both sacred and valuable.

> The Quraysh came to him and said, "This is the well of our father Ishmael, and we have a right to it, so give us a share in it." "I will not," he answered. "I was specially told of it and not you, and I was the one to be given it." They said, "Do us justice, for we shall not leave you until we have got a judicial decision in this matter." He said, "Appoint anyone you like as umpire between us." He agreed to accept a woman diviner of the Banu Sa'd Hudhaym, who dwelt in the uplands of Syria. So Abd al-Muttalib, accompanied by some of his relations and a representative from all of the tribes of the Quraysh, rode away. (Ibn Ishaq 1955, p. 62)

A tribal dispute and an appeal to a holy person from a distant locale to arbitrate it—suddenly we are in the same circumstances that carried Muhammad to Medina in 622 A.D. Here the parties were going to the seer, however, though they did not have to complete their journey. In the course of their trip, when all the travelers were threatened by death from thirst, it came about that it was Abd al-Muttalib who discovered water. This was accepted by the Quraysh accompanying him that God's judgment had indeed rested upon Abd al-Muttalib.

Ibn Ishaq supplies another version with more circumstantial detail on the actual discovery of the well:

> The next day Abd al-Muttalib and his son al-Harith . . . went and found the ants' nest and the raven pecking beside it between the two idols Asaf and Na'ila at which the Quraysh used to slaughter their sacrifices. He brought a pick-axe and began to dig where he had been commanded. The Quraysh, seeing him at work, came up and refused to allow him to dig between their two idols where they sacrificed. Abd al-Muttalib then told his son to stand by and protect him while he dug, for he was determined to carry out what he had been commanded to do. When they saw he was not going to stop work, they left him severely alone.
>
> He had not dug deeply before the stone top of the well appeared, and he gave thanks to God knowing that he had been rightly informed. As the digging went further, he found the two gazelles of gold which the Jurhum had buried there when the left Mecca. He also found some swords and coats of mail from

Qal'a.[5] The Quraysh claimed they had a right to share in this find.

Once again Abd al-Muttalib agreed to submit the dispute to divine judgment, though in this version it is to a form of divina- ⌄ tion through the casting of arrows.

> Abd al-Muttalib said he would make two arrows for the Ka'ba, two for them [that is, the Quraysh] and two for himself. The two arrows which came out from the quiver would determine to whom the property belonged. This was agreed, and he made two yellow arrows for the Ka'ba, two black ones for himself and two white ones for the Quraysh. They were then given to the priest in charge of the divinatory arrows, which were thrown down beside. Hubal was an image in the middle of the Ka'ba, indeed, the greatest of the images . . .
>
> Abd al-Muttalib began to pray to God, and when the priest threw the arrows, the two yellow ones for the gazelles came out in favor of the Ka'ba. The two black ones allotted the swords ⌁ and coats of mail to Abd al-Muttalib, and the two arrows of the Quraysh remained behind (in the quiver). Abd al-Muttalib made the swords into a door for the Ka'ba and overlaid the door with the gold from the gazelles. This was the first golden ornament of the Ka'ba, or so they allege. Then Abd al-Muttalib took charge of the supply of Zamzam water to the pilgrims. (*Ibid.*, p. 64)

It is difficult to know whether to credit the story. Other sources tell us that Abd al-Muttalib was already in inherited possession of the *siqaya*, the right to provide water to the pilgrims. In Islamic times, or perhaps even from this juncture forward, the stories about the *Hajj* or the Haram inevitably identify the *siqaya* with the Zamzam, which, as this story testifies, it clearly was not for a long stretch of Meccan history.[6] Again, the "discovery" story does not much avert to the fact that in or near that same place the early inhabitants used to cast their votive offerings to the gods of the Ka'ba,[7] and that what Abd al-Muttalib most likely "discovered"—other accounts add swords and jewels to the gazelles—was the treasury of the sanctuary.[8]

The Binding of Abdullah

The cleromantic practice of divination through arrows reappears in connection with another famous story told, though manifestly not with Ibn Ishaq's complete confidence, about the Prophet's grandfather.[9]

> It is alleged, and God only knows the truth, that when Abd al-Muttalib encountered the opposition of the Quraysh when he was digging up the Zamzam, he vowed that if he should have ten sons to grow up and protect him, he would sacrifice one of them to God at the Ka'ba. Afterwards, when he had ten sons who could protect him, he gathered them together and told them about his vow and called on them to keep faith with God. They agreed to obey him and asked what they were to do. He said that each one of them must get an arrow, write his name on it, and bring it to him. This they did, and he took them before Hubal in the middle of the Ka'ba. Hubal stood by a well there. It was that well in which gifts made to the Ka'ba were stored.

> Abd al-Muttalib said to the man with the arrows, "Cast the lots for my sons with these arrows," and he told him of the vow he had made. Each one gave him the arrow on which his own name was written. Now Abdullah was his father's youngest son. . . . It is alleged that Abdullah was Abd al-Muttalib's favorite son, and his father thought that if the arrow missed him, he would be spared. (He was the father of the Apostle of God.) When the man took the arrows to cast lots with them, Abd al-Muttalib stood by Hubal praying to God. Then the man cast lots and Abdullah's arrow came out. His father led him by the hand and took a large knife; then be brought him up to Asaf and Na'ila, two idols of the Quraysh at which they slaughtered sacrifices, to sacrifice him. (Ibn Ishaq 1955, pp. 66–67)

This was not to be, however, as we might have suspected since the Abdullah in question was the future father of the Prophet. On the advice of the Quraysh, Abd al-Muttalib consulted a female seer at Medina—or the Jewish oasis of Khaybar, as others said. She advised him to take the standard bloodprice of ten camels and cast lots between them and his son. If the lot fell upon his son, he was to add ten more camels to the price and cast again until the Lord should be satisfied at the price and so allow the lot to fall upon the camels. Abd al-Muttalib returned to Mecca and did as he had been advised. When the bloodprice finally reached the sum of 100 camels, the Lord caused the lot to fall on the camels rather than Abdullah, and Abd al-Muttalib redeemed his son for that price. As for the camels, "they were duly slaughtered and left there and no man was kept back or hindered (from eating them)."

An act of divine providence, which had first apparently condemned Abdullah to death, now brings him salvation, this time
mediated through the activity of yet another female seer. Are we
to understand that there were human sacrifices at Mecca no more
than twenty-odd years before the birth of the Prophet? It may be
so because there is parallel and contemporary evidence for such
practices elsewhere among the Arabs.[10] Or it may be we are simply in the presence of a moral tale, one with a distant echo of
Abraham's near sacrifice of his son.

ABRAHA

There is no hint in any of this of the tumultuous events taking
place in the Yemen: the first Abyssinian invasion, Dhu Nuwas's
violent reaction to Christian Abyssinian hegemony in his land,
and a second intervention from across the Red Sea. Only with the
withdrawal of this second Abyssinian force and the rise to power
in Himyar of the Negus' deputy Abraha do the careers of the
Hijaz and the Yemen begin to draw together in the sources.

Once again Procopius supplies the details of what occurred in
Himyar after Ella Asbeha returned to Ethiopia after his invasion
in 525 A.D.:

> In the Ethiopian army there were many slaves and others of a
> lawless disposition who did not wish to follow the king. Left
> behind, they stayed there (in South Arabia) out of a desire to
> acquire the land of the Himyarites, for it is extremely rich. Not
> long after this mob, together with some others, revolted against
> Esimiphaios [that is, Samu Yafa'] and put him in prison in one
> of the fortresses in that land, appointing another king for the
> Himyarites, by name Abraha.
>
> This Abraha was indeed a Christian, but a slave of a Roman
> citizen in an Ethiopian city, Adulis, staying there to conduct his
> commercial undertakings by sea.
>
> On hearing of these events Ella Asbeha wished to requite
> Abraha and the rebels for their treatment of Samu Yafa', sent an
> army of 3,000 men against them and one of his family as ruler.
> This army, which was composed of men who were no longer
> willing to do their duty and return home but inclined rather to
> stay on in a rich land, opened negotiations with Abraha without
> the knowledge of the king, and came to terms with their adver-
> saries. When the battle was joined they killed the ruler (sent out
> with them), joined the enemy army and stayed on there.

In great anger Ella Asbeha sent out another army, which eventually fought an engagement against the followers of Abraha. But they were defeated and shortly thereafter returned home. Thereafter out of fear the Ethiopian king sent no more expeditions against Abraha.

When Ella Asbeha was dead, Abraha agreed to pay tribute to his successor in the rule over the Ethiopians and in that way Abraha secured legitimate rule . . . (Procopius, Wars, vol. 1, 20.2–8)

The death of Ella Asbeha, and so the recognition of Abraha, likely occurred sometime after 535 A.D., when, as Procopius says, "he was most securely established." Somewhat later, perhaps in 544 A.D., Justinian made to the new ruler of Himyar the same request he had to his predecessors; namely, to take up arms against the Persians. And Abraha's response was identical to the others': "Even Abraha, later when he was most securely established as a ruler, though he frequently promised the Emperor Justinian to raid Persian territory, only started out on that expedition on one occasion, and retired immediately . . . " (Procopius, *Wars*, vol. 1, 20.13).

THE MEN WHO HAVE THE ELEPHANT

The pre-Islamic Arabs had no fixed annual dating system of their own, and so the Muslim authorities were uncertain in precisely what year the Prophet was born.[11] One tradition connects it, not entirely implausibly, with an event that shook the Mecca of that era, a march against the holy city from the Yemen. It was led by Abraha, the former Abyssinian viceroy who was now established as the independent and aggressive ruler of Himyar.

Muhammad's biographer Ibn Ishaq, who had traced Abraha's rise to power in the wake of the destruction of Dhu Nuwas, now resumes his narrative:

Then Abraha built the church in San'a (in the Yemen), such a church as could not be seen elsewhere in any part of the world at that time.

He wrote to the Negus [that is, the ruler of Abyssinia] saying, "I have built a church for you, O king, such as has not been built for any king before you. I shall not rest until I have diverted the Arabs' pilgrimage to it." When the Arabs were talking about this letter of his, one of the calendar intercalators was enraged. He was of the Banu . . . Kinana. The intercalators are those who used to adjust the months for the Arabs in the Age of Ignorance. They would make one of the holy months profane, and make one of the profane months holy to balance the calendar. It was about this that God sent down the verse "Postponement (of a sacred month) is but an added infidelity by which those who disbelieve are misled. They make it (the month) profane one year and make it sacred the next, that they may make up the number of months that God has made sacred." (Quran 9:37) . . . 12

9:37

The Kinanite went forth until he came to the church (at San'a) and defiled it. Then he returned to his own country. Hearing of the matter, Abraha made inquiries and learned that the outrage had been committed by an Arab who had come from the shrine in Mecca where the Arabs went on pilgrimage, and that he had done this in anger at Abraha's threat to divert the Arabs' pilgrimage to the church, showing thereby that it was unworthy of reverence. Abraha was enraged and swore that he would go to this shrine and destroy it . . . 13

So he commanded the Abyssinians to prepare and make ready, and sallied forth with the elephant. News of this incident plunged the Arabs into alarm and anxiety and they decided that it was incumbent upon them to fight against him when they heard he meant to destroy the Ka'ba, God's Holy House. (Ibn Ishaq 1955, pp. 21–23)

After some local opposition from a member of the former royal house, Dhu Nafr, whom he captured and held, Abraha proceeded, according to Ibn Ishaq, to the outskirts of Mecca.

Arrived here, Abraha sent an Abyssinian . . . with some cavalry as far as Mecca, and the latter sent off to him the plunder of the people of the Tihama, the Quraysh and others, among it 200 camels belonging to Abd al-Muttalib ibn Hashim [the Prophet's grandfather], who at that time was the leading shaykh of the Quraysh. At first the Quraysh, Kinana, Hudhayl and others who were in the holy place meditated battle, but seeing that they had not the power to offer resistance, they gave up the idea.

Abraha sent Hunata the Himyarite to Mecca instructing him to inquire who was the chief notable of the country and to tell him that the king's message was that he had not come to fight them, but only to destroy the shrine. If they offered no resistance, there would be no cause for bloodshed, and if he wished to avoid war he would return with him. On reaching Mecca Hunata was told that Abd al-Muttalib ibn Hashim ibn

Abd Manaf ibn Qusayy was the leading notable, so he went to
him and delivered Abraha's message. Abd al-Muttalib replied:
"God knows that we do not wish to fight him for we have no
power to do so. This is God's sanctuary and the shrine of His
friend Abraham—or words to that effect. If He defends it
against Abraha, it is His shrine and His sanctuary; and if He lets
him have it, by God we cannot defend it!" Hunata replied that
he must come with him to Abraha, for he was ordered to bring
him back with him. (Ibn Ishaq 1955, p. 23)

Abd al-Muttalib is now portrayed by Ibn Ishaq as the ruler of
Mecca, and through the good offices of Dhu Nafr, whom he knew
and who was under arrest in Abraha's camp, he gained an audience with Abraha at the latter's camp.

Abraha sat upon his carpet and made Abd al-Muttalib sit beside
him there. Then he told his interpreter to inquire what he
wanted, and the reply was that he wanted the king to return the
200 camels of his which he had taken. Abraha replied through
the interpreter: "You pleased me much when I saw you; then I
was much displeased with you when I heard what you said. Do
you wish to talk to me about 200 camels of your which I have
taken and say nothing about your religion and the religion of
your forefathers which I have come to destroy?" Abd al-Muttalib replied: "I am the owner of the camels but the shrine has
its own owner who will defend it." . . .
      When they left Abraha, Abd al-Muttalib went back to the
Quraysh and having given them the news ordered them to with-
draw from Mecca and take up defensive positions on the peaks
and in the passes of the mountains for fear of the excesses of the
soldiers. Abd al-Muttalib took hold of the metal knocker of the
Ka'ba, and a number of Quraysh stood with him praying to
God and imploring His help against Abraha and his party. . . .
Abd al-Muttalib then let go of the knocker of the door of the
Ka'ba and went off with his Quraysh companions to the mountain tops where they took up defensive positions waiting to see
what Abraha would do when he occupied Mecca.

Thus, the way the story is made to unfold, it is up to Allah, the
Lord of the Ka'ba, to defend His own House. The point is clear:
there will be no human intervention; all is in the hands of God.

In the morning Abraha prepared to enter the town and made his
elephant ready for battle and drew up his troops. His intention
was to destroy the shrine and then return to the Yemen. When

they made the elephant—its name was Mahmud—face Mecca, Nufayl ibn Habib came up to its flank and taking hold of its ear said: "Kneel, Mahmud, or go straight back whence you came, for you are in God's holy land!" He let go of its ear and the elephant knelt, and Nufayl made off at top speed for the top of the mountain. The troops beat the elephant to make it get up but it would not; they beat its head with iron bars; they stuck hooks into its underbelly and scarified it; but it would not get up. Then they made it face the Yemen and immediately it got up and started off. When they faced it towards the north and the east it did likewise, but as soon as they directed it toward Mecca, it knelt down. (Ibn Ishaq 1955, pp. 25–27)

After describing the quite exemplary prayer habits of Abraha's elephant—like a good Muslim of a later generation, it bows down in veneration only in the direction of the Ka'ba—Ibn Ishaq turns to an early verse in the Quran that the Muslim tradition construed—again, the Quran provides no context—as a reference to Abraha's expedition:

"Did you not see how your Lord dealt with the men who have the elephant? Did He not reduce their guile to sheer terror? And He sent upon them flocks of birds, throwing hard clay stones upon them, making them as blades of grain that have been devoured." (Quran 105)

Then [Ibn Ishaq continues] God sent upon them birds from the sea like swallows and starlings; each bird carried three stones, like peas and lentils, one in its beak and two between its claws. Everyone who was hit died, but not all were hit. They withdrew in flight the way they came, crying out for Nufayl ibn Habib to guide them on the way to the Yemen. . . . As they withdrew they were continually falling by the wayside, dying miserably by every waterhole. Abraha was smitten in his body, and as they took him away his fingers fell off one by one. Where the fingers had been there arose an evil sore exuding pus and blood, so that when they brought him to San'a he was like a young fledgling. They allege that as he died, his heart burst from his body.[14]

And then in a final note, Ibn Ishaq offers, almost as an aside, what may have actually befallen the expedition: "Ya'qub ibn Utba told me that he was informed that that year was the first time that measles and smallpox had been seen in Arabia . . . " (Ibn Ishaq 1955, p. 27).

When did all this occur? The question is an important one not only for the history of Mecca but for the career of Muhammad because a substantial part of the Muslim historical tradition places the birthdate of Muhammad in this very same "Year of the Elephant." The following Sabean inscription was found at the well of Murayghan in South Arabia, and though the site is far to the east of the ways connecting the Yemen and Mecca, it describes a military encounter at a place called *Taraban*, a known oasis only 100 kilometers east of Ta'if. Indeed, the inscription appears to commemorate a part of the very same campaign recalled in Sura 105 of the Quran.[15]

> By the power of the Merciful and His Messiah. The king Abraha Za Bayman, king of Saba and Dhu Raydan and Hadramawt and Yamamat, and his Arabs, on the high plateau and the open coast, have written this document when the Ma'add undertook their spring raiding, in the month of Dhu Tabtan, while all the Banu Amir rose up. And the king placed Abgabar at the head of the Kinda and the Al, and Bashir, son of Husn, at the head of the Sa'id. And they struck (?) and joined battle at the head of the troop: Kinda against the Banu Amir and . . . Murad and Sa'id in the valley (?) on the route of Turaban. And they were killed and taken prisoner. And those who fled was struck by the king at Haliban. And the Mu'add disappeared like a cloud. And they gave pledges. And afterwards Amr, the son of Mundhir, gave his guarantee, and he [Mundhir?] seconded his son to them and set him up as governor over the Ma'add. And they returned from Haliban by the power of The Merciful, in the year 662 (of the Sabean era). (Ry. 506 = Ryckmans 1953, p. 278)

That is, in 552 A.D. or thereabouts Abraha directed, or rather sent, an expedition made up not of his own troops but of the Kinda and other bedouin allies against the Arab Ma'add, who were by then the vassals of the Persians. And in connection with the same northern campaign, an Abyssinian force seems to have unsuccessfully attacked Mecca, an event that was still being recalled in that latter city a half-century later and gave its name to the "Year of the Elephant."

THE SECURITY OF THE QURAYSH

Ibn Ishaq connected the assault of the "men who have the elephant" with two different *suras* of the Quran, the first, as we have seen, is Sura 105, with its apparently direct reference to the confrontation; the second is the *sura* immediately following it, of which notice has already been taken in connection with Hashim. Sura 106 of the Quran, the one called "The Quraysh," had, in fact, a critical role, perhaps *the* critical role, in the later Muslims' view of their ancestors at Mecca, and through them, in the modern interpretation of the entire Meccan enterprise before Islam.

> For the covenants of security of the Quraysh,
> The covenants (covering) the journey of winter and of
>   summer,
> Let them worship the Lord of this House,
> Who provides them with food against hunger and security
>   against fear. (Quran 106)

This is the by now standard translation-interpretation of the *sura*, which might be paraphrased as "Because the Lord granted (or perhaps guaranteed) the treaties enjoyed by the Quraysh, treaties that have made possible their annual commercial journeys, let the Quraysh recognize this and worship the Lord of the Ka'ba who has, through these treaties and their consequences, provided the Quraysh with both sustenance and security." This is intelligible in English, but the Arabic of the *sura* has posed serious linguistic and syntactical problems that have bothered commentators from the beginning.[16] The *sura* begins (1) abruptly—early *suras* commonly open with some type of adjuration—(2) with an subordinate clause, and (3) with a term, *ilaf*, that was apparently so difficult to construe that a number of secondary readings were quickly put forward. A secondary tradition in both texts and commentaries suggests, on the other hand, that Suras 105 and 106 were once a single unit, a juncture that would solve most of the linguistic and interpretative difficulties that surround the latter and, in addition, provide a somewhat different interpretation of the whole:

> Do you not see how the Lord dealt with the men of the
>   elephant?
> Did He not make their treacherous plan go astray?
> And He sent against them flights of birds,
> Striking them with stones of baked clay.
> Then He made them like an empty field of stalks and
>   straw, all eaten up,
> So that He might make the Quraysh secure,
> The security of the journey of winter and of summer,

So let them worship the Lord of this House,
Who provides them with food against hunger and security
    against fear.

The primary emphasis of God's benevolence shifts, then, away
from the "treaties" of the Quraysh to the providential destruction
of Abraha, which in turn permitted to the Quraysh the "easement" of the winter and summer journey. Another consequence of
joining the suras is that there is an easier and more natural sense
to the *ilaf* of the opening verse of 106, a word that has been variously understood as "covenants" or "commercial treaties," a
technical usage induced by the difficult reading. In the new construction the technical term disappears, to be replaced by the ordinary sense of *ilaf* as "protection" or "easement," with the nature
of that easement spelled out in the following clause, "their easement of the journey of winter and of summer."[17]

The widespread understanding of *ilaf* as "treaties" appears to
have affected the interpretation of the following "journey of winter
and of summer" as commercial enterprises, an interpretation that
reflected backward not only upon *ilaf* but upon the entire history
of Qurayshite Mecca since the days of Hashim, the alleged founder
of those international "commercial treaties." As has recently been
pointed out,[18] there is little evidence or even likelihood for such
international trade under either Hashim or one of his successors in
Mecca, and our conviction is strengthened when we understand
that the same Quranic commentators who were certain that the
"journey of winter and of summer" were trading ventures had no
clear idea of either their timing or their destination.[19]

The Arab accounts of the expedition of Abraha reveal something else. The Abyssinians had Arab allies against Mecca, tribesmen from both the north and the south, the same putative *ilaf*
confederates in the Meccan trading company.[20] Mecca apparently
did not yet enjoy its special status at that point, which is precisely
the point of the combined Suras 105–106, and Ibn Ishaq underlines the implication. "When Allah turned back the Abyssinians
from Mecca, and inflicted upon them His vengeance, the Arabs
admired Quraysh and said: "They are the people of Allah. He has
fought for them, and spared them the trouble of their enemies."
(Ibn Ishaq 38 = Ibn Ishaq 1955, p. 28).

This is exactly how a number of exegetes understood Sura
106; here, for example, Ibn Qutayba:

The meaning of the *sura* is that the Quraysh were secure within the Haram from the danger of being attacked in it by the enemies, and from any harassment when they went out of it for their trade. The people said, "The Quraysh are the inhabitants of the Haram of Allah, they are the people of Allah and the custodians of His House . . . " They had two journeys each year, a journey to the Yemen in winter and journey to Syria in the summer. Were it not for these journeys, they would not have survived at Mecca, and were it not for the protection derived from their dwelling near the House they would not have been able to conduct their affairs. (Ibn Qutayba, *Mushkil* 413)[21]

All of this came together, we are told, because of the newly enhanced prestige of the Quraysh in the wake of the battle against Abraha and the "men who have the elephant." The Quraysh were recognized as the genuine "people of the House," who shared in the sanctity of the place whose guardians they were. The result, the Quran tells us, was that the Lord of the House provided them with "food against hunger and security against fear" (Quran 106: 4).

The Muslim commentators read the last verse of Sura 106 as a consequence of what preceded, the "journey of the winter and the summer," which were in turn understood to be commercial caravan trips to Syria and the Yemen. When and where the journeys took place was not clearly understood, as we have seen, nor was it entirely clear how they were "eased" for the Quraysh, and how that "easement" was connected with a guaranteed food supply, as Sura 106 asserts. Tabari's attempt at clarification, taken from Ibn Abbas, is not untypical:

> Allah ordered them to worship the Lord of this House, and He spared them the hardships. Their journey took place in winter and summer, and they did not have rest during winter nor during summer. Afterwards he provided them with food against hunger and protected them against fear, and (henceforth) they journeyed at their pleasure, i.e., if they wished they set out, and if they wished they remained (at Mecca). This belonged to the benevolence of Allah towards them. (Tabari, *Tafsir*, vol. 2, p. 198)[22]

In Ibn Abbas's mind the two journeys were connected with subsistence and were a matter of necessity. Then, "afterward," presumably after the battle with the Abyssinians, the Quraysh had no longer to travel for (or to earn?) food because it was provided by God, and so the need of the journeys passed. Ibn Abbas makes it sound as if the Quraysh had to travel to get food, but other commentators convert the journeys into capital ventures that earned the Quraysh wealth with which to buy food. Neither is very convincing. The Quran itself seems to offer a far better explanation. In 2: 126 Abraham begged God to "make this a secure land and sustain its people with fruits," and again in Sura 14: "O our Lord, I have made some of my offspring dwell in this valley without cultivation, by Your sacred House, in order that they might establish prayer-services. So fill the hearts of some men with yearning for them, and sustain them with fruits . . . " (Quran 14: 37).

Abraham's prayer for sustenance for his descendants was answered by the Quraysh's victory over Abraha, which guaranteed security to the Meccan sanctuary, and the connection between a "secure sanctuary" and Mecca and the Meccans being provided with the food necessary for life is most clearly established in Sura 38, where God declares: "Have We not established for them a secure sanctuary (haram amina), to which are brought as tribute fruits of all kinds, a sustaining provision from Us" (Quran 28: 57).

This verse brings together all the complex notions of God, Mecca and its sanctuary that are scattered throughout the Quran and the prophetic traditions.[23] Through God's mercy Mecca was made into a haram. This may have been done originally for Abraham and his immediate descendents (14: 35; 2: 126), but in some of its early passages, the lesson of that benevolence is being underlined for the benefit of its contemporary beneficiaries. According to Sura 106, no other than the Quraysh now, after the defeat of Abraha, enjoy God's providence. Mecca, in its "valley without cultivation," had no resources of its own, and the inhabitants would surely have perished, the Quran assures them, except for the fact that Mecca is a "secure sanctuary," of which the Quraysh, the "people of the House" (ahl al-bayt), were the masters and guardians.

BUYING AND SELLING IN THE SACRED MONTHS

Not everyone read the "two journeys," which God had "eased" and to which the prosperity of the Quraysh was linked, as an expanded opportunity for trade. Al-Razi for one thought that the "journey of winter and of summer" referred to the traveling of pil-

grims to Mecca, the one referring to the *'umra* of the month Rajab
and the other to the *Hajj* of the month Dhu al-Hijja.[24] If it was a
guess, it was an inspired one. Muslim commentators, who lived in
an era and a society without intercalation and so without seasonal
festivals, would have difficulty in imagining seasonal pilgrimages,
as all such were in pre-Islamic days. Such pilgrimages would
surely have been "eased" if they took place under the authority
and protection of the now saintly Quraysh. Thus, in this reading
of the Quran, every year, twice a year during the sacred months,
pilgrims were drawn to Holy Mecca on pilgrimage, and their fee
of homage was the provisions, on which the Quraysh and the
other Meccans lived. Trade enters nowhere in this equation, particularly not the long-distance trade read by some of the commentators into verse 2 of Sura 106.

Trade may have been a background issue, however, or rather
the Quraysh's participation in it; and some of Muhammad's audience appear to have opposed it, or such seems to be the sense of
verse 198 in Sura 2, "It is no fault for you to aspire to the Lord's
bounty," immediately preceded and followed by detailed prescriptions regarding the pilgrimage "in the well-known months." The
historians had a good deal of information on the circumstances
and places where the "Lord's bounty" was reaped by interested
parties; namely, the holy-day fairs (*mawasim*). That trade should
be tied to the pilgrimage was natural to most of the participants,
save perhaps to the puritanical *Hums* with their fierce and, as we
shall see, exclusive devotion to Mecca. Peoples who, by reason or
danger or distance, did not normally associate came together in
and around Mecca under the protection of the truce of God, to
worship and, it seems clear, to trade.

Al-Azraqi's is the most detailed sketch of the market fairs:

> . . . And the *Hajj* was in the month of Dhu al-Hijja. People
> went out with their goods and they ended up in Ukaz on the day
> of the new moon of Dhu al-Qa'da. They stayed there twenty
> nights during which they set up in Ukaz their market of all col-
> ors and all goods in small houses. The leaders and foremen of
> each tribe oversaw the selling and buying among the tribes
> where they congregate in the middle of the market.
> After twenty days they leave for Majanna, and they spend
> ten days in its market, and when they see the new moon of Dhu
> al-Hijja they leave for Dhu al-Majaz, where they spend eight
> days and nights in its markets. They leave Dhu al-Majaz on the

"day of *tawarih*," so called because they depart from Dhu al-Majaz for Urfa after they have taken water (for their camels) from Dhu al-Majaz. They do this because there is no drinking water in Urfa, nor in Muzdalifa.

The "day of *tawarih*" was the last day of their markets. The people who were present at the markets of Ukaz and Majanna and Dhu al-Majaz were merchants, and those who wanted to trade, and even those who had nothing to sell and buy because they can go out with their families. The non-merchants from Mecca left Mecca on the "day of *tawarih*." (Azraqi 1858, p. 129)

Pilgrims, then, who were making the pre-Islamic *Hajj* traded at various locations in the vicinity of the pilgrimage sites before performing their rituals and, as seems likely, at Mina and Arafat as well, a practice that did not extend, as we shall see, to Mecca. Therefore the wealth of the pre-Islamic Quraysh had nothing to do, as it certainly did in the Islamic era, with trading with pilgrims at Mecca during the Hajj season. If Meccans traded, it was elsewhere, either at the fairs outside of Mecca—fairs they did not themselves control[25]—or else as a function of the regional trading network set up as a result of Hashim's arrangements with the bedouin and the Quraysh's own status as a holy tribe, a condition formally institutionalized not long before Muhammad's birth by the confederation known as the *Hums*.

A RELIGIOUS SODALITY: THE *HUMS*

The Meccan historian al-Azraqi provides a succinct definition of the pre-Islamic religious association that the Muslims later remembered as *Hums:*

... we are the people of the Haram. We do not leave the Haram. We are *Hums*, and the Quraysh become *Hums* and all who are born to the Quraysh. *Humsis* and the tribes that became *Humsis* with them were so called because they were strict fundamentalists in their religion, and so an *ahmasi* (sing.) is a man who is religiously conservative.[26] (al-Azraqi 1858, p. 115)

A great many additional more historical and ritualistic nuances to the portrait can be supplied from Ibn Ishaq:

I do not know whether it was before or after the Year of the Elephant [that is, 552 A.D.] that the Quraysh invented the idea of *Hums* and put it into practice. They said, "We are the sons of Abraham, the people of the holy territory, the guardians of the shrine and the citizens of Mecca. No other Arabs have rights like ours, or a position like ours. The Arabs recognize none as they recognize us, so do not attach the same importance to the outside country as you do to the sanctuary, for if you do, the Arabs will despise your taboo and will say 'They have given the same importance to the outside land as to the sacred territory'." So they [that is, the *Hums*] gave up the halt at Arafat and the departure from it, though they recognized that these were institutions of the *Hajj* and the religion of Abraham. They considered that other Arabs should halt there and depart from the place, but they said, "We are the people of the sanctuary, so that it is not fitting that we should go out from the sacred territory and honor other places as we, the Hums, honor that; for the Hums are the people of the sanctuary." They then proceeded to deal in the same way with the Arabs who were born within and without the sacred territory. Kinana and Khuza'a joined them in this.

The *Hums* were, then, tribesmen of the Quraysh, the Kinana, the Khuza'a, and the Amir ibn Sa'sa'a who embraced, or perhaps had even newly embraced, what was later called *the religion of Abraham*, Muhammad's own later phrase to describe Islam, and which the members strongly identified with the cult of the Ka'ba in Mecca, even to the exclusion of the other pilgrimage rituals, chiefly the *Hajj*, which was focused on other places, like Mina and Arafat.[27] In this view, and we have no reason to doubt it, the original *Hajj* had nothing to do with the "religion of Abraham," and the Quraysh as *Hums* did not recognize the *Hajj* because some of its rituals took place outside the Haram, as appears from this passage in Ibn Ishaq which seems to draw the *Hums* definition of the Haram somewhat short of Arafat:

> The *Hums* used to say, "Do not respect anything profane and do not go outside the sacred area during the *Hajj*." So they cut short the rites of pilgrimage and the halt at Arafat, it being in the profane area, and would not halt at it or go forth from it. They made their stopping place at the extreme end of the sacred territory at Namira at the open space of al-Ma'ziman, stopping there the night of Arafat and sheltering by day in the trees of Namira and starting from it to Muzdalifa. When the sun tur-

baned the tops of the mountains, they set forth. They were
called *Hums* because of the strictness of their religion. (Ibn
Ishaq 1955, p. 115)

These limited cult excursions outside of Mecca may have been
by way of concession to some of the bedouin members of the
sodality, or to newcomers who found it difficult to break old
habits, because other reports stress the *Hums'* narrower definition
as the area *immediately* around the Ka'ba, as in this from Muqatil
ibn Sulayman:

> The *Hums*—they were Quraysh, Kinana, Khuza'a and Amir ibn
> Sa'sa'a—said: "The Safa and the Marwa do not belong to the
> sacred sites of Allah." In the Age of Barbarism there was on
> (Mount) Safa an idol named Na'ila and on (Mount) Marwa an
> idol named Asaf.[28] They [that is, the *Hums*] said: "It is
> improper for us to make a turning (*tawaf*) between them," and
> therefore they did not make a turning between them. (Muqatil,
> *Tafsir*, ms. 1:25b)[29]

If we are to believe this, the *Hums* attempted, perhaps not
entirely successfully,[30] to exclude even Safa and Marwa, within a
stone's throw from the Ka'ba, from their own particular rites. Or
perhaps not. Muslim commentators were continuously attempting to supply the historical background for the Quran's great
number of verses without context. One such directly addresses
Safa and Marwa and what appears to be a group of Meccans who
hesitated to accept the cult there: "Safa and Marwa are among the
indications of Allah. It is therefore no sin for him who is on pilgrimage to the House of God, or visiting it, to go round them . . ."
(Quran 2: 158).

Limiting their cult rituals to the Haram of Mecca was only
one aspect of *Hums'* observance. There were dietary and domestic
taboos and a great deal of emphasis upon the clothes connected
with the ritual:[31]

> The *Hums* went on to introduce innovations for which they had
> no warrant. They thought it wrong to eat cheese made of sour
> milk or clarified butter while they were in a state of ritual taboo.
> They would not enter tents of camel-hair or seek shelter from
> the sun except in leather tents while they were in this state. They
> went further and refused to allow those outside the Haram to
> bring food in with them when they came on the great or little
> pilgrimage. Nor could they circumambulate the House except in

the garment of the *Hums*. If they had no such garments they had to go round naked. If any man or woman felt scruples when they had no *Hums* garments, then they could go round in their ordinary clothes; but they had to throw them away afterwards so that neither they nor anyone else could make use of them. The Arabs called these clothes "the cast-off." They imposed all these restrictions on the Arabs, who accepted them and halted at Arafat, hastened from it, and circumambulated the house naked. The men at least went naked, while the women laid aside all their clothes except a shift wide open back and front . . . (Ibn Ishaq 1955, p. 87)

. . . When the Quraysh let an Arab marry one of their women, they stipulated that the offspring should be an *ahmasi* following their religion. . . . The Hums strictly observed the sacred months and never wronged their proteges therein nor wronged anyone therein. They went round the Ka'ba wearing their clothes. If one of them before and at the beginning of Islam was in a state of taboo, if he happened to be one of the housed-wellers, that is, living in the houses or villages, he would dig a hole at the back of his house and go in and out by it and not enter by the door. . . . The year of Hudaybiyya the Prophet was entering his house. One of the Ansar (from Medina) was with him and he stopped at the door, explaining that he was an *ahmasi*. The Apostle said "I am an *ahmasi* too. My religion and yours are the same," so the Ansari went into the house by the door as he saw the Apostle do. (al-Azraqi 1858, p. 115)

If the report of Muhammad's claim that he too was a member of the *Hums* has any credibility, it must refer to his other later boast that he was an adherent of the "religion of Abraham" because, at Medina at least, he did not venerate the Quraysh, he did not exclude Arafat from the Islamic *Hajj*, nor did he appear to practice any of the *Hums'* clothing taboos described by Azraqi:

Abu Abbas said: there were Arab tribes, among them the Banu Amir (ibn Sa'sa'a), who circumambulated the House naked, the men during the day and the women during the night. When one of them reached the entry of the Haram, he would say to the *Hums*, "Who will lend clothes to a man who needs them?" If an *ahmasi* gave him his clothes he would circumambulate in them, otherwise he would throw off his own clothes at the entry of the Haram and then circumambulate seven times naked. And they used to say, "We cannot circumambulate in our own clothes because we have committed sins in them." . . . Some of their women used to take belts with them which they hung around their loins in order to cover themselves. (al-Azraqi 1858, p. 124)

If a man or a woman went to the *Hajj* without being a member of the *Hums*, they could not circumambulate the House unless they were either naked or wearing the clothes of the *ahmasi*, which they borrowed or rented. Such a man (not of the *Hums*) would stand at the entry to the Haram and say: "Who will lend someone an outfit?" If one of the *Hums* lends him an outfit, or if he is able to rent one, then he can circumambulate; else he will have to remove his (own) clothes outside the Haram and then enter naked. He starts from Asaf and moves to the Black Stone;[32] then he turns right and circumambulates seven times, returning to the pillar, and then on to Na'ila to end the circumambulation. He goes out (of the Haram) and there finds his clothes just as he left them . . .

The *Hums* used to circumambulate in their own clothes, and if a non-*Humsi* noble, a man or a woman, wanted to circumambulate and had another set of clothes, he can circumambulate in one outfit and then throw away what he was wearing between Asaf and Na'ila and no one would touch (the first set) and no one use them until they disintegrated from being under foot and from the sun and rain and wind. (*Ibid.*, p. 121)

Finally, we can approach the belief system of the *Hums* from another side. Among the liturgical acclamations called *talbiyya*—"We are present (*labbayka*), O Lord, We are present"—is one purporting to be the ritual cry of the *Hums*.[33] In it Allah is addressed not only as "Lord of the Ka'ba," as we might aspect, but also as "Lord of Manat, al-Lat, and al-Uzza," and even as "Lord of Sirius." Both sentiments are expressed in the Quran, the first in references to the goddesses as the "daughters of Allah," a notion that was embraced on at least one occasion—that of the "Satanic verses" (see later)—and the second as part of a kind of a credo (Quran 53: 49) associated with a scriptural monotheist.[34] Allah, we seem to be told in this *labbayka,* was not the only god, but he was assuredly the master of the other gods, another sentiment exactly echoed in the Quran:

Do they attribute to Him as partners things that can create nothing but are themselves created? No aid can come from them, nor can they even aid themselves. If you call them for guidance, they will not obey. As for you, it is all the same whether you call upon them or hold your peace. In truth, those

whom you call upon besides Allah are servants (of Allah) like
yourselves . . . (Quran 7: 191–194)

THE PERSIAN OCCUPATION OF
THE KINGDOM OF HIMYAR

According to the Arab-Muslim tradition, Abraha, once the
viceroy of the Abyssinian Negus in the Yemen and more recently
an autonomous king there, met his death in a vain attempt to take
Mecca, with important effects on that latter city, as we shall see.
The attack was said to have taken place in the same year as
Muhammad's birth, which, if it placed in 570 A.D., leaves little
time for the succession of two of Abraha's sons in turn, Yaksum
and Masruq.[35]

> When Abraha died, his son Yaksum became king of the
> Abyssinians. [Tabari, *Annals*, vol. 1, p. 945: Himyar and the
> tribes of the Yemen were humiliated under the heel of the
> Abyssinians. They took their women and killed their men and
> seized their young men to act as interpreters.] When Yaksum
> ibn Abraha died his brother Masruq ibn Abraha reigned over
> the Abyssinians in the Yemen. (Ibn Ishaq 1955, p. 31)

The rule of the Abyssinian occupiers eventually was by then
intolerable to the local Himyarite aristocracy, and during the reign
of Masruq one of them, Sayf ibn dhi Yazan went to Constantinople to seek help from the unbalanced Justin II (r. 565–578).

> When the people of the Yemen had long endured oppression,
> Sayf ibn Dhi Yazan, the Himyarite, who was known as Abu
> Murra, went to the Byzantine emperor and complained of his
> troubles, asking him to drive out the Abyssinians and take over
> the country. He asked him to send what forces he pleased and
> promised him the kingdom of the Yemen.

Failing to gain a hearing in Byzantium, Sayf made contact
with the Lakhmid prince of al-Hira, Amr ibn Mundhir,[36] who
introduced him to the shah's court. He complained that his country had been taken over by "ravens," that is, blacks. From
Abyssinia or Sind, Khusraw wanted to know. Abyssinians, he was
told. "And I have come to you for help and that you may assume
the kingship of my country." Though he composed a poem "in the
Himyarite language" in praise of the shah, he received no firm

commitment from Khusraw, who remarked: "Your country is far distant and has little to attract me. I cannot endanger a Persian army in Arabia and there is no reason why I should do so" (Ibn Ishaq 1955, p. 31).

Sayf died at the shah's court while still awaiting a response, but his son Ma'di-karib appears to have had somewhat better luck with Khusraw.[37] An army was put together from 800 tough prisoners rousted out of Iranian jails, and they set sail for the Yemen under an elderly knight, Vahriz (ar. Wahriz).[38]

> Khusraw gathered his advisers together and asked their opinion about the man and his project. One of them reminded the king that in his prisons were men condemned to death. If he were to send them (to the Yemen) and they were killed, that would merely be the fate determined for them; on the other hand, if they conquered the country, he would have added to his empire. Thereupon Khusraw sent those who were confined in his prisons to the number of 800 men.
>
> He put in command of them a man called Wahriz who was of mature age and of excellent family and lineage. They set out in eight ships, two of which foundered, so that only six reached the shores of Aden . . . (Ibn Ishaq 1955, pp. 31–32)

Despite these loses en route, the Persian expeditionary force found some local support for Ma'di-karib and removed Masruq from the scene (575 A.D.) Vahriz returned to Iraq with a great deal of gold, but before leaving, he instructed his new client on his responsibility for levying land and poll taxes and sending the proceeds to the shah, which was exactly the practice followed in the Hijaz.[39]

Ma'di-karib's reign lasted no more than two years; in 577 he was assassinated by an Abyssinian conspiracy. Khusraw had once again to send out Vahriz, this time with 4000 Persian regular troops.

> When the Persian king heard of this (insurrection against his Himyarite client) he sent Wahriz with 4,000 Persians and ordered him to kill every Abyssinian or child of an Abyssinian and an Arab woman, great or small, and not leave alive a single man with crisp curly hair. Wahriz arrived and in due course carried out these instructions and wrote to tell the king he had done so. The king then gave him viceregal authority and he ruled under Khusraw until his death. (Ibid., 1955, p. 34)

After this bloody massacre of the Abyssinians Vahriz was in the Yemen to stay as the shah's regent and tax collector.[40] What followed thereafter is difficult to discern. Tabari says that Vahriz's son and grandson ruled the Yemen in the shah's name. But at least one of them was called *marzban*, which has suggested to one scholar that the Yemen was organized as a frontier province of the Sasanian Empire and governed by a possibly hereditary Persian military governor.[41]

These events took place in the late 570s, during the earliest years of Muhammad at Mecca, if we accept the traditional dating of the Prophet's birth to the "Year of the Elephant." It makes no difference, however, if the Persian occupation of the Yemen took place just before or just after Muhammad's birth. The results were the same. The shah of Iran now controlled not only the overland trade routes to the Farther East but the Middle East's own primary sources of spices, the former "Araby the Blest" in the Yemen. The occupation of the richest corner of Arabia should have been an enormous commercial boon for the Sasanians, but there is no sign that it was in fact such. What the available evidence does show is that after the first decades of the sixth century South Arabia was in a state of political, social and economic disarray: its agriculture was in ruin,[42] and its affiliated Arab tribes were moving out of their sedentary ways back into the nomadic life of the steppe. By the mid-sixth century Arabia was in the full grip of what has been called *the bedouinization of Arabia*.[43]

THE BIRTH OF MUHAMMAD IBN ABDULLAH

It is alleged in popular stories—and only God knows the truth—that Amina, daughter of Wahb, the mother of God's Apostle, used to say when she was pregnant with God's Apostle that a voice said to her, "You are pregnant with the lord of this people, and when he is born, say: 'I put him in the care of the One from the evil of every envier'; then call him Muhammad." As she was pregnant with him she saw a light come forth from her by which she could see the castles of Bostra in Syria. Shortly afterwards Abdullah, the Apostle's father, died while his mother was still pregnant.

Thus rapidly does Muhammad's father pass from history, the same Abdullah nearly sacrificed by his own father, Abd al-Muttalib.

> The Apostle was born on Monday, the 12th of First Rabi' in the Year of the Elephant. . . . It is said that he was born in the house known as Abu Yusuf's, and it is said that the Apostle gave it to Aqil ibn Abi Talib who kept it until he died. His son sold it to Muhammad ibn Yusuf, the brother of al-Hajjaj, and he incorporated it into the house he built. Later Khayzuran separated it therefrom and made it into a mosque.[44] (Ibn Ishaq 1955, pp. 69–70)

This apparently confident chronology is belied by most of the other information we possess about the life of Prophet. To begin with, not all the authorities date his birth in the so-called Year of the Elephant.[45] Muhammad, like most others of his contemporaries and people in similar circumstances for many centuries after, had little or no idea when he was born and thus of his exact age at his death. Most of the authorities make him anywhere between 60- and 65-years-old when he died, a quite advanced age in that culture and quite at odds with the impression given by the sources of his vitality and of the unexpectedness of his death when it did occur.[46]

As it turns out, the reported age of Muhammad was a function not of the memory of his followers, who had no way of knowing it, but of a *calculation* based on quite another set of considerations. This is one example:

> The Quraysh reckoned (time), before the (beginning of the) era of the Prophet, from the time of the Elephant. Between the Elephant and the Sinful Wars, they reckoned forty years. Between the Sinful Wars and the death of Hisham ibn al-Mughira they reckoned six years. Between the death of Hisham and the (re)building of the Ka'ba they reckoned nine years. Between the (re)building of the Ka'ba and the departure of the Prophet for Medina, they reckoned fifteen years; he stayed five years (of these fifteen) without receiving the revelation. Then the reckoning (of the usual chronology) was as follows . . . [47] (Ibn Asakir, *Ta'rikh*, vol. 1, p. 28)[48]

One nonhistorical element in the calculation was the notion that the Prophet should have been at the ideal age of 40 when he received his first revelation,[49] and another, less frequently invoked, is that he should not have yet reached the age of responsibility when he took part, as we shall see, in the so-called Sinful Wars.[50] The consequent calculations have led to numerous anom-

alies, like obliging Khadija to bear Muhammad eight children
after she had passed the age of 40.[51]

Later Muslim authorities seem to give tacit recognition to the
uncertainty of any of the chronological indications passed on
about the Prophet's life at Mecca. They, like us, must have felt
that the historical ground grew firm only at Muhammad's migration to Medina;[52] it was that date, in any event, that they chose to
begin the Muslim calendrical era.[53]

We return to Ibn Ishaq's canonical account of the early years
of Muhammad, what has been called the *Infancy Gospel of
Islam*,[54] filled, as it appears, with the same miracles and presenti-
ments of the future as are found in the opening pages of Matthew
and Luke:

> Salih ibn Ibrahim . . . said that his tribesmen said that Hassan
> ibn Thabit said, "I was a well-grown boy of 7 or 8, understand-
> ing all that I heard, when I heard a Jew calling out at the top of
> his voice from the top of a fort in Yathrib [that is, Medina]: 'O
> company of Jews' until they all came together and called out,
> 'Confound you, what is the matter?' He answered: 'Tonight has
> risen a star under which Ahmad is to be born.' . . . "
>
> After his birth his mother sent to tell his grandfather Abd
> al-Muttalib [Muhammad's father, it will be recalled, died before
> he was born] that she had given birth to a boy and asked him to
> come and look at him. When he came she told him what she had
> seen and what was said to her and what she was ordered to call
> him. It is alleged that Abd al-Muttalib took him before Hubal in
> the middle of the Ka'ba, where he stood and prayed to Allah
> thanking him for this gift. Then he brought him out and deliv-
> ered him to his mother, and he tried to find foster mothers for
> him. (Ibn Ishaq 1955, pp. 69–70)

A foster mother was found for the newborn, a certain Halima
from among the tribe of the Banu Sa'd ibn Bakr, and this suckling
interval in his life was the setting for some of the more extraordinary stories that grew up around Muhammad.

> Thawr ibn Yazid, from a learned person who I think was Khalid
> ibn Ma'dan al-Kala'i, told me that some of the Apostle's com-
> panions asked him to tell them about himself. He said: "I am
> what Abraham my father prayed for and the good news of my
> brother Jesus. When my mother was carrying me she saw a light
> proceeding from her which showed her the castles of Syria. I
> was suckled among the Banu Sa'd ibn Bakr, and while I was

with a brother of mine behind our tents shepherding our lambs, two men in white raiment came up to me with a gold basin full of snow. Then they seized me and opened up my belly, extracted my heart and split it; then they extracted a black drop from it and threw it away; then they washed my heart and my belly with that snow until they had thoroughly cleaned them. Then one said to the other, "Weigh him against ten of his people." They did so and I outweighed them. Then they weighed me against a hundred and then a thousand and I outweighed them. He said, "Leave him alone, for by God, if you weighed him against all his people, he would outweigh them."[55]

The Apostle of God used to say, "There is no prophet but has shepherded a flock." When they said, "You too, Apostle of God?," he said "Yes."

The Apostle of God used to say to his companions, "I am the most Arab of you all. I am of the Quraysh and I was suckled among the Banu Sa'd ibn Bakr. It is alleged by some, but God knows the truth, that when his foster mother brought him to Mecca, he escaped her among the crowd while she was taking him to his people. She sought him and could not find him, so she went to Abd al-Muttalib and said: "I brought Muhammad tonight and when I was in the upper part of Mecca he escaped me and I don't know where he is." So Abd al-Muttalib went to the Ka'ba praying to God to restore him. They assert that Waraqa ibn Nawfal and another man of Quraysh found him and brought him to Abd al-Muttalib saying 'We have found this son of yours in the upper part of Mecca.' Abd al-Muttalib took him and put him on his shoulder as he went round the Ka'ba confiding him to God's protection and praying for him; then he sent him to his mother Amina."

A learned person told me that what urged his foster mother to return him to his mother, apart from what she told his mother, was that a number of Abyssinian Christians saw him when she brought him back after he had been weaned. They looked at him, asked questions about him, and studied him carefully, then they said to her, "Let us take this boy and bring him to our king and our country; for he will have a great future. We know all about him." The person who told me this alleged that she could hardly get him away from them. (Ibn Ishaq 1955, pp. 72–73)

CHAPTER 5

The Gods and the Shrine

The Muslims of the first and second century after the Hijra looked back upon time of their ancestors before the revelation of Islam and labeled it the *Era of Ignorance* or *The Barbarism* (*al-jahiliyya*). They laid upon it their own version of a "sacred history" that is merely hinted at in the Quran, and thus the older religious traditions of Mecca were to a large extent rewritten, or misrepresented, or simply forgotten in the light of a new revelation that had annulled the beliefs and practices of an earlier age. Those beliefs and practices were, however, the milieu that, if it did not produce Islam, certainly bore witness to its birth; and so to attempt to reconstruct it is nothing less than to supply the context out of which Muhammad and God's Quran came.

THE GODS AND WORSHIP AT MECCA

The Meccans and their neighbors in the Hijaz worshipped the way they lived; the small settled population venerated their gods at fixed shrines in towns and oases, and the bedouin worshipped in transit: like the ancient Israelites crossing Sinai, they carried their gods with them.[1] The objects worshipped were principally stones and trees and heavenly bodies,[2] or rather, the gods thought to reside in them or possibly were represented by them. What is reasonably clear is that in the more recent Arabian past sacred stones were increasingly being shaped into human likenesses, rough or fine, and that by Muhammad's day many of them had distinctive names and personalities. The expert on the subject, Hisham ibn al-Kalbi (d. 819), describes what one of them might have looked like, this on the authority of his scholar father, who is posing the question in the following passage:

> I requested Malik ibn Haritha, "Describe to me (the god) Wadd in such a way which would make it appear vividly before me."

105

Malik replied: "It was the statue of a huge man, as big as the largest of human beings, covered with two robes, clothed with the one and cloaked with the other, carrying a sword at his waist and a bow on his shoulder, and holding in one hand a spear to which had been attached a standard, and in the other a quiver full of arrows. (Ibn al-Kalbi, *Book of Idols*, p. 56 = Ibn al-Kalbi 1952, p. 49)

However the devotees thought of it, Arabian cultus was exceedingly fluid, the deities often sharing characteristics, or being harmonized into families, or passing now into the possession of this tribe and now of that. There is a distinctly tribal notion to the Arabs' worship of the gods. On the basis of the South Arabian evidence, with which the more meager Arab tradition concurs, each tribe or tribal confederation had a divine patron whose cult gave the group a focus for its solidarity. And in a practice that points directly to what was occurring at Mecca, each of these "federal deities" was the "lord" of a shrine that served as the cult center of the federation. The bedouin came into the towns to worship at the fixed shrines (*masajid*)—the same word the Muslims will use for their places of prayer—of the gods there. The incentive may have been principally commercial, because fairs are a consistent feature of such urban shrines; and undoubtedly a conscious policy was at work: the movement of the effigy of a popular into a town shrine meant that its worshippers would eventually follow—cult followed cult objects—if certain conditions could be guaranteed. The chief of those was security, and the solution was the usual one of the "truce of God," sacred months when hands and weapons were restrained by divine injunction. Under such security tribes came together, worshipped and traded, and then returned to their other, more normal ways.

When it comes to speak of these matters of pre-Islamic religion in the Hijaz, our authorities are all later Muslims authors, and it was obviously important to them, because Muhammad had either taken over or adapted into Islam certain of the cult practices in the Mecca of his day, to maintain some kind of continuous link with the Abrahamic, and so manifestly authentic, past.

Among these devotional practices (of the Arabs) were some which had come down from the time of Abraham and Ishmael, such as the veneration of the House and its circumambulation, the *Hajj*, the *'umra* [or lesser pilgrimage], the "standing" on Arafat and Muzdalifa, sacrificing she-camels, and raising the voice (*tahlil*) (in acclamation of God) at the *Hajj* and '*umra*, but they introduced into the latter things that did not belong to it.

Ibn al-Kalbi then supplies an example of just such an "unorthodox" innovation, a pre-Islamic "acclamation" (*talbiyya*): "Here we are (*labbayka*), O Lord! Here we are! Here we are! You have no partner save the one who is yours; you have dominion over him and whatever he possesses."

Ibn al-Kalbi immediately provides his own Islamic gloss on the practice: "Thus they declared His [that is, Allah's] unity through the *talbiyya* and at the same time associated their gods with Him, placing their [that is, their gods'] affairs in His hands . . . " (Ibn al-Kalbi, *Book of Idols*, pp. 6–7 = Ibn al-Kalbi 1952, pp. 4–5)

Allah and His Associates

Amidst the profusion of idols in this West Arabian pantheon, one stands out as the chief god of the Meccans. The cult of the deity termed simply *the god* (*Allah* < *al-ilah*) was known throughout southern Syria and northern Arabia,[3] and was obviously of central importance in Mecca, where the building called the Ka'ba was indisputably his house. Indeed, the Muslim profession of faith, "there is no *ilah* except *al-ilah*," attests to precisely that point: the Quraysh were being called upon to repudiate the very existence of all the other gods save this one alone. It seems equally certain that Allah was not merely a god in Mecca but was widely regarded as the "high god," the chief and head of the entire Meccan pantheon, whether this was the result, as has been argued, of a natural progression toward henotheism, or of the growing influence of Jews and Christians in the peninsula.[4] The most convincing piece of evidence that it was the latter at work is the fact that of all the gods of Mecca, Allah alone was not represented by an idol.

How did the pagan Meccans view their god Allah? The Quran provides direct and primary evidence.

> If you ask them [that is, the pagan Quraysh] who created the heavens and the earth and made subject the sun and the moon, they will certainly reply "Allah." . . . And indeed if you ask them who sends down the rain from the sky and so restores life to the earth after its death, they will certainly reply, "Allah." (Quran 29: 61, 63)

> And if you ask them who created them, they will certainly reply, "Allah." . . . (Quran 43: 87)

Say: Who is it that sustains you from the sky and from the earth? Or who is it who has power over hearing and sight? And who is it who brings out the living from the dead and the dead from the living? And who is it who rules and regulates all affairs? They will soon answer, "Allah."

But Allah is not alone in the worship of the Meccans, it soon appears. "If you ask them who created the heavens and the earth, they will certainly say "Allah." Say: Those (female) things you call upon apart from Allah, do you think that if God wills evil to me, they can remove this evil, or, if He wills mercy to me, they can hold back this mercy?" (Quran 39: 38)

In this last verse the "high god" relationship is quite marked. On the one hand, there is Allah, the creator, sustainer, and ruler of the universe, and on the other, a host of minor deities—the "daughters of Allah" among them—who intercede with the lord of the gods.

The most powerful of the idols with whom Allah shared the sanctuary of Mecca was undoubtedly the well-known Arab god Hubal. How he came to be in Mecca is explained by the Meccan historian al-Azraqi. Abraham, we are told, had dug a pit inside the Ka'ba, and it was here that the Khuza'i Amr ibn Luhayy set up the idol of Hubal:

> Amr ibn Luhayy brought with him (to Mecca) an idol called Hubal from the land of Hit in Mesopotamia.[5] Hubal was one the Quraysh's greatest idols. So he set it up at the well inside the Ka'ba and ordered the people to worship it. Thus a man coming back from a journey would visit it and circumambulate the House before going to his family, and he would shave his hair before it.
>
> Hubal is the idol to which Abu Sufyan[6] said on the day of (the battle of) Uhud, "Tower up, O Hubal," that is, manifest you religious power," while the Prophet said, "Tower up, O Unique One." The name of the well inside the Ka'ba was al-Akhsaf; the Arabs used to call it al-Akhshaf . . . (al-Azraqi 1858, 73)

> Muhammad ibn Ishaq said that Hubal was (made of) cornelian pearl in the shape of a human. His right hand was broken off and the Quraysh made a gold hand for it. It had a vault for the sacrifice, and there were seven arrows cast (on issues relating to) a dead person, virginity and marriage. Its offering was a hundred camels. It had a custodian (hajib) . . . [7] (Ibid., p. 74)

The usually reliable antiquarian Ibn al-Kalbi supplies some interesting additional details on the kind of activity that was associated with Hubal at Mecca:

> The Quraysh had several idols in and around the Ka'ba. The greatest of these was Hubal. It was made, as I was told, of red agate, in the form of a man with the right hand broken off. It came into the possession of the Quraysh in this condition, and they therefore made for it a hand of gold. . . . It stood inside the Ka'ba, and in front of it were seven divinatory arrows. On one of these was written the word "pure," and on another "associated alien." Whenever the lineage of a newborn was doubted, they would offer a sacrifice to Hubal and then shuffle the arrows and throw them. If the arrows showed the word "pure," the child would be declared legitimate and the tribe would accept him. If, however, the arrows showed "associated alien," the child would be declared illegitimate and the tribe would reject him. The third arrow had to do with divination concerning the dead, while the fourth was for divination about marriage. The purpose of the three remaining arrows has not been explained. Whenever they disagreed concerning something, or proposed to embark upon a journey, or undertake some other project, they would proceed to Hubal and shuffle the divinatory arrows before it. Whatever result they obtained they would follow and do accordingly. (Ibn al-Kalbi, *Book of Idols*, pp. 28–29 = Ibn al-Kalbi 1952, pp. 23–24)

Finally, among the pictures that decorated the interior of the Ka'ba in pre-Islamic days, there was one, as Azraqi says, "of Abraham as an old man." But because the figure was shown performing the divination by arrows, the chief activity with which Hubal is associated at Mecca,[8] it seems likely that it was Hubal that was so portrayed, a suspicion that is strengthened by the fact that when Muhammad finally took over the sanctuary he permitted the picture of Jesus to remain but had that of "Abraham" removed with the dry comment, "what has Abraham to do with arrows?"[9]

Has Hubal depicted as "Abraham the Ancient" anything to do with the "Ancient House," as the Ka'ba is often called? Or, to put the question more directly, was Hubal rather than Allah "Lord of the Ka'ba"?[10] Probably not, else the Quran, which makes no mention of Hubal, would certainly have mentioned the contention. Hubal was, by the Arabs' own tradition, a newcomer to both Mecca and the Ka'ba, an outsider introduced by the ambitious Amr ibn Luhayy, and the tribal token around which the Quraysh later attempted to construct a federation with the surrounding Kinana, whose chief deity Hubal was. Hubal was introduced into the Ka'ba but he never supplanted the god Allah, whose House it continued to be.

Manat ··· The other popular deities of the Meccans and their neighbors, the so-called daughters of Allah, were named Manat, al-Lat, and al-Uzza; and Ibn al-Kalbi knew a good deal about their pre-Islamic history: "All the Arabs used to venerate her [that is, Manat] and sacrifice before her, in particular the Aws and Khazraj, and so too the inhabitants of Medina and Mecca and their vicinities used to venerate Manat, sacrifice before her and bring her their offerings . . . "

The devotees of Manat also participated in the Meccan cult:

> The Aws and Khazraj, as well as those Arabs among the people of Yathrib [Medina] and other places who followed their way of life, were accustomed to go on *Hajj* and observe the "standing" at all the appointed places, but not shave their heads. At the end of the *Hajj*, however, when they were about to return home, they would set out to the place where Manat stood, shave their heads and stay there a while. (Ibn al-Kalbi, *Book of Idols* = Ibn al-Kalbi 1952, pp. 12–13)

al-Lat If Manat was the favored goddess of the Aws and Khazraj of Medina, al-Lat's chief devotees in the Hijaz were the Thaqif of Ta'if, where she had her principal shrine.

> Al-Lat stood in al-Ta'if and was more recent than Manat. She was a cubic rock beside which a certain Jew used to prepare his barley porridge. Her custody was in the hands of the Banu Attab ibn Malik of the Thaqif, who built an edifice over her. . . . The Quraysh, as well as all the Arabs, were wont to venerate al-Lat. They used to name their children after her, calling them Zayd al-Lat and Taym al-Lat. (Ibn al-Kalbi, *Book of Idols*, p. 16 = Ibn al-Kalbi 1952, p. 14)

al-Uzza Of the three "daughters of Allah," al-Uzza was the most recent arrival,[11] but apparently the dearest to the Meccans—Ibn al Kalbi calls her "the greatest idol among the Quraysh"—and her shrine was in a valley called Hurad not very far to the east of Mecca, complete with a *Haram* and a sacrificial altar.[12] And just as the cult of other two goddesses forged political connections between the Meccans and their neighbors, so too the Hurad shrine of al-Uzza was where the Quraysh strengthened their ties with the Sulaym and other tribes of the eastern hinterland. Ibn al-Kalbi sums up:

> The Quraysh as well as the other Arabs who inhabited Mecca did not give to any of the idols anything similar to their veneration of al-Uzza. The next in order of veneration was Al-Lat and then Manat. Al-Uzza, however, received from the Quraysh the exclusive honor of visitation and sacrifice. This I believe was because of her close proximity. The Thaqif, on the other hand, were accustomed to offer to al-Lat the exclusive honor (of visitation and sacrifice) in the same way the Quraysh offered it to al-Uzza, while the Aws and the Khazraj favored Manat therewith. All of them, though, venerated al-Uzza. (Ibn al-Kalbi, *Book of Idols*, p. 27 = Ibn al-Kalbi 1952, pp. 22–23)

Despite the fact that their principal shrines lay north and east of Mecca, al-Lat, al-Uzza, and Manat were all worshipped by the Quraysh of Mecca, and before his "conversion," al-Uzza numbered no less than Muhammad himself among her worshippers.[13] And as we shall see later, at one dark point in his career he may have contemplated accepting the cult of all three of the "daughters of Allah" into Islam.

Al-Lat, Uzza, and Manat represent one order of those gods and goddesses whom the Quraysh "associated" with the high god Allah, and presumably others of the same rank from Ibn al-Kalbi's catalogue enjoyed a similar relationship with the Lord of the Ka'ba. But beside and below these named Semitic deities were other supernatural beings who, if they did not have a cult at Mecca, were certainly part of the religious landscape there. The Quran has a developed "angelology," much of it similar to Jewish and Christian beliefs about such beings. They are, for example, God's creatures who serve as His winged messengers (15: 8; 35: 1), as individual guardians of humans (13: 11, 82: 10–12), and singers of God's praises around his heavenly throne (40: 7; 42: 5). Gabriel and Michael are identified by name (2: 97–98). How many of these notions the Quraysh were already familiar with or shared is difficult to ascertain. But there some issues where Muhammad and his compatriots parted company on the subject of angels. Indeed, there may have been some confusion between the "daughters of Allah" and angels (cf. 21: 26) because the same argument about God having daughters is common to both: "Ask them their opinion. Has your

Lord only daughters while they themselves have sons? Or that We created angels female as they bear witness?" (Quran 37: 149–150).

And in another place the Quraysh are quite explicitly accused of worshipping angels, and in the form of women: "And they make into female angels (beings) who themselves are servants of al-Rahman. Did they witness their creation?" (Quran 43: 19).

Close to the angels stood the more native *jinn*, "spirits thought to haunt desolate, dingy and especially dark places in the desert"; and though they were the subject of considerable apprehension, they were not normally the objects of the kind of cult associated with the gods. They are fully integrated into Quranic theology—on one occasion (72: 1–19; 46: 29–32) they overheard the Quran being revealed, as they had earlier heard the Torah, and were converted to Islam—but once again they are merely creatures, Muhammad insists against the Quraysh, who worshipped them: "Yet they make the *jinn* equal to God, though God created the *jinn*. And in their ignorance they falsely attribute to Him sons and daughters . . . " (Quran 6: 100).

The Cultus

Like their Semitic and Arab fellows elsewhere in the Near East, the Arabs of the Hijaz used sacrifice as a primary way of forging and maintaining a relationship with the realm of the divine. "To every people," the Quran says, "did We appoint rites of sacrifice that they might celebrate the name of God over the sustenance He gave them from animals." (22: 34) This is said with clear approval, but the immediately preceding verses are considerably more obscure, though apparently on the same subject: "But if someone holds in esteem the (sacrificial) tokens (*sha'a'ir*) of God, that esteem should come truly from piety of the heart. In them [the sacrificial animals?] you have benefits for an appointed term, but then their place (of sacrifice) is toward the Ancient House" (Quran 22: 32–33).

There then follow more precise directions on the benediction and the consuming of the animal sacrifice, again reflecting on what seems to have been the current practice:

> The sacrificial camels we have made the tokens of God for you; in them is much good for you. So pronounce the name of God over them as they line up. When they are down on their sides (after slaughter), eat of them and give of them to eat such as live

in contentment and such as beg with due humility. Thus have We made animals subject to you, that you might be grateful. (*Ibid.* 36)

The sacrifice of animals disappeared out of the Haram in Islamic times but continued to be practiced at Mina during the Hajj. The principal Quranic injunction to sacrifice occurs in Sura 108, which reads in its entirety: "Behold, we have given you abundance. So pray to your Lord and sacrifice. In truth, it is the one who hates you who is suffering loss."

Despite its apparently straightforward command linking prayer and sacrifice, the second verse raised considerable debate among the Muslim commentators,[14] chiefly on the grounds of its occurrence in a Meccan *sura* and thus apparently commands the Prophet to participate in a pagan ritual, possibly connected with the Hajj and possibly not, before the later "Islamicization" of the Pilgrimage.[15]

More than one form of sacrifice was known to the Arabs. The Muslim authorities tell us of animals simply offered to the gods and kept within their sacred precincts without being sacrificed, and the Quran seems to refer to the practice of animal offerings in 5: 106, as part of a repertoire of pagan ritual practices: "And was it not God who made the (custom of) a slit-ear she-camel, or a she-camel let loose for free pasture, or sacrifices for twin births, or stallion camels (freed from work)?" (Quran 5: 106).

Ibn al-Kalbi also comments on the practice of setting aside not only livestock but produce for a god:

The Khawlan had in the land of Khawlan an idol call Amm-Anas. They were accustomed to set apart a portion of their livestock property and land produce and to give one part to it and the other to Allah. Whatever portion of the part allotted to Amm-Anas made its way to the part set aside for Allah, they would restore to the idol; but whatever portion of the part consecrated to Allah made it way to the part allotted to the idol they would leave to the idol. (Ibn al-Kalbi, *Book of Idols*, p. 44 = Ibn al-Kalbi 1952, p. 37)

In addition to animal sacrifice, grain and milk were offered to the gods, as well as the captured arms of enemies, and precious objects like the golden gazelles kept in the treasure pit of the Ka'ba.[16]

Each devotee offered his own victim, and though animals sacrificed in the desert might sometimes be simply left behind, as they often were at Mina throughout Islamic times, in town the animal was usually cooked and eaten as part of a common meal, a practice that created problems for Muslims as it had earlier for Christians. Among the things forbidden to the believer by the Quran is "that which has been sacrificed upon a stone (*nusub*)" (5: 4). Such stones (*ansab*) are described as "abominations," and the "work of Satan" (5: 93). These are familiar objects indeed, already known from the story of Jacob's betyl in Genesis (35: 14). Stones on which one poured out the blood of sacrifice were widely used among the ancient Arabs, not only as here in the vicinity of the Ka'ba, but even as tombstones and boundary markers for sacred enclosures;[17] and because with the coming of Islam their use constituted a form of idolatry, the believer might not share in the food.

Calling upon God

There is little or no reference to the practice of formal liturgical prayer in Meccan paganism, not in its later Islamic sense, at any rate. We have already seen one quite unmistakably pagan doxology in the *talbiyya*, and in the story of Muhammad's temptation to permit the cult of al-Lat, al-Uzza, and Manat there may occur another. He is reported to have said of the goddesses, "These are the high-flying cranes; verily their intercession is to be hoped for."[18] What precisely is to be understood by *exalted cranes*? The Muslim authorities were uncertain what *gharaniq* meant, as are we,[19] but what they did know was that this was the refrain—"Al-Lat, and al-Uzza and Manat, the third, the other; indeed these are exalted (or lofty, '*ula*) *gharaniq*; let us hope for their intercession"—that the Quraysh used to chant as they circumambulated the Ka'ba."[20] It is as close as we shall come, perhaps, to a Qurayshite prayer formula, offered up to Allah—clearly not the goddesses in question—as the devotes moved in a processional liturgy around His Holy House.

These indications apart, we must assemble the evidence for pagan worship as best we can, and most of it emerges, somewhat indistinctly, from the Quran, which is, of course, derisive of the pagans' veneration of the gods, and the Quraysh's prayer (*salat*) at the Holy House is described as "nothing but whistling and clapping" (8: 35). The word used in this verse, *salat*, is the same as that employed for the Muslim's own canonical prayer,[21] but there is a somewhat more authentic Arabic word, *du'a*, a "calling (upon God)," an "invoking," and one verse of the Quran seems addressed to reassuring the Muslims' on the efficacy of their own practice of "calling": "When My servants ask you concerning Me, (say) then: I am near, I answer the call of the caller when he calls (*da'wat al-da'i idha da'ani*). So let them respond to Me and believe in Me. O may they go straight!" (Quran 2: 186).

The "calling" was a personal prayer of supplication, directed in pre-Islamic days to the various idols worshipped by the Arabs. All in vain, the Quran asserts: the idols can neither hear nor answer:

> To Him alone is there true calling (*du'a*); the others whom they call upon besides him hear them no more than if they were to stretch out their hands toward water for their mouths but it reaches them not. The calling of the unbelievers is nothing but straying in error. (Quran 13: 14)

> They call upon such deities besides God as can neither hurt nor help them. That is straying far indeed. (*Ibid.*, 22: 12)

The exact content of such pagan prayers is not preserved, though it is not difficult to reconstruct, particularly in the light of the many graffiti that the Thamud and other bedouin have left scattered on stones across the steppe. They bear the name of the god, the name of the suppliant and a formula of supplication, a request for help, a cure, prosperity.[22]

The Thamudic and Safaitic graffiti indicate that the worshipper might invoke his god where he chose, but there is other evidence that suggests that in some circumstances at least there were special places of prayer. The South Arabian inscriptions refer to the construction or reconstruction of places called *places of prostration* (*mdhqn*),[23] obviously some sort of a building. The word is closely parallel to the Quran's own term, *masjid*, again "a place of prostration." This pre-Islamic shrine is also a building. The term is used to refer to the Ka'ba (22: 25: "the sacred shrine," *al-masjid al-haram*), and in one place it is put (in the plural) in series with other sacred buildings: "Did not God check one set of people by means of another? There would surely have been pulled-down monasteries, churches, synagogues and shrines (*masajid*) in which the name of God is commemorated in abundant measure" (*ibid.*, 22: 40).

There are signs too that in addition to their impromptu supplications, the pagan Arabs prayed at some fixed times as well. The

Quraysh and other Arabs apparently prayed at dawn and sunset. The bedouin were noted for their sunrise prayers, and some of the *Hajj* rituals—the sacrifices at Mina, the departures from Muzdalifa to Mina and from Arafat to Muzdalifa—originally took place at either dawn or sunset, and Muhammad went to particular pains to sever his own ritual practice from those precise hours in order to underscore his rejection of pagan cult.[24]

THE PILGRIMAGE BEFORE ISLAM

The best known of pre-Islamic rituals taken over into Islam is that of the *Hajj* or pilgrimage. The pre-Islamic pilgrimage was not a single act but a complex of rituals joined in a manner, and for reasons, we cannot easily discern. The later Muslim tradition "harmonized" the Islamic version of the complex by identifying each of its elements with some incident in the Abraham legend, which was itself in turn enriched by association with otherwise inexplicable practices in the *Hajj* ritual. As we have already seen, the construction of the Ka'ba is described in the Quran as the work of Abraham and Ishmael (2: 127), and the circumstantial evidence suggests that this may have been a common belief among the pre-Islamic Quraysh. There is, however, no evidence, Quranic or circumstantial, that such a claim was being made by Muhammad, or had been accepted by the pagan Quraysh, for the various *Hajj* rituals. Their association with Abraham appears to have come into circulation well after the acceptance of the *Hajj* as a legitimate and meritorious way for a Muslim to worship God (Quran 2: 197; 3: 97).

Absent the Abrahamic motif, the *Hajj* of Muhammad's Mecca disintegrates into an obscure series of acts centering not on Mecca but on the mount called Arafat eleven miles east of the city. The *Hajj*, it has been maintained, originally had nothing to do with Mecca, as even the Islamic version of the ritual testifies: the climax of the Muslim *Hajj* was and is the "standing" at Arafat followed by a procession to Mina and sacrifice there, after which the pilgrim was free to remove his ritual vestments.[25] More, it was common knowledge that it was not the Quraysh but the Sufa, and later the Tamim, who held the religious offices, granting the so-called permission (*ijaza*) at Arafat and Mina.[26] And not only was Mecca not part of the original *Hajj*, there may have been no trading in the city in connection with its own rituals. Such at any rate seem to be the conclusion to be drawn from the fact that the famous "pilgrimage fairs"—and Mecca is never numbered among them—are associated with Arafat and Mina and the Quraysh seem to play no major role in them.[27] Therefore the Meccan ritual was at some point joined to the Arafat complex, probably by Muhammad himself, because the Quran raised the point whether Muslims, who, if their religious orientation was toward Mecca, were not accustomed to linking commerce with ritual, were permitted to indulge in trade like the *Hajj* habitués of Arafat and Mina.

It was in this context that the revelation preserved in Quran 2: 198 was made public: "It is no fault for you if you seek the bounty of the Lord," in verses that leave little doubt that it referred to the pilgrimage season. Somebody, then, was objecting to the practice of mixing commerce and the pilgrimage ritual, a practice for which Muhammad is announcing God's explicit permission. We obviously do not know everything behind the objection,[28] but what does seem reasonably clear is that, although previously pilgrimage trading had been restricted to the "fairs," of which Mecca apparently was not one,[29] after the revelation of this verse at Medina, Mecca was sanctioned as a pilgrimage trading center, even though the Muslims could not take full advantage of the permission until after the capture of Mecca not long before Muhammad's death.[30]

If the *Hajj* was not Meccan, the Quraysh had their own holy days, the Spring festival called the *'umra* and celebrated in the month of Rajab.[31] Under Islam it lost its seasonal aspect with the ban on intercalation, and some of its distinctive character—its sacrifices, for example[32]—disappeared in its combination with the *Hajj*,[33] but the *'umra* of Rajab preserved its special, and peculiarly Meccan, identity well into Islamic times, as we shall see.

THE WORSHIP OF THE ONE TRUE GOD

Allah, we can be sure, was neither an unknown nor an unimportant deity to the Quraysh when Muhammad began preaching His worship at Mecca. What is equally certain it that Allah had what the Quran disdainfully calls "associates," other gods and goddesses who shared both his cult and his shrine. The processional chant of the pagans of the "Era of Barbarism" was, we are told, "Here I am, O Allah, here I am; you have no partner except such a λ partner as you have; you possess him and all that is his."³⁴ The last clause may reflect what we have already seen was an emerging tendency toward henotheism, the recognition of Allah as the "High God" of Mecca, but it was not sufficient for Muslims who put in its place their own manifestly monotheistic hymn: "Here I am, O Allah, here I am; You have no partner; the praise and the grace are Yours, and the empire; You have no partner."

Abraham

On the prima facie witness of the Quran, Muhammad's preaching introduced this new monotheistic urgency into the Meccan cult: the Quraysh are relentlessly chastised for "partnering God," and from what we otherwise know of Muhammad's Mecca, the charge is not an unjust one. But a closer look reveals that the matter was by no means so simple. While he was still at Mecca,³⁵ Muhammad had begun to invoke the example of Abraham, the Israelite patriarch who was later to play a crucial role in his own self-identification.

As we have already seen, the Quran credits Abraham and Ishmael with the construction of the Ka'ba. The claim appears, however, in Sura 2: 127, a revelation made at Medina, and likely at the point of Muhammad's first break with the Jews there. The Abraham of the Prophet's Meccan period has a somewhat different profile, however. Note, for example, what amounts to a doublet of Abraham's Sura 2 prayer in 14: 35 ff.,³⁶ and particularly 37–40:

> O my Lord, I have made some of my offspring to dwell in this valley without cultivation, by Your Sacred House, in order, O Lord, that they may establish prayer (*salat*). So fill the hearts of some with love towards them and feed them with fruits so that they may give thanks . . .
>
> Praise be to God, who has granted me in old age Ishmael and Isaac, for truly the Lord is He, the Hearer of the Supplication.
>
> O my Lord, make me one who establishes prayer (*salat*), and likewise among my offspring. O our Lord" Accept my supplication (*du'a*). (Quran 14: 37–40)

If it is true, as the argument has been made, that this represents the original, Meccan connection of Abraham with Mecca,³⁷ it is noteworthy that it contains no reference to Abraham or Ishmael's construction of the Ka'ba; indeed, it appears from 14: 37 that Abraham had settled his offspring "by Your Sacred House," a building already in existence. Nor is any particular emphasis given to Ishmael, who is here (14: 39) simply linked with his brother Isaac.

Verse 14: 39 is itself anomalous. All the other prayer verses between 35 and 41 begin with the archaic formula "Our Lord" or "My Lord," whereas 14: 39 uses what eventually becomes the normal reference to God as "Allah." The point is worth noting because in its earliest understanding, the Quran appears to have regarded Isaac and *Jacob* as Abraham's sons, as in 19: 50, a Meccan revelation. It describes God's regard for Abraham after his rejection of his family's paganism: "When he [that is, Abraham] had turned away from them and from those whom they worshipped besides God, We bestowed on him Isaac and Jacob, and each one of them we made a Prophet."

Ishmael is in fact mentioned in the same *sura*, in verse 54, following Moses, and with no apparent connection with Abraham: "And mention in the Book Ishmael; verily he was true to his promise. And he was an Apostle, a Prophet. He used to enjoin on his people prayer and almsgiving, and he was acceptable in the sight of his Lord."

The immediate connection of Isaac and Jacob with Abraham and Ishmael's separation from all three is not an isolated occurrence. It appears again in lists in 6: 84–86, 21: 72–85, 38: 45–48, where Ishmael appears without note or particular importance amidst a miscellany, and not always the same miscellany, of prophets. The conclusion seems inescapable. While still at Mecca Muhammad was under the impression that Isaac and Jacob were Abraham's sons, then at some point, probably at Medina, he corrected the genealogy (14: 39), and eventually, for reasons more theological and polemical, placed the emphasis on Ishmael (2: 125, 127).[38]

To return to Abraham, the evidence is strong that even at Mecca he played an important role in Muhammad's self-perception. In Sura 87: 18–19 Muhammad's preaching of the Last Judgment is immediately connected with "the earliest Scriptures, the Scriptures of Abraham and Moses." Likewise in 53: 36 he chides a pagan unconvinced by his own message that he must be unacquainted with what is in Scriptures of Moses and Abraham. And to this duo is later added Jesus in the late Meccan Sura 42: 13:

"The same religion has he established for you as that which he enjoined on Noah, the same which We have sent by inspiration to you, and which we enjoined on Abraham, Moses and Jesus . . . "

And at Mecca too the connection between Abraham the *hanif* and Muhammad's own religion was established. In almost exactly the same words that Abraham is made to characterize his beliefs 6: 79, Muhammad responded to doubters in the Meccan Sura 10: 105: "Set you face toward religion in the manner of the *hanif*."[39]

The "religion of Abraham" was not, then an unknown concept at Mecca. There are, as we shall see, traditions that others in the city had connections with Abraham, connections that centered, as Muhammad's own did,[40] on the Meccan Ka'ba. Was Muhammad aware at Mecca that Abraham had built that Sacred House? There is no evidence that he did: Abraham had settled his offspring in Mecca near the Ka'ba, but it was not until Muhammad arrived in Medina that the Quranic assertion appears that Abraham and Ishmael had actually built the House.

The statue of Hubal was inside the building during the "Era of Barbarism," it is true, but the ritual performed there was the Abrahamic one of circumcision,[41] and a great many Abrahamic associations, all of them pre-Islamic, clustered around the Ka'ba.[42] The origin of these associations is difficult to trace through every stage of their development, but there are scattered signs along the way. That the pre-Islamic Arabs circumcised their young was well known, though not on the eighth day like the Jews; and Josephus was confident he knew where they had gotten the custom: the Arabs "circumcise after the thirteenth year because Ishmael, the founder of their nation, who was born to Abraham of the concubine (Hagar), was circumcised at that age."[43] Josephus was not telling his readers something of which they were unaware: that the Arabs were descended from the biblical Ishmael and had lapsed from their original faith into forms of idolatry was a commonplace in the history of both the post-Exilic Jews and the Christians.[44] This, for example, is how the ecclesiastical historian Sozomen of Gaza explained the matter in the midfifth century A.D. The author had just been discussing "Saracens," a common name for Arabs before and after Islam:

> This tribe (of Saracens) takes its origins from Ishmael the son of Abraham and had that appellation as well: the ancients called them Ishmaelites from their ancestry. And avoiding the charge

of bastardy and the low birth of the mother of Ishmael, they called themselves "Sara-cens" as if descended from Abraham's wife Sarah. Possessing this kind of descent, all of them are circumcised like the Hebrews and abstain from the flesh of swine and observe among themselves many of the latter's customs. Nor should one think that they have always lived in the same manner, whether by reason of the passage of time or by their intercourse with the surrounding peoples. For it was long after them that Moses legislated, and then only for those who went out of Egypt. Those who lived near the Ishmaelites, being demon-worshippers, likely destroyed the Ishmaelites' ancestral way of life, the only norm by which the ancient Hebrews lived before the Mosaic legislation, relying on unwritten customs. Those same demons the Ishmaelites too doubtless reverenced and they especially honored them and called upon them in the manner of the cult practices of their neighbors and so demonstrated the reason why they neglected their ancestral laws. The passage of a long time caused them to forget some and allow others to grow antiquated.

Afterwards some of them became acquainted with the Jews and learned whence they had come. They reverted back to their ancestry and took up the Hebrew customs and law. From that time many among them still live in the Jewish fashion. (Sozomen, *Church History* VI, 38, 1–13)

Sozomen, then, writing in southern Palestine no more than century and a half before Muhammad, knew that the Arabs were Abrahamites in their ancestry and that "many among them still live in the Jewish fashion." It is not the Hijaz, but it is very close.

The Men Who Found God

In emphasizing the Abrahamic strain in Islam, the Quran calls Abraham a *hanif*, a somewhat mysterious term,[45] but one that the Quran contextually identifies with *muslim* in referring to Abraham, and which is, like Abraham himself, explicitly distinguished from Jew or Christian on the one hand and from the idolators or "associators" on the other. It is all summed up in a single verse of the Quran: "Abraham was not a Jew, nor yet a Christian, but was a *hanif*, a *muslim*, and was not one of the 'associators'" (Quran 3: 67).

And it is precisely in Abraham's footsteps as a *hanif* that Muhammad and his followers are commanded to worship God:

They say: "Become Jews or Christians if you want the guidance." You say: "No, I prefer the religion of Abraham the *hanif*, who was not one of the 'associators'." (Quran 2: 135)

God speaks the truth: follow the religion of Abraham, the *hanif*, who was not one of the "associators." (Quran 3: 95)

Who can be better in religion than one who submits (*aslama*) his self to God, does good and follows the religion of Abraham the *hanif*, for God took Abraham as a friend. (Quran 4: 125)

Muslim scholars took the word *hanif*, and its abstract noun, *hanifiyya*, in two senses: first, as a synonym for historical Islam, the religion revealed to Muhammad and practiced by Muslims; and second, in the sense that the Quran meant it, as a form of "natural" monotheism of which Abraham was the chief, though not the sole, practitioner. And it was in this latter sense that the Muslim tradition recalled that there were in Mecca and environs just such monotheists without benefit of revelation before Islam. Ibn Ishaq presents them to his readers in what is obviously a schematized setting:

One day when the Quraysh had assembled on a feast day to venerate and circumambulate the idol to which they offered sacrifices, this being a feast which they held annually, four men drew apart secretly and agree to keep their counsel in the bonds of friendship. They were Waraqa ibn Nawfal . . . ibn Jahsh . . . Uthman ibn Huwarith . . . Huwarith . . . and Zayd ibn Amr. . . . They were of the opinion that their people had corrupted the religion of their father Abraham, and that the stone they went around was of no account; it could neither see, nor hear, nor hurt, nor help. "Find yourselves a religion," they said; "for by God you have none." So they went their several ways in the lands, seeking the Hanifiyya, the religion of Abraham.

Waraqa attached himself to Christianity and studied its Scriptures until he had thoroughly mastered them. Ubaydallah went on searching until Islam came; then he migrated with the Muslims to Abyssinia, taking with him his wife who was a Muslim, Umm Habiba, the daughter of Abu Sufyan. When he arrived there he adopted Christianity, parted from Islam and died a Christian in Abyssinia. . . . After his death the Prophet married his widow Umm Habiba. Muhammad ibn Ali ibn Husayn told me that the Apostle sent Amr ibn Umayya to the Negus to ask for her and he married him to her. He gave her as a dowry, on the Apostle's behalf, 400 dinars . . .

Uthman ibn Huwarith went to the Byzantine emperor and became a Christian. He was given high office there.

Zayd ibn Amr stayed as he was: he accepted neither Judaism nor Christianity. He abandoned the religion of his people and abstained from idols, animals that had died, blood and things offered to idols.[46] He forbade the killing of infant daughters, saying that he worshipped the God of Abraham and he publicly rebuked the people for their practices. (Ibn Ishaq 1955, pp. 98–99)

This and similar accounts of "natural" Arabian monotheists have not been universally accepted by modern scholars. Some are doubtless the result of special pleading—the stories surrounding Waraqa ibn Nawfal, for example, Khadija's cousin who serves as a kind of John the Baptist in the accounts of Muhammad's early revelations—but others ring quite true, particularly when they have to do with men known to have opposed Muhammad to the end.[47] And if they are true, we have another important clue to the existence of "a national Arabian monotheism which was a preparatory stage for Islam and which, in any examination of the possible stimuli that made themselves felt on Muhammad, cannot be ignored."[48]

Two prominent opponents of Muhammad who are also described as *hanifs* are Abu Amir Abd Amr ibn Sayfi and Abu Qays ibn al-Aslat.[49] The first was a prominent Aws leader at Medina who was identified with the man behind the mysterious affair—mysterious to us, though doubtless well known to the Quran's audience—of the "mosque of schism" built at Medina "in preparation for one who warred against God and His Apostle aforetime" (Quran 9: 107). According to Ibn Ishaq, he used to practice *tarahhub* and was called *al-rahib*, "the monk," both apparent references to the practice of some kind of Christian asceticism,[50] although other accounts connect his *hanifiyya* with beliefs and practices close to Jewish ones. There is in Ibn Ishaq an interesting report of a direct confrontation at Medina between Abu Amir and Muhammad:

Abu Amir came to the Apostle in Medina to ask him about the religion he had brought. "The *hanifiyya*, the religion of Abraham," (Muhammad answered). "That is what I follow," (said Abu Amir). "You do not." Yes I do. But you, Muhammad, have introduced into the *hanifiyya* things which do not belong to it." "I have not," (Muhammad answered,) "I have brought it white and pure." . . . (Ibn Ishaq 1955, p. 278)

In the sequel Abu Amir led his men to Mecca and allied himself there with the Quraysh. After Muhammad's conquest of Mecca in 630 he went to Ta'if and eventually to Syria.

Muhammad's other *hanif* opponent, Abu Qays, is the reputed author of some verses preserved by Ibn Ishaq, which, if they are authentic,[51] provide another view of what constituted pre-Islamic *hanifiyya*:

> Lord of mankind, serious things have happened/the difficult and the simple are involved.
> Lord of mankind, if we have erred/guide us to the good path.
> Were it not for our Lord we should be Jews/and the religion of the Jews is not convenient.
> Were it not for our Lord we should be Christians/along with the monks on Mount Jalil.
> But when we were created, we were created/with our religion distinct from (that of) any other generation.
> We lead the sacrificial animals walking obediently in iron/their shoulders exposed under the clothes.
> (Ibn Ishaq 1955, p. 201)

Some of the motifs are familiar. Abu Qays's beliefs are very close to, but not identical with, those of the Jews and the Christians, but again, he regarded the *hanifiyya*, just as the Quran did, as a natural, or here, an innate religious system. What is less familiar is Abu Amir's description in the last verse of what must be a *hanif* ritual. The details are obscure, but the word for "sacrificial animals" is the Quran's own term (5: 3, 100) for the "garlanded" animals sacrificed at the "Sacred House," and other allusions in the traditions add to the certainty that the *hanifs* conducted their rituals at the Ka'ba at Mecca.[52]

It appears, then, that *hanifiyya* was, in fact, the "religion of Abraham" extoled in the Quran, to which was connected, as we might well expect, a veneration of the Meccan Ka'ba, doubtless as the Holy House built by Abraham; and finally, and perhaps crucial for the development of Islam out of this matrix, a devotion to the Quraysh as the authentic guardians of the sacred precinct in Mecca.[53] Where the *hanifs*, and Muhammad, may have differed from the Quraysh was in their refusal to "associate" other gods with the Lord of the Ka'ba, a difference that was apparently acceptable to the Quraysh. What eventually separated Muhammad from the *hanifs* was their view of the Quraysh. Far from accepting the Quraysh as the untouchable guardians of the Haram, Muhammad repudiated and attacked them.

A Hanif *Poet*

One of the *hanifs* who had a direct and important connection with Muhammad was Zayd ibn Amr, the Meccan who resisted not only Judaism and Christianity but even Islam, and for that very reason reports about him, especially those that put him in conflict with the Prophet, enjoy a higher degree of probability than many other *hanif* stories. Ibn Ishaq's *Life* preserves some of Zayd ibn Amr's poetry, and one at least of his poems gives us some idea of how he rebuked the Quraysh for their idolatry. Both the images and ideas are similar to those expressed in the Quran—what might perhaps be described as biblical monotheism—and apparently with equally negligible success:

Zayd also said:

To God I give my praise and my thanksgiving,
A sure word that will not fail as long as time lasts,
To the heavenly King—there is no God beyond Him
And no lord can draw near to Him.
Beware, O men, of what follows death!
You can hide nothing from God.
Beware of putting another beside God,
For the upright way has become clear.
Mercy I implore, others trust in the jinn,
But Thou, my god, art our Lord and our hope.
I am satisfied with Thee, O God, as a Lord,
And will not worship another God beside Thee.
Thou of Thy goodness and mercy
Sent a messenger to Moses as a herald.
Thou saidst to him, Go thou and Aaron
And summon Pharaoh the tyrant to turn to God
And say to him, "Did you spread out this (earth) without
    a support,
Until it stood fast as it does?"
Say to him, "Did you raise this (heaven) without support?
What a fine builder you were then!"
Say to him, "Did you set the moon in the middle thereof,
As a light to guide when night covered it?"

Say to him, "Who sent forth the sun by day
So that the earth it touched reflected its splendor?"
Say to him, "Who planted seeds in the dust
That herbage might grow and wax great,
And brought forth its seeds in the head of the plant?"
Therein are signs for the understanding.
Thou in Thy kindness did deliver Jonah
Who spent nights in the belly of the fish.
Though I glorify Thy name, I often repeat:
"O Lord, forgive my sins.
O Lord of creatures, bestow Thy gifts and mercy on me
And bless my sons and property." (Ibn Ishaq 1955, pp.
      100–101)

Nor is this all. Ibn Sa'd reports a tradition concerning Zayd and how he worshipped: "This [that is, the Ka'ba] is the *qibla* of Abraham and Ishmael. I do not worship stones and do not pray toward them and do not sacrifice to them, and do not eat what is sacrificed to them, and do not draw lots with arrows. I will not pray toward anything but this House till I die."

If this sounds remarkably like the Prophet's own preaching— Muhammad may have wavered briefly on the question of the *qibla* or prayer direction, however—it is likely Muhammad who learned it from Zayd rather than vice versa. According to a famous, though much edited, tradition,[54] it was the young Muhammad who was the pagan and Zayd ibn Amr who was the monotheist. It was sometime before the beginning of the Prophet's revelations, and in this version the report is told on the authority of Zayd ibn Haritha, who was present and later told the story to his son.

The Prophet slaughtered a ewe for one of the idols (*nusub min al-ansab)*; then he roasted it and carried it with him. Then Zayd ibn Amr ibn Nufayl met us in the upper part of the valley; it was one of the hot days of Mecca. When we met we greeted each other with the greeting of the Age of barbarism, *in'am sabahan*. The Prophet said: "Why do I see you, O son of Amr, hated by your people?" He said" "This (happened) without my being the cause of their hatred; but I found them associating divinities with God and I was reluctant to do the same. I wanted (to worship God according to) the religion of Abraham. . . . The Prophet said, "Would you like some food?" He said, "Yes." Then the Prophet put before him the (meat of the ewe). He [that is, Zayd ibn Amr] said: "What did you sacrifice too, O Muhammad?" He said, "To one of the idols." Zayd then said: "I am not the one to eat anything slaughtered for a divinity other than God." (al-Khargushi, *Sharaf al-mustafa*)[55]

This tradition in one form or other is likely to be true—it flies in the face of later Muslim sentiments about the impeccability of the Prophet even prior to his call—and confirms the information passed on by Ibn al-Kalbi, that Muhammad offered a ewe to al-Uzza, "in accordance with the religion of the people."[56]

A Monotheist's Creed

There is a passage in Sura 53 of the Quran that points towards the same, vaguely scriptural monotheism that the later Muslim tradition thought it detected in Arabia. The verses appear to be directed at a specific individual, and whoever it is—the Quran itself provides no clue as to his identity, though the commentators are filled with guesses—he is being chastised not for his beliefs, with which Muhammad is in agreement, but because of his failure to live up to them. "Do you see the one who turns his back? Who gives little and then hardens his heart? Has he knowledge of the unseen, so that he sees? Has he not been informed of what is in the books (*suhuf*) of Moses, and of Abraham, who kept faith? . . . "

Whoever is being singled out here has, then, a knowledge of Scripture, though not necessarily a reading knowledge ("has he not been informed"), it appears, even though the reference is to something written (*suhuf*). The fact is not remarked upon as unusual but simply to make the failing more grave: the miscreant is about to be read out a scriptural lesson that he should have known, *and that the Quran's audience in general was expected to be familiar with.*[57] The text continues:

Namely, that no burdened soul can bear the burdens of another, and that man has nothing to his credit save what he has himself striven for, and that the fruit of his striving will surely become manifest, and thereafter he shall be rewarded for it with most complete reward; that to your Lord the final end belongs, and that it is He who has given laughter and tears, He who grants life and death, He who created the two sexes, male and female, from a drop of seed when it passed into the womb; and that with Him rest the Second Creation, that it is He who gives wealth and possessions . . .

These are presumably the contents, in whole or in part, of the books of Moses and Abraham that the addressee was presumed to be familiar and with which Muhammad's own teaching is identical. None of the teaching occurs in such form in the Bible, it seems,[58] nor should we expect it to because the reference is to the "books of Abraham" (cf. Quran 87: 18–19) and thus to a tradition of scriptural apocrypha. The teaching is indeed the Quran's own, though here acknowledged as present in other, and current, revealed sources: Allah is the God of Creation and of the Resurrection; all things come from Him and will find their final reckoning from His hand.

Then, somewhat surprisingly, the following three verses take us, without a break, away from the biblical world to that of the Arabian prophets: "And that He is the lord of Sirius,[59] and it is He who brought destruction to the former Ad and upon the Thamud and spared them not . . . "

And then, just as quickly, the thematic line returns to the biblical exempla of Noah and the Cities of the Plain: " . . . and upon the tribesmen of Noah before them.—truly these were yet more imperious and rebellious, and (it was He who) destroyed the Overturned Cities and overwhelmed them with His overwhelming" (Quran 53: 33–54).

PERSONAL DEVOTIONS

When Ibn Ishaq comes to speak of how and where Muhammad received his first revelations, he inadvertently lifts one corner of the veil that covers most of what might be called *religion* in pre-Islamic Mecca:

> The Prophet used to sojourn on Mount Hira for a month every year.[60] That was the *tahannuth* which the Quraysh used to practice in the period of the Era of Barbarism. The Prophet used to sojourn during that month every year, feeding the poor who called upon him.[61] After the conclusion of that month of sojourn, before entering his house, he would go to the Ka'ba and circumambulate it seven times or as many times as it pleased God. When the month came when God wished to grant him His grace, in the year when God sent him and it was the month of Ramadan, the Prophet went out to al-Hira as was his custom for his sojourn. With him was his family. (Ibn Ishaq 1955, p. 105)

There is another, somewhat different, version of this tradition in Bukhari, reported on the authority of Muhammad's later wife Aisha, who was not yet born when the events described took place. It reads:

> Then he was made to cherish solitude and he sojourned alone in the cave of al-Hira and practiced *tahannuth* a number of nights before he returned to his family; and he used to take provisions for it [that is, the sojourn]. Then he would go back to Khadija and take provisions for a similar (period of sojourn). So things went till the Truth came upon him when he was in the cave of Hira. (Bukhari, *The Sound*, 1, 5)[62]

There was, then, no great agreement among the early authorities on either *tahannuth* or the Prophet's own practice, whether it was a shared annual custom or Muhammad's private devotion, whether solitary or accompanied by his family, whether or not it was in a cave, or whether the devotions included feeding the poor. The word *tahannuth* itself was not perfectly understood because later generations glossed it in a variety of ways: to do deeds of kindness, to perform acts of worship, or simply, as Ibn Ishaq's editor Ibn Hisham preferred, "to act like a *hanif*."[63] Modern opinion, which early on noted these obviously important traditions about Muhammad's religious background, had no greater conviction than its medieval antecedents. *Tahannuth* was described as "leading a solitary life" or "acts of devotion," or more specifically as "an ascetic practice that the Meccans observed in Ramadan on Hira: fasting and sexual abstention." Finally, the parallel to the Hebrew *tehinnoth*, "prayers," that is, *voluntary* devotions, was noted.[64]

Other texts, not generally noted in this connection, have, however, come to light; and they somewhat enlarge our understanding of the pre-Islamic *tahannuth*. One describes Abd al-Muttalib as the man who initiated the practice:

> He was the first who practiced *tahannuth* at Hira. . . . When the moon of Ramadan appeared he used to enter (Mount) Hira and did not leave till the end of the month and fed the poor. He was distressed by the iniquity of the evil of the people of Mecca and would perform circumambulation of the Ka'ba many times. (Baladhuri, *Ansab al-Ashraf*, vol. 1, p. 84)[65]

Another tradition from the same source speaks more generally of the Quraysh:

When the month of Ramadan began people of the Quraysh—those intending *tahannuth*—used to leave for (Mount) Hira and stayed there a month and fed the poor who called on them. When they saw the (new) moon of Shawwal they (descended and) did not enter their homes until they had performed the circumambulation of the Ka'ba for a week. The Prophet used to perform it [that is, this custom]. (*Ibid.*, vol. 1. p. 105)[66]

Tahannuth, then, was a Quraysh practice, apparently in the month of Ramadan and somehow connected with Mount Hira—how or why we do not know—and included both charitable deeds like feeding the poor or freeing slaves and ritual acts like the circumambulation of the Ka'ba. It was, in a sense, a novelty, an innovation, or, at least a complex of practices restricted to a few of the Quraysh, but not without precedent or parallel. There occurs in the Quran, in the midst of a series of verses concerning the fast of Ramadan, the injunction, "do not have sexual relations with your wives *while you are in retreat in the shrines*" (2: 187). The practice, whatever it was—the verb apparently means to attach oneself to something, to stay in one place—must have been well known to the Muslims, though its meaning is nowhere established in the Quran. It appears in 2: 125 as one of God's purposes in having Abraham and Ishmael build the Ka'ba, "for those on retreat," followed immediately by "and for those who bow and prostrate themselves."

We can conclude, then, that there was a pre-Islamic practice of "retreat" (*'ukuf*), in which the devoté withdrew for a period of time, possibly a night, possibly longer, to a shrine for supplicatory prayer (*du'a*) and fasting in proximity to the god,[67] and that the practice could be combined with the *Hajj* or the *'umra*. It seems unlikely that this was identical with Muhammad's own practice—why else would the sources have recalled the odd and forgotten word *tahannuth*?—but it must have been very close. There may well have been a shrine (*masjid*) on Mount Hira, just as there were at Arafat, Mina, and Muzdalifa, where there were "standings" in pre-Islamic days;[68] and Muhammad spent his nights there, probably with his family—so the implication of 2: 187—in prayer and fasting, though whether it was during Ramadan remains to be seen.

MUHAMMAD AND MECCAN PAGANISM

There were, then, monotheists at Mecca before Islam, and Muhammad, the man who practiced *tahannuth* on Mount Hira, would eventually be reckoned one of them. But what of the other beliefs and practices of Meccan paganism? Did Muhammad share them as well? On the face of the Quran's testimony it would appear so. In some verses in the early Sura 93 and in the context of Muhammad's attempting to reassure himself, the Quran comes as close to providing a biographical sketch of the Prophet as it ever does.

> Did He not find you an orphan and give you shelter?
> Did He not find you erring and give you the Guidance?
> Did he not find you in need and make you rich?
>   (Quran 93: 6–8)

Verse 7 is closest to our purpose here, and the Arabic words for "erring" (*dalla*) and "guiding" (*hada*) leave little doubt that the "error" is not simply confusion but that Muhammad was immersed in the same cult practices in which the Quraysh persisted even after God had sent the "Guidance" to them as well.[69] Though this interpretation is confirmed by story of Zayd ibn Amr's admonition and the tradition from Ibn al-Kalbi,[70] and there are other remarks and notices to the same point, the Muslim tradition found it increasingly difficulty to accept that Muhammad had been, perhaps for most of his life before his call, a pagan. The doctrine of Muhammad's "impeccability," was grounded, like its Christian counterpart, Mary's perpetual virginity, on the principle of *quod decet*. It began to affect exegesis, and sometime about a century after the Prophet's death was driving the older traditions of Muhammad's prerevelational paganism out of the commentaries.[71]

The same point emerges from an investigation of the reading of another early *sura*, 108, which begins: "We have granted you the abundance, so pray to your Lord and sacrifice." The later exegetical tradition either understood *sacrifice* as a mere gloss on "pray" or else insisted that it referred to the *Hajj* sacrifice at Mina. But nothing in the Quran suggests that, and in fact it never mentions in the *Hajj* in the Meccan *suras*. Sura 108 must clearly be read as the protasis of the firm repudiation of paganism in 109: "Say: O you who are unbelievers, I do not worship not what you worship, nor will you worship what I worship; And I will not worship what you have been worshipping, nor will you worship what I worship. To you your religion and to me mine" (Quran 109: 1–6).

Sura 109 may refer simply to Muhammad's discontinuance of his practice of making the *Hajj*,[72] but not, if it is closely associated with Sura 108, of the customary sacrifices at Mecca.[73] Or, if it falls somewhat later, it may mark his complete break with Meccan paganism, probably announced after the beginning of his public preaching, with what we shall see was an enlarged understanding of what was required by submission to God.

CHAPTER 6

A Prophet at Mecca

COMING OF AGE IN MECCA

If the stereotypical "recognition" stories in Muhammad's infancy narratives inspire little historical confidence, there appears to be some factual kernel embedded in anecdotes like the following:

> The Apostle lived with his mother Amina daughter of Wahb and his grandfather Abd al-Muttalib in God's care and keeping like a fine plant, God wishing to honor him. When he was 6 years old his mother Amina died. . . . Thus the Apostle was left for his grandfather for whom they made a bed in the shade of the Ka'ba. His sons used to sit round the bed till he came out to it, but none of them sat upon it out of respect for him. The Apostle, still a boy, used to come and sit on it and his uncles would drive him away. When Abd al-Muttalib saw this he said: "Let my son alone, for by God he has a great future." Then he would make him sit beside him on his bed and would stroke his back with his hand. It used to please him to see what he did.
>
> When the Apostle was 8 years of age, eight years after the Year of the Elephant, his grandfather died. . . . When Abd al-Muttalib died his son al-Abbas took charge of Zamzam and the watering of the pilgrims, though he was the youngest of his father's sons. When Islam came it was still in his hands and the Apostle confirmed his right to it and so it remains in the family of al-Abbas to this day. . . . The Apostle lived with his uncle Abu Talib, for (so they allege) the former had confided him to his care because he and Abdullah, the Apostle's father, were brothers of the same mother. . . . It was Abu Talib who used to look after the Apostle after the death of his grandfather and he became one of his family. (Ibn Ishaq 1955, pp. 73, 78–79)

We have already seen how Muhammad was recognized and acknowledged by both the Jews, at the moment of his birth, and later by certain Abyssinian Christians, as God's own Apostle. A similar recognition takes place in a meeting at Mecca with an itinerant fortune-telling pagan seer (Ibn Ishaq 1955, p. 79), and indeed there are extended passages in the *Life* devoted to this theme (Ibn Ishaq 1955, pp. 90–98).[1] But by all accounts the most famous and detailed of all these recognition incidents is the one that occurred during Muhammad's adolescence in the course of a commercial journey to Bostra in Syria.[2]

> Abu Talib had planned to go on a merchant caravan to Syria, and when all preparations had been made for the journey, the Messenger of God, so they allege, attached himself closely to him so that he took pity on him and said that he would take him with him. . . . When the caravan reached Busra in Syria there was a monk there in his cell by the name of Bahira, who was well versed in the knowledge of the Christians. . . . They had often passed by him in the past and he never spoke to them or took any notice of them until this year, and when they stopped near his cell they made a great feast for them . . . and sent word to them, "I have prepared food for you, O men of Quraysh, and I should like you all to come, great and small, bond and free." One of them said to him, "By God, Bahira, something extraordinary has happened today; you used not to treat us so, and we have often passed by you. What has befallen you today?" He answered, "You are right in what you say, but you are my guests and I wish to honor you and give you food so that you may eat."
>
> So they gathered together with him, leaving the Messenger of God behind with the baggage under the tree, on account of his extreme youth. When Bahira looked at the people he did not see the mark which he knew and found in his books, so he said, "Do not let one of you remain behind and not come to my feast." . . . One of the men of Quraysh said, "By al-Lat and al-Uzza, we are to blame for leaving behind the son of Abdullah ibn Abd al-Muttalib." Then he got up and embraced him and made him sit with the people. When Bahira saw him he stared at him closely, looking at his body and finding traces of his description (in the Christian books). When people had finished eating and had gone away, Bahira got up and said to him, "Boy, I now ask you by al-Lat and al-Uzza to answer my question." Now Bahira said this only because he had heard his people swearing by these goddesses. They allege that the Messenger of God said to him, "Do not ask me by al-Lat and al-Uzza, for by God nothing is more hateful to me than those two." Bahira answered, "Then, by God, tell me what I ask." He replied, "Ask me what you like," so he began to question him about

what happened in his waking and in his sleep, and his habits and affairs generally, and what the Messenger of God told him coincided with what Bahira knew of his description. Then he looked at his back and saw the seal of prophethood between his shoulders in the very place described in his book.

When he had finished he went to his uncle Abu Talib . . . and said "Take your nephew back to his country and guard him carefully against the Jews, for, by God! if they see him and knew about him what I know, they will do him evil; a great future lies before this nephew of yours, so take him home quickly." (Ibn Ishaq 1955, pp. 79–81)

One of the few events in the history of pre-Islamic Mecca in which the youthful Muhammad was reportedly involved was the so-called Sinful Wars, which fall somewhat uncertainly in the period of his life before his marriage, reportedly at age 25, to Khadija. Both Ibn Ishaq and Tabari pass quickly over the events of these "wars" in their biographies of the Prophet, but there seems little doubt that the conflict did occur, whatever the role the future Prophet of Islam was assigned by the sources to play in it.[3] The issue was a violation, or rather, a series of violations of the "truce of God" during the holy months, whence the name *the Sinful Wars*. The parties were the Kinana and the Hawazin, and the occasion was the fair at Ukaz at its accustomed time in Dhu al-Qaʿda. What started as a personal quarrel escalated into armed tribal conflict that lasted over more than one season at Ukaz. The Quraysh were drawn in first as peacemakers, as their own best interests dictated, and then eventually as combatants in what came to be called *the Fourth Sinful War*, which was not a scuffle or a dispute but full-scale hostilities.

A man named Barrad, we are told, one of the Kinana, was expelled by his own tribe on account of being a drunkard and a troublemaker. He came to Mecca, where was granted the protection of Harb ibn Umayya by becoming his protected ally. Barrad continued to misbehave, and Harb insisted he leave the city, though still formally an ally. He went to Hira where he was commissioned to escort a caravan of Nuʿman's to Ukaz and protect it, possibly as an ally of the untouchable Quraysh, against the Kinana along the way. But Barrad was soon replaced by Urwa al-Rahhal, of the Banu Amir, who had been mocking him as an outlaw and persuaded Nuʿman to give him the job instead. Barrad trailed the caravan and murdered Urwa and took the goods. He then notified the Quraysh because he feared that Urwa's tribal group, the Hawazin, who take their vengeance on a Quraysh leader—Barrad himself was of no consequence because he was an outlaw. Which is precisely what the Hawazin attempted to do over the next four years in pitched battles between the themselves and the Kinana at various places, and then for a time after that by assassinations until finally peace was made. The Quraysh were participants in the field on four separate occasions and were victorious in only one, though the Meccan accounts reckon the affair a Quraysh success.

Though Muhammad was generally thought to have taken part in one or more of the engagements, the sources were uncertain what he did and, more important from the point of dogma, how old he was at the time. The entire business of the "Sinful Wars" was obviously a violation of customary religious law at the time; and Muhammad's participation in it raised serious questions, particularly in what later developed as the doctrine of the Prophet's "impeccability," his freedom from sin even before his prophetic call.[4]

Marriage to Khadija

This is as much as we know about the adolescence of Muhammad. The next event in his life is his marriage, traditionally at about the age of 25, to the widow Khadija:

> Khadija was a merchant woman of dignity and wealth. She used to hire men to carry merchandise outside the country on a profit-sharing basis, for the Quraysh were a people given to commerce. Now when she heard about the Prophet's truthfulness, trustworthiness and honorable character, she sent for him and proposed that he should take her goods to Syria and trade with them, while she would pay him more than she paid others. He was to take a lad of hers called Maysara. The Apostle of God accepted the proposal and the two of them set forth till they came to Syria.

There then occurs in Ibn Ishaq's narrative another recognition scene, or likely a doubling of the Bahira story, because here too the agent is a Christian Syrian monk, though anonymous in this version. Ibn Ishaq's account then continues to describe a transaction the appears to be barter, the exchange of goods for goods, and may represent what actually occurred in Meccan commercial transactions of that era:

Then the Prophet sold the goods he had brought and bought what he wanted to buy and began the return journey to Mecca. The story goes that at the height of noon, when the heat was intense as he rode his beast, Maysara saw two angels shading the Apostle from the sun's rays. When he [that is, Muhammad] brought Khadija the property she sold it and it amounted to double or thereabouts. Maysara for his part told her about the two angels shaded him and of the monk's words. Now Khadija was a determined, noble and intelligent woman possessing the properties with which God willed to honor her. So when Maysara told her these things she sent to the Apostle of God and—so the story goes—said: "O son of my uncle I like you because of our relationship and your high reputation among your people, your trustworthiness and good character and truthfulness." Then she proposed marriage. Now Khadija was at that time the best born woman in the Quraysh, of the greatest dignity and, the richest as well. All her people were eager to get possession of her wealth if it were possible . . .

The Apostle of God told his uncles of Khadija's proposal, and his uncle Hamza ibn Abd al-Muttalib went with him to Khuwaylid ibn Asad [that is, Khadija's father] and asked for her hand and he married her.

She was the mother of all the Apostle's children except Ibrahim, namely al-Qasim—whereby he [that is, Muhammad] was known as Abu'l-Qasim—al-Tahir, al-Tayyib . . .

As the Muslim commentators themselves point out, these latter two designations are not names but epithets—"the Pure," "the Good"—applied to the one son, al-Qasim. " . . . (and the girls) Zaynab, Ruqayya, Umm Kulthum and Fatima. Al-Qasim, "the Pure and the Good," died in paganism. All his daughters lived into Islam, embraced it, and migrated with him to Medina"[5] (Ibn Ishaq 1955, pp. 82–83).

The results of this marriage with one of Mecca's more successful entrepreneurs were extremely fortunate for Muhammad, as the Quran itself seems to recognize:

By the morning brightness, and the night when it is still, your Lord has not forsaken you, nor does He hate you. And truly, the last is better for you than the first. And truly the Lord will give to you, so that you will be content. Did He not find you an orphan, and He gave you refuge? He found you wandering and guided you? He found you poor and made you rich . . . (Quran 93: 1–8)

This reading of the *sura* did not find much favor among the commentators. As we have seen, its open acknowledgment that Muhammad was once orphaned and poor as well as a pagan ("wandering") were not popular themes among later Muslims. Ibn Ishaq's *Life* makes no mention of the Prophet's poverty during the guardianship of Abd al-Muttalib and Abu Talib, and though it reports the marriage to Khadija, there is no reflection on the riches or even prosperity that followed from it. There was no room in the "legend of Muhammad" for suffering or poverty,[6] and so none for the precise point of 93: 8: God found Muhammad poor and made him rich, not by the performance of some miracle but his providential marriage to the wealthy and successful Khadija.[7]

In 605 A.D., if we follow the traditional chronology, when Muhammad was 35-years-old, as Ibn Ishaq tells us, a memorable event occurred in Mecca, the reconstruction of the Ka'ba, the only stone building in that town.

> The Quraysh decided to rebuild the Ka'ba when the Apostle was 35 years of age. . . . They were planning to roof it and feared to demolish it, for it was made of loose stones above a man's height, and they wanted to raise it and roof it because men had stolen part of the treasure of the treasure of the Ka'ba which used to be in a well in the middle of it. The treasure was found with Duwayk, a freedman of the Banu Mulayh ibn Amr of the Khuza'a. The Quraysh cut his hand off; they say that the people who stole the treasure deposited it with Duwayk . . .
>
> Now a ship belonging to a Greek merchant had been cast ashore at Jidda and became a total wreck. They took its timbers and got them ready to roof the Ka'ba. It happened that in Mecca there was a Copt who was a carpenter, so everything they needed was ready at hand. Now a snake used to come out of the well in which the sacred offerings were thrown and sun itself every day on the wall of the Ka'ba. It was an object of terror because whenever anyone came near it, it raised its head and made a rustling noise and opened its mouth, so that they were terrified of it. While it was thus sunning itself one day, God sent a bird which seized it and flew off with it. Thereupon the Quraysh said, "Now we may hope that God is pleased with what we propose to do. We have a friendly craftsman, we have got the wood and God has rid us of the snake. . . .
>
> The people were afraid to demolish the temple, and withdrew in awe from it. Al-Walid ibn al-Mughira said, "I will begin

the demolition." So he took a pick-axe and went up to it, saying the while, "O God, do not be afraid. [Note: The feminine form indicates that the Ka'ba itself is addressed.] O God, we intend only what is best." Then he demolished the part at the two corners. That night the people watched, saying, "We will look out; if he is smitten, we will not destroy any more of it and we will restore it as it was; but if nothing happens to him then God is pleased with what we are doing and we will demolish (the rest of) it." In the morning al-Walid returned to the work of demolition and the people worked with him, until they got down to the foundation of Abraham. They came upon green stones like camel's humps joined one to another . . .

I was told the Quraysh found in the corner a writing in Syriac. They could not understand it until a Jew read it for them. It was as follows: "I am Allah the Lord of Bakka. I created in on the day that I created heaven and earth and formed the sun and the moon, and I surrounded it with seven pious angels. It will stand while its two mountains stand, a blessing to its people with milk and water," and I was told that they found in the *maqam* a writing, "Mecca is God's holy house; its sustenance comes to it from three directions; let its people not be the first to profane it . . . "

The tribes of the Quraysh gathered stones for the building, each tribe collecting them and building by itself until the building was finished up to the black stone, where controversy arose, each tribe wanting to lift it to its place, until they went their several ways, formed alliances and got ready for battle. The Banu Abd al-Dar brought a bowl full of blood, then they and the Banu Adi ibn Ka'b pledged themselves unto death and thrust their hands into the blood. For this reason they were called the "blood-lickers." Such was the state of affairs for four or five nights, and the Quraysh gathered in the mosque and took counsel and were equally divided on the question.

A traditionist alleged that Abu Umayya ibn al-Mughira, who was at that time the oldest man of the Quraysh, urged them to make the first man to enter the gate of the mosque umpire in the matter of the dispute. They did so and the first one to come in was the Apostle of God. When they saw him they said, "This is the trustworthy one. We are satisfied. This is Muhammad." When they came to him and informed him of the matter, he said "Give me a cloak," and when they brought it to him, he took the black stone and put it inside it and said that each tribe should take hold of an end of the cloak and they should lift it together. They did this so that when they got it into position he placed it with his own hand, and then building went on above it. (Ibn Ishaq 1955, pp. 84–85)

Ibn Ishaq's was not the only version of the Ka'ba project.[8] Al-Azraqi, Mecca's premier local historian, has his own account. According to him, there was a particularly destructive flood in that year—not an implausible event, given the history of the town[9]—and the Ka'ba, which sat directly in the torrent bed, was undermined. "Downpours were many, and Mecca had its share of torrential rains and floods. One of these flooded the Ka'ba and its walls were cracked to the point that the Quraysh were afraid on the one hand to use the place and on the other to destroy or rebuild it for fear that some evil would befall them" (al-Azraqi 1858, p. 107).

It was then that an Egyptian ship was wrecked near Shu'ayba, then the nearest port to Mecca on the Red Sea. One of the survivors was a Greek or Coptic carpenter, or perhaps more generally an artisan, named Baqum—Pachomius—who was capable of putting a new roof on the Ka'ba. The Quraysh, Muhammad among them, cooperated by collecting stones for the new edifice.

> When it came time to tear down the remains of the old building, a certain anxiety arose, and it was dispelled only by a divine sign—a bird flew over and removed the serpent that had protected the sanctuary and its treasure for more than 500 years. One of the older Quraysh, who explained he had nothing to lose, began the work, but the others held back until they saw that nothing had happened. Nothing, that is, until they reached the Abrahamic foundations. When they tried to remove these lightening struck and an earthquake shook Mecca. They left them alone. The four factions among the Quraysh each built its own side. It was on that occasion that the door, formerly on ground level, was raised. When it was time to replace the stone they had to summon, "Amin," the trustworthy Muhammad, adjudicate. He used his mantle as described by Ibn Ishaq and all were satisfied.
>
> Baqum then built the roof and inside made pictures of the Prophets, including Abraham and Mary and the Child Jesus. The "golden gazelle" and treasures which were kept in the house of Abu Talha during the reconstruction and the idols, stored the in Zamzam, were returned to their accustomed places inside the Ka'ba. (al-Azraqi 1858, pp. 108–109)

In another already cited passage al-Azraqi supplies some additional details on the representations inside the reconstructed Ka'ba, including "pictures of trees and pictures of angels."

> There was a picture of Abraham as an old man and performing divination by the shaking of arrows, and a picture of Jesus son of Mary and his mother, and a picture of angels. On the day of the conquest of Mecca, the Prophet entered the House and he sent al-Fadl ibn al-Abbas to bring water from Zamzam. Then he asked for a cloth which he soaked in water, and ordered all the pictures to be erased, and this was done. . . . Then he looked at the picture of Abraham and "May God destroy them! They made him cast the divining arrows. What does Abraham have to do with divining arrows?"
>
> Ata ibn Abi Rabah said that he saw in the House a decorated statue of Mary with a decorated Jesus sitting on her lap. The House contained six pillars . . . and the representation of Jesus was on the pillar next to the door. This was destroyed in the fire at the time of Ibn al-Jubayr. Ata said he was not sure that it was there in the time of the Prophet but he thought it was. (al-Azraqi 1858, p. 111)

THE PROPHETIC SUMMONS

So it was as we might have suspected before we began: the young man Muhammad, not the 40-year-old of tradition, had made little or no mark on his native Mecca before his emergence into the political limelight. He was married—his earliest followers remembered his wife, and fondly, it would appear—and thanks to this providential connection, he was, like most Meccans, engaged in the local regional commerce in skins and raisins. How far afield that took him, we cannot say because the Quran's awareness, or interest in, events in the contemporary world is severely limited.[10] Basing itself on such passages as Quran 7: 157 and 158, the later Muslim tradition insisted that Muhammad could not read or write.[11] The insistence appears apologetic—an illiterate Prophet could not "steal" the writings of the Jews and Christians—nor does the word in question, *ummi*, bear quite that burden of meaning.[12] The point may well be moot. If Muhammad was engaged in commerce, it is likely that he possessed some literate skills, however modest; it is even more certain that he had never literally "read," nor was likely capable of reading, the Sacred Books of the Jews and Christians.[13] He had heard, of course, the current Meccan stories about Abraham and the Kaʻba, and he prayed and sacrificed in the civil manner of his fellow Quraysh. But Muhammad was apparently something more: he was caught up, like some few others there, in a more private and personal and exclusive devotion to the Lord of Kaʻba, and he found, on the advice and with the encouragement of some of those close to him, that he had received a special summons from on high.

If we rely solely on the testimony of Quran, it is impossible to say which of the revelations contained in it was the first, though there is some evidence of how, if not precisely when, the summons to prophecy occurred. On two occasions, Suras 53 and 81: 19–17 Muhammad himself describes two visions he had had. In both *suras* the experience is described as having happened in the past and the visions are being referred to, somewhat reluctantly, to defend his current activity—here described only as "speaking"[14]— and perhaps even to his own followers:

> By the star when it goes down, your companion has not wandered[15] nor has he erred, nor does he speak of his own inclination. It was nothing less than inspiration that inspired him. He was taught by one mighty in power, one possessed of wisdom, and he appeared while in the highest part of the horizon. Then he approached and came closer, and he was at a distance of two bow lengths or closer. And he inspired his servant with what he inspired him. His heart did not falsify what it saw. Will you then dispute with him over what he saw? (Quran 53: 1–12)

The same *sura* immediately continues: "Indeed he saw him descending a second time, near the lotus tree that marks the boundary. Near it is the garden of the dwelling, and behold, the lotus tree was shrouded in the deepest shrouding. His sight never swerved, nor did it exceed its limits. Indeed, he saw the signs of his Lord, the Greatest" (*ibid.*, pp. 13–18).

None of the pronouns is identified in these verses, though there is little doubt that the recipient of the vision was Muhammad. Who was seen is less clear, and if Muhammad's being referred to as his "servant" in verse 10 suggests that is God Himself, the Muslim tradition preferred to understand that it was Gabriel in all the other instances, chiefly because later in his own career Muhammad, as we shall see, had unmistakably come to the same conclusion. But there is no other mention of Gabriel in the Meccan *suras*, and it appears far more likely that God Himself first appeared to

Muhammad "on the high horizon" and then on a second occasion by the lotus tree near the "garden of the dwelling" to show him "the signs of his Lord." Muhammad was clearly earthbound when he had his first experience, but where the latter vision took place, whether in a known locality near Mecca or, as is often thought, in some heavenly venue,[16] is not further indicated. Neither is there anything to suggest that it was on either of these occasions that ∨ Muhammad received the words of the Quran.[17]

If Sura 53: 1–18 seems to say that Muhammad believed that on two distinct occasions he had had a vision of God, who thereby prompted him and showed to him His signs, the second vision is referred to only briefly in passing:

> Truly it is the speech of a noble messenger, one possessing power with the master of the established throne, obeyed and trustworthy. Your comrade is not *jinn*-possessed. He saw him on the clear horizon; he does not withhold knowledge of the unseen, nor is it the word of a stoned Satan. So where will you go? It is nothing else than a reminder to the worlds. (Quran 81: 19–27)

Although verse 10 appears to refer back to the same vision "on the high horizon" mentioned in 53: 7–9, the Muslim commentators saw in the first three verses of this passage from Sura 81 ∙ an unmistakable reference to Gabriel. But there is abundant evidence that Muhammad not only did not identify Gabriel as the agent of revelation until his Medina days, but that while at Mecca he was criticized for the fact that God had *not* sent an angelic messenger: "They said: 'If your Lord had so pleased, He would certainly have sent down angels; as it is, we disbelieve your mission'" ⸂ (Quran 41: 14).

Muhammad's earliest response did not encourage them to think that there was in fact an angel in God's revelation to him:

> They say: "You to whom the Reminder is being sent down, truly you are *jinn*-possessed! Why do you not bring angels to us if you are one of those who possess the truth?" We do not send down the angels except when required, and if they came, there would be no respite. (*Ibid.*, 15: 6–8)

> And before you as well the Messengers we sent were but men, to whom We granted inspiration. And if you do not understand that, ask the people who possess the Reminder. (*Ibid.*, 16: 43)

A HEAVENLY JOURNEY

And finally, this celebrated Quranic passage also seems to refer to a supernatural vision granted to Muhammad: "Glory be to Him who carried His servant by night from the sacred shrine to the distant shrine, whose surroundings We have blessed, that We might show him some of Our signs (ayat)" (Quran 17: 1).

That the subject is God and that the object of God's nocturnal activity, "His servant," is Muhammad is certain because the expressions conform to standard Quranic usage, as does the reference to Mecca as "the sacred shrine" (al-masjid al-haram). In Sura 53 an earthbound Muhammad is merely a passive beholder of both God and the supernatural signs; here, however, he is carried off on a journey to another place, "the distant shrine" (al-masjid al-aqsa) and there shown what God wished.

The reading of this opening verse of Sura 17, whose aberrant rhyme makes it appear to be a later addition to the rest of the sura, depends principally on how one understands the "distant shrine." The Muslim tradition had it both ways. It first took it to refer to heaven, then to Jerusalem—this soon became, and remains, the majority view—and in the end produced a harmonizing version that described how Muhammad was first carried to the Temple Mount in Jerusalem on a mythical beast called Buraq, and thence into the seventh heaven and the presence of God, and this was the occasion, it was later thought, that the Quran was revealed to him.

None of this is immediately apparent in the verse; indeed, there are what appear to be earlier denials of the possibility of a heavenly journey in connection with the revelation to Islam, and indeed in this same sura:

> They say: "We shall not believe you until you cause a spring to gush forth for us from the earth, or until you a garden of date-trees and vines and cause rivers to gush forth in their midst, carrying abundant water. Or you cause the sky to fall to pieces, as you day, against us, or you bring God and the angels before us face to face. Or you have a house adorned with gold, or you mount a ladder into the skies. No, we shall not even believe in your mounting until you send down to us a book that we could read." Say: "Glory to my Lord! Am I aught but a man, an apostle?" (Quran 17: 90–93)

And the same disclaimer is made in Sura 6: 35, where God is addressing and consoling Muhammad, "Even if you were to seek a tunnel in the ground or a ladder to the skies and bring them a sign (*aya*), (what good?)."

The evidence is, however, strong that the "distant shrine" of 17: 1 in fact refers to heaven[18] and that the verse refers unmistakably to a heavenly journey that God had granted to his Messenger. We can only conclude that at some point in his career, after first denying the possibility, Muhammad conceded his own experience of a heavenly journey connected with the revelation—the seeing of the supernatural signs exactly echoes the point of the vision in 53: 18—and the opening verse was accordingly added to Sura 17.[19]

There was a great deal of uncertainty about this in Muslim circles and even a century after the Prophet's death, his biographer was still expressing both historical and theological reservations about the pastiche he had composed out of the varying information that had come to him:

> The following account reached me from Abdullah ibn Mas'ud and Abu Sa'id al-Khudri, and Aisha the Prophet's wife, and Mu'awiya ibn Abi Sufyan, and al-Hasan ibn Abi'l Hasan al-Basri, and Ibn Shihab al-Zuhri and Qatada and other traditionists, and Umm Hani bint Abi Talib. It is pieced together in the story that follows, each one contributing something of what he was told about what happened when he was taken on the night journey. The matter of the place [or: time] of the journey and what is said about it is a searching test and a matter of God's power and authority wherein is a lesson for the intelligent; and guidance and mercy and strengthening to those who believe. (Ibn Ishaq 1955, p. 181)

And later, after a brief discussion of whether Muhammad was physically transported to Jerusalem—Aisha, the Prophet's wife used to maintain that "the Apostle's body remained where it was but God removed his spirit by night"—Ibn Ishaq adds his own finis to the controversy: "I have heard that the Apostle used to Say: 'My eyes sleep while my heart is awake.' Only God knows how revelation came and he saw what he saw. But whether he was asleep or awake, it was all true and actually happened" (*ibid.*, p. 183).

Much earlier in Muhammad's life, as we have seen, when he was 3- or 4-years-old perhaps, Ibn Ishaq places an event that was filled with Prophetic significance.

> While I was with a brother of mine, (Muhammad is reported to have said) behind our tents shepherding the lambs, two men in

white raiment came to me with a gold basin full of snow. Then
the seized me and opened my belly, extracted my heart and split
it; then they extracted a black drop from it and threw it away;
then they washed my heart and my belly with that snow until
they had thoroughly cleaned them . . . (*Ibid.*, p. 72)

This is the celebrated "opening of Muhammad's breast," the
cleansing of his heart of any vestiges of sin and paganism in preparation for his prophetic mission. It finds its chief Scriptural justifi-
cation in Quran 94: 1: "Have We not expanded your breast and
removed from you your burden which weighed down your back
and exalted your fame?" and is typical of prophetic and priestly
initiations in many religious cultures.[20] What is noteworthy here,
however, is its location early in the Prophet's life, a dogmatic dislocation from where it typologically belongs, to wit, as a preface
to his ascension into heaven.[21] This is precisely where it occurs in
the more explicit traditions preserved in Tabari's *Annals*:

> Ibn Humayd . . . from . . . Anas ibn Malik: At the time when
> the Prophet became a Prophet, he used to sleep around the
> Ka'ba, as did the Quraysh. On one occasion two angels, Gabriel
> and Michael, came to him and said: "Which of the Quraysh
> were we ordered to come to?" Then they said, "we were
> ordered to come to their chief," and went away. After this they
> came from the *qibla* [the direction of Jerusalem?] and there
> were three of them. They came upon him as he slept, turned him
> on his back, and opened his breast. Then they brought water
> from Zamzam and washed away the doubt, or polytheism, or
> pre-Islamic beliefs, or error, which was in his breast. Then they
> brought a golden basin full of faith and wisdom, and his breast
> and belly were filled with faith and wisdom. (Tabari, *Annals*,
> vol. 1, p. 1157 = Tabari 1988, p. 78)

Then, without any mention of Jerusalem, Muhammad is
borne directly to heaven:

> Then he was taken up to the earthly heaven. Gabriel asked for
> admittance, and they said, "Who is it?" "Gabriel," he said.
> "Who is with you?" they said. "Muhammad," he answered.
> "Has his mission commenced?" they asked. "Yes," he said.
> "Welcome," they said and called down God's blessings upon
> him. (*Ibid.*, p. 1158 = Tabari 1988, p. 78)

In this first or terrestrial heaven Muhammad is introduced to
Adam, in the second heaven John and Jesus, in the third the Patri-

arch Joseph, in the fourth the Prophet Idris (Quran 19: 56; 21: 85), in the fifth Aaron, in the sixth Moses, and in the seventh Abraham. Finally Muhammad is permitted to enter Paradise itself, whose description is integrated with the elements of the current exegesis of the visionary experiences in Sura 53: 7–15 and the "river of Paradise" in 108: 1. "Then his Lord drew nigh, 'till He was distant two bows' lengths or nearer,'" Tabari quotes from Quran 53: 9. "God made revelation to His servant, caused him to understand and know, and prescribed for him fifty prayers (daily)." On his return descent, Muhammad once again encounters Moses who advises him to ask God to reduce the number of daily prayers. This is repeated five times until it is reduced to what later became the canonical five daily prayers.[22]

THE EARLIEST *SURA?*

This, then, is what was available to the Muslim community regarding Muhammad's call to prophecy: somewhat oblique Quranic references and later traditions that professed to explain them. The Muslim commentators looked at the material and attempted, much as we do, to assemble it into a coherent whole, and with a notable lack of success. The Muslim authorities were as uncertain as we are about which of the revelations recorded in the Quran was the earliest received by the Prophet,[23] and which, if any, of the early *suras* describe the actual experience of revelation. One manner of proceeding was to single out what must have appeared to be—it is clear that no one knew for certain—the earliest *sura* in the Quran and then construct out of the available tradition what was a plausible "occasion" for such a revelation. This, for example, is what Ibn Ishaq assembled on the subject:

> Al-Zuhri related from Urwa ibn Zubayr that Aisha told him that when God desired to honor Muhammad and have mercy on His servants by means of him, the first signs of prophethood vouchsafed to the Apostle was true visions, resembling the brightness of daybreak, which were shown to him in his sleep. And God, she said, made him love solitude so that he liked nothing better than to be alone . . .

The first part of Aisha's report—clear visions, given in sleep—can be inferred from the Quran, but the love or pursuit of solitude cannot and may represent an independent tradition. Ibn Ishaq continues: "Wahb ibn Kaysan, a client of the family of al-Zubayr, told me: I heard Abdullah ibn al-Zubayr say to Ubayd ibn Umayr . . . 'O Ubayd, tell us how began the prophethood which was first bestowed on the Apostle when Gabriel came to him'."

Ubayd's remarks on *tahannuth* during Ramadan, already cited in Chapter 4, are then quoted, after which Ibn Ishaq turns to another authority:

> Wahb ibn Kaysan told me that Ubayd said to him: Every year during that month the Apostle would pray in seclusion and give food to the poor that came to him. And when he completed the month and returned from his seclusion, first of all before entering his house he would go to the Ka'ba and walk around it seven times or as often as it pleased God; then he would go back to his until in the year when God sent him, in the month of Ramadan in which God willed concerning him what He willed of His grace, the Apostle set forth for Hira as was his wont, and his family with him.
>
> When it was the night on which God honored him with his mission and showed mercy on His servants thereby, Gabriel brought him the command of God. "He came to me," said the Apostle of God, "while I was asleep, with a coverlet of brocade on which there was some writing, and said, "Recite!." I said, "What shall I recite?" He pressed me with it so tightly that I thought it was death; then he let me go said "Recite!" I said, "What shall I recite?" He pressed me with it again so that I thought it was death; then he let me go and said, "Recite!" I said, "What shall I recite?" He pressed me with it a third time so that I thought it was death and said "Recite" I said, "What then shall I recite"—and this I said only to deliver myself from him, lest he should do the same again." He said:
>
> Recite in the name of thy Lord who created,
> Who created man of blood coagulated.
> Read! Thy Lord is most beneficent,
> Who taught by the pen,
> Taught that which they knew not to men.
> (Ibn Ishaq 1955, pp. 105–106)

What Muhammad was bidden to recite are, according to this tradition, the opening lines of what was later numbered as the 96th *sura* of the Quran, and here it is being plausibly put forward as the earliest of Muhammad's revelations, as indeed it may have been,[24] though the preceding Gabriel story—Gabriel is not identified as the bringer of revelation until the Medina era (2: 91)—has the appearance of an invention designed to lead into it.[25]

Ibn Ishaq continues with Muhammad's own account, still on the authority of Ubayd ibn Umayr:

> So I read it and he departed from me. And I awoke from my sleep, and it was as though these words were written in my heart. . . . When I was midway on the mountain, I heard a voice saying, "O Muhammad, you are the Apostle of God and I am Gabriel." I raised my head toward heaven to see and lo, there was Gabriel in the form of a man with his feet astride the horizon saying, "O Muhammad, you are the Apostle of God and I am Gabriel." I stood gazing at him, moving neither forward nor backward; then I began to turn my face away from him, but towards whatever region of the sky I looked, I saw him as before. I continued standing there, neither advancing nor turning back, until Khadija sent her messengers in search of me and they gained the high ground above Mecca and returned to her while I was standing in the same place. Then he parted from me and I from him, returning to my family.

This tradition too is exegetical, assuring the Muslim that the unidentified presence in Sura 53: 5–10, which is obviously the inspiration for this story, was not God, as we have reason to suspect, but Gabriel, as Muhammad later asserted and as the entire Muslim tradition after him maintained.

Sura 96 was not the only candidate for the oldest revelation in the Quran. Another equally prevalent tradition preferred 74: 1–7 and told the following story to lead into it. On the authority of Jabir ibn Abdullah Muhammad is reported to have said:

> I sojourned in Hira and when I had finished my sojourn, I descended to the bottom of the wadi. I heard a voice calling me, and I looked all round me and could see no one. Then I looked above my head, and there He was sitting upon the Throne. I was burdened thereby and went to Khadija, saying "cover me with a mantle," which she did. Then there came down to me the words: "O you wrapped in a mantle, arise and deliver your warning. Magnify your Lord; keep your garments free from stain and shun idolatry. And do not expect increase for yourself, but be patient in the Lord's (cause)." (Quran 74: 1–7)

Given the widely differing opinions of his followers, can we retrieve anything reliable about Muhammad's earliest prophetic experience? If we follow the Quran, it began with a vision, or a number of visions, that Muhammad first thought was of God Himself, though he later had occasion to modify that impression. There is also a fairly constant tradition, and one that displays no obvious motivation for invention, that it took place during sleep and while Muhammad was in one of his periods of seclusion. We can connect the two and describe the seclusion as a form of Meccan ritual and therefore the sleep as a type of incubation. The seclusion ritual is described by the Muslim authorities as *tahannuth*, a word they were unsure of and so is likely authentic. We know as little of *tahannuth* as they, but its connection with another form of ascetic retreat has already been noted,[26] and it seems likely that Muhammad was engaged in that or a closely related spiritual exercise. The content of his vision(s) we do not know except that he had an awareness of the presence of God and that he "saw" the prophetic signs of his Lord's choosing. Despite the Muslim tradition, Muhammad does not seem to say that he received the Quran in that fashion. How or when the Quran was sent down is left undescribed, save for the fact that it was obviously intended as some sort of liturgical recitation, probably on a Jewish or Christian scriptural model, and that it was sent down gradually. The latter was obviously an issue with the Meccans, who used the piecemeal nature of the Quran to attack it authenticity:

> Those who disbelieve say: "Why is not the Quran revealed to him all at once?" "It is sent down thus so that We may strengthen your heart, and We have arranged it gradually." (Quran 25: 32)

> It is a Quran and We have divided it (into parts) that you might recite it to the people at intervals; We have sent it down gradually. (*Ibid.* 17: 106)

The commentators were not sure who were the "disbelievers" of Sura 25: 32, the Quraysh or the Jews,[27] but if it was the first, the question was certainly inspired by the (Jewish) conviction that revelation is single act, a conviction that Muhammad himself would eventually come to share.[28]

We return to Ibn Ishaq's account and to the events that followed Muhammad's first experience of revelation.

> And I came to Khadija and sat by her thigh and drew close to her. She said, "O Abu al-Qasim,[29] where you been? By God, I

sent my messengers in search of you and they reached the high ground above Mecca and returned to me." Then I told her what I had seen; and she said, "Rejoice, O son of my uncle, and be of good heart. Verily, by Him in whose hand is Khadija's soul, I have hope that you will be the prophet of this people."

Then she rose and gathered her garments about her and set forth to her cousin Waraqa ibn Nawfal . . . who had become a Christian and read the Scriptures and learned from those that follow the Torah and the Gospel. And when she related to him what the Apostle of God had told her he had seen and heard, Waraqa cried, "Holy! Holy! Holy! Verily by Him in whose hand is Waraqa's soul, if you have spoken to me the truth, Khadija, there has come unto him the greatest *Namus*, who came to Moses aforetime, and lo, he is the prophet of this people. Bid him be of good heart." (Ibn Ishaq 1955, pp. 106–107)

A later generation of Muslims also understood *Namus*, the Greek *nomos* or law, as the Angel Gabriel. It is not clear in this passage whether either Muhammad or Waraqa so understood it; it might well have meant, via a previous (Jewish?) personification of the Law-Torah, something akin to "God's Holy Spirit."[30]

Revelation came fully to the Apostle while he was believing in Him and in the truth of His message. He received it willingly, and took upon himself what it entailed, whether of men's good-will or anger. Prophecy is a troublesome burden—only strong, resolute messengers can bear it by God's help and grace, because of the opposition which they meet from men in conveying God's message. The Apostle carried out God's orders in spite of the opposition and ill-treatment which he met.

Khadija believed in him and accepted as true what he brought from God, and helped him in his work. She was the first to believe in God and His Apostle and in the truth of his message. He never met with contradiction and charges of false-hood, which saddened him, but that God comforted him by her when he went home. She strengthened him, lightened his burden, proclaimed his truth and belittled men's opposition. May God almighty have mercy on her . . .

Then the revelations stopped for a time so that the Apostle was distressed and grieved.[31] Then Gabriel brought him the *Sura* of the Morning (Sura 93), in which his Lord, who had so honored him, swore that He had not forsaken him and did not hate him . . . (Ibn Ishaq 1955, pp. 111–112)

These momentous events were dated by the tradition to the month of Ramadan in the Prophet's fortieth year,[32] thus, in the standard chronology, 610 A.D.

MUHAMMAD'S PUBLIC PREACHING

Muhammad's public preaching may not have begun immediately after he received his revelation; rather, it appears to have been confined to his immediate family circle for three years.[33] So at least the Muslim tradition believed, and the belief is reflected in Ibn Ishaq's *Life*:

> People began to accept Islam, both men and women, in large numbers until the fame of it spread throughout Mecca, and it began to be talked about. Then God commanded His Apostle to declare the truth of what he had received and to make known His commands to men and call them to Him. Three years elapsed from the time that the Apostle concealed his state until God commanded him to publish his religion, according to information which has reached me. Then God said, "Proclaim what you have been ordered and turn away from the polytheists." (Sura 15: 94) . . . (Ibn Ishaq 1955, p. 117)

Ibn Ishaq averts, though not terribly emphatically, to a religious reaction to the new message:

> When the Apostle openly displayed Islam as God ordered, his people did not withdraw or turn against him, so far as I have heard, until he spoke disparagingly of their gods. When he did that, they took great offense and resolved unanimously to treat him as an enemy, except those whom God had protected by Islam from such evil, but they were a despised minority. Abu Talib his uncle treated the Apostle kindly and protected him, the latter continuing to obey God's commands, nothing turning him back. (*Ibid.*, p. 118)

According to Ibn Ishaq, then, there was no general outcry or marked hostility when Muhammad first began to deliver his message, or perhaps, more appropriately, began his "speaking," as he himself calls it in the early Sura 53: 3. What was that first message? In 1956 Harris Birkeland wrote a study of five *suras*—93, 94, 108, 105, and 106—all of which we have already seen in one historical context. They share, Birkeland argued, common characteristics.

They all bear the telltale denominative of *Lord* as the name of God,[34] and more telling, they contain a single moral theme, God's providential guidance and man's grateful response.[35] There is no insistence on monotheism, no ethical prescriptions, no mention of the Judgment, all characteristic teachings of the somewhat later Muhammad the "warner." Finally, one *sura* (108) shows Muhammad still practicing at least some of the rituals of paganism, and two (105, 106) indicate that he was still on friendly terms with his fellow Quraysh.[36] Here, then, if anywhere, is the original form of Islam, the fruit, we may guess, of Muhammad's earliest experiences of God, which He disclosed only later (Sura 53) to silence his critics.

One of those who accepted the "Submission" was Muhammad's cousin Ali, the son of the same Abu Talib who had raised the orphaned Muhammad.

> Ali was the first male to believe in the Apostle of God, to pray with him and to believe his divine message, when he was a boy of 10. God favored him in that he was brought up in the care of Apostle before Islam began. Abdullah ibn Abi Najih told me on the authority of Mujahid ibn Jabr that God showed his favor and goodwill towards him when a grievous famine overtook the Quraysh. Now Abu Talib had a large family, and the Prophet approached his uncle Al-Abbas, who was one of the richest of the Banu Hashim, suggesting that in view of Abu Talib's large family and the famine which affected everyone, they should go together and offer to relieve him of the burden of some of his family. Al-Abbas agreed and so they went to Abu Talib offering to relieve him of the responsibility of two of his boys until conditions should improve. Abu Talib said, "Do as you like so long as you leave me Aqil." So the Apostle took Ali and kept him with him and Al-Abbas took Ja'far. Ali continued to be with the Apostle until God sent him forth as a Prophet. Ali followed him, believed him, and declared his truth, while Ja'far remained with Al-Abbas until he became a Muslim and was independent of him . . . (Ibn Ishaq 1955, p. 114)

Ali's embrace of Islam was followed by other, almost equally consequential conversions, Muhammad's freedman Zayd, and then the redoubtable Abu Bakr:[37]

> Zayd the freedman of the Apostle was the first male to accept Islam after Ali. Then Abu Bakr ibn Abi Quhafa, whose name was Atiq, became a Muslim. . . . When he became a Muslim he

showed his faith openly and called others to God and His Apostle. He was a man whose society was desired, well liked and of
easy manners. He knew more about the genealogy of the Quraysh
than anyone else and of their faults and merits. He was a merchant of high character and kindness. His people used to come to
him to discuss many matter with him because of his wide knowledge, his experience in commerce and his sociable nature. He
began to call to God and to Islam all whom he trusted of those
who came to him and sat with him. (Ibn Ishaq 1955, p. 115)

But there were not many such converts. The Quraysh were
skeptical, and principally, it would appear, of the content of
Muhammad's preaching. The notion of the resurrection of the
dead was a particular target of sarcasm. How could God assemble
the bones of their dead ancestors, they asked (Quran 77: 11–15).
Muhammad countered these charges by simply reiterating that
both the resurrection and the Last Judgment are realities, and well
within the power of an omnipotent God.

THE WARNING

At the end of his historical sketch of Mecca in the era that the
Muslims later came to call *The Ignorance* or *The Barbarism,* Ibn
Ishaq offers his appreciation of how and to what extent God's
new envoy altered the religious life of the city and of the Arabs:

> This state of affairs [that is, the pagan practices of the Arabs of
> Mecca] lasted until God sent Muhammad and revealed to him
> when He gave him the laws of His religion and the customs of
> the pilgrimage: "Then hasten onward from the place whence
> men hasten onwards, and ask pardon of God, for God is forgiv-
> ing, merciful." (Quran 2: 195). The words are addressed to the
> Quraysh and "men" refer to the Arabs. So in the regulation of
> the *Hajj* he hastened them up to Arafat and ordered them to
> halt there and then to hasten thence.
>
> In reference to their prohibition at the shrine of food and
> clothes brought in from outside the sacred territory, God
> revealed to him: "O sons of Adam, wear your clothes in every
> mosque and eat and drink and be not prodigal, for He loves not
> the prodigal. Say: who has forbidden the clothes which God has
> brought forth for His servants and the good things which He
> has provided? Say: they on the day of resurrection will be only
> for those who in this life believed. Thus do we explain the signs

for people who have knowledge." (Quran 7: 29) Thus God set aside the restrictions of the *Hums* and the innovations of the Quraysh against men's interests when He sent His Apostle with Islam. (Ibn Ishaq 1955, p. 88)

By adducing those Quranic verses, Ibn Ishaq seems to suggest that Muhammad's first interest was in changing the *Hajj*. The Quran itself gives an entirely different view, however: what are reckoned the second earliest *suras* reflect not so much ritual concerns as theological and eschatological ones. It is belief the Quran enjoins, belief that God is one—the God Muhammad refers to as his "Lord"—belief in the unlimited power of the One God and now in the fact that that power will be manifested in God's reckoning of humankind on the Last Day. Change your thinking and your life, the Quran warns, because a sure Hell awaits the sinner and a bounteous reward the just.

> You, wrapped in a mantle! Arise and warn! And magnify your Lord! Keep your garments free of stain and shun the abomination of idolatry. Do not expect any increase, but be persevering in your Lord. For when the trumpet is sounded, that will be—that day—a day of distress, far from easy for the unbelievers. Leave to Me the creature I have created isolated and alone, to whom I granted resources in abundance, and sons to be at his side, for whom I made the way smooth and comfortable. Yet he is greedy that I add more . . .
>
> He [that is, the sinner] turned his back and was haughty. Then he said: "This is nothing but ancient magic. This is nothing but the saying of a mortal man!" Soon I will cast him into the Fire, and what will make you understand what the Fire is? It permits none to endure and none does it spare, darkening and changing the color of a man . . .
>
> I swear by the moon, and by the night as it disappears, and by the dawn as it shines forth, this is one of the mighty things, a warning to mortals, to any of you who chooses to press forward or to follow behind, every soul will held as security for its deeds, all save the Companions of the Right Hand; in the Garden they will question each other, and of the sinners: "What led you into the Fire?" And they will say: "We were not among those who made prayer, nor of those who fed the poor, but we talked vanities with the vain, and we denied the Day of Judgment, until there came upon us the Certainty." Then no intercession of intercessors will avail them, So why do they turn away from admonition as if they were frightened asses fleeing from a lion.

No, each one of them wants a scroll (of revelation) spread before him. It will not be so, but they do not fear the Hereafter. No, this is surely a warning, and let who will remember it . . . (Quran 74: 1–15, 23–29, 32–55)[38]

GOD ON HIGH

Whatever might have been his beliefs and practices before his visionary experience, the Muhammad who began publicly to preach the "warning" and the "good news" of Islam in Mecca had a new understanding of God. It unfolds in some of the early *suras* of the Quran.[39] It is not the Allah of the pagan Quraysh, nor yet the Allah of the assertive Prophet of Medina. What is chiefly remarkable, perhaps, is that in the early Meccan *suras* Muhammad almost invariably refers to the deity not as *Allah* but rather, as we have seen, as *Lord* or, because God is often the speaker, *your Lord*.[40] It is patently not the name of some new divinity, some god whose presence at Mecca was previously unknown; rather, it is an appellative, a reference to a familiar.[41] Who is Muhammad's "Lord"? It is not at all clear, not at any rate at this point, though later it is unmistakably the Allah of the Quraysh and, of course, of the Jews and Christians.[42]

Allah, Rahman, and Musaylima

The Muslim savants who studied the Quran admitted no development or evolution in Muhammad's thinking about God: the Quran is all and only revelation, all of it eternally simultaneous to God. But on the more secular premise that the mind of Muhammad as well as the providence of God is being revealed in its pages, a change does seem to occur across the admittedly tentative chronology of the *suras*, or at least a tentative step in an apparently new direction. Sometime after the beginning of his preaching, perhaps after two years,[43] Muhammad begins to use the name *al-Rahman*, "The Merciful One," for his God, and conspicuously, in Suras 56, 68, 78, 89 and 93 Lord and *Rahman* are used side by side, with no mention of Allah. Unlike *Lord*, *Rahman* is a name, always used with the article and quite different from the various other appellatives applied to God in the Quran.[44] And it is a name with a history, a history unconnected with Mecca, where the pre-Islamic cult of "*al-Rahman*" remains unattested. Where *Rahman* was worshipped was in the Yemen[45] and even more interesting, because there is a direct connection with Muhammad, in the area of central Arabia known as al-Yamama.

The name *al-Rahman* appears more than fifty times in the suras of the so-called second Meccan period, and often with explicit reference to the fact that the Meccans found the name strange or the deity somehow unacceptable.

> When the unbelievers see you [Muhammad], they treat you only with ridicule. "It is the one who talks of your gods?" (they say). And they profess unbelief at the mention of *al-Rahman*. (Quran 21: 36)

> When it is said to them, "Prostrate yourselves (in adoration) before *al-Rahman*," they say, "What is *al-Rahman*? Shall we prostrate ourselves before that which you command us?" And it increases their flight. (Quran 25: 60)

> Thus have We sent you among a people before whom a people has passed away, in order that you might communicate to them what We sent down on you by revelation. Yet do they disbelieve in *al-Rahman*. Say, He is my lord and there is no god but He; in him do I trust and to him do I turn. (Quran 13: 30)

Therefore Muhammad's choice of the name *al-Rahman* to designate the "Lord" who was sending him revelations caused confusion and objections among the Quraysh. Some may have thought that Muhammad's *Rahman* and their own *Allah* were two distinct gods, as they might well have been. We can see the beginnings of a reconciliation in Sura 17 or, more accurately, what appears to be a concession on Muhammad's part, in the context of deciding an issue in ritual prayer: "Say: Pray to *Allah* or pray to *al-Rahman*; whichever you call upon, to Him belong the most beautiful names. And do not be loud in your prayer, nor speak it softly [as if in secret], but find a way between" (Quran 17: 110).

After that, there are no more mentions of *al-Rahman*, not, at any rate, as the unique name of God. Thenceforward that name was the familiar *Allah* of Mecca, and *Rahman* is reduced to one of His characterizations, enshrined in the formula that stands at the head of every sura save one of the Quran: "In the name of Allah, the Merciful (*al-Rahman*), the Compassionate (*al-Rahim*)."

The Quran says nothing about the source of Muhammad's interest in *Rahman* or how he came to his devotion to this deity. What is conceded by the Muslim tradition is that, in the distur-

Musaylima

bances across Arabia following the death of Muhammad in 632 A.D., there arose a number of other prophetic claimants and that among them was a certain Musaylima of the Banu Hanifa who rallied his people around him in the name of the deity "al-Rahman." Musaylima claimed that he had received revelations from this god,[46] revelations urging a political program, embodying a severe moral code, and promising eschatological salvation:

> "To us (Musaylima said) belong the prayers of a pious community who are neither damned nor morally insolent, who pray by night and fast by day for the very great god, the god of clouds and rain. . . . " He also said: "When I saw their faces were beautiful and their complexions pure and their hands tender, I told them: You do not approach women nor do you drink wine, but you are pious community that fasts one day and imposes duties (upon yourself) another. Praise be to God for the life you will live when you live again (in the resurrection) and how you will ascend to the king of heaven. In truth, be it only the weight of a grain of mustard seed, there will nonetheless be a witness who knows what is in the hearts of men; and most men are destined for destruction."
>
> Among the other things that Musaylima prescribed for them was that whoever has a male offspring cannot have sex with a woman unless that son should die. Then he may attempt to have (another) son but he has to desist (from sexual activity) once he has one. Thus he forbade women to those who (already) had male children. (Tabari, *Annals*, vol. 1, pp. 1916–1917)

Musaylima is touched upon twice in the *Life* by Ibn Ishaq, on both occasions lightly, but in both instances with a full recognition that there had been such a man and that he was a prophetic rival of Muhammad in al-Yamama in central Arabia. The first reference occurs in an account of the various tribal delegations that came to the Prophet in the wake of his successes at Mecca and Ta'if. One of them was from the Banu Hanifa, the paramount tribe of the Yamama and the people of Musaylima. It was thought fitting by the later Muslim chroniclers not only that Musaylima should be among that delegation but that he should have come in contact, however slight, with the Prophet of Islam. Ibn Ishaq gives, without any great conviction, two accounts of the meetings—neither one quite face to face—and of Musaylima's conversion along with the rest of the delegation. In the second Muhammad is alleged to have said of him, "His position is no worse than yours," an odd remark that Musaylima was thought to have turned to his own advantage:

> When they [that is, the Banu Hanifa] reached al-Yamama the enemy of God (Musaylima) apostatized, gave himself out as a prophet and played the liar. He said, "I am a partner with him [that is, Muhammad] in the affair," and then he said to the delegation who had been with him, "Did he not say to you when you mentioned me to him, 'His position is no worse than yours.' What can that mean except that I am a partner with him in the affair?" Then he began to utter rhymes in *saj'* [that is, the rhymed prose characteristic of both pre-Islamic seers and the early parts of the Quran] and speak in imitation of the style of the Quran. "God has been gracious to the pregnant woman; He has brought forth from her a living being that can move; from her very midst." He permitted them to drink wine and to fornicate, and let them dispense with prayer, yet he was acknowledging the apostle as a prophet, and the Hanifa agreed with him on that. But God knows what the truth is. (Ibn Ishaq 1955, pp. 636–637)

The reports on Musaylima's ethical teaching in this account are clearly tendentious; elsewhere, as we have seen, he is said to have required fasting every other day, abstention from wine, and continence within marriage after the birth of a son. This strict moral teaching was complemented by a belief in individual resurrection and a Final Judgment. Finally, we know that he prescribed formal prayers three times daily and urged recognition of a *haram* at Hajr in al-Yamama.[47] There are obvious similarities with Muhammad's teachings, but what is less obvious is the connection between the two men and the direction in which the influences, if any, flowed. The Muslim sources insist that Musaylima "borrowed" or "stole" from Muhammad, particularly in matters of style,[48] and if this seems likely enough, it is difficult to imagine that Musaylima "borrowed" *al-Rahman* from the earlier and not notably successful Muhammad of Mecca and then succeeded in rallying the Banu Hanifa around the supposititious deity. It is easier to assume that *al-Rahman* had a genuine and long-standing cult in al-Yamama, in the vicinity of modern Riyadh, a cult to which Muhammad too may have been drawn.

"They Are Only Names"

Muhammad had had an experience of God, and his passage from identifying the source of that experience first with his "Lord," then with *al-Rahman*, and finally with Allah is only one example, and not the most striking, of the modification of his beliefs over a period of time. We have already noted the presence of the goddesses al-Lat, al-Uzza, and Manat at Mecca. The same three goddesses appear—and then disappear—in an extremely curious and much-discussed passage in Sura 53 of the Quran. The exact context of the *sura* is unknown, but Muhammad was still at Mecca and was apparently feeling the pressures of the Quraysh resistance to his message:

> When the Messenger of God saw how his tribe turned their backs on him and was grieved to see them shunning the message he had brought to them from God, he longed in his soul that something would come to him from God that would reconcile him with his tribe. With his love for his tribe and his eagerness for their welfare, it would have delighted him if some of the difficulties which they made for him could have been smoothed, and he debated with himself and fervently desired such an outcome. Then God revealed (Sura 53) . . . and when he came to the words "Have you thought al-Lat and al-Uzza and Manat, the third, the other?" (vv. 19–20), Satan cast on his tongue, because of his inner debates and what he desired to bring to his people, the words: "These are the high-flying cranes; verily their intercession is to be hoped for."
>
> When the Quraysh heard this, they rejoiced and were happy and delighted at the way in which he had spoken of their gods, and they listened to him, while the Muslims, having complete trust in their Prophet with respect of the message which he brought from God, did not suspect him of error, illusion or mistake. When he came to the prostration, having completed the *sura*, he prostrated himself and the Muslims did likewise. . . . The polytheists of the Quraysh and others who were in the mosque [that is, the Meccan *haram*] likewise prostrated themselves because of the reference to their gods which they heard, so that there was no one in the mosque, believer or unbeliever, who did not prostrate himself. . . . Then they all dispersed from the mosque. The Quraysh left delighted at the mention of their gods . . . (Tabari, *Annals*, vol. 1, pp. 1192–1193 = Tabari 1988, pp. 108–109)

There then followed the "sending down" of a new "corrected" verse, the one actually in our Quran: "These are only names which you and your fathers have invented. No authority was sent down by God for them. They only follow conjecture and wish-fulfillment, even though guidance had come to them already from the Lord" (Quran 53: 23).

This is the indubitably authentic story—it is impossible to imagine a Muslim inventing such an inauspicious tale—of the notorious "Satanic verses." The implications of a Quranic verse being uttered and then withdrawn are profound for Islamic scriptural theology and jurisprudence, but what is important here is what they reveal of the contemporary regard for the three goddesses. What was first granted and then rescinded was permission to use the three goddesses as intercessors with Allah. It was, as has been suggested, a critical moment in Muhammad's understanding of the distinction between Allah as simply a "high god," the head of the Meccan or Arabian pantheon where the lesser gods and goddesses might be invoked as go-betweens,[49] and the notion that eventually prevailed: Allah is uniquely God, without associates, companions, or "daughters." The goddesses were, as the revision put it, "nothing but names," invented by the Quraysh and their ancestors.[50]

The Daughters of Allah

The Quran takes up the theme of the "daughters of Allah" on a number of different occasions, including the very lines into which the "satanic verses" were inserted and then removed: "Have you considered al-Lat and al-Uzza, and another, Manat, the third? What, males for you and females for Him [Allah]? That would surely be an unjust division!" (Quran 53: 19–22).

What precisely is meant by an *unjust division* is spelled out elsewhere:

> Is it that He chooses daughters (for Himself) from all He has created while He honors you with sons? Whenever one of them [that is, a mortal man] receives news of what he ascribes to al-Rahman [i.e., that a daughter has been born to him], his countenance becomes dark and he is filled with inward grief. (Quran 43: 16–17)

> Then ask for their opinion: Does your Lord have daughters and they sons? . . . Is it not their own invention when they say:

> "Allah has begotten"? But they are surely liars! Would He
> choose daughters rather than sons? . . . (Quran 37: 149–153)

It is in this way that the Quran establishes that the three goddesses were not the "daughters of Allah"—if God had offspring
they would surely be sons—and it raises, but does not here
directly address, the more basic question: if they are not His offspring, what is the relationship of the various gods and goddesses
in the Meccan pantheon to the High God Allah? Are they, and
may they be called upon, as intercessors of some sort? One answer
is given a few lines later in the same *sura*: "How many angels there
may be in the heavens, their intercession avails nothing except as
Allah gives permission to whomever He pleases—to those who are
acceptable to Him. Those who do not believe in the hereafter
name the angels with female names" (Quran 53: 26–27).

The last verse shows the direction in which Muhammad's
thinking was going: the three goddesses, and perhaps others as
well, are actually angels, the Quran argues, whose intercession *is*
permitted by God, and to whom the unbelievers have unknowingly given female names.[51] The point is made explicitly in
another early *Rahman* text:

> And they have made into females the angels, who are them-
> selves servants of al-Rahman. What, did they [that is, the poly-
> theists] witness their creation? Their testimony will be written
> down and they will be questioned. And they say: "If al-Rahman
> had willed, we would not have worshiped them." But they have
> no knowledge about that; they are only guessing. (Quran 43:
> 19–20)

The Lesser Demons

If the first disparagement of the goddesses in the Meccan pantheon served to reduce them from the status of progeny of Allah to
the rank of angels, a further downgrading is evident elsewhere in
the Quran. The scene in Sura 34 depicts God interrogating the
angels at the Judgment. "He will say to the angels: 'Was it you
these (polytheists) were worshiping?' And they will answer:
'Glory be to You! You are our protector apart from them.' No,
rather they worshiped the *jinn*, in whom most of them believed"
(Quran 34: 40–42).

And again, "They have ascribed a kinship between Him and
the *jinn*. But the *jinn* know they will be arranged, glory be to God,

high above those they ascribe (to Him as fellow-gods)!" (Quran 37: 158–159).

And finally, and most explicitly: "Yet they [that is, the poly-theists] ascribe to Allah as associates the *jinn*, even though He cre-ated them, and they impute to him sons and daughters without having any knowledge. Glory be to Him. May He be exalted high above all they associate (with Him)" (Quran 6: 100).

The gods of Mecca were, then, even lower than the angels; they were the demonic *jinn*, mistakenly, and perhaps even unknowingly, worshiped by the Quraysh and others as authentic gods.[52] They are servants, like men, and worse, they are impotent:

> Do they ascribe to Him as partners things that can create noth-ing but are themselves created? They cannot aid them and they cannot aid themselves. If you call to them for the Guidance, they will not obey: it is all the same for you whether you pray to them or are silent. In truth, those you pray to apart from God are servants like yourselves. Pray to them and see if they pay heed if you are truthful. Do they have feet to walk with or hands to grasp with? Or eyes to see with? Or ears to hear with? . . . (Quran 7: 191–195)

All of these positions eventually yielded, late in Muhammad's Meccan period,[53] to a more distinct monotheism in which the very existence of other or lesser gods is denied. The denizens of the Meccan pantheon were, as Quran 53: 26 amended, "nothing but names," and the Medinese *suras* are filled with statements about the unqualified uniqueness of God.[54]

Along with this more severe and profound understanding of monotheism toward the end of his stay at Mecca went an appar-ent change in Muhammad's understanding of all the familiar demonic staples of pre-Islamic Mecca, the *jinn*, satans, and assorted angels that are granted some status and credibility in the earliest *suras* of the Quran. In the Meccan *suras* it is taken for granted not only that the *jinn* exist but that they are linked in some way to human destiny: of the forty-eight mentions of *jinn*, twenty occur in the phrase "*jinn* and mankind" and sixteen describe someone, including Muhammad himself, as "*jinn* pos-sessed."[55] But shortly after the Hijra, the term disappears: the *jinn* had ceased to exist for the Prophet of Islam. The same is true for a related but slightly different notion, the *shaytans* or satans.[56] Though Muhammad had found the term useful to characterize his opponents, that notion too disappeared from his religious glossary a couple of years after arriving in Medina.

THE CALL TO PRAYER

The Arabs prayed before Islam, as we have seen, and if their "calling upon the god" was sometimes impromptu and sometimes at fixed moments like dawn and sunset, they generally took place in the vicinity of the deity, in the shrines (*masjid/masajid*) whose very name, a "place of prostration," indicates that the supplication was accompanied by appropriate postures. Of liturgies we have seen two, the processional verses addressed to the "daughters of Allah," probably as part of a circumambulation ritual, and the doxology (*talbiyya*) directed toward Allah and the associated gods. We do not always know the contexts in which the Quraysh venerated their gods in this fashion, which prayers went with which sacrifices or how the "retreat" with its prayer and fasting was combined with the pilgrimage ritual. But pray and worship they certainly did, and so when the Quran derisively dismisses it as "nothing but whistling and hand-clapping" at the Holy House (8: 35), or has the Quraysh describe themselves in the Quran as those who "were not among those who made prayer," (74: 43) and so were cast into Hell, the judgments are being made from a particularly Islamic perspective.

Prayer, a certain kind of prayer, is, in fact, one of the earliest and most persistently urged elements of Muhammad's message, and prayer precisely as understood by the contemporary Jews and Christians. The word that is used is *salat*, a word taken over into Arabic from the Aramaic lingua franca of those other two communities,[57] where it refers precisely to *liturgical* prayer, a public worship of God in the form of audibly uttered words—"Do not be loud in your prayer," Muhammad advises the Muslims, "nor speak it softly (as if in secret), but find a way between" (Quran 17: 110)—accompanied by the traditional gestures or postures and, eventually, at certain fixed times.

What Muhammad did himself and what he required of others at Mecca is open to doubt.[58] The few Muslims lived alone and isolated in a hostile pagan milieu, and it would have been difficult to practice any type of public prayer that would have set them off from their relatives, friends and neighbors, and it may well have been that their prayers were identical in form and setting with the Quraysh's own or else were done privately and spontaneously.[59] A number of prayer injunctions are in the Meccan *suras*, but they may as likely be addressed by God to Muhammad himself as prescriptions for general practice. There is an early reference, for example, to one of the pagans there attempting to prevent "the servant" from praying (96: 9–10), a term often used in the singular of Muhammad.

The early traditionist Waqidi is somewhat more explicit about the Quraysh reaction to Muhammad's prayer in Mecca:

> The Prophet used to go out to the Ka'ba at the beginning of the day and perform the *duha* prayer. It was a prayer with which the Quraysh did not find any fault. When he afterwards prayed during the rest of the day, Ali and Zayd used to sit and keep guard on him. When it was the time of the *'asr* the Prophet and his companions used to scatter in the ravines, one by one and in pairs; they used to pray (the prayers of) the *duha* and the *'asr*. (Maqrizi, *Imta'*, vol. 1, pp. 16–17)[60]

The *duha* was a prayer performed shortly after sunrise,[61] and the *'asr* was a prayer before sunset, and why the Quraysh objected to one and not the other is not entirely clear.[62] But we are shown Muhammad praying at the Ka'ba in the manner and time of the Quraysh. And the Prophet had received at Mecca some rather distinct instructions of when this was to be done: "Stand at (or establish) the prayer *(salat)* from the sinking of the sun until the darkness of the night and the morning recitation *(quran)*, for the morning recitation is witnessed to" (17: 80). *Standing* or *taking up one's place* at prayer is a commonplace expression in the Quran, as it is in the Bible, and one is reminded of the fact that the "standing-place of Abraham" *(maqam Ibrahim)* was a notable and pre-Islamic feature of the Meccan Haram.[63]

The times seem clear in this passage, a morning and an evening prayer is to be made, though other Meccan verses like 11: 116 ("Stand at prayer at the two ends of the day and at the approaches of the night") indicate that Muhammad may have prayed three times daily, and if that suggests Jewish practice, the fact that it included night prayer speaks more strongly to Christian custom, particularly in the light of the Quran's remark in 73: 20: "In truth your Lord knows that you stand (at prayer) nearly two-thirds of the night, or a half, or a third, as does a party of those who are with you." Though this last may owe something to the ill-understood pre-Islamic "retreat," it seems to be no ordinary liturgical practice, and certainly not on a Jewish model, though it does accord with the customs of Christian monks, with whose lives Muhammad was well acquainted.[64] It was not, in any event, obligatory because the verse makes clear that not all Muslims were practicing it.

At Medina the Muslims' prayer custom seems to have grown closer to that of the Jews' practice of morning, midday, and evening prayers.[65] The voluntary night vigils were abrogated in a revelation that was included in the same verse 20 of Sura 73, and a noonday prayer adopted, an addition reflected in the late Sura 2: 239: "Keep to your practice of the *salats* and also the middle *salat*."[66] By the Medina period formal bowing (*rukku'*) was certainly part of the prayer ritual (48: 29, 22: 76 etc.), and Quran 77: 48, "And when it said to them, 'bow down' they do not bow down," addressed to the pagan Quraysh strongly suggests that it was so from the beginning.

In the Quranic verse 17: 80 already cited, *salat* seems to be identified as "recitation," apparently of God's own words as indited in "The Recitation" par excellence, *al-Quran*. Here too we are in the presence of a Syriac loan-word (*qeryana*),[67] and if the frequent reference to the Quran as "The Book" speaks to the Jewish and Christian tradition of revelation as formal written Scripture (*biblion, graphe*), *qeryana*, the Syriac prototype of the word Quran itself, speaks to the oral recitation (*lectio, miqra*) of God's same words in a liturgical context.[68] Contemporary Jewish and Christian liturgical traditions both enshrined the Book—the presence of the synagogue Torah niche and processional entry of the Gospels into the church sanctuary would be apparent to the most casual of observers—and used its recitation as a form of prayer to God. But even without this powerful lexicographical evidence, the same conclusion would impose itself from the style and substance of the Quran. The early Meccan *suras* bear all the stylistic and rhetorical earmarks of what was intended to serve, from the beginning, as prayers.[69]

CHAPTER 7

The Migration to Medina

THE OPPOSITION OF THE QURAYSH

Following the traditional account in Ibn Ishaq's *Life*, Muham-mad's preaching soon roused the spiteful wrath of his Quraysh kinsmen. The Quran provides at least a hint, though typically an extremely allusive one, as to their point of view:

> Have We given them a previous Book to which they are adher-ing? Not at all! They say: "We found our fathers following a certain religion (*ala ummatin*), and we are guiding ourselves by their footsteps." Just in the same way, whenever we have previ-ously sent a Warner to any people, the wealthy ones among them said: "We found our fathers following a certain religion (*ala ummatin*), and we are certainly following in their foot-steps." (Quran 43: 22–23)

The Quran thus characterizes the Quraysh as stubborn reac-tionaries, but it seems to be more than just blind traditionalism that roused his fellow Meccans against the new preacher who had arisen in their midst. The verse just cited categorizes the oppo-nents of the Warning as "the rich among them," or "the well-off," which has suggested to some that there was a strain of social and economic tension in the Quraysh resistance. The "rich among them" might indeed resist the oft-repeated warning that each man was but a custodian of his wealth and would be called upon to give an account of his stewardship on the Day of Judgment.[1]

> For him who gives in charity and guards against evil and believes in goodness, We shall smooth the path of salvation; but for him who neither gives nor takes and disbelieves in goodness, We shall smooth the path of affliction. When he breathes his last, his riches will not avail him. The Guidance is Ours; Ours is the Next World, Ours the present. I warn you, then, of the blazing fire, in which none shall burn save the hardened sinner, who denies the

Truth and pays no heed. But the good man who purifies himself through almsgiving shall avoid it; and so shall he who does good works for the sake only of the Most High, seeking no recompense. Such men shall be content. (Quran 92: 4–21)

These are delicate implications: there is no naming of names in the Quran, no direct criticism, and Muhammad certainly gives no impression that he was zealous to turn the money-changers out of the Temple or that he was essaying the role of a Meccan Savonarola. We obviously do not have the whole story, but on purely "spiritual" grounds, the eventually violent Meccan rejection of Muhammad remains as mysterious as the kind of opposition that led to the execution of Jesus.

Other less spiritual motives have been advanced, however, why the Quraysh might have objected so strenuously to the message of the fellow Meccan. Some have argued that it was the fear that Muhammad would overturn the prevailing combination of piety and commerce that constituted the *Hajj*, whereas others have insisted that there is no evidence that Muhammad had any intention of such, nor that the Quraysh anticipated the dismantling of the religious and commercial arrangement bringing them whatever degree of prosperity they enjoyed.[2] It is indeed true that Muhammad showed no sign of ever intending entirely to abolish the *Hajj* as such, but there are at least suggestions that he may have had problems with some of the Meccan ritual proper, as when he somewhat grudgingly allows—"it is no sin"—the circumambulation of Marwa and Safa in 2: 158, and we are certain that he originally banned the cult of the three goddesses, all of whom had been gathered into the Meccan Haram, and then, to appease the anxieties of the Quraysh, permitted it for a time—hence the "Satanic verses." We cannot tell if those anxieties were religious or commercial, but Meccan polytheism and its cultus seem to have been at issue in Muhammad's preaching and the Quraysh's reception of it. These two early reports seems to confirm it:

The Messenger of God—God bless him and preserve him— summoned to Islam secretly and openly, and there responded to God whom He would of the young men and weak people, so that those who believed in Him [or "him"] were numerous and the unbelieving Quraysh did not criticize what he said. When he passed by them as they sat in groups, they would point to him and say "There is the youth of the clan of Abd al-Muttalib who speaks (things) from heaven."[3] This lasted until God (in the Quran) spoke shamefully of the idols they worshiped other than Himself and mentioned the perdition of their fathers who died in disbelief. At that they came to hate the Messenger of God— God bless him and preserve him—and to be hostile to him. (Ibn Sa'd I/1, p. 133)[4]

There is another account of this critical juncture in Muhammad's career. It is preserved by the tenth century historian Tabari, who is quoting from a document of the late seventh century, seventy-odd years after the events it purports to describe:[5]

Hisham ibn Urwa related to us on the authority of Urwa that he wrote to Abd al-Malik ibn Marwan [Caliph 685-705 A.D.]): " . . . Now as for him, that is, the Messenger of God—God bless him and preserve him—when he called upon his tribe to accept the Guidance and the light revealed to him, which were God's purpose in sending him, they did not hold back from him when first he summoned them, but were almost won over until he mentioned their idols. Then there came from Ta'if certain of the Quraysh who owned property there, and hotly argued with him in their disapproval of his message and they stirred up against him those who had followed him. Thus most of the people turned back away from him and deserted him, except those of them whom God kept safe, who were few in number. Things remained like that for such time as God determined they should so remain. Then their leaders took counsel how they might seduce from the religion of God those of their sons and brothers and fellow-clansmen who had followed him [that is, Muhammad]. This was a time of extreme trial and upheaval for the people of Islam who followed the Messenger of God—God bless him and preserve him. Some were seduced but God kept safe whom He would . . . (Tabari, *Annals*, vol. 1, pp. 1180–1181)

What Manner of Man Is This?

We have no reason to think that Muhammad did not participate in the annual trading fairs—he was, after all, a trader—even after the Quran began to be sent down. We cannot say if the following incident, alleged to have occurred on the eve of one such fair, is authentic. It may have been imaginatively reconstructed for apologetic purposes, but it does have the value of presenting a menu of contexts in which the Quraysh might have located Muhammad:

When the fair was due, a number of the Quraysh came to al-Walid ibn al-Mughira, who was a man of some standing, and he addressed them in these words:

"The time of the fair has come round again and representatives of the Arabs will come to you and they will have heard about this fellow of yours, so agree upon one opinion without dispute so that none will give lie to the other."

They replied: "You give us your opinion of him."

He said: "No, you speak and I will listen."

They said: "He is a seer *(kahin)*."

He said: "By God, he is not that, for he has not the unintelligent murmuring and rhymed speech of the *kahin*."

"Then he is *jinn*-possessed," they said.

"No, he is not that," he said. "We have seen the *jinn*-possessed and here is no choking, spasmodic movements and whispering."

"Then he is a poet," they said.

"No, he is no poet, for we know poetry in all its forms and meters."

"Then he is a sorcerer."

"No, we have seen sorcerers and their sorcery, and here is no spitting and no knots."

"Then what are we to say, O Abu Abd Shams?" they asked.

He replied: "By God, his speech is sweet, his root is a palm tree whose branches are fruitful, and everything you have said would be known to be false. The nearest thing to the truth is your saying that he is a sorcerer, who has brought a message that separates a man from his father, or from his brother, or from his wife, or from his family."

At this point they left him, and began to sit on the paths which men take when they come to the fair. They warned everyone who passed them about Muhammad's doings. . . . So these men began to spread this report about the Apostle with everyone they met so that the Arabs went from that fair knowing about the Apostle, and he was talked about in the whole of Arabia. (Ibn Ishaq 1955, pp. 121–122)

The entire passage from Ibn Ishaq is a good example of the later Muslim biographer at work. What he or his original source had before him is likely no more than the Quran, from whose own pages emerge the very charges to which the *Life* then supplies little more than an expanded exegesis. The accusations are found in two early revelations:

Therefore remind! By the Lord's bounty you [that is, Muhammad] are not a soothsayer (*kahin*) nor are you jinn-possessed (*majnun*). Or do they say, "He is a poet for whom we expect the accidents of the fates." Say: "Expect! I shall be with you among the expectant." (Quran 52: 29–31)

And again, at about the same time:

No! I swear by what you see and by what you do not see: It is indeed the discourse of a noble Messenger—It is not a poet's discourse (little do you believe!) nor a seer's (*kahin*) discourse (little do you recall!)—a sending down from the Lord of the Worlds. (Quran 69: 38–43)

Why did his contemporaries think they were in the presence of a seer or poet? As Ibn Ishaq concedes, both types of charismatics were familiar in early seventh century Arabia,[6] and on the basis of the available evidence, Muhammad's earliest utterances at Mecca did in fact sound like the rhyming speech of the poets, similar enough, at any rate, to suggest to his listeners that he was one of that company.[7] Though Ibn Ishaq is far more defensive, the Quran does not deny the formal or stylistic resemblance; it attacks rather the underlying supposition: the Prophet's inspiration is from God by way of God's "trusted spirit" (Quran 26: 192–193)—somewhat later identified with Gabriel—and not, as in the cases of those pagan *vates*, from the *jinn* or even a demon.

It is indeed the discourse of a noble Messenger, one having power and with the Lord of the Throne firmly placed, one to be obeyed there and trustworthy. Your comrade [that is, Muhammad] is not *jinn*-possessed (*majnûn*): He did see him on the clear horizon. Nor with the Mystery (*al-ghayb*) is he stingy. It is not the discourse of an accursed demon (*shaytan*). (Quran 81: 19–25)

The Open Persecution of the Muslims

Ibn Ishaq traces the deteriorating state of affairs between Muhammad and the notables among the Quraysh:

When the Quraysh saw that he [that is, Muhammad] would not yield to them and withdrew from them and insulted their gods and that his uncle treated him kindly and stood up in his defense and would not give him up to them, some of their leading men went to (Muhammad's uncle and patron) Abu Talib. . . . They said, "O Abu Talib, your nephew has cursed our gods, insulted our religion, mocked our way of life and accused our forefathers of error; either you must stop him or you must let us get at him, for you yourself are in the same position as we in opposition to him and we will rid you of him." He gave them a conciliatory reply and a soft answer and they went away.

The Apostle continued on his way, publishing God's religion and calling men thereto. In consequence his relations with the Quraysh deteriorated and men withdrew from him in enmity. They were always talking about him and inciting one another against him. Then they went to Abu Talib a second time and said, "You have a high and lofty position among us, and we have asked you to put a stop to your nephew's activities but you have not done do. By God, we cannot endure that our fathers should be reviled, our customs mocked and our gods insulted. Until you rid us of him we will fight the pair of you until one side perishes," or words to that effect. Thus saying they went off. Abu Talib was deeply distressed at the breach with his people and their enmity, but he could not desert the Apostle and give him up to them . . .

A simple turning away no longer satisfied the frayed sensibilities of the Quraysh. If they could not get at Muhammad, who stood under family protection, they found more accessible targets among his less fortunate followers.

The Quraysh incited people against the companions of the Apostle who had become Muslims. Every tribe fell upon the Muslims among them, beating them and seducing them from their religion. God protected His Apostle from them through his uncle, who, when he saw what the Quraysh were doing, called upon the Banu Hashim and the Banu Abd al-Muttalib to stand with him in protecting the Prophet. This they agreed to do so, with the exception of Abu Lahab, the accursed enemy of God. (Ibn Ishaq 1955, pp. 118–120)

At this point the persecution became not only overt but violent:

Then the Quraysh showed their enmity to all who followed the Apostle; every clan which contained Muslims attacked them, imprisoning them, beating them, allowing them no food or drink, and exposing them to the burning heat of Mecca, so as to seduce them from their religion. Some gave way under pressure of persecution, and others resisted them, being protected by God . . .

Social pressure, economic boycott, and physical force were all invoked against the new believers:

> It was that evil man Abu Jahl who stirred up the Meccans against them. When he heard that a man had become a Muslim, if he was a man of social importance and had relations to protect him, he reprimanded him and poured scorn on him, saying, "You have forsaken the religion of your father who was better than you. We will declare you a blockhead and brand you a fool and destroy your reputation." If he was a merchant, he said "We will boycott your goods and reduce you to beggary." If he was a person of no social importance, he beat him and incited the people against him." (Ibn Ishaq 1955, p. 143)

Migration to Abyssinia

There then occurred what is to us a quite unexpected event, but one that makes sense: a number of the believers—eighty-two or -three men according to one account, eleven men and four women according to another—were sent across the Red Sea to the Christian kingdom of Abyssinia. The best account is that provided by Tabari on the authority of al-Zuhri:

> When the Muslims were treated in this way (by the Quraysh), the Messenger of God commanded them to emigrate to Abyssinia. In Abyssinia there was a righteous king called the Negus in whose land no one was oppressed and who was praised for his righteousness. Abyssinia was a land with which the Quraysh traded and in which found an ample living, security and a good market. When the Messenger of God commanded them to do this, the main body of them went to Abyssinia because of the coercion they were being subjected to in Mecca. *His fear is that they would be seduced from their religion.* He himself remained and did not leave Mecca. Several years passed in this way, during which the Quraysh pressed hard upon those of them who had become Muslims. (Tabari, *Annals*, vol. 1, pp. 1180–1181 = Tabari 1988, pp. 98–99)

The Quraysh decided to pursue, an act that would make little sense unless the presence of even a relatively small number of Muslims in Abyssinia might threaten an important connection, almost certainly a commercial connection, that the Meccans enjoyed with Abyssinia.

> When the Quraysh saw that the Prophet's companions were safely ensconced in Abyssinia and had found security there, they

decided among themselves to send two determined men of their number to the Negus to get them sent back so that they could seduce them from their religion and get them out of the home in which they were living in peace. . . . Leatherwork was especially prized there, so they collected a great many skins so they were able to give some to every one of his generals. (Ibn Ishaq 1955, pp. 150–151)

The Quraysh's instructions to the two envoys were that they were to distribute their presents of leather goods, likely the only thing of value the Meccans had to offer, and attempt to prevail upon the Negus to extradite the Muslims before he had an opportunity to speak to them in person. The design did not sit well with the sovereign.

The Negus was enraged and said, "No by God, I will not surrender them. No people who have sought my protection, settled in my country, and chosen me rather than others shall be betrayed, until I summon and ask them about what these two men allege. . . . " Then he summoned the Apostle's companions. . . . When they came into the royal presence, they found that the king had summoned his bishops with their sacred books exposed around him. He asked them what was the religion for which they had forsaken their people without entering his religion or any other. Ja'far ibn Abi Talib answered: "O king, we were an uncivilized people, worshiping idols, eating corpses, committing abominations, breaking natural ties, treating guests badly, and our strong devoured our weak. Thus we were until God sent us an Apostle whose lineage, truth, trustworthiness and clemency we know. He summoned us to acknowledge God's unity and to worship Him and to renounce the stones and images which we and our fathers formally worshiped. He commanded us to speak the truth, be faithful to our engagements, mindful of the ties of kinship and friendly hospitality, and to refrain from crimes and bloodshed. He forbade us to commit abominations and to speak lies, and to devour the property of orphans, to vilify chaste women. He commanded us to worship God alone and not to associate anything with Him, and he gave us orders about prayer, almsgiving and fasting. . . . Our people attacked us, treated us harshly and seduced us from our faith to try to make us go back to the worship of idols instead of the worship of God. . . . We came to your country, having chosen you above all others. Here we have been happy in your protection, and we hope that we shall not be treated unjustly while we are with you, O king."

The Negus asked them if they had with them anything that had come from God. When Ja'far said that he had, the Negus commanded him to read it to him, so he read him a passage from KHY'S [that is, Sura 19]. The Negus wept till his beard was wet and his bishops wept until their scrolls were wet, when they heard what he read to them. Then the Negus said, "Of a truth, this and what Jesus [var. Moses] brought have come from the same niche. You two may go, for by God I will never give them up to them and they shall not be betrayed." (*Ibid.*, pp. 151–152)

This was in fact a small triumph, and the motive that prompted it, despite the Negus's weeping at the recitation of the Arabic Quran, is not entirely clear.[8] The sources say that Muhammad feared for the faith of those who were sent, that they were, in other words, the weakest or the least likely to be able to stand up to Quraysh intimidation. There is some truth to the allegation because there is reason to believe that, when some of the emigrants finally did return after Muhammad was safely established in Medina, they had to argue the case that they were not apostates, and those who never did return were certainly regarded such.[9] Western scholars have proposed other reasons for the emigration, trade, for example, or an attempt to draw the Abyssinians into an alliance, or perhaps even the beginning of schismatic differences within the tiny new Muslim community in Mecca.[10]

Abyssinia may in fact have been the only port of call still open to the Meccans. In 614, four years after Muhammad's first revelation, disaster struck both the Great Powers of the Fertile Crescent in turn. First the Persians burst through the ill-guarded frontier and occupied all the eastern Roman provinces, including Syria, Palestine and Egypt; the international consumer market had collapsed. The occupation did not last very long. While Muhammad was suffering a boycott at Mecca, the emperor Heraclius was collecting a new army in Armenia, the instrument with which he soon broke the Persians in return and overran their empire. By 632, the year of Muhammad's death in Medina, the two powers lay exhausted in political, social, and economic disarray.

We have a few literary accounts of these events, principally of the fall of Jerusalem in 614 and the massacres there, but the more graphic testimony is what happened to the fragile border areas, where bedouin and settler came in contact. The Negev of southern Palestine, which up to that time had somehow managed to survive growing imperial neglect, tumbled rapidly into ruin.[11] The Arab tradition, which appears isolated and had few precise memories of these momentous events, did remember that the arable land of southern Syria was a landscape of ruined cities and deserted olive groves, "a pastureland for camel herders."[12]

Thus whatever commercial hopes the Meccans harbored may have lain in Abyssinia and the western coast of the Red Sea, which were not in any event very distant from the Hijaz in military and economic terms, as the previous and subsequent history of the two places bears abundant witness. Nor did a wide religious gulf separate Muhammad's biblical monotheism—or what might be even be called his brand of *Judeo-Christianity*—from current practices in the kingdom of the Negus.[13] Muhammad may have been too ambitious a Hijazi politician to entertain thoughts of a permanent home for himself and his followers in Abyssinia, but he was also quite enough of a universal prophet to think that the Christian Abyssinians might offer not so much a refuge as highly promising missionary ground for the spread of Islam, the same perhaps as he later expected to find among the Jews of Medina.

Whatever the reason for their departure, most of those Muslims who went out eventually returned, the first batch because of a rumor:

> The Apostle's companions who had gone to Abyssinia heard that the Meccans had accepted Islam and they set out for their homeland. But when they got near Mecca they learned the report was false, so that they entered the town under the protection of a citizen or by stealth. Some of those who returned to him (on this occasion) stayed at Mecca until they migrated to Medina and were present at (the battles of) Badr and Uhud with the Apostle; others were shut away from the Prophet until Badr and other events had passed; and others died in Mecca. . . . The total number of his companions who came to Mecca from Abyssinia [on this occasion?] were thirty-three men. (*Ibid.*, 168–169)

The Boycott

Rumors to the contrary, the Quraysh had not been converted wholesale, but there were perhaps some encouraging signs at Mecca. Before the migration and then shortly after it, the faith of Muhammad did win two powerful and energetic converts from a among the Quraysh, Hamza ibn Abd al-Muttalib and Umar ibn al-Khattab, the latter of whom would follow Abu Bakr as the Prophet's successor as head of the Muslim community. However modest a success these conversions represented, they provoked a severe response from the principal men of the Quraysh:

> When the Quraysh perceived that the Apostle's companions had settled in a land in peace and safety and that the Negus had protected those who had sought refuge with him, and that Umar had become a Muslim and that he and Hamza were on the side of the Messenger and his companions, and that Islam had begun to spread among the tribes, they came together and decided among themselves to write a document in which they would put a boycott on the Banu Hashim and the Banu Muttalib to the effect that no one should marry their women nor give women for them to marry; and that no one should either buy from them or sell to them, and when they agreed on that they wrote it in a deed. Then they solemnly agreed on the points and hung the deed up in the middle of the Ka'ba to remind them of their obligations. (Ibn Ishaq 1955, p. 159)

The point of the boycott does not appear so much to starve Muhammad and his followers into submission as to exclude them from the commercial life of that very commercial city.[14]

> ... Meanwhile the Messenger was exhorting his people night and day, secretly and publicly, openly proclaiming God's command without fear of anyone. His uncle and the rest of the Banu Hashim gathered round him and protected him from the attacks of the Quraysh, who when they saw they could not get at him, mocked and laughed and disputed with him. The Quran began to come down concerning the wickedness of the Quraysh and those who showed enmity to him, some by name and some only referred to in general ...
>
> The Banu Hashim and the Banu al-Muttalib were in the quarters which the Quraysh had agreed upon in the document they wrote, when a number of the Quraysh took steps to annul the boycott against them. None took more trouble in this than Hisham ibn Amr. ... He went to Zuhayr ibn Abi Umayya ... and said: "Are you content to eat food and wear clothes and marry women while you know the condition of your maternal uncles? They cannot buy or sell, marry or give in marriage. ... " He said, "Confound you, Hisham, what can I do? I am only one man. By God, if I had another man to back me, I would soon annul it." ...

Hisham went round the city and drummed up some additional support.

> They all arranged to meet at night on the nearest point of al-Hajun above Mecca, and there they bound themselves to take up the question of the (boycott) document until they had secured its annulment. Zuhayr claimed the right to act and speak first. So on the morrow when the people met (publicly) together, Zuhayr clad in a long robe went round the Ka'ba seven times; then he came forward and said: 'O people of Mecca, are we to eat and clothe ourselves while the Banu Hashim perish, unable to buy or sell? By God, I will not sit down until this evil boycotting document is torn up!' Abu Jahl, who was at the side of the mosque, exclaimed, "You lie, by God. It shall not be torn up." Zama'a said, "You are a greater liar; we were not satisfied with the document when it was written." . . . (*Ibid.*, pp. 161, 172)

Nor were others, apparently. The opposition of Abu Jahl was overridden and it was agreed that the boycott instrument should be annulled and destroyed. But at a point at which it might seem that his enemies were losing their resolve, in 619 A.D. Muhammad's psychological and legal defenses collapsed under two almost simultaneous and rapidly descending blows.

THE DEATHS OF KHADIJA AND ABU TALIB

> Khadija and Abu Talib died in the same year, and with Khadija's death troubles followed fast on each other's heels, for she had been a faithful support for him in Islam, and he used to tell her all his troubles. With the death of Abu Talib he lost a strength and stay in his personal life and a defense and protection against his tribe. Abu Talib died some three years before he migrated to Medina, and it was then that the Quraysh began to treat him in an offensive way which they would not have dared to follow in his uncle's lifetime. (Ibn Ishaq 1955, p. 191)

Muhammad had married Khadija in 595 A.D. when, we are told, somewhat implausibly, that he was 25 and she 40. She bore him four daughters, Zaynab, Ruqayya, Umm Kulthum and Fatima, as well as a number of sons, all of the latter dying in infancy. Shortly after the death of Khadija Muhammad married Sawda, the wife of one of his followers who had gone to Abyssinia and died there. There was some question that the Prophet might have contracted to marry Aisha, the daughter of Abu Bakr, while they were both still at Mecca, but it seems likely that the marriage was not consummated till he had emigrated to Medina, when Aisha was reportedly 9.[15] At Medina he also married Umar's daughter Hafsa, Hind, Zaynab daughter of Jahsh,[16] Umm Salama, Juwayriyya, Ramla or Umm Habiba, Safiyya, and Maymuna.[17] None of them bore him children, however, though he had a son, Ibrahim, by his Coptic concubine Mary. Ibrahim too died an infant.

AN INVITATION FROM A DISTANT OASIS

Despite the collapse of the formal boycott, Muhammad's affairs now became increasingly desperate. Abu Talib had stood like a stout tribal shield between the Prophet and his opponents, but at his death Muhammad had to seek protection, even conditional protection, in other quarters. An appeal to the Thaqif of nearby Ta'if, long-time rivals of the Quraysh, proved unavailing, as did visits to the bedouin collected at the local fairs.

> His people opposed him more bitterly than ever, apart from the few lower-class people who believed in him. . . . The Apostle offered himself to the tribes of Arabs at the fairs whenever the opportunity came, summoning them to God and telling them that he was a prophet who had been sent. He used to ask them to believe in him and protect him until God should make clear to them the message with which He had charged His prophet . . .

Muhammad's own growing desperation was matched by the implacable opposition of Abu Lahab. The conflict between the two men had by now descended to a deep personal animosity:

> I heard my father telling Rabi'a ibn Abbad that when he was a youngster with his father in Mina the Apostle used to stop by the Arab encampments and tell them that he was Apostle of God who ordered them worship Him and not associate anything with Him and to renounce the rival gods which they worshiped, and believe in His Apostle and protect him until God made plain His purpose in sending him. There followed him an artful spruce fellow with two sidelocks of hair and wearing an Aden cloak. When the Apostle finished his appeal, he used to say: "This fellow wishes only to get you to strip off al-Lat and

al-Uzza from your necks. . . . Don't obey him and take no notice of him." I asked my father who the man was who followed the Apostle and contradicted what he said, and he answered that it was his uncle Abd al-Uzza ibn Abd al-Muttalib known as Abu Lahab. (Ibn Ishaq 1955, pp. 194–195)

The petitioning finally paid off, however. Among those who heard the Prophet's pleas were visitors from the oasis of Yathrib, some 275 miles to the north of Mecca. Yathrib, later named *The City (madina) of the Prophet*, or simply Medina, was an agricultural settlement of mixed Arab and Jewish population. Ibn Ishaq regarded both the encounter and the presence of Jews at Yathrib as providential:

> When God wished to display His religion openly and to glorify His Prophet and to fulfill His promise to him, the time came when he met a number of "Helpers" [that is, future Medinese converts to Islam] at one of the (Meccan) fairs. . . . They said that when the Apostle met them he learned by inquiry that they were of the (tribe of the) Khazraj and were allies of the Jews (there). He invited them to sit with him and he expounded to them Islam and recited the Quran to them.
>
> Now God had prepared the way for Islam in that they [the Khazraj] lived side by side with the Jews (of Medina), who were people of the Scriptures and knowledge, while they themselves were polytheists and idolaters. They had often raided them in their district and whenever bad feelings arose the Jews used to say to them, "A Prophet will be sent soon. His day is at hand. We shall follow him and kill you by his aid just as Ad and Iram perished." So when they [the Khazraj] heard the Apostle's message they said to one another, "This is the very Prophet of whom the Jews warned us. Don't let them get to him before us!"

What is first portrayed as simple self-protection—"If we do not quickly get the new Prophet on our side, the Jews will use him to our destruction"—is quickly broadened out to embrace what may have been the true grounds for Muhammad's attractiveness to these Medinese: this charismatic holy man might indeed be the one to put an end to the civil strife at Medina, a brutal close-quarters warfare that, as we shall see, had in fact nothing to do with Arab-Jewish animosity.

> Thereupon they accepted his teaching and became Muslims, saying, "We have left our people, for no tribe is so divided by hatred and rancor as they. Perhaps God will unite them through

you. So let us go to them and invite them to this religion of yours; and if God unites them in it, then no man will be mightier than you." Thus saying they returned to Medina as believers.

In the next pilgrimage season, without indication of any contact in the interval, another group came down from Medina and embraced Islam, though this time the conditions of conversion are laid out.

> In the following year twelve "Helpers" attended the fair and met at al-Aqaba [that is, a place near Mecca]—this was the "First Aqaba"—where they gave the Messenger the "pledge of women."[18] . . . "I was present at Aqaba (one of the participants reported). There were twelve of us and we pledged ourselves to the Prophet after the manner of women, and that was before (the obligation of) war was enjoined. The undertaking was that we should associate nothing with God; we should not steal; we should not commit fornication, nor kill our offspring; we should not slander our neighbors; we should not disobey him [Muhammad] in what was right. If we fulfilled this, Paradise would be ours; if we committed any of these sins, it was for God to punish us or forgive us as He pleased.
>
> When these men left the Apostle sent with them Mus'ab ibn Umayr and instructed him to read the Quran with them, and to teach them Islam, and to give them instruction about religion. (Ibn Ishaq 1955, pp. 197–199)

Mus'ab did not confine himself to what was standard practice at Mecca—note that the Quran, which at this point comprised only the Meccan *suras,* is already regarded as both Scripture and a liturgical text—but went a very large step forward:

> . . . And Mus'ab had them recite the Quran and taught them. He then wrote to the Messenger of God asking permission to perform with them the Friday service. The Prophet gave his consent and wrote to them: "On the day when the Jews make public (preparations) for their Sabbath and when the sun is setting, draw near God with two bows and deliver a sermon." Then Mus'ab ibn Umayr held the Friday prayer with them in the abode of Sa'd ibn Khaythama . . . (Ibn Sa'd, *Tabaqat* III/1, p. 83)

What we conclude from this report, if it is true,[19] is that permission was granted to the few Muslims at Medina to make a public prayer at sunset on Friday in the manner of the Jews, effectively the first prescriptive prayer service in Islam in the first environment where it was possible. What is highly unlikely is that Mus'ab delivered a sermon. The "sermons" that were later delivered in Medina on that day had in fact no intrinsic connection with the pre-Sabbath prayers that were already being conducted at Medina. They were Muhammad's weekly address to his followers at Medina, apparently on a variety of topics and delivered in the courtyard of his home, which was the natural center of the movement.[20] Friday became the Prophet's preferred day, it has plausibly been suggested, not to separate himself from the Jewish Sabbath or the Christian Sunday, but because this was the chief market day in Medina.[21] That Friday should have become such in Medina—there is no indication that Friday had any particular significance for either Muhammad or the Quraysh at Mecca—seems to have had to do, as this tradition explicitly admits, with the Jews' Sabbath preparations on the eve of that holy day; indeed, the *suq* of the Jewish tribe of the Banu Qaynuqa' served as the market place for the entire oasis,[22] which collected there on what was likely called, even before Muhammad began to use the day for his own political purposes, *yawm al-jum'a*, the "day of assembly," the later standard Muslim designation for Friday.[23]

That the Friday "day of assembly" at Medina had an urgent commercial context is revealed in the only Quranic passage in which the day is mentioned:

> O you who believe, when you are summoned to prayer (*salat*) on the day of assembly, hasten to the remembrance of God and leave off your trading. That is best for you, if you only knew.
>
> But when the prayer is finished, then you may scatter through the land and seek the bounty of God. Celebrate the praises of God often that you may prosper.
>
> And when they see some merchandise or some amusement, they disperse in its direction and leave you standing there . . . (Quran 62: 9–11)

To return to Mus'ab, even if his duties were chiefly religious, he was almost certainly given a political commission as well, to scout the ground at Yathrib/Medina.[24] The oasis, which was an agricultural and not a commercial settlement, does not seem to have been well known or to have attracted much notice at Mecca; and the Medinans coming to the annual fairs near Mecca are far more likely to have known about Muhammad than the latter about the politics of the distant oasis.

The following year the new Muslim "Helpers" returned to the fair, seventy-three men and two women, and pledged their support. Muhammad was apparently invited to Medina, though there were questions. If he did came to Medina, how long did he intend to stay? And what of his followers? We do not find much discussion of them. The Medinans had little need for them—it was the holy man who was going to solve their problems—but if they too were coming, as Muhammad must have insisted, how did he intend they were to live?[25] And finally, there was the matter of the Jews, which Muhammad's religious program, not the Medinans' political agenda, had raised.

> "O Apostle, [one of the Medinese said] we have ties with other men—he meant the Jews—and if we sever them, perhaps when we have done that and God will have given us victory, will you return to your people and leave us?" The Messenger smiled and said, "No, blood is blood, and blood not to be paid for is blood not to be paid for. I am of you and you are of me. I will war against those who war against you and be at peace with those at peace with you." (Ibn Ishaq 1955, p. 204)

It was a prophecy that did not turn out to be true.

A TURN TO ARMED RESISTANCE

In the period of time that elapsed between the two meetings at the place near Mecca called *the Defile (al-Aqaba),* another event commemorated in the Quran may have occurred, or so Ibn Ishaq would have us believe. It was in any event one with enormous political consequences for the nascent Islamic community: A formal rejection of passive resistance to the persecution of the Muslims and a turn to the use of force.

> The Messenger had not been given permission to fight or allowed to shed blood before the second (pledge of) Aqaba. He had simply been ordered to call men to God and to endure insult and forgive the innocent. The Quraysh had persecuted his followers, seducing some from their religion and exiling others from their country. They had to choose whether to give up their religion, be mistreated at home, or to flee the country, some to Abyssinia, others to Medina.
> When the Quraysh became insolent toward God and rejected His gracious purpose, accused His Prophet of lying,

and ill treated and exiled those who served Him and proclaimed His unity, believed in His Prophet and held fast to His religion, He gave permission for His Messenger to fight and protect himself against those who wronged them and treated them badly.

The first verse which was sent down on this subject, from what I have heard from Urwa ibn al-Zubayr and other learned persons, was: "Permission is given to those who fight because they have been wronged. God is well able to help them—those who have been driven out of their houses without right only because they said God is our Lord. Had not God used some men to keep back others, cloisters and churches and oratories and mosques wherein the name of God is constantly mentioned would have been destroyed. Assuredly, God will help those who help Him. God is Almighty. Those who if We make them strong in the land will establish prayer, pay the poor tax, enjoin kindness and forbid iniquity. To God belongs the end of matters" (Quran 22: 39–41).

This is Ibn Ishaq's positioning of the context of Quran 22: 39–41, and a highly unlikely guess on the face of it. During his last years at Mecca Muhammad had few followers and even fewer resources to fight against the Quraysh, even if he had wished to do so. Force became an option for Muslims only after their arrival in Medina, and even then not immediately.

Having provided what he or someone else believed was the occasion of the revelation, Ibn Ishaq then goes on to explain its meaning:

The meaning is: "I have allowed them to fight only because they were unjustly treated, while their sole offense against men is that they worship God. When they are in the ascendent they will establish prayer, pay the poor tax, enjoin kindness and forbid iniquity, that is, the Prophet and his companions, all of them." Then God sent down to him (the verse): "Fight so there is no more persecution," that is, until no believer is seduced from his religion, "and the religion is God's," that is, until God alone is worshiped. (Quran 2: 193). (Ibn Ishaq 1955, pp. 212–213)

This permission to fight, to turn from passive to active resistance to the Quraysh, was, whenever granted, no trifling matter, as its divine sanction shows. The Quraysh's commercial enterprises were protected by their own religiously sanctioned prohibitions against violence and bloodshed during the sacred months surrounding the pilgrimage and the annual fairs that were connected to it, but now the community of Muslims had its own God-given sanction for violence, something that put military teeth in the agreement with the Medinans. Force now had to be discussed because it was no longer a matter of conversion: Muhammad and his followers were entering a *political compact* with the Medinans, though the latter could hardly have imagined that when their new leader spoke of war, he was referring to what was to them distant, and unimportant, Mecca. "When God gave permission to His apostle to fight, the second Aqaba (agreement) contained conditions involving war which were not in the first act of fealty. Now they bound themselves to war against all and sundry for God and His apostle, while he promised them for faithful service thus the reward of Paradise" (*ibid.*, p. 208)

THE HIJRA (622 A.D.)

The agreement was not that the Medinans should protect Muhammad in his native Mecca but that he and his followers should come to Medina and effect a political settlement there, probably by reconciliation, as they thought, because the Medinans neither bargained for nor got a band of mercenary soldiers— there were such in the Hijaz—but a bedraggled lot of dispirited refugees. But first they had to get themselves out of Mecca.

> When God had given permission to fight, and this clan of the "Helpers" (from Medina) had pledged their support to him in Islam and to help him and his followers, and the Muslims had taken refuge with them, the Messenger commanded his companions to emigrate to Medina and to link up with their brethren, the "Helpers": "God will make for you brethren and houses in which you may be safe." So they went out in companies, and the Messenger stayed in Mecca waiting for the Lord's permission to leave Mecca and migrate to Medina . . . (Ibn Ishaq 1955, pp. 212–213)

The arrangements were now complete and the migration of Muslims to Mecca began, quietly and prudently, and its final stage it had to be undertaken with great caution:

> After his companions had left, the Messenger stayed at Mecca waiting for permission to emigrate. Except for Abu Bakr and Ali, none of his (Meccan) supporters remained behind, except those who were being restrained [that is, had not yet received

⌐permission] and those who had been forced to apostatize. The former kept asking the Messenger for permission to emigrate and he would answer, "Do not be in a hurry; it may be that God will give you a companion." Abu Bakr hoped that it would be Muhammad himself.

And then. with the benefit of a great deal of historical hindsight:

When the Quraysh saw that the Messenger (now) had a party and companions not of their tribe and outside their territory, and that his companions had migrated to join them, and when they realized that the Muslims had settled in a new home and had gained protectors, they feared that the Messenger might join them, since they knew that he had decided to fight them. So they assembled in their council chamber, the house of Qusayy ibn Kilab, where all their important business was conducted, to take counsel what they should do in regard to the Apostle, for they were now in fear of him.

So Quraysh took counsel on how to deal with this new and potentially dangerous development. After a discussion of various possibilities, Muhammad's archrival Abu Jahl took the floor. He knew well how to play upon at least the religious anxieties of his fellow Quraysh: "Muhammad alleges that if you follow him you will be kings of the Arabs and the Persians. Then after death you will be raised to gardens like those of the Jordan.[26] But if you do not follow him you will be slaughtered, and when you are raised from the dead you will be burned in the fire of hell . . . "

Abu Jahl had a plan, however:

. . . Each clan should provide a young, powerful, well-born aristocratic warrior; that each of them should be equipped with a sharp sword; and that each of them should strike a blow at him and kill him. Thus they would be relieved of him, and the responsibility for his blood would lie on all the clans. The Banu Abd Manaf could not fight them all and would accept the blood-money to which they would all contribute. . . . Having come to a decision, the people dispersed.

Then Gabriel came to the Messenger and said, "Do not sleep tonight on the bed on which you usually sleep." Before much of the night had passed they [the deputized assassins] assembled at his door waiting for him to go to sleep so they might fall upon him. When the Messenger saw what they were doing, he told Ali to lie on his bed and wrap himself in his green Hadrami mantle; for no harm would befall him. He himself used to sleep in that mantle . . .

The ruse worked. Muhammad and Abu Bakr were safely on the way to Medina by the time the would-be assassins discovered the sleeping Ali.

According to what I have been told none knew when the Messenger left except Ali and Abu Bakr and the latter's family. I have heard that the Messenger told Ali about his departure and ordered him to stay behind in Mecca in order to return goods which men had deposited with the Apostle, for anyone in Mecca who had property which he was anxious about left it with him because of his notorious honesty and trustworthiness.

When the Messenger decided to go he came to Abu Bakr and the two of them left by a window in the back of the latter's house and made for a cave on Thawr, a mountain below Mecca. Having entered, Abu Bakr ordered his son Abdullah to listen to what people were saying and to come to them by night with the day's news. . . . The two of them stayed in the cave for three days. When the Quraysh missed the Messenger they offered a hundred she-camels to anyone who would bring them back. During the day Abdullah was listening to the plans and conversations and would come at night with the news. (Abu Bakr's freedman) Amir used the pasture his flocks with the shepherds of Mecca and when night fell would bring them to the cave where they milked them and slaughtered some. . . .

Muhammad ibn Ja'far ibn al-Zubayr from Urwa ibn al-Zubayr from Abd al-Rahman ibn Uwaymir ibn Sa'ida told me, saying, men of my tribe who were the Apostle's companions told me: When we heard that the Messenger had left Mecca and we were eagerly expecting his arrival, we used to go out after morning prayers to the lava tract beyond our land to await him. This we did until there was no more shade left, then we went indoors in the hot season. On the day the Messenger arrived we had sat as we always had until there being no more shade we went inside, and it was then that the Prophet arrived. The first to see him was a Jew. He had seen what we were in the habit of doing and that we were expecting the arrival of the Apostle, and he called out at the top of his voice, "O Banu Qayla, your luck has come!" So we went out to greet the Apostle, who was in the shadow of a palm tree with Abu Bakr, who was of like age. Now most of us had never seen the Messenger and as the people

crowded around him they did not know him from Abu Bakr
until the shade left him and Abu Bakr got up with his mantle
and shielded him from the sun, and then we knew.

Ali stayed in Mecca for three days and nights until he
restored the deposits which the Prophet held. This done, he
joined the Messenger . . . (Ibn Ishaq 1955, pp. 221–229)

Later, when the Muslim community chose the Prophet's
migration (*hijra*) as the starting point of the Muslim era, they were
constrained to attempt to date the event with some accuracy:

Abu Ja'far (al-Tabari): The Messenger of God received his call
to prophethood at the age of 40. According to Sha'bi, Israfil was
associated with the Messenger of God's prophethood, for three
years, this being before he was commanded to call people to
Islam and to proclaim it openly. We have already quoted the
narratives and stories to this effect. After three years Gabriel
was associated with his prophethood, and he commanded him
to summon people openly to God. He did this for ten years
while resident in Mecca, and then emigrated to Medina in (the
month of) First Rabi' fourteen years after becoming a prophet.
He left Mecca on a Monday and arrived in Medina on Monday
the 12th of First Rabi' [that is, September 24, 624]. (Tabari,
Annals, vol. 1, p. 1255 = Tabari 1988, p. 162)

There is more than one problem here, the most obvious being
that the standard dating of the "migration" places it on July 16,
622, of the Christian era. July 16 is intelligible because those who
set the system "rounded off" the date of the event to the first day
of the lunar year, the first of Muharram, of that same year, which
was not, however, a Monday, as Tabari says, but a Friday. Our
confusion on the matter is that we cannot be sure how the later
Muslims handled the dating of events that occurred before
Muhammad forbade the practice of intercalation during his
"Farewell Pilgrimage" in March of 632 A.D. Did they retroject
their own purely lunar calendar onto the years 622–632 or did
they recall them according to the old intercalation system?[27]

If that is our confusion, it is clear that the early Muslims were
themselves confused about the chronology of events in Muhammad's career at Mecca.[28] The later chronology can be pegged to
the various battles that were fought by the Muslim armies, but
there were no such publicly recalled events for the Meccan period,
and few if any hints in the early *suras* of the Quran.[29] As has

already been noted, some attempted to tie the birth of Muhammad with the year of the "Battle of the Elephant," though there is no general agreement that the latter took place in 570 A.D., or that Muhammad was in fact born in that same year.

CHAPTER 8

The City of the Prophet

With the removal of Muhammad from Mecca to Medina, it is possible to reconstruct a somewhat firmer chronology for the remembered events of his life. It must have been recalled that he died in the year 632 of the Christian era—at what age no one was certain—and that he had been in Medina for some ten years. Between those two points unfolded the events that became the landmarks of Islam: the battles of Badr and Uhud and the siege of Medina, the raid to Mu'ta, the victories at Hunayn and Ta'if and the raid to Tabuk. Three of them are circumstantially referred to in the Quran (Badr at 3: 13, Uhud at 3: 121, and, less certainly Hudaybiyya at 48: 1), and both Badr (3: 123) and Hunayn (9: 25) are mentioned by name. Even the most severe critic of the Muslim sources felt compelled to accept both the events and the traditional sequence.[1]

YATHRIB

All of these landmark occurrences took place at Yathrib, the most important of the villages that formed the agglomerate named Medina (*madina*),[2] an oasis complex 275 miles north of Mecca. Medina lies on an elevated plain covered in most places by rough lava blocks, the *harras*, which on the western side of town extended right up to the city's medieval walls. On the other three sides, and particularly toward the south, the land was arable and under intense cultivation, chiefly in date palms, for which the city was celebrated well into the nineteenth century.[3] It is no longer so, of course, but in the early nineteenth century the cultivated areas extended from six to eight miles from the eastern and southern sides of town,[4] and the condition was probably similar in Muhammad's time. The Medinese saw their settlement as made up of the arable land on what were known as "The Heights" and the poor and unhealthy lots situated on "The Bottom."[5]

The urban units of Medina were a mixture of residences and cultivated land. The principal type of dwelling is what the sources call an *abode (dar)*, actually a complex of connected residences that served as both a farmstead and clan preserve.[6] The attached palm groves and fields of each *dar* were divided into clan holdings and individually owned garden plots. Within the *dar* lived the extended, single-residence families (*ahl bayt*) that constituted the clan. The *dar* was an asylum for all the members of the clan but there were in addition forts placed here and there around the oasis for the protection of women in children during the periods of civil strife that racked the settlement.[7]

JEWS AND ARABS

The ancient history of the peoples who inhabited the oasis of Medina is as obscurely shadowed with legend as that of Mecca. As at Mecca, the task of the Muslim historian was to account for the condition of the city at the appearance of Islam, and in the case of Medina, that meant explaining the presence of the two chief Arab clans of the Aws and the Khazraj and the origins and history of the various Jewish tribes who then inhabited the oasis and who had apparently been present for an extended period.[8]

By all accounts, the Jews of Medina, even though they were not the original settlers of the oasis, were present there before the Aws and Khazraj. How they came or when was and remains a matter of dispute. There were well-attested Jewish populations in all the major oases of Western Arabia north of Medina, a pattern that has suggested to many that there had been a migration southward from Palestine into Arabia. This certainly seems to have been the Muslim view, and when the antiquarians attempted to construct genealogies for the Jewish tribes of Medina, they managed to trace them back to "Lawi" (Levi), or even Abraham himself, though through Isaac rather than Ishmael.[9] Few European scholars were convinced, however, at least as it concerned the Jews of Medina; most thought that they were far more likely Judaized Arabs, converts made by active Jewish missionaries elsewhere.[10]

Whether converts or not, the "Jewish" tribes of Medina—the three chief ones known as the Nadir, Qurayza, and Qaynuqa', as well as a number of lesser clans[11]—enjoyed, and were acknowledged to possess, a higher degree of culture than the other settlers

in the oasis. Their number has been estimated at 36,000–42,000,[12]
and they were craftsmen, merchants, and skilled agriculturalists
rather than scarcely sedentarized bedouin like the Aws and
Khazraj. "The Banu Qurayza were people of high lineage and of
properties," said an early Muslim, "whereas we were but an Arab
tribe who did not possess any palm trees nor vineyards, being people of only sheep and camels."[13] The bedouin in fact used to be
hired by the Jews of Medina to carry the dates off on their camels
to nearby markets. Most surprising of all, perhaps, is the report
that the Banu Nadir and Banu Qurayza served as the tax-collectors
for the shah of Iran in Medina during the period of Persian sovereignty over parts of the Hijaz.[14] The Jews also appear to have been
the most literate part of the population. They spoke their own language, perhaps Persian but far more likely some form of Aramaic,
which they could also write. In the minds of the later Muslims they
had not only books but rabbis and possibly schools.[15]

When Muhammad reached Medina in 622 A.D. the Jewish
tribes were allied as subordinates to the two major Arab tribes of
Aws and Khazraj,[16] known collectively as the Banu Qayla. They
were newcomers, immigrants from the south as part of the large
group called the Azd. How or when they displaced the Jewish tribes
from their position of hegemony in Medina is unknown, though it
appears not to have been a formal or protracted struggle, and the
mid-sixth century, probably after Abraha's attack on Mecca, seems
to be plausible date for the change in the balance of power.[17]

> When the Aws and Khazraj were on their way and arrived at
> Medina, they settled in the *harras*. Then they began to spread
> out: some took refuge in the unwatered and uninhabited areas
> and settled there; others took refuge in the settled hamlets and
> lived with the inhabitants. The Aws and Khazraj remained
> where they had settled, living in poverty and wretchedness with-
> out either camels or goats because Medina was unsuitable for
> pasturage. They owned neither palm groves nor arable land,
> except some few who possessed some palms or small fields that
> had no owners. The prosperous farms belonged to the Jews.
> (*Kitab al-Aghani*, vol. 19, pp. 95–96)

The Jews of Medina found themselves in a new and uncom-
fortable position:

> The Jews were now powerless and despondent and gripped with
> great fear. And if one of the Aws or the Khazraj grew angry at a

Jew because of some offense, the latter did not go to one of his fellow Jews but to one of his Arab protectors, in whose midst he lived, and said: "We are your protégés and associates." And so all the Jewish families took refuge with a family group of the Aws or Khazraj and sought their protection. (*Ibid.*, 97)[18]

Once the Arab newcomers became paramount, peace still did not come to the oasis. The Banu Qayla fell to fighting among themselves, Aws and Khazraj, with each side attempting to court the assistance of the Jewish tribes, and Yathrib was torn by civil strife for nearly a century before the Prophet was summoned from Mecca to intervene. And the chief motive, it appears, was the possession of the limited arable land, the chief source or Medina's prosperity. The struggles of the Aws and Khazraj, and perhaps Muhammad's own quarrels with the Jews of the oasis, had principally to do with land.[19]

MUHAMMAD SETTLES IN

We have seen the dangerous circumstances surrounding Muhammad's departure from his native city. His arrival in his newly adopted—and permanent—home was considerably more auspicious. There are many embellished versions of it, and the following brief summary is that of the historian Tabari:

> We shall now mention the other noteworthy events of this year, the first year of the Hijra. Among these is his holding the Friday prayer with his [that is, Muhammad's] companions on the day on which he left (the Medinese suburb of) Quba for Medina. This was on a Friday, and the time for prayer—the Friday prayer—overtook him in the territory of the Banu Salim ibn Awf in the bed of a wadi belonging to them, and this was used a mosque that day. This was the first Friday prayer which the Messenger of God held in Islam.[20] (Tabari, *Annals*, vol. 1, p. 1256 = Tabari 1987, pp. 1–2)

Muhammad chose his dwelling place in Medina in much the same way as he had in the suburb of Quba five days previously: he gave his camel her head, and where she stopped, there he would live. By one account the site was a drying-floor for dates, but Tabari preferred a different version.

The site of the mosque (and living quarters) of the Prophet belong to the Banu al-Najjar and contained palm trees, cultivated land and pre-Islamic graves. The Messenger of God said to them, "Ask me a price for it," but they said, "We do not want a price for it, but only the reward we shall receive from God." The Messenger of God then gave orders concerning the cite; the palm trees were cut down, the cultivated land levelled, and the graves dug up. Before this mosque was completed the Messenger of God used to pray in sheep enclosures or wherever the time of prayer overtook him. (*Ibid.*, vol. 1, pp. 1259–1260 = Tabari 1987, p. 5)

All these traditions assert or suggest that Muhammad's first intention in Medina was to found a mosque (*masjid*). It seems highly improbable on the face of it. As far as we can ascertain from the Quranic evidence, a *masjid* was a shrine, a cult building rendered sacred by the ground upon which it was built or the idol that it housed. The place where Muhammad chose to live in Quba or Medina was neither; it was a *dar* like the other family dwellings in Medina,[21] and though Muhammad may have prayed in the open courtyard and naturally addressed his followers there, the functions of the building were primarily domestic, as is amply attested to by a great number of traditions that describe what went on there, including dogs' eating the family's food scraps, the stabling of camels, and even bedouin urinating in the corners.[22]

What it might have looked like to begin with appears in a number of traditional accounts, like this from the traveler Ibn Battuta:

The site of the mosque was an enclosure used for drying dates. The Apostle of God—God bless him and give him peace—bought this drying ground . . . then built the mosque, himself working on it with his Companions, and put a wall around it, but gave it neither roofing nor pillars. He made it square in shape, its length being a hundred cubits and its breadth the same, though some say that its breadth was a little less, and fixed the height of the wall at the stature of a man.

Later on, when the heat grew intense, his Companions spoke of roofing it, so he set up for this purpose a number of columns formed of trunks of palms, and made its roof of their branches. Then when it rained the mosque dripped, so the Companions of the Apostle of God—God bless him and give him peace—spoke to him about making it with clay, but he said "On no account! A booth like the booth of Moses," or "A shelter like the shelter of Moses, and man's estate is even less enduring than that."[23] On being asked, "What is the shelter of Moses like?" he replied: "When he stood up, the roof struck his head." He made three gateways in the mosque, but the southern gateway was blocked up when the prayer-direction was changed [from Jerusalem on the north side of the mosque to Mecca on the south]. (Ibn Battuta 1958, p. 168)

That Muhammad's dwelling in Medina was precisely that throughout his lifetime, and perhaps for some time afterward,[24] was unimaginable not only to Ibn Battuta, who calls it a "mosque" throughout, but to all the later traditionists and theologians who had long since systematized both Muslim prayer and the etiquette of the mosque, and who had, moreover, witnessed the architectural magnification of what had once been a modest courtyard house into a grandiose monument to the Prophet of Islam and his final resting place. It was, in any event, a somewhat slow process, and according to the tenth century geographer Muqaddasi, the building appears to have undergone some enlargement but little alteration under the earliest caliphs.

The mosque . . . is at the side of the cemetery of al-Gharqad, made like the mosque in Damascus, and not very large. It and the Damascus mosque were constructed by al-Walid ibn Abd al-Malik and the Abbasids enlarged it. . . . The first Umar enlarged it from the pillars to which the lattice-work grill is today attached as far as the south wall. Then Uthman enlarged it toward the south as far as it now reaches. (Muqaddasi, vol. 3: p. 80)

By all accounts the caliph al-Walid (r. 705–715), his deputy, and the future caliph, Umar ibn Abd al-Aziz, transformed the Prophet's home into a genuine shrine. Walid was, like his caliph father, an ambitious builder. Neither father nor son, who were active in Jerusalem and Damascus, undertook any substantial changes at Mecca, but Walid had far-reaching plans for the Prophet's mosque in Medina, as reported in Tabari's more circumstantial account of his work under the year 707 A.D.:

This year al-Walid ibn Abd al-Malik ordered the demolition of the mosque of the Prophet and the demolition of the apartments of the wives of the Prophet and their incorporation into the mosque. Muhammad ibn Umar reported that Muhammad ibn Ja'far ibn Wirdan, the builder, had said: "I saw the messenger sent by Abd al-Malik. He arrived in First Rabi' of 88 [February–March 707], his face covered, and people wanted to know why he had come. He went and gave to Umar ibn Abd al-Aziz the letter bidding him incorporate the apartments of the wives of the Prophet into the mosque of the Prophet and acquire (the buildings) behind and around the mosque so that it would measure 200 by 200 cubits. He said to him: Push back the south wall if you can—and you can—back to the place where your maternal uncles live, since they will not oppose you. If any of them resists, order the local people to calculate a fair price (for the property), tear it down and pay the owner its value. You have the authentic precedent of Umar and Uthman to guide you . . .

The local property owners offered no resistance, however. They took their payments and surrendered their houses to the mosque renewal project.

> Muhammad ibn Umar said . . . on the authority of Salih ibn Kaysan: "When the letter of al-Walid arrived from Damascus after a trip of fifteen days,[25] Umar ibn Abd al-Aziz took the work in hand." Salih also said: "He put me in charge of the demolition and reconstruction of the mosque. . . . We set about demolishing it with laborers from Medina, beginning with the apartments of the wives of the Prophet. Then there arrived the workers sent by al-Walid. . . . We began the demolition of the mosque of the Prophet in Safar of 88 [that is, January 707]. Al-Walid had sent and informed the Byzantine ruler that he had given orders for the demolition of the mosque of the Prophet and that he should assist in this enterprise. The latter sent him 100,000 *mithqals* of gold, a hundred artisans and forty loads of *tesserae* for the mosaics. He had given orders that the *tesserae* should be recovered from ruined towns and sent them to Walid, who sent them on to Umar ibn Abd al-Aziz. (Tabari, *Annals*, vol. 2, pp. 1192–1194)

Muhammad's building himself a house has received the major share of the historians' and traditionists' attention because that residence eventually became the second holiest place in Islam after Mecca. But Muhammad had, as we have seen, no idea that he was building a mosque, much less his own tomb, and in his own mind something else he attempted may have at that time seemed far more important. According to a number of important traditions,[26] Muhammad attempted to set up his own market in Medina:

> The Prophet pitched a tent in the cemetery al-Zubayr and said: "This is your market." Then (the Jewish leader) Ka'b ibn al-Ashraf came up, entered inside and cut its ropes. Then Prophet then said: "Indeed, I shall move it into a place which will be

more grievous for him than this place." And he moved into the place of the "Market of Medina" [scil. to the place that was later the market of Medina]. Then he said: "This is your market. Do not set up sections in it and do not impose taxes for it." (Samhudi, Wafa' al-wafa', vol. 1, p. 540)[27]

The reasons for Ka'b's objection appears elsewhere. Muhammad, it is said, was attempting to set up on the open and unoccupied site of a former cemetery in the quarter of Banu Sa'ida a market to replace, or at least to compete with, what was then the principal suq of Medina, that of the Jewish tribe of the Banu Qaynuqa'. Eventually it would make little difference to Muslim fortunes because a string of military victories rapidly made the new believers rich from booty rather than local trade. But at the outset at least it appears that Muhammad intended to establish a kind of free trade zone in Medina, perhaps on the model of places like Ukaz, and to do it at the expense of Jewish commercial interests.

THE MEDINA AGREEMENT

Ibn Ishaq said: And the Apostle of God wrote a document (kitab) between the Migrants and the Helpers, and in it he made a peace (wada'a) with the Jews and a pact ('ahada) with them, and he confirmed/established them according to their religion/law ('ala dinihim) and properties and laid down obligations due to them, and imposed obligations upon them. (Ibn Ishaq 1955, p. 231)

Thus Ibn Ishaq introduces in his Life of the Apostle of God a document, or, more likely, a collection of documents,[28] that purports to record the political arrangements contracted not, as Ibn Ishaq seems to emphasize, between Muhammad and the Jews of Medina, but rather dictated by Muhammad and regulating the political arrangements between his partisans from Mecca and all the inhabitants of Yathrib, Muslims, pagans, and Jews:

In the Name of God, the Compassionate, the Merciful. This is a document from Muhammad the Prophet (concerning the relations) between the believers and Muslims of the Quraysh and Yathrib [Medina], and those who followed them and joined them and labored with them. They are one community (umma) to the exclusion of all men . . . (Ibn Ishaq 1955, pp. 231–232)

There is little reason to doubt the authenticity of the collection.[29] Its earliest and central elements represent a type of political
contract whereby Muhammad unexpectedly—from the point of
view of a later Muslim—agrees that the signatories, the Muslims,
pagans, and Jews of Medina, shall henceforward constitute a single *political* community, albeit under the supervision—one
scarcely knows what word to use in describing Muhammad's own
role—of someone who is patently a holy man (*nabi*). It reveals
why in fact Muhammad was invited to Medina in the first place,
to reconcile the murderous differences between the two chief Arab
factions and their respective Jewish allies, and how he attempted
to accomplish it. In place of the old tribal units he fashioned a new
community united by little else, it appears, than their willingness
to accept his divinely derived authority: "Whenever you differ
about a matter, it must be referred to God and Muhammad."

To describe this new community Muhammad and the document uses a term, *umma*, that was already commonplace in the
Quran. But how the document's core elements—the so-called
Documents A and B—understood "community" (*umma*) is quite
different from the Quran's, which generally regards an *umma* as a
religious community united by its belief in the One True God (e.g.,
Quran 10: 47), one to which a messenger has been sent (Quran
23:44), and more particularly, the community of the Muslims,
described in Quran 3: 110 as "the best of communities that has
been raised up for mankind, enjoining what is right, forbidding
what is wrong, and having faith in God."[30] It is not even certain
that the Medina agreement, which is the cornerstone of Muhammad's presence and authority in Medina, is even mentioned in the
Quran.[31]

This was no *hums* arrangement, with its stringent cultic regu-
lations; the contracting parties did not embrace Islam: they did
agree to recognize the authority of Muhammad, to accept him as
the community leader and to abide by his political judgments. In
so doing they were acknowledging, as was the Prophet himself,
that they were one community or *umma* under God, Muhammad's God, not yet uniquely composed of Muslims, but committed to defend its own joint interests, or what was now newly
defined to be the common good. It was, transparently, the result
of some very hard bargaining.[32]

After the brief descriptive preamble, there follow either the
terms of the agreement, forty-seven in all according to the by now

standard numeration or, more likely, a series of other arrangements agreed upon in Medina at various times,[33] though most of
the provisions likely date from a few months after Muhammad's
arrival in Medina:[34]

[12] A believer shall not take as an ally the client of
another Muslim against him.

[13] The God-fearing believers shall be against the rebellious or him who spreads injustice, or sin or enmity or corrup-
tion between believers.

[14] A believer shall not slay a believer for the sake of an
unbeliever, nor shall he aid an unbeliever against a believer.

[15] God's protection (dhimma) is one, the least of them
may give protection to a stranger on their behalf. Believers are
patrons and clients one to the other to the exclusion of outsiders.

[16] To the Jew who follows us belongs the same help and
support (as the believers), so long as he is not wronged nor his
enemies aided.

[17] The peace of believers is indivisible and no separate
peace shall be made when believers are fighting in the way of
God, except insofar as the conditions are fair and equitable . . .

[20] No pagan is to offer protection of goods or person to
the Quraysh (of Mecca), nor to intervene in the latter's favor
against a believer.

[23] Wherever there is anything about which you differ, it
is to be referred to God and Muhammad.

[24] The Jews must bear their expenses so long as they are
fighting alongside the believers.[35]

Then follows a clause that has raised considerable interpretative difficulties: "[25] The Jews of Banu Awf are a community
(umma) along with the believers. To the Jews their religion (din)
and to the Muslims their religion (din).[36] (This applies) both to
their clients and themselves, except those who have behaved
unjustly or acted treacherously. He brings evil only on himself and
his household."

Din is used very early in the Quran to describe not only
Muhammad's religion but that of the pagans of Mecca: "You
have your din and I have my din," Quran 109: 6 affirms. In the
full range of its Quranic citations, din is used to refer simply to a
personal commitment as well as in the "reified" sense of a system
of rites, beliefs, and teachings. If the Jews were permitted from the
outset to practice their religion within the newly constituted

umma, then Muhammad's original Medina "community" was a ꜩ purely secular one, and the word *umma* was being used in a sense different from its Quranic occurrences. Or else the clause dates from a later period, after the expulsion of the most aggressively hostile Jews from the oasis, when it was politically safe to allow those who remained to constitute a minor, and protected, *umma* of their own, the prototype of the later *dhimmi* status.[37]

Articles 26–35 includes various other Jewish tribes or clans in the same provision.

Article 39 of the document of Medina constitutes the oasis and its vicinity the same kind of "protected" enclave found elsewhere in Arabia, though in this instance the sanctuary notion is constituted not around a shrine, as at Mecca, for example, but on the authority of a recognized "holy man," the Meccan *nabi* Muhammad, now openly called in Article 42, *the Messenger of God.*

> [39] The center of Yathrib is sacred for the people of this document . . .
>
> [42] Whenever among the people of this document there occurs any dispute or controversy likely to cause trouble, it should be referred to God and to Muhammad, the Messenger of God. God is the most scrupulous and trues (guarantor) of what is in this document. (Ibn Ishaq 1955, pp. 232–233)

Ibn Ishaq's placement of the Medina document, which he regards as unity, in the frame of his narrative suggests that it was agreed upon shortly after Muhammad's arrival in Medina in 622, perhaps merely a matter of months after the "migration." So it may have been, in its original form, but the Muslim tradition remembered somewhat otherwise with respect to the "haramization" of Medina referred to in Article 39. It occurred, according to the Medinese historian Samhudi,[38] after the successful expedition to Khaybar, that is, sometime about September 628 A.D., at a point when Muhammad's confidence would have been immeasurably higher, at witnessed by the his overt characterization as "Messenger of God."[39]

The text says "the center" or "hollow" (*al-jawf*) of Medina was declared a *haram*. The phrase is somewhat limiting and clearly excludes the possibility that we are here dealing with what was later called a *hima* or "inviolate pasture"; Medina was to be a very urban *haram,* and because Muhammad at that juncture could have had no thought that he would one day overwhelm

Mecca and the surrounding tribes, the new *haram* may have been intended as the home ground for a new tribal amphictyony or even some sort of commercial venture, perhaps on the model of Mecca, and certainly in competition with it.[40]

INNOVATIONS

Almost as soon as the Prophet and his followers had settled down in Medina, or Yathrib, as it was still called at that time, his relations with the Jews of the place began to deteriorate. Eventually many Jews were killed or expelled from the oasis, as we shall see. None of those tribes are mentioned in the just cited document, however, a condition that strongly suggests that many of the articles, 25 and following, for example, with their emphasis on wrongdoing and treachery, were drawn up *after* the conflict between the Prophet and chief Jewish clans and so represent an arrangement with the reduced numbers of Jews who continued to live in Medina.[41]

Muhammad's relationship with the Jews of Medina turned violent soon after his first great victory over his Meccan rivals at Badr Wells in 624, as we shall see, but commercial, religious, and psychological differences may have surfaced even earlier. We have already seen, for example, how he may have attempted to carve out an economic place at Medina for his fellow "migrants" at the expense of the Jews of the oasis. And Muhammad was, after all, claiming to be a prophet in the tradition of Moses and the Torah, and in the Jewish community of Medina, he encountered, perhaps contrary to his own expectations, a rebuff from the contemporary partisans of that same tradition:

> About this time the Jewish rabbis showed hostility to the Messenger in envy, hatred and malice, because God had chosen His Messenger from the Arabs. They were joined by men from (the Arab tribes of) al-Aws and al-Khazraj who had obstinately clung to their heathen religion. They were hypocrites, clinging to the polytheism of their fathers, denying the resurrection; yet when Islam appeared and their people flocked to it they were compelled to accept it to save their lives. But in secret they were hypocrites whose inclination was towards the Jews because these latter considered the Messenger a liar and strove against Islam.[42] (Ibn Ishaq 1955, p. 239)

The Jews of Medina obviously rejected his claims, but did Muhammad in fact expect their recognition of his prophetic mission? It is not unreasonable to think so, first in the light of the strong biblical, and more specifically Abrahamic, emphases of his Meccan preaching. The chronology of the *suras* is uncertainly deceptive here. Though Abraham's connection with the Ka'ba is likely Meccan, we cannot be certain that the notion of Abraham as a *hanif* or that Muhammad was doing nothing more than reestablishing the "religion of Abraham" date from the same early period and so are prior to any real contact with Jews. The assertion that Abraham was not a Jew (2: 140; 3: 67) seems, on the ⊬ other hand, to be directed against a Jewish polemicist, and so plausibly to date from the Prophet's earliest years at Medina.[43] There is also Muhammad's marked *political* animosity toward the Jews of Medina after the battle at the Badr wells in 624. That too is part of the conviction that at first Muhammad offered himself as a prophetic reformer to the Jews of Medina, and then, when they rejected him, turned his back on them and began to refashion "Islam" as an *alternative* to Judaism.

Rethinking the Quran

But before that turning away from the Jews occurred, room must be made for the appearance of other notions absent from the Meccan *suras* and indicative of a positive and more appreciative sense of the Jewish religious experience. There is, for example, this tradition about fasting on "The Tenth" (*ashura*) preserved by Tabari among others:

> According to Abu Ja'far (al-Tabari): In this year [2 A.H., that is, 624 A.D.], it is said, the fast of Ramadan was prescribed, and it is said that it was prescribed in Sha'ban. When the Prophet came to Medina he saw the Jews fasting on the day of *Ashura*. He questioned them and they told him it was the day on which God drowned the people of the Pharaoh and so saved Moses and those with him from them. "We have a better right to Moses than they have," and he fasted and ordered people to fast with him. When the Fast of Ramadan was prescribed, he did not order them to fast on *Ashura*, nor did he forbid them to do so. (Tabari, *Annals*, vol. 1, p. 1281 = Tabari 1987, pp. 25–26)

There is another version as well, reported on the authority of Aisha:

Aisha, may God be pleased with her, reported that the Quraysh used to fast on the day of *Ashura* in the pre-Islamic days and the Messenger of God, may peace be upon him, also observed it. When he migrated to Medina he himself observed the fast and commanded (others) to observe it. But when fasting during the month of Ramadan was made obligatory, he said: "He who wishes to observe the fast (of *Ashura*) may do so and he who wishes to abandon it may do so." (Muslim, *Sahih* 6.423.2499)

Although the first of the traditions has the coloring of somewhat later anti-Jewish polemic,[44] there may be something authentic in the second, with its overt admission that Muhammad observed the fast of "the Tenth" even before Islam. The "Tenth" in question is not the later tenth of Muharram but the Jews' tenth of Tishri, that is, Yom Kippur.[45] And according to this tradition, Muhammad continued the apparently *obligatory* practice of sanctifying that day until shortly after his arrival in Medina—and a hostile confrontation with the Jews there?—when the fast of Ramadan was prescribed and that of *Ashura* made optional. The veneration of *Ashura* continued, however, but was effectively severed from its Jewish prototype, which was a seasonally adjusted holy day that annually fell at the end of September, when before his death Muhammad forbade Jewish-type calendar adjustments to Muslims, and *Ashura* began to be celebrated on the tenth day of the first Muslim month, Muharram.[46]

If this tradition is true, as it almost certainly is, why did Muhammad prescribe fasting on the tenth day of the first month of the Jewish calendar, the solemn day the Jews called the Day of Atonement or Yom Kippur, and known in the Arab tradition as "the Tenth," *Ashura*? The reason asserted in the first version of the tradition is Muhammad's claim of kinship with Moses. The Prophet's sense of the identity of his mission with that of Moses before him is already explicitly asserted in the Meccan *suras*, in 11: 17, for example, "Before it [the Quran] there was the Book of Moses, given as a guide and an act of mercy, and this (Quran) is a book confirming it in the Arabic language"; or this in Sura 28: 48–49: They say "Why are there not come (signs) like those sent to Moses?" Do they not disbelieve (also) in what was earlier sent to Moses? They say: "Two sorceries assisting each other." And they say, "As for us, we reject all (such)." Say: "Then make come a Book from God which is a better guide than these two."

If these are Meccan insights, what Muhammad may have learned new at Medina is that the Jews had a solemn day, "the Tenth," on which they commemorated the "sending down" of the Torah on Sinai.[47] That would explain not only the new fast of *Ashura*, but the appearance of another new idea in the Quran, the "sending down" of the Quran on a single night, though it is no longer being identified as *Ashura* but in what must be a Medina *sura* as the "Night of Destiny":[48]

> We have indeed sent it down in the Night of Destiny (*laylat at-qadr*). And what will explain to you (sing.) what is the Night of Destiny? The Night of Destiny is better than a thousand months. Therein come down the angels and the Spirit by permission of their Lord on every errand (*min kulli amrin*). (Therein is) peace until the dawn. (Quran 97: 1–5)

Sura 44 begins with what seems to be reference to the same event: "By the clear Book! We sent it down in a blessed night. Verily, We are ever warning. In it is discerned [or: decided] every wise matter (*kullu amrin hakimin*) by a command from Our presence Verily, we are ever sending Envoys [or: revelations] as a mercy from your Lord. He is the Hearer, the Knower" (*ibid.*, 1–6)

The "Night of Destiny," that "blessed night," is a new expression, or rather, an old occasion newly employed. From its generic descriptions in Suras 97 and 44, the Night of Destiny has been identified as a typical New Year's day observance, the occasion when, as on Rosh ha-Shana, God's judgments for the following year are determined, written in the Heavenly Book,[49] or, as the Quran puts it, "the angels and the Spirit descend[50] and, on one such annual night, with the Quran itself.

There is no further identification of the night, though it is clear that it is no longer the Jews' *Ashura*, the day on which Muhammad first fasted when he came to Medina. The appearance of the Night of Destiny in the divine economy of Islam must be after the discontinuance of the celebration of *Ashura*, but before the notion of a connection between the Quran and Ramadan that appears after the battle at the Badr wells and is expressed in Sura 2:185 ("Ramadan is the month in which We sent it down . . . ").[51] The replacement of the Jew's *Ashura* as the "moment" of revelation with the old Arabian New Year "Night of Destiny" is transparently another function of Muhammad's initial attraction to Jewish practices and his subsequent distancing from them, all in the brief interval between his arrival in Medina period and the battle of Badr some two years later.[52]

There was another consequence. Earlier in his preaching Muhammad had insisted, even in the face of severe objections from the Quraysh, that the Quran had been revealed piecemeal: "Those who disbelieve say: why is not the Quran revealed to him all at once (*jumlatan wahidatan*) . . . we have rehearsed it to you in slow, well-arranged stages, gradually" (Quran 25: 32). This was not a new idea introduced to oppose the Jewish—and what he understood to be the Christian—contention that Scripture should be revealed all at once. It conforms with the Quran's descriptions of his early visions and what every Muslim knew, that the Prophet continued to receive revelations right down to the very end of his life. Now, however, it was being asserted that the Quran had in fact, like the Torah, been revealed on a single occasion, first, we hypothesize, on Ashura, the very same day at the Torah, and then, after his break with the Jews, on the old Arabian New Year's "Night of Destiny."[53]

Linked with this new assertion of a single revelation of the Quran was another notion that might also have been Jewish inspired, that an angel, specifically Gabriel, was the agent of that revelation. This too had been thrown up to him earlier (6: 8) but he dismissed it (16: 43). Now, however, at Medina, he concedes that Gabriel was the messenger for his revelations—an assertion that of course caused later Muslims to read the visions of Sura 53 as referring not to God but to an angel.[54] But if the identification of Gabriel was intended to make the Quran more "scriptural," it did not satisfy the "enemies of Gabriel," probably the Jews of Medina who preferred to see Michael as the guardian of Scripture: "Say: Who is an enemy of Gabriel? For he it is who revealed it [that is, the Quran] to your heart by God's permission, confirming what was before it, and a guidance and glad tidings to believers" (Quran 2: 97).

Here too, at the beginning of his stay at Medina, and in the same context of contact with the Jews, Muhammad apparently began to formulate the notion that the Quran was not merely a "recitation," but a Book, like the Torah a copy of a heavenly prototype, in which were inscribed all God's decrees. The Medinese Sura 2 is filled with legislation, most of it introduced by the word "prescribed" (*kutiba 'ala*), and the *sura* itself opens with the state-

ment: "Alif, Lam, Mim. This is the Book, in which there is no
doubt, a guidance for the pious." The first three expressions are
letters of the Arabic alphabet, the mysterious letters that precede
twenty-nine *suras* of the Quran,[55] and indeed all the *suras* that up
to this point have such letters attached to them (3, 7, 10, 11, 12,
13, 14, and 15) begin with a statement about the Book, a fact that
has suggested to some that these constituted the nucleus, or at
least the beginning, of what Muhammad conceived of as genuine
scriptural Book on the Torah model.[56]

"Turn Your Face Toward the Sacred House"

Though on some matters—the Book, the single revelation, perhaps the times of prayer—there was no turning back, the evolution of Islamic practice did not long continue along this path parallel to Jewish ritual. Muhammad, it is said, had a falling out with
the Jews of Medina, and critical to this point is the issue of the
qibla, the point toward which the worshiper should face in
addressing his prayers to God. The Quran itself recognizes it as an
almost absolute external characteristic of membership in a religious community (Sura 2: 143, 145), and so the question of
Muhammad's direction of prayer, and the changes that all concede it underwent, receives an extended treatment both in the
Quran, where it seems to represent a serious problem, and by the
later commentators who were constrained to make some sense of
the Quran's own turnings on the subject.

While still at Mecca, and even after his arrival at Medina,
Muhammad is said to have prayed "toward Syria." *Toward Syria,*
as a good many Muslims understood it, meant Jerusalem, a custom that would have unmistakably aligned the Prophet with the
practice of the Jews who, as 1 Kings 8: 44 tells us, faced toward
the Temple there when they prayed. Muhammad may have done
so as well, but his own developed sense that his religion was—and
perhaps had always had been, some would add—Abrahamic
rather than Jewish, gave birth to a number of traditions that
Muhammad originally prayed toward the Ka'ba while at Mecca,
and that he switched his *qibla* briefly to Jerusalem after his arrival
at Medina in an effort to conciliate the Jews.[57] By the time Ibn
Ishaq came to write his *Life of the Apostle of God,* a least one version of the story had become "harmonized": Muhammad, we are
told, prayed facing *both* Jerusalem and the Ka'ba! "While he [that

is, Muhammad] was in Mecca he faced Syria in prayer, and when he prayed, he prayed between the southern corner and the black stone, putting the Ka'ba between himself and Syria . . . " (Ibn Ishaq 1955, p. 135).

But a little later in the same work there appears what is probably the more authentic version:

> And when the prayer-direction was changed from Syria to the Ka'ba—it was changed in (the month of) Rajab at the beginning of the seventeenth month after the Apostle's arrival in Medina—Rifa'a ibn Qays (and a number of others from among the Jews of Medina) . . . came to the Apostle asking why he had turned his back on the *qibla* he used to face when he alleged that he followed the religion of Abraham. If he would return to the *qibla* in Jerusalem they would follow him and declare him to be true. (Ibid., pp. 258–259)

The Jews' sole intention, Ibn Ishaq or some other editorial hand adds, "was to seduce him from his religion." And this, according to the same editors, was the occasion that prompted the revelation of those Quranic verses that do not so much announce as defend the decision to change his prayer direction:[58]

> The foolish among the people will say, "What has turned them away from the direction of prayer toward which they formerly prayed?" Say: "To God belongs the East and the West, and He guides whom He wills in the straight way."
>
> Thus We have made you a community of the middle path in order that you may be witnesses over humankind and that the Messenger be a witness over you. We appointed the prayer-direction to which you formerly prayed only to make known those who follow the Messenger and those who would turn back on their heels. It (that is, the change in the direction of prayer) is indeed a grave matter, except for those whom God has guided aright. As for you, God would never count your faith for naught. Truly God is Gracious and Compassionate toward mankind.
>
> We have seen you turning your face about toward heaven. We shall therefore direct you toward a prayer-direction which would please you. Turn your face toward the Sacred House of Worship; wherever you may be, turn your faces toward it. As for those who were given the Scriptures, they know well that it is the truth from their Lord, nor is God unaware of what they do.

Even if you were to bring those who were given the Scriptures every manifest sign, still they would not follow your prayer-direction, nor will you follow theirs, nor yet will they follow each other's. If therefore you were to follow their desires after the knowledge that has come to you, you would surely be one of the wrongdoers. (Quran 2: 142–145)

The uncertainty of later Muslims regarding these verses, or the circumstances that promoted them, is illustrated by the traditions preserved in Tabari's classic tenth-century commentary:

> On the authority of Ikrima and Hasan al-Basri: The first injunction which was abrogated in the Quran was that concerning the direction of prayer. This is because the Prophet used to prefer the Rock of the Holy House of Jerusalem, which was the prayer-direction of the Jews. The Prophet faced it for seventeen months [after his arrival in Medina] in the hope that they would believe in him and follow him. Then God said: "Say, 'To God belong the east and the west . . . '."

> Al-Rabi' ibn Anas relates on the authority of Abu al-Aliya: The Prophet of God was given his choice of turning his face in whatever direction he wished. He chose the Holy House in Jerusalem in order that the People of the Book would be conciliated. This was his prayer-direction for sixteen months (after his arrival in Medina); all the while, however, he was turning his face towards the heavens until God turned him toward the House [that is, the Ka'ba].

> It is related, on the other hand, on the authority of Ibn Abbas: When the Apostle of God migrated to Medina, most of whose inhabitants were Jews, God commanded him to face Jerusalem, and the Jews were glad. The Prophet faced it for some time beyond ten months, but he loved the prayer-direction of Abraham [that is, the Ka'ba]. Thus he used to pray to God and gaze into the heavens until God sent down (the verse) "We have seen you turning your face toward heaven." (2: 144). The Jews became suspicious and said, "What has turned them away from the direction of prayer toward which they formerly prayed?" Thus God sent down (the verse) "Say, To God belongs the east and the west . . . '." (Tabari, *Tafsir, ad loc.*)

The "Religion of Abraham"

It was during this same critical interval that Muhammad must have began to invoke a powerful new notion, that what the Quran

was propagating was none other than the "religion of Abraham."
The idea occurs in its clearest and most urgent form in the Medina
Sura 2: 124–135,[59] and it begins by hearkening back to the
Covenant and, somewhat less explicitly,[60] to the binding of Isaac:
"Remember that Abraham was tried by his Lord with certain
commands, which he fulfilled. He said: 'I will make you a leader
(*imam*) to the people.' He [that is, Abraham] pleaded: 'And also
(leaders) from my offspring.' He answered: '(Yes), but My
promise is not within the reach of evil-doers'."

There then follows the earlier cited verses (2: 125–127)
describing Abraham and Ishmael's settling at Mecca and building
of the Ka'ba at God's command.

The text then continues with the prayer of the patriarch and
his son:

> Our Lord, make us *muslims* (submitted) to You, and make of
> our offspring a *muslim* people (submitted) to You. And show us
> our places and turn toward us, for You are the Oft-Returning,
> the Merciful.
>
> They say "If you would have the Guidance, become Jews or
> Christians." Say instead, "No! (For me) the religion of Abra-
> ham the *hanif*." (Quran 2: 135)

> Strive truly in His cause. He has chosen you and imposed no dif-
> ficulties on you in religion: it is the religion of Abraham, and it
> is He who named you *muslims*,[61] both earlier and in this (reve-
> lation) . . . (Quran 22: 78)

And in a verse that establishes the continuity of the "religion
of Abraham" through the line of the prophets to his own preaching: "He has established for you the same religion that He
enjoined on Noah—and which We revealed to you—and that He
enjoined on Abraham, Moses and Jesus—namely, that you remain
steadfast in the religion and make no divisions in it . . . " (Quran
42: 13).

CHAPTER 9

Fighting in God's Cause

The Quraysh at Mecca were doubtless well informed on what was happening at Medina, though there was little in the events of 622 or 623 to make them anxious for their own security: Muhammad had come to somewhat uncertain and uneasy terms with the Medinese, though there continued to be tensions between the Meccan Muslim "Migrants" (*muhajjirun*) and the local Medinese believers called *Helpers* (*ansar*).[1] More encouraging, Muhammad was apparently encountering difficulties with the Jews of the oasis. There were, in addition, tensions. At that point the Prophet took the boldest political step in his career, an attack upon Mecca's commerce.

The battle of Badr in 624 A.D. is a turning point in Islamic history, and Muhammad's decision to attack a Meccan caravan there on its way home at first seems to have been abruptly and even impetuously taken. In reality there had been small-scale skirmishing between Muslims from Medina and the Quraysh caravaneers almost from the beginning: raiding parties of twenty to eighty armed and mounted Migrants were sent out by Muhammad, or even on occasion led my him, to harass, and perhaps reconnoiter the acknowledged enemy. The Muslim historians propose no particular motive for these expeditions. They may have been merely an attempt to provoke the Quraysh,[2] but more likely they represented Muhammad's attempt at finding a means of supporting his own people, unconnected newcomers to the Medina oasis who were not agriculturalists by training or inclination and had no capital with which to become traders. Raiding was a quick remedy for poverty, though not perhaps an easy one, as the lack of success of these expeditions testifies. No great damage appears to have been done, in any event, but Muhammad, with power now in his own hands, set his community onto the path of aggressive political violence, a course urged and underlined in the Quran: "Permission is given to those who fight because they have suffered wrong—truly God is most powerful in their aid—and those who have been expelled from their homes in defiance of right, only because they have said 'Our Lord is God'" (Quran 22: 39–40).

And then somewhat later: "Fight in the cause of God, and know that God hears and knows all things" (Quran 2: 244).

VIOLENCE IN THE SACRED MONTH

The first real fighting between the Migrants and the Quraysh took place in December of 623 and provoked a moral crisis. Muhammad had sent out a raiding party of only eight Muslims with sealed orders. The orders commanded them to spy out the Quraysh at Nakhla on the road between Mecca and Ta'if and "find out for us what they are doing."[3] What the Quraysh were doing was transporting, under very light escort, camel-loads of raisins and leather from Ta'if to Mecca. Ibn Ishaq continues the story:

> When the caravan saw them [that is, the Muslims] they were afraid because they had camped nearby. Ukkasha [that is, one of the Migrants], who had shaved his head (like a pilgrim after the *'umra*), looked down on the Quraysh, and when they saw him they felt safe and said: "They are pilgrims; we have nothing to fear from them."
>
> The raiders took counsel among themselves, for this was the last day of Rajab, and they said: "If we leave them alone tonight, they will get into the *haram* and will be safe from us; and if we kill them, we will kill them in a sacred month." So they were hesitant and feared to attack them.

Finally the Muslims decided to attack, holy month or not. Some of the Quraysh were killed and the caravan was taken back to Medina together with two captives. They had set aside a fifth of the booty for the Prophet—this was reportedly the first time this practice, which later became customary, was followed—and divided the rest among themselves, but on their entry into Medina they found a cold reception:

> When they came to the Apostle, he said: "I did not order you to fight in the sacred month," and he held the caravan and the two prisoners in suspense and refused to take anything from them. When the Apostle said that, the men were in despair and thought they were doomed. Their Muslim brethren reproached

them for what they had done, and the Quraysh said, "Muhammad and his companions have violated the sacred month, shed blood therein, taken booty and captured men. . . . The Jews of Medina turned this raid into an ill omen against the Apostle. . . . And when there was much talk about it, God sent down to His Apostle:

"They ask you concerning fighting in the prohibited month. Say: 'Fighting therein is a grave offense; but graver it is in the sight of God to prevent access to the path of God, to deny Him, to prevent access to the sacred shrine and drive out its members. Tumult and oppression are worse than slaughter' . . . " (Quran 2: 217)

. . . And when the Quran came down about that and God relieved the Muslims of their anxiety in the matter, the Apostle took the caravan and the prisoners. (Ibn Ishaq 1955, pp. 287–288)

THE BATTLE AT THE BADR WELLS

This is the background against which a major military operation unfolded in March of 624 A.D. News came to Muhammad that a very large caravan was on its way southward from Palestine to Mecca. Muhammad summoned the Muslims of Medina and said, "This is the Quraysh caravan containing their property. Go out and attack it; perhaps God will give it as prey." The people answered his summons, some eagerly, others reluctantly because "they had not thought that the Messenger would go to war"[4] The Quraysh heard of the intended attack and mobilized their own forces, and thus there came about the first major confrontation between the Muslims and their opponents at Mecca. The fighting began and at first it went badly for the outnumbered Muslims. The Prophet rallied his troops, however, with this promise: "Then the Messenger went forth to the people and incited them saying, 'By God in whose hand is the soul of Muhammad, no man will be slain this day fighting against them (the Quraysh) with steadfast courage, advancing and not retreating, but God will cause him to enter Paradise'" (Ibn Ishaq 1955, p. 300).

The Muslims were in the end victorious, with a great effect on their own and the Quraysh's morale for the rest of the struggle between them.

The Angels of Badr

In a rare historical aside, the Quran itself twice celebrates the event the victory at Badr Wells: "There has already been a sign for you in the clash of the two forces, one fighting in the way of God and the other disbelieving. And they [that is, the latter] saw twice the force before their eyes . . . " (Quran 3: 13).

The allusion here is not entirely clear to us, even though it must have to been to Muhammad's listeners, as the Quran's own gloss on itself reveals some verses later in the same *sura*:

> God had helped you at Badr, when you were a contemptible lit-
> tle band. So fear God and thus show your gratitude. Remember
> when you said to the Believers: "Is it not enough for you that
> your Lord helped you with 3,000 angels sent down? Yes, and if
> you remain firm and aright, even if the enemy should come
> against you here in hot haste, your Lord would help you with
> 5,000 angels on the attack." (Quran 3: 123–125)

The angels that miraculously appeared to swell the Muslims' numbers at Badr were familiar creatures not only to the Muslims but to the Quraysh as well. Though they do not appear in the very earliest revelations, angels, or supernatural creatures we assume to be angels, appear in a variety of roles in the Meccan and Medinese *suras*, as witnesses of both the Creation (2: 30–34) and the Judgment (25: 25), as "watchers" who record human deeds, and as God's messengers, to Abraham (11: 69–73, etc), for example, and to Mary, the mother of Jesus (19: 19). At the time of Badr they were coming more directly to the assistance of Muslims, not only in battle, as has been noted, but to the Prophet himself in an otherwise unspecified family quarrel (61: 3–4).[5]

That the angels were not merely a feature of Islam but were a part of the inherited belief system of the Meccans is revealed in Sura 15, which begins: "These are the signs of the Book,[6] of the manifest Quran."

The Quraysh were unwilling to accept such signs; they required something more traditional and more visibly convincing: "They say: 'You upon whom the Remembrance is sent down, surely you are *jinn*-possessed.! If you speak the truth, why do you not bring the angels to us?'" (Quran 15: 6–7).

"No," God retorts, "the angels are not sent down except in a just cause" (*ibid*. 15: 8), and just such a cause provoked the invisible presence of the angels at Badr. No longer do the angels appear to people in human form, however; in Quranic accounts of the angels after the battle of Badr, their presence is unseen and humans are no longer aware of their operations, a shift signalling not only a new sense of the role of angels but of the relationship between God, angels and men.[7]

"Fasting Is Prescribed for You"

As we have already seen, there was a tradition that Muhammad took up for himself and others the Jewish custom of fasting on "The Tenth" (*ashura*) of the month of Tishri, the day known as *Yom Kippur* or *The Day of Atonement*. It was, as the name itself suggests, a day of penitence, but it marked as well the annually celebrated anniversary of the giving of the Torah to Moses on Sinai. Muhammad discontinued the *Ashura*, or at least made it purely voluntary, and on the apparent testimony of the Quran substituted for it the fast of the full month of Ramadan. And the reason is the same as that which had made the *Ashura* attractive in the first place, a connection with the revelation of the Quran: "Ramadan is the month in which was sent down the Quran as a guide for the people, clear signs of that Guidance and of the Deliverance. So whoever of you is present that month, let him fast it. But whoever is sick or on a journey, than a number of other days . . . " (Quran 2: 185).

The passage in question occurs, however, in a whole series of verses with considerable internal contradictions. They begin thus: "O you who believe, fasting (*siyam*) is prescribed for you,[8] as they were prescribed for those before you. O, may you be God-fearing!"[9] (Quran 2: 183).

"Those before you" naturally excited the interest of the Quranic commentators, as it does our own. Tabari among others thought the reference was to the Christians' Lent, but as we have seen, a far more likely precedent is the Jewish *Ashura* fast, which does not last a month, assuredly, but was not uncommonly extended backward by pious Jews to cover the entire first ten days of the month of Tishri.[10] And this latter provides a clue for the most enigmatic of the fasting verses, which occur immediately after the preceding and serves as an adverbial clause to the initial prescription: "Fasting is prescribed for you . . . (2: 183) . . . for the counted days (2: 184)." What the *counted* or *numbered* days were eludes easy explanation. The Muslim commentators generally took it as an oblique reference—"some days"—but we are confronted from both the Jewish and the pre-Islamic Arab sides with evidence of a ten-day period of fast and abstinence to which the Quran itself seems to allude. "By the dawn!" begins the Meccan Sura 89, followed immediately by another oath: "By the ten nights!"

Further down in the same *sura* the evidence points to the Arab rather than the Jewish practice. In the midst of a long verse (2: 187) explaining that sexual activity is *now* permitted during the nights of the fasting period—"God knows what deceptions you practiced among yourselves and He has forgiven you"—and that the Muslim is permitted to eat and drink after sunset as well, there occurs an explicit exception: "But do not have intercourse while you are in seclusion ('*akifun*) in the shrines (*masajid*). These are limits set to you by God, so do not approach them" (Quran 2: 187).

We have already seen in Chapter 5 that the pre-Islamic practice of the '*ukuf*-retreat, days of prayer, fasting, and abstinence that were probably connected with the *ihram* or taboo periods of the '*umra* of Rajab and the *Hajj* of Dhu al-Hijja, and centered in the first on its holiest day, the "Night of Destiny," and in the second on the "Day of Arafat."[11] It was this period of ten days, it has been suggested,[12] immediately before the "Night of Destiny" in Rajab that constituted the prescribed fast of the "counted days" for the Muslims. It was intended to replace the *Ashura*, and it was quickly replaced in turn with the month-long fast of Ramadan, though it left traces of its brief existence in verses 184 and 187 of Sura 2 of the Quran.[13]

None of this has any apparent connection with Ramadan, and yet the Quran is quite explicit in Sura 2: 185 in prescribing a fast in that month and connecting it with the Quran, there described as a Guidance and what has here been translated as "the Deliverance." The word for the latter is *al-Furqan*, another baffling term for the Muslim commentators, probably because it was another Aramaic-Syriac loan-word in Arabic, whereas the Muslims' unshakable conviction that this was a "clear Arabic Quran" inevitably led them to discover meanings exclusively within the repertoire of Arabic lexicography. The Arabic *faraqa* points to "criterion"; the Judeo-Christian *purqana* to "salvation," "redemption," "deliverance."[14] It occurs elsewhere in the Quran, in two instances as something given to Moses and Aaron with (or as) as a light and a reminder (21: 48), and more specifically, with (or as) the Book given to Moses (2: 53). Elsewhere it is something quite similar "sent down" to Muhammad:

> He has sent down to you the Book with the truth, confirming what went before it, and He sent down the Torah and the Gospel before this as the Guidance for the people and He sent down the *Furqan*. (Quran 3: 3)

> Blessed be He who sent down the *Furqan* upon His servant that he might be to the worlds a warner. (Quran 25: 1)

Most significant, perhaps, are the cluster of references that connect the *Furqan* with the battle of Badr. In one of them the *Furqan* appears in a context where it is being promised to the Muslims before Badr: "O you believers, if you show piety toward God, he will appoint to you to you a *Furqan* and will absolve you from your evil deeds and forgive you" (Quran 8: 29).

And then, in the same *sura*, as something that has been accomplished at the event and on the day of Badr itself, "when the two parties met": " . . . if you have believed in God and what We sent down to Our servant on the day of the *Furqan*, the day when the two parties met" (Quran 8: 41).

The battle of Badr took place in Ramadan, and Sura 2: 185 all the elements are tied together: the date, the revealed Book. "Ramadan is the month in which the Quran was sent down as a guide for the people, clear signs of the Guidance and the *Furqan*. So whoever is wakeful that month, let him fast it . . . " (Quran 2: 185).

This Medinan verse is our first indication that the Quran was revealed in either whole or in part in the month of Ramadan. In Sura 97: 1–5 we had been told that it had been sent down on the "Night of Destiny," apparently a New Year's night with no known connection with Ramadan. The key may lie in the notion of *Furqan*. The day of Badr was indeed a "deliverance," much as the escape from Egypt had been for Moses and his people, and it was at the same time, as it had been for Moses, not the Book itself but a confirmation of the Book. "If you show piety toward God," the Muslims had been told (8: 29) on the eve of Badr, "He will appoint to you a *Furqan*." They had believed and the *Furqan* had been granted, not in the form of the Book, which they had had for some time, but in a stunning victory over the Meccans, and as an equally stunning confirmation of the Book. To mark the event the Muslims are commanded to fast during that now glorious month, a fast that replaced that of the "counted days."[15] Later, perhaps with ban on intercalation, the actual date of the "Night of Destiny" must have been lost, and because of the obscurity or misunderstanding of the word *furqan* (like *hanif*), the Muslims begin to think that the Quran was *revealed*, and not simply *confirmed* in Ramadan.

FROM BADR TO THE BATTLE OF THE TRENCH

After the success at Badr, the issue of the Jews of Medina surfaced once again, or at least as it concerned one tribe of them, the prosperous Banu Qaynuqa', who are accused of breaking a pact with Muhammad, though precisely under what circumstances is not specified.[16] Whatever the provocation, Muhammad and his followers attacked the Banu Qaynuqa' in their fortified positions in Medina and defeated them. The surviving Qaynuqa' were then expelled from the settlement, leaving their property behind, presumably to the benefit of the new "Migrants" from Mecca.

The triumph of Badr was followed early in the next year by a full-scale attack of 3,000 foot soldiers and 200 cavalry mustered by the Quraysh for an assault on Medina, and commemorated in Muslim history as the Battle of Uhud. It ended in a severe setback for the Muslims, which also seems to be mentioned in the Quran: "Recall to them that morning when you left your household early to post the Believers at their stations for battle and how God hears and knows all things. Recall how two of your parties had cowardice in mind but that God was their protector and that the Believers should ever put their trust in God" (Quran 3: 122–123).

Thus once again Muhammad is rehearsing history, specifically Muslim, and so familiar, history, to strengthen the faith of the believers. Ibn Ishaq retells it in a more formal fashion:

> The Muslims were put to flight and the enemy slew many of them. It was a day of trial and testing in which God honored several with martyrdom, until the enemy got at the Messenger who was struck with a stone so that he fell on his side and one of his teeth was smashed, his face gashed and his lip injured. The man who wounded him was Utba ibn Abi Waqqas . . .
>
> According to what Salih ibn Kaysan told me, Hind, the daughter of Utba and the women with her stopped to mutilate the Apostle's dead companions. They cut off their ears and noses and Hind made them into anklets and collars. . . . She cut out Hamza's liver and chewed it, but she was not able to swallow it and threw it away. Then she mounted a high rock and shrieked at the top of her voice:

"We have paid you back for Badr,
And a war that follows a war is always violent.
I could not bear the loss of Utba
Nor my brother and his uncle and my first-born.
I have slaked my vengeance and fulfilled my vow . . . "

When (the Quraysh leader) Abu Sufyan wanted to leave, he went to the top of the mountain and shouted loudly, saying, "You have done a fine work. Victory in war goes by turns: today is in exchange for the day of Badr. Show your superiority, Hubal," that is, vindicate your religion. The Messenger told Umar to go up and answer him and say, "God is most high and most glorious. We are not equal: our dead are in paradise, yours are in hell." At this answer Abu Sufyan said to Umar, "Come up here to me." The Messenger told him to go and see what Abu Sufyan was up to. When he came Abu Sufyan said, "I adjure you by God, Umar, have we killed Muhammad?" "By God, you have not, he is listening to what you are saying right now," Umar replied. Abu Sufyan said, "I regard you as more truthful and reliable than Ibn Qami'a," referring to the latter's claim that he had killed Muhammad. (Ibn Ishaq 1955, pp. 380–386)

Just as in the sequel of Badr Muhammad turned to the Jewish tribe of the Qaynuqa', so the direct or indirect consequence of Uhud was the expulsion of a second Jewish tribe from the Medina association, the Banu al-Nadir. In this case the provocation was the report of a threat by members of the Banu al-Nadir against the Prophet's life.[17] The response was prompt and direct, an assault on their redoubts in the Medina oasis.

The Jews took refuge in their forts and the Messenger ordered the palm-trees should be cut down and burnt. And they [that is, the Banu al-Nadir] called out to him, "O Muhammad, you have prohibited wanton destruction and blamed those guilty of it. Why then are you cutting down and burning our palm-trees?" Now there were a number of the (Arab tribe of the) Banu Awf ibn al-Khazraj . . . who had sent to the Banu al-Nadir saying, "Stand firm and protect yourselves, for we will not betray you. If you are attacked we will fight with you and if you are turned out we will go with you." Accordingly they waited for the help they had promised, but they [the Banu Awf] did nothing and God cast terror into their hearts. The Banu al-Nadir then asked the Messenger to deport them and to spare their lives on condition that they could retain all their property which they could carry on camels, armor excepted, and he agreed. So they loaded their camels with what they could carry. Men were destroying

their houses down to the lintel of the door, which they put on
the back of their camels and went off with it. Some went to
Khaybar and others went to Syria . . .

If this was the end of the Banu al-Nadir in Medina, it went
bravely:

> Abdullah ibn Abi Bakr told me that he was told that the Banu
> al-Nadir carried off their women and children and property
> with tambourines and pipes and singing girls playing behind
> them. . . . They went with such pomp and splendor as had never
> been seen in any tribe in their days. They left their property to
> the Messenger and it became his personal possession to dispose
> of as he wished. He divided it among the first emigrants (from
> Mecca to Medina), to the exclusion of the "Helpers" . . . (Ibn
> Ishaq 1955, pp. 437–438)

It was at this point in Muhammad's career that occurred the
first of the raids against Dumat al-Jandal, the present day oasis of
al-Jawf. The Muslim geographers measured Dumat at ten
marches from Kufa, ten from Damascus and thirteen marches
from Medina.[18] Though distant from the Muslim base, the oasis
was well known to the Arabs because tradition recorded that it
too was the site of an annual fair and was protected by the same
guarantees of security as the other marts.[19] Ibn Ishaq passes over
the Duma expedition of 626 with the briefest of mentions, but
others supply additional details. The raid, if such it was, took
place in the month of First Rabi' of the fifth year of the Hijra, and
the Prophet remained there for about a month.[20] Indeed, the entire
affair has about it the air of a reconnaissance in force—there were
a thousand Muslims, a considerable force, but hardly enough to
take a fortified oasis—or of an opportunistic foray that had found
no opportunity along the caravan routes and had simply came to
rest at Dumat al-Jandal.[21]

The abortive expedition to Dumat al-Jandal, which produced
neither booty nor even a sense of success, was Muhammad's only
political act during a stretch of nearly eighteen months in
625–627 A.D. The long period of quietude, and the absence of any
tangible profits from what had at first appeared an enormously
successful enterprise, may have emboldened the opposition once
again to attempt to unseat the Prophet. The lead was taken in
March 627 by some of the Banu al-Nadir who had gone into exile
at Khaybar:

A number of Jews who had formed a party against the Apostle . . .
went to the Quraysh at Mecca and invited them to join them in an
attack upon the Messenger so they could get rid of him together.
The Quraysh said, "You, O Jews, are the first people of Scripture
and know the nature of our dispute with Muhammad. Is our religion the best or is his?" They replied that certainly the Quraysh's
religion was better than Muhammad's and had a better claim to
be in the right. And it was in this connection that God sent down
[the verses of the Quran]: "Have you not considered those to
whom a part of Scripture was given and yet believe in idols and
false deities and say to those who disbelieve, these are more
rightly guided than those who believe? . . . We gave the family of
Abraham the Scripture and the wisdom and we gave them a great
kingdom and some of them who believed in it and some of them
turned from it, and hell is sufficient for (their) burning." (Quran
4: 51–54)

These words (of the Jews) rejoiced the Quraysh and they
responded gladly to their invitation to fight the Apostle, and
they assembled and made their preparations. Then that company of Jews went off to Ghatafan of Qays Aylan and invited
them to fight the Messenger and told them that they would act
in concert with them and that the Quraysh had followed their
lead in the matter; so they to joined in with them . . .

When the Messenger heard of their intention he drew a
trench around Medina and worked at it himself, encouraging
the Muslims with hope of reward in heaven. The Muslims
worked very hard with him, but the disaffected held back and
began to hide their real object by working slackly and stealing
away to their families without the Apostle's permission or
knowledge . . .

When the Messenger had finished the trench, the Quraysh
came and encamped where the torrent beds of Ruma meet
between al-Juruf and Zughaba with 10,000 of their black mercenaries and their followers from the Banu Kinana and the people of Tihama. Ghatafan too came with their followers from
Najd and halted at Dhanab Naqma towards the direction of
Uhud. The Messenger and the Muslims come out with 3,000
men having Sal' at their backs. He pitched his camp there with
the trench between him and his foes, and he gave orders for the
women and children to be taken up to the forts (of the oasis) . . .

The situation became serious and fear was everywhere. The
enemy came at them from above and below until the believers
imagined vain things and disaffection was rife among the disaffected, to the point that Mu'attib ibn Qushayr said, "Muham-

mad used to promise that we would eat the treasures of Khusraw and Caesar and today not one of us can feel safe going to
the privy!" It reached such a point that Aws ibn al-Qayzi, one of
the Banu Haritha ibn al-Harith, said to the people, "Our houses
are exposed to the enemy"—this he said before a large gather-
ing of his people—"so let us go out and return to our home, for
it is outside Medina." The Messenger and the polytheists
remained (facing each other) twenty days and more, nearly a
month, without fighting except for some shooting with arrows,
and the siege. (Ibn Ishaq 1955, pp. 450–454)

Muhammad and his followers were dispirited, but the morale
in the camp of the Quraysh was at an even lower pitch. Soon the
alliance began to disintegrate, and in the end the siege was broken
off and the attackers returned to their homes. If it was a victory
for the Muslims, it was an attenuated one.[22]

THE BANU QURAYZA

According to the Muslim tradition, the Banu Qurayza, the last
major surviving Jewish presence in Medina, had bound themselves by treaty not to assist the enemies of the Prophet. Which is
precisely what the Qurayza had done, it was alleged, at the instigation of Huyayy ibn Akhtab, the leader of the banished Banu al-
Nadir. But there was little need for political reasons for what followed; the motivation is said to have come from on high:

> According to what al-Zuhri told me, at the time of the noon
> prayers Gabriel came to the Messenger wearing an embroidered
> turban and riding on a mule with a saddle covered with a piece
> of brocade. He asked the Messenger if he had abandoned fight-
> ing, and when he said he had, Gabriel said that the angels had
> not yet laid aside their arms and that he had just come from pur-
> suing the enemy. "God commands you, Muhammad, to go to
> the Banu Qurayza. I am about to go to them and shake their
> stronghold . . . "
> The Messenger besieged them for twenty-five nights until
> they were sore pressed and God cast terror into their hearts. . . .
> And when they felt sure that the Messenger would not leave
> them until he had made an end to them, (their leader) Ka'b ibn
> Asad said to them: "O Jews, you can see what has happened to
> you. I offer you three alternatives. Take which you please. We
> will follow this man and accept him as true, for by God it is
> plain to you that he is a prophet who has been sent and that it is

he that you find mentioned in your Scripture; and then your lives, your property, your women and children will be saved." They said, "We will never abandon the laws of the Torah and never change it for another." He said, "Then if you won't accept this suggestion, let us kill our wives and children and send men with their swords drawn against Muhammad and his companions, leaving no encumbrances behind us, and let God decide between us and Muhammad. If we perish, we perish, and we shall not leave children behind us to cause anxiety. If we conquer, we can acquire other wives and children." They said, "Should we kill those poor creatures? What would be the good of life when they were dead?" He said, "Then if you will not accept this suggestion, tonight is the eve of the Sabbath and it may well be that Muhammad and his companions will feel secure from us, so come down and perhaps we can take Muhammad and his companions by surprise." They said, "Are we to profane our Sabbath and do on the Sabbath what those before us of whom you well know did and were turned into apes?" He answered, "Not a single man among you from the day of your birth has ever passed a night resolved to do what he knows ought to be done."

Then the Banu Qurayza sent to the Messenger saying, "Send us Abu Lubaba [of the Banu Aws]—for they were allies of the Aws—"that we may consult him." So the Messenger sent him to them, and when they saw him they got up to meet him. The women and children went up to him weeping in his face, and he felt pity for them. They said, "O Abu Lubaba, do you think we should submit to Muhammad's judgment?" He said "Yes," but pointed his hand to his throat, signifying slaughter. Abu Lubaba (later) said, "My feet had not moved from the spot before I knew that I had been false to God and His Apostle." Then he left them and did not go to the Messenger but bound himself to one of the pillars in the mosque saying, "I will not leave this place until God forgives me for what I have done," and he promised that he would never go to the Banu Qurayza and would never be seen in a town in which he had betrayed God and His Apostle . . . (Ibn Ishaq 1955, pp. 461–462)

When the Aws, the former patrons of the Banu Qurayza somewhat hesitantly asked for leniency—they recalled what had happened in the case of the other Jewish clients at Medina— Muhammad asked them if they would be content if one of their own number passed judgment on the Banu Qurayza. They said they would. A certain Sa'd ibn Mu'adh was chosen.

Sa'd said: "I give judgment that the men should be killed, the
X property divided, and the women and children taken as captives . . . "

Then the Banu Qurayza surrendered themselves and the
Messenger confined them in the compound of Bint al-Harith, a
woman of the Banu al-Najjar. Then the Messenger went out to
the market of Medina—which is still the market today—and
dug trenches in it. Then he sent for them and struck off their
heads in those trenches as they were brought out to him in
batches. Among them was the enemy of God Huyayy ibn Aktab
and Ka'b ibn Asas their chief. There were 600 or 700 in all,
though some put the figure as high as 800 or 900. as they were
being taken out in batches to the Apostle, they asked Ka'b what
he thought would be done to them. He replied, "Will you never
understand? Don't you see that the summoner never stops and
Y those who are taken away never return? By God, it is death!"
This went on until the Messenger made an end to them . . . (Ibn
Ishaq 1955, p. 464)

The penalty was a harsh one, and perhaps even somewhat surprising in the light of Muhammad's earlier treatment of the Jews
of Medina, but the later Muslim jurists took their cue from Sura 8
of the Quran, which they took to refer to this case:

The worst of beasts in the sight of God are those who reject
Him: they will not believe. They are those with whom you made
a pact, then they break their compact every time and they fear
not God. So if you come up against them in war, drive off
through them their followers, that they may remember. And if
you fear treachery from any group, dissolve it [that is, the pact]
with them equally, for God does not love the treacherous.
(Quran 8: 55–58)

This is precisely what happened, the Muslims jurists argued:
A the Banu Qurayza had broken their treaty with the Prophet by
assisting the Azhab at the Battle of the Trench and so Muhammad
was justified in dissolving the pact and declaring a state of war
against the Qurayza.[23]

A NEW TACTIC

Muhammad's political career seems to follow no predictable
course of action. The violent purge of the Banu Qurayza was fol-

lowed by a surprising announcement: the Prophet intended to
return to Mecca, not as an attacker but as a pacific pilgrim intending only to make the '*umra*:24

> The Messenger stayed in Medina during the months of
> Ramadan and Shawwal [in 628 A.D.] and then went out on the
> '*umra* (or lesser pilgrimage) in Dhu al-Qa'da with no intention
> of making war. He called together the Arabs and the neighbor-
> ing bedouin to march with him, fearing that the Quraysh (in
> Mecca) would oppose him with arms or prevent his visiting the
> shrine, as they actually did. Many of the Arabs held back from
> him, and he went out with the Migrants and the Helpers and
> such of the Arabs as stuck to him. He took the sacrificial victims
> with him and donned the pilgrim garb so that all would know
> that he did not intend war and that his purpose was to visit the
> shrine and venerate it . . .
>
> In his tradition al-Zuhri said: When the Messenger had
> rested (at Hudaybiyya near Mecca), Budayl ibn Warqa al-
> Khuza'i came to him with some men of the Khuza'a and asked
> him what he had come for. He told them he had not come for
> war but to go on pilgrimage and visit the sacred precincts. . . .
> Then returned to the Quraysh and told them what they had
> heard; but the Quraysh suspected them and spoke roughly to
> them, "He may not come out wanting war, but by God, he will
> never come in here against our will nor will the Arabs ever see
> that we allowed it." The Khuza'a were in fact the Apostle's con-
> fidants, both the Muslims and the non-Muslims among them,
> and they kept him informed of everything that went on in
> Mecca . . .
>
> . . . Then they (the Quraysh of Mecca) sent Urwa ibn
> Mas'ud al-Thaqafi to the Apostle. . . . He came to the Messen-
> ger and sat before him and said: "Muhammad, you have col-
> lected a mixed people together and then brought them against
> your own people to destroy them? By God, I think I see you
> deserted by these people here tomorrow." Now Abu Bakr was
> sitting behind the Messenger and he said, "Go suck al-Lat's tits!
> Should we desert him?" . . . Then Urwa began to take hold of
> the Apostle's beard as he talked to him. Al-Mughira ibn Shu'ba
> was standing by the Apostle's head clad in mail and he began to
> hit Urwa's hand as he held the Apostle's beard saying, "Take
> your hand away from the Apostle's face before you lose it!"
> Urwa said, "Confound you, how rough and rude you are!" The
> Messenger smiled and when Urwa asked who the man was he
> told him that it was his brother's son Urwa ibn Shu'ba, and

Urwa said, "You wretch, it was only yesterday that I was wiping your behind!"

The Messenger told him what he told the others, namely that he had not come out for war. Urwa then got up from the Apostle's presence, having noted how his companions treated him. Whenever he performed his ablutions, they ran to get the water he used; if he spat, they ran to it; if a hair of his head fell out, they ran to pick it up. So he returned to the Quraysh and said, "I have seen Khusraw in his kingdom and Caesar in his kingdom and the Negus in his kingdom, but never have I seen a king among a people like Muhammad is among his companions."

Muhammad decided to try a more direct approach, to send one of his own followers into Mecca to convince the Quraysh of his peaceful intentions. The one chosen was Uthman, the future third caliph of Islam (r. 644–656 A.D.), and a man well connected in Mecca.

As Uthman entered or was about to enter Mecca, Aban ibn Sa'id met him and carried him in front of him (on his mount) and gave him protection until he could convey the Apostle's message to them. Having heard what Uthman had to say, the Quraysh said: "If you wish to circumambulate the shrine, then go ahead." He for his part said he would not until Muhammad did so, and so the Quraysh kept him prisoner with them. The Messenger and the Muslims were informed, however, that Uthman had been killed.

Abdullah ibn Abi Bakr told me that when the Messenger heard that Uthman had been killed, he said that he would not leave until they fought the enemy, and he summoned the men to pledge themselves to this. The pledge of al-Ridwan took place under a tree. Men used to say that Muhammad took their pledge unto death, but Jabir ibn Abdullah said that it was not a pledge unto death but an undertaking not to run away. . . . Then the Messenger heard that the news about Uthman was false. (Ibn Ishaq 1955, pp. 499–504)

Whatever gave rise to the rumors of foul-play, Uthman's mission was a success:

Then the Quraysh sent Suhayl ibn Amr to the Messenger with instructions to make peace with him on condition that he returned (to Medina) this year so that none of the Arabs could say that he had made a forcible entry. . . . After a long discussion peace was made and nothing remained but to write the document. Umar leaped up and went to Abu Bakr saying, "Is he not God's Messenger and are we not Muslims, and are not they polytheists?" to which Abu Bakr agreed, and he went on, "Then why should we agree to what is demeaning to our religion?" Abu Bakr replied, "Follow what he says, for I bear witness that he is God's Apostle." Umar said, "And so do I." Then he went to the Messenger and put the same questions, to which the Messenger answered, "I am God's slave and His Apostle. I will not go against His commandment and He will not make me a loser." Umar used to say (afterwards), "I have not ceased giving alms and fasting and praying and freeing slaves because of what I did that day and for fear of what I had said, when I hoped that (my plan) would be better."

Then the Messenger summoned Ali and told him to write, "In the name of God, the Compassionate, the Merciful." Suhayl said, "I do not recognize this; write rather, 'In thy name, O God.'" The Messenger told Ali to write the latter and he did so. Then he said, "Write, This is what Muhammad, Messenger of God, has agreed with Suhayl ibn Amr." Suhayl said, "If I confessed that you were God's Messenger I would not have fought you. Write your own name and the name of your father." The Messenger said, "Write, this is what Muhammad ibn Abdullah has agreed with Suhayl ibn Amr: they have agreed to lay aside war for ten years during which men can be safe and refrain from hostilities on condition that if anyone comes to Muhammad without the permission of his guardian he will return him to them; and if anyone of those with Muhammad returns to the Quraysh they will not return him to him. We will not show enmity one to another and there shall be no secret reservation or bad faith. He who wishes to enter into a bond or agreement with Muhammad may do so and whoever wishes to enter into a bond or agreement with the Quraysh may do so." ...

When the Messenger had finished the document he summoned representatives of the Muslims and the polytheists to witness the peace.... The Apostle was encamped in the profane territory, and he used to pray in the sacred area. When the peace was concluded he slaughtered his victims and sat down and shaved his head. ... When the men saw what the Messenger had done, they leapt up and did the same ...

It was an odd business, this coming to terms with the "unbelievers," and on transparently unfavorable terms,[25] but Ibn Ishaq tried to put the best face on it:

No previous victory in Islam was greater than this. There was nothing but battle when men met; but when there was an armistice and war was abolished and men met in safety and held discussion, none talked about Islam intelligently without entering it. In those two years double or more than double as many entered Islam as ever before. (Ibn Ishaq 1955, pp. 504–507)

The Quran too confirmed that this was a triumph, at least in the minds of those later believers who read this verse of the *sura* called "Victory" as referring to the truce of Hudaybiyya: "In truth We have given you a manifest victory that God may forgive you your past sin and the sin to come, and may complete His favor upon you and guide you on the straight way" (Quran 48: 1–2).

THE NORTHERN OASES

After the arrangement at Hudaybiyya, Muhammad returned to Medina and waited there until the expiration of the sacred months in the early summer of 628. Then with the Quraysh bound by the terms of Hudaybiyya to refrain from any hostility against the Muslims of Medina, Muhammad was free to turn elsewhere without fear of interference or reprisal.[26] His target in the summer of 627 were the oases to the north of Medina, and most particularly the Jewish settlement at Khaybar about 100 miles to the north. We have already seen some of the theories to account for a Jewish presence in the Hijaz, how after the fall of Jerusalem to the Babylonians some of the Israelite tribes migrated south into Arabia and settled at Medina and, among other places, the oasis at Khaybar.[27]

When the Muslims' attack fell upon the oasis, the resistance at Khaybar was determined but unavailing, and the terms of the capitulation were not lost on the occupants of Fadak, another nearby oasis:

The Messenger besieged the people of Khaybar in their two forts al-Watih and al-Salalim until when they could hold out no longer he asked them to let them go and spare their lives, and he did so. Now the Messenger had already taken possession of all their property . . . except what belonged to these two forts. When the people of Fadak heard of what had happened they sent to the Messenger asking them to let them go (as well) and to spare their lives and they would leave him their property, and he did so. . . . When the people of Khaybar surrendered on these conditions they asked the Messenger to employ them on the property, with a half share of (future) produce saying, "We know more about it than you and are better farmers." The Messenger agreed to this arrangement on the condition that "if we wish to expel you, we will expel you." He made a similar arrangement with the men of Fadak, except that Khaybar became war spoils for all the Muslims, while Fadak was the personal property of the Messenger because they had not attacked it with horses and camels. (Ibn Ishaq 1955, pp. 515–516)

And it was after Khaybar, we are told, that another contingent of emigrants to Abyssinia, sixteen males and their wives and children, returned and rejoined the community of Muslims.[28]

THE 'UMRA FULFILLED

The point of Hudaybiyya was not forgotten, however, in the successful flush of Khaybar:

When the Messenger returned from Khaybar to Medina he stayed there from the first Rabi' until Shawwal, sending out raiding parties and expeditions. Then in Dhu al-Qa'da—the month in which the polytheists had prevented him from making the pilgrimage (in the preceding year)—he went out to make the "fulfilled pilgrimage" in place of the 'umra from which they had excluded him. Those Muslims who had been excluded with him went out in A.H. 7 [February 629 A.D.], and when the Meccans heard it, they got out of his way. The Quraysh said among themselves, "Muhammad and his companions are in destitution, want and privation."

A man I have no reason to suspect told me that Ibn Abbas said: "They gathered at the door of the *Dar al-Nadwa* to look at him and his companions, and when the Prophet entered the sanctuary he threw the end of his cloak over his left shoulder leaving his right upper arm free. Then he said, 'God have mercy on a man who shows them today that he is strong.' Then he embraced and kissed the stone and went on trotting, as did his companions, until the point where the temple concealed him from them and he had embraced and had kissed the southern corner he walked to kiss the Black Stone. Then he trotted in the same fashion for three circuits and walked the rest."

If the somewhat tortured manner of expressing the ritual actually performed by the Prophet on this occasion suggests that other considerations were later steering the passage, Ibn Ishaq immediately confirms the suspicion: early on, likely in the generation after

Muhammad, there had been a debate about the ritual of circum-ambulation, or perhaps only the "embracing and kissing" (*ista-lama*) part of it. "Ibn Abbas used to say 'People used to think that this practice was not incumbent on them because the Prophet only did it for this clan of the Quraysh because of what he had heard about them until the farewell pilgrimage, when he adhered to it and the *sunna* carried it on'" (Ibn Ishaq 1955, pp. 530–531).

The issue of the ritual of a Muslim *Hajj* was determined, then, at least according to Ibn Abbas's report, by Muhammad's "cus-tomary practice" (*sunna*), here defined by his ritual acts during the famous "farewell pilgrimage" that, as we shall see, the Prophet led in person in March of 632 A.D.

Circumambulation was not the only legal problem connected with the *'umra* of February 629. There is strong evidence that Muhammad offered the customary animal sacrifices on this occa-sion,[29] and more, he took another wife, an act that was, according to one report, consummated while the Prophet was in a state of *ihram* or ritual purity, when normally all sexual acts were forbid-den.[30] Ibn Ishaq allows the reader to have it both ways:

> . . . The Messenger married Maymuna daughter of al-Harith on that journey when he was in a state *ihram*. [His uncle] al-Abbas ibn Abd al-Muttalib gave her to him in marriage [and probably became a Muslim at the same time.] The Messenger remained three days in Mecca. Huwaytib ibn Abd al-Uzza with a few Quraysh came to him on the third day because the Quraysh had entrusted him with the duty of sending the Messenger out of Mecca. They said, "Your time is up, so get out from among us." The Messenger answered, "How would it harm you if you were to let me stay and I gave a wedding feast among you and pre-pared food and you came too?" They replied, "We don't need your food, so get out." So the Messenger went out and left Abu Rafi' his client in charge of Maymuna until he brought her to him in Sarif . . . (Ibn Ishaq 1955, p. 531)

A DARING RAID INTO SYRIA

After the *'umra* of February 629 Muhammad returned to Medina where the remained quietly throughout the next five or six months. Then in September of that year he attempted a military move more ambitious and provocative than anything he had done since Badr, a raid deep into Byzantine territory in Syria.

Muhammad ibn Ja'far ibn al-Zubayr from Urwa ibn al-Zubayr said: The Messenger sent his expedition to Mu'ta in (the month of) First Jumada in the year 8 [September, 629 A.D.] and put Zayd ibn Haritha in command; if Zayd were slain, then Ja'far ibn Abi Talib was to take command, and if he were killed then [the Helper] Abdullah ibn Rawaha. The expedition got ready to the number of 3,000 and prepared to start. . . . They went on their way as far as Ma'an in Syria, where they heard that Heraclius had come down to Ma'ab in the Balqa with 100,000 Greeks [that is, Byzantine troops] joined by 100,000 men from the Banu Lakhm and Judham and al-Qayn and Bahra' and Bali commanded by a man of Bali of Irasha called Malik ibn Zafila . . . (Ibn Ishaq 1955, p. 532)

The Muslims were clearly caught unawares—they had not expected opposition—and were uncertain what to do. In the end they had to face the Byzantines, however, and with disastrous results:

The people went forward until, when they were on the borders of the Balqa', the Greek and Arab forces of Heraclius met them in a village called Masharif. When the enemy approached, the Muslims withdrew to a village called Mu'ta. . . . When fighting began Zayd ibn Haritha fought holding the Messenger's standard, until he died from a loss of blood among the spears of the enemy. Then Ja'far took it and fought with it. When the battle hemmed him in he jumped off his roan and hamstrung her and fought until he was killed . . . (Ibn Ishaq 1955, p. 534)

There are a great many uncertainties in this sketchy report of a raid to the vicinity of a distant village in what is today Jordan. The numbers are obviously exaggerated—Ibn Ishaq, who reports them, finally tallies the Muslim dead at eight—and there are no grounds for thinking the Byzantine emperor Heraclius was anywhere in the vicinity. But it was noted in Byzantium in some fashion; the raid to Mu'ta was, at any rate, the first event in the history of Muhammad and his community to be reported in an outside source, in this case, the Byzantine historian Theophanes (d. 818):[31]

Muhammad was already dead,[32] but he appointed four amirs to wage war on the Christian Arabs. The Muslims marched against a town called Moucheon, in which Theodore the Vicar was stationed, and wished to attack the Arabs on the day on which they were to sacrifice to their idols;[33] when he learned this from a member of the Quraysh tribe who was in his

employ, Theodore collected all the soldiers of the desert gar-
risons, and since he knew the day on which the Muslim forces
intended to attack, he anticipated them in a place called Moth-
ous, where his forces killed three of their amirs and most of
their army; one of their amirs, Khalid, whom they called "the
sword of God," escaped. (Theophanes, *Chronography, sub
anno* 6133)

Though we are not entirely certain how to connect the two
events, the account of Theophanes then passes directly to another
piece of information, and one that, in the sequel might have been
far more important than the abortive Muslim raid on Mu'ta:

There were some of the nearby Arabs who received small
money allowances from the emperors for guarding the "gateways" of the desert. . . . A certain eunuch came to give their
allowance to the soldiers, and the Arabs arrived to collect their
stipend as usual. The eunuch drove them away, saying that the
ruler had scarcely enough pay for his soldiers, much less his
dogs. Offended, the Arabs went to their fellow tribesmen and
led them to the very rich region of Gaza, it being a "gateway" of
the desert extending toward Sinai. (Theophanes, *Chronography, sub anno* 6123)

The place is obviously Sinai and the Negev, and it was here,
and perhaps elsewhere along the southeastern steppe frontier of
the empire, Heraclius chose to discontinue the stipend he had been
paying his Arab allies to guard the "gateways" (*stomia*), the passes,
and natural corridors whereby the bedouin passed between the
desert and the sown. And the consequences were clear, at least to
Theophanes, the destructive attack on Gaza that occurred when
the empire's former allies led their "fellow tribesmen" through the
"gateway" they had formerly been paid to protect against just such
raids.

Another Byzantine historian, Nicephorus, also knew of
Sergius's defeat and drew the same conclusion: the Byzantine com-
mander had himself brought on the disaster. " . . . he induced Heraclius not to accede to sending the Saracens their customary
allowance of thirty pounds of gold in commercial exchange [that
is, in the form of commodities worth thirty pounds of gold] from
the Roman government; henceforward they began to inflict out-
rages on Roman territory" (Nicephorus, *Opuscula historica* p. 23)

The Muslims in Medina in September of 629 knew nothing of

this, of course. The raid to Mu'ta, or whatever was its goal, was not only a community failure; it was a personal tragedy in which he lost his freedman and close personal friend Zayd ibn Haritha.

CHAPTER 10

"The Truth Has Come and Falsehood Has Passed Away"

The breaking of the armistice concluded between Muhammad and the Quraysh of Mecca at Hudaybiyya in 628 A.D. came about not through the principals themselves but because of an altercation between two of their bedouin allies. The violation might have been settled in other ways—the Quraysh appeared willing to negotiate—but in January 630 A.D. Muhammad judged the occasion fit and the time appropriate for settling accounts with the polytheists of Mecca for once and for all.

> The Messenger ordered preparations to be made for a foray and Abu Bakr came in to see his daughter (and Muhammad's wife) Aisha as she was moving some of the Apostle's gear. He asked her if the Messenger had ordered her to get things ready and she said he had and that her father had better get ready too. She told him that she did not know where the troops were going, however. Later the Messenger informed the men that he was going to Mecca and ordered them to make preparations. He said, "O God, take their eyes and ears from the Quraysh that we may take them by surprise in their land," and the men got themselves ready. (Ibn Ishaq 1955, p. 544)

THE FALL OF MECCA

The surprise prayed for by Muhammad was granted him, along with other good fortune—Abu Sufyan, the Quraysh leader, was captured by chance before the Muslims reached Mecca and persuaded, despite continuing doubts, to save himself and embrace Islam—and the Meccans' will to resist was at a low ebb. "The Messenger had instructed his commanders when they entered Mecca only to fight those who resisted them, except for a small number who were to be killed even if they were found beneath the curtains of the Ka'ba itself . . . "

235

According to other traditions there may have been only four such casualties. Ibn Ishaq continues:

> The Messenger after arriving in Mecca, once the populace had settled down, went to the shrine and went round it seven times on his camel, touching the Black Stone with a stick which he had in his hand. This done, he summoned Uthman ibn Talha and took the keys of the Ka'ba from him, and when the door was opened for him, he went in. There he found a dove made of wood. He broke it in his hands and threw it away. . . . [According to another account] the Messenger entered Mecca on the day of the conquest and it contained 360 idols which Iblis (or Satan) had strengthened with lead. The Messenger was standing by them with a stick in his hand saying, "The truth has come and falsehood has passed away." (Quran 17: 81) Then he pointed at them with his stick and they collapsed on their backs one after another.

Though the following material is also found in the preserved version of Ibn Ishaq, the material appears not to have come from him or his sources but to have been added by his later editor, Ibn Hisham (d. 833):[1]

> When the Messenger had prayed the noon prayer on the day of the conquest (of Mecca), he ordered that all the idols which were around the Ka'ba should be collected and burned with fire and broken up. . . . The Quraysh had put pictures in the Ka'ba including two of Jesus son of Mary and Mary, on both of whom be peace. Ibn Shihab said: Asma' the daughter of Shaqr said that a woman of the Banu Ghassan had joined in the pilgrimage of the Arabs and when she saw a picture of Mary in the Ka'ba she said: "My father and my mother be your ransom! (Mary), you are surely an Arab woman!" The Messenger ordered that the pictures be erased, except those of Jesus and Mary.[2]
>   A traditionist told me that the Messenger stood at the door of the Ka'ba and said: "There is no god but God alone; He has no associates. He has made good His promise and helped His servant. He alone has put to flight the confederates. Every claim of privilege or blood or property are abolished by me except the custody of the shrine and the watering of the pilgrims. . . . O Quraysh, God has taken from you the haughtiness of paganism and its veneration of ancestors. Man springs from Adam and Adam from dust." Then he recited them this verse: "O men, we created you male and female and made you into peoples and tribes that you may know one another; in truth, the most noble

of you in God's sight is the most pious . . . " to the end of the passage. (Quran 49: 13). Then he added, "O Quraysh, what do you think I am about to do to you?" They replied, "Good, for you are a noble brother, son of a noble brother." He said, "Go your way; you are freed." (Ibn Ishaq 1955, pp. 550–553)

THE SMASHING OF THE IDOLS

The cleansing of the Meccan Haram was only part of a general campaign to destroy the idols of Arabian paganism, and the operation began almost immediately after the fall of Mecca. The first to go was the powerful al-Uzza, and her potency in Quraysh eyes may explain the oddly tentative quality in Ibn al-Kalbi's account of her destruction:

Al-Uzza was a she-devil which used to frequent three trees in the valley of Nakhla. When the Prophet captured Mecca he despatched Khalid ibn al-Walid saying, "go to the valley of Nakhla; there you will find three trees. Cut down the first one." Khalid went and cut it down. On his return to report, the Prophet asked him, "Have you seen anything there?" Khalid replied, "No." The Prophet ordered him to return and cut down the second tree. He went and cut it down. On his return to report the Prophet asked him a second time, "Have you seen anything there?" Khalid replied, "No." Thereupon the Prophet ordered him to return and cut down the third tree. When Khalid arrived on the scene he found an Abyssinian woman with dishevelled hair and her hands placed on her shoulders, gnashing and grating her teeth. Behind her stood Dubayya al-Sulami who was then the warden of al-Uzza. . . . Turning to the woman Khalid dealt her a blow which severed her head in two, and behold, she crumbled into ashes. He then cut down the tree and killed Dubayya the warden, after which he returned to the Prophet and reported to him his exploit. Thereupon the Prophet said, "That was al-Uzza. But she is no more. The Arabs shall have none after her. Verily she shall never be worshipped again." (Ibn al-Kalbi, *Book of Idols*, pp. 25–26 = Ibn al-Kalbi 1952, pp. 21–22)

Manat too came to a violent end,[3] but al-Lat appears to have posed a more serious political problem. The Thaqif from around Ta'if possessed what Ibn Ishaq described as "the proud spirit of opposition." They were willing to "make their submission and accept Islam on the Apostle's conditions provided they could get a document guaranteeing their land and their people and their animals." They got their document, but that was by no means the end of the matter. The text from Ibn Ishaq's *Life* continues:

> Among the things they asked the Messenger was that they should be allowed to retain their idol al-Lat undestroyed for three years. The Messenger refused and they continued to ask him for a year or two (grace), and he refused. Finally they asked for a month (dispensation) after their return home, but he refused to agree to any set time. All that they wanted, as they were trying to show, was to be safe from their fanatics and women and children by leaving al-Lat, and they did not want to frighten their people by destroying her until they had (all) accepted Islam. The Messenger refused this, but he sent Abu Sufyan and al-Mughira to destroy her (for them). They also asked him that he would excuse them from prayer and that they would not have to break the idol with their own hands. The Messenger said: "We excuse you from breaking your idols with your own hands, but as for prayer, there is no good in a religion which has no prayers." They said that they would perform them, though they were demeaning. (Ibn Ishaq 1955, pp. 613–614)

Other authors supply additional details. When Muhammad sent Abu Sufyan ibn Harb and Mughira ibn Shu'ba to destroy the idol, the former remained on his own property in Ta'if, where the sounds of Mughira's sledge-hammer caused him bitter regrets over the destruction; the latter went to the task despite the opposition of his family who feared for his life. The women of the Thaqif came out to watch the work unveiled and grieving. When Mughira finished the destruction, he took possession of the treasure of the sanctuary, which consisted of jewels, gold and onyx.[4]

HUNAYN, TA'IF AND THE *'UMRA*

The "opening" of Mecca appears by hindsight to have been an easy triumph and the course of Islam seemed on a direct course to total victory when suddenly, scarcely a month after the capture of his native city, there came the last real challenge to Muhammad's political supremacy: a bedouin confederation mustered its forces and marched against the Prophet. The encounter occurred in February 630 A.D. at a place called Hunayn,[5] and though at first there was panic in the Muslim ranks, their numerical superiority finally prevailed and the bedouin were routed on a day that merited reference in the Quran itself:

> God has given you victory on many fields, and on the day of Hunayn, when you exulted in your numbers, though they availed you nothing, and the earth, vast as it was, was straitened for you. Then you turned back in flight. Then God sent down His peace of reassurance on His Messenger and upon the believers, and sent down hosts you could not see, and punished those who did not believe. Such is the reward of disbelievers. (Quran 9: 25–26)

Among the allies of the Hawazin at Hunayn were members of the Banu Thaqif of al-Ta'if who fled back to the protection of their city in the wake of the Muslims' victory. The Thaqif barricaded themselves in what was then a walled city, and despite the Muslims' possession of some recently acquired siege weapons, the taking of a walled town was still beyond their powers.[6] When they finally realized this, Muhammad ordered the siege broken off and retired to Ji'rana close to Mecca to divide the spoils of his victory over the Hawazin. He remained there from February 24 to March 9, 630, and then set out for Mecca to make the *'umra*.

> The Apostle left Ji'rana to make the *'umra* and . . . having completed the pilgrimage he returned to Medina. He left Attab ibn Asid in charge of Mecca. He also left behind with him Mu'adh ibn Jabal to instruct the people in religion and to teach them the Quran . . .
>
> The Apostle's *'umra* was in Dhu al-Qa'da [March] and he arrived in Medina towards the end of that month or in Dhu al-Hijja. The people made the *Hajj* that year in the way the (pagan) Arabs used to do. Attab made the *Hajj* with the Muslims that year, A.H. 8 [that is, April 630]. The people of Ta'if continued in their polytheism and obstinacy in their city from the time the Apostle left in Dhu al-Qa'da of the year 8 until Ramadan of the following year [that is, January 631]. (Ibn Ishaq 1955, p. 597)

THE MALINGERERS

Even before the occupation of Mecca Muhammad had been casting his net of raids and expeditions in an ever wider arc, most notably at Mu'ta, and after the battle of Hunayn, toward the end of that same eventful year of 630 A.D.—his last surviving son, the infant Ibrahim, born of the Egyptian Christian concubine named Mary, also died in that year—he prepared his troops for a long-distance expedition northward, into the sphere of influence of the Byzantine Empire, for reasons that at least one tradition understood as primarily economic. Abu Umama al-Bahili said: I have heard the Messenger of God say, "Verily God has turned my face toward Syria and my back toward the Yemen, and said to me, 'O Muhammad! I have made what is behind you a reinforcement for you and what faces you a booty and a livelihood.'" (Ibn Asakir, *Ta'rikh Dimashq*, vol. 1, p. 378)

This time the thrust carried Muslim arms to Tabuk in the far north of the Hijaz.[7] The immediate motive for this venture, we are told, is that the Byzantines had collected a large army and were preparing to march into the Hijaz,[8] a most unlikely enterprise. A more probable incentive is something close to what was reported by Ibn Asakir, that the Muslim community in Medina had become dependent on (or perhaps simply accustomed to) the booty from the Prophet's raids, and that this, like the forays against Dumat al-Jandal and Mu'ta, was simply a predatory "fishing" expedition.[9]

Whatever the motives behind it, Ibn Ishaq's account in the *Life*, as well as parts of Sura 9 of the Quran, that are thought to refer to the malingerers in this enterprise, leave no doubt that a great many Muslims were in no mood for this particular raid.

> Those who were left behind rejoiced in their inaction behind the back of the Apostle of God; they hated to strive and fight with their goods and persons in the cause of God. They said, "Do not go forth in the heat." Say: "The fire of hell is fiercer in heat." If only they could understand!
>
> Let them laugh a little; much will they weep in recompense for what they do.
>
> If, then, God bring you back to any of them, and they ask your permission to go out with you (on a raid), say: "Never shall you go out with me or fight an enemy with me. For you preferred to sit inactive on the first occasion. So sit now with those who lag behind." (Quran 9: 81–83)

When a *sura* comes down enjoining them to believe in God and to strive and fight with His Apostle, those with wealth and influence among them ask you for exemption, and say: "Leave us behind; we would rather be with those who sit at home." They prefer to be with the women who remain behind. Their hearts are sealed and so they do not understand. (*Ibid.*, 9: 86-87)

It was not fitting for the people of Medina and for the bedouin in the vicinity to refuse to follow God's Apostle, nor to prefer their own lives to his, because everything that they would suffer or do would be accounted to their credit as a deed of righteousness—whether they suffered thirst or fatigue or hunger in the cause of God or trod paths to anger the unbelievers or received any injury. (Quran 9: 120)

Ibn Ishaq makes no mention of an actual engagement at Tabuk and speaks instead of the sequel, which unfolded at Ayla, the later Aqaba, at the head of the Aelanatic Gulf:

When the Messenger reached Tabuk, Yuhanna ibn Ru'ba, governor of Ayla, came and made a treaty with him and paid him the poll-tax. The people of Jarba' and Adhruh also came and paid the poll-tax.[10] The Messenger wrote for them a document which they still have. He wrote to Yuhanna ibn Ru'ba thus:

"In the name of God, the Compassionate and Merciful. This is a guarantee from God and Muhammad the prophet, the Messenger of God, to Yuhanna ibn Ru'ba and the people of Ayla, for their ships and their caravans by land and sea. They and all that are with them, men of Syria and the Yemen, and seamen, all have the protection of God and the protection of Muhammad the prophet. Should any one of them break the treaty by introducing some new factor then his wealth shall not save him; it is the fair prize of him who takes it. It is not permitted that they shall be restrained from going down to their wells or using their roads by land or sea." (Ibn Ishaq 1955, p. 607)

Beginning in the late third century a Roman legion had been stationed at Ayla, a sign of the city's importance to Roman commerce and political order in the region,[11] but when the Muslims threatened the city in 630, it had no visible defenses—the legion had long since been withdrawn—and the negotiations for its submission were carried out by Yuhanna ibn Rub'a, who, though Ibn Ishaq does not identify him as such—he is called *ruler* or *king* in the Arab sources—was apparently the Christian bishop of the city, a not entirely untypical example of the lapse of secular political authority in seventh century Syria-Palestine.[12]

So ended the extraordinary adventure that carried Islam's troopers deep across the frontiers of the Byzantine empire to the town of Tabuk. Though it may have revealed to Muhammad the weakness of his international rivals, the raid was not an entirely successful enterprise, either in its organization or its fulfillment, as many passages in Sura 9 of the Quran testify.

THE ESTABLISHMENT OF AN ISLAMIC *UMMA*, WITH DUES

The Hijri year beginning April 630 A.D. is called the *Year of the Delegations* in the Muslim tradition, and with some justice. The news of the capitulation of Mecca and the defeat of the tribal confederation at Hunayn had spread rapidly across western Arabia where the tribes began to realize that they must now come to terms with the new political reality there. Coming to terms meant membership in the *umma*, the Prophet's community. An *umma* had been established shortly after Muhammad's arrival in Medina, but it was, as we have seen, essentially a political arrangement, and despite the fact that the signatories accepted the authority of Muhammad, "the Prophet," and his God, their obligations remained political, with an aim to maintaining the peace, rather than credal or cultic, with an eye toward salvation. Over the years Muhammad's power had grown, and with it the tacit acceptance of a different kind of relationship. The "hypocrites" were no longer crypto-pagans but occasionally unenthusiastic Muslims; the recalcitrant Jews had gone to death or exile, and their more complaisant fellows were simply clients of a now exclusively Muslim *umma*.[13] We do not know if the *umma* conditions were formally altered along with the understanding, but after the fall of Mecca, membership in the *umma* meant the acceptance of Islam.

> In deciding their attitude to Islam the Arabs were only waiting to see what happened to this clan of the Quraysh and the Apostle. For the Quraysh were the leaders and guides of men, the people of the sacred shrine (of Mecca), and the pure stock of Ishmael son of Abraham; and the leading Arabs did not contest this. It was the Quraysh who had declared war on the Messenger and opposed him; and when Mecca was occupied and the Quraysh became subject to him and he subdued them to Islam, and the Arabs knew they could not fight the Messenger or display enmity towards him, they entered into God's religion "in batches" as God said,[14] coming to him from all directions . . . (Ibn Ishaq 1955, p. 638)

"Entering God's religion" was not simply a matter of pro-
nouncing a creed; those who entered the new, exclusively Muslim
umma were required to pay a tax, the *sadaqa* or *zakat*, into the
treasury of the community. This alms tax was different from the
political tribute levied on non-Muslims who came under Muslim
sovereignty: the *zakat* was a *religious* obligation, one of the five
basic elements that made up what were later called the "pillars of
Islam." Thus are the newcomers to the *umma* to be treated: "If
they repent, establish regular prayers and pay the tithes—they are
your brothers in religion. Thus do we explain the signs [or verses]
for those who understand."

And then, in a prescient anticipation of what would in fact
happen after Muhammad's death: "But if they violate their oaths
after they have pledged, and taunt you for your religion, fight the
leaders of unbelief, for their oaths are nothing to them" (Quran 9:
11–12).[15]

The payment was not left to the good will or the consciences
of the new members of the *umma*: Muhammad despatched agents
to all the tribes and charged them with the collection of the
sadaqa-zakat, and Ibn Sa'd provides a list of both the tribes and
the tax-collectors sent out to them on this year, though no source
mentions the actual collection of the *zakat* until much later.[16]

THE *HAJJ* OF YEAR 9: THE BREAK WITH THE PAGANS

> The Apostle remained there [that is, in Medina] for the rest of
> the month of Ramadan and Shawwal and Dhu al-Qa'da. Then
> he sent Abu Bakr in command of the *Hajj* in the year 9 (of the
> *Hijra*) to enable the Muslims to perform their *Hajj* while the
> polytheists were at their pilgrimage stations. Abu Bakr and the
> Muslims then duly departed. (Ibn Ishaq 1955, p. 617)

The rest of this chapter of Ibn Ishaq's *Life* is devoted to a
lengthy explanation of another momentous change in the relations
between Muslims and non-Muslims that was signalled, the tradition asserts, in the verses of Sura 9 revealed on this occasion:[17]

> A declaration of immunity from God and His Apostle is given
> to the pagans with whom you have contracted alliances.
>   Go about safely in the land for four months and know that
> you cannot frustrate God, and that God is about to humiliate
> unbelievers.

> And a proclamation from God and His Apostle on the Day of the Great Pilgrimage—that God and His Apostle dissolve treaty obligations with the pagans . . .
> Except those pagans with whom you made treaties and who have not afterward failed you in any regard and have not supported anyone against you. As for them, respect their treaty till the end of their term. God loves those who obey.
> And when the sacred months are passed, kill the pagans wherever you find them, and take them and surround them and lie in wait for them in every spot. But if they repent, and observe the ritual prayers and pay the alms-tithe, then leave them alone. God is forgiving, compassionate. (Quran 9: 1–5)

There was a final caution sounded in Sura 9. If the non-believers were excluded from the pilgrimage, would this not threaten the livelihood of the Muslims of Mecca?

> It is not for the pagans to operate [or "visit"] the shrines of God while they witness against their own souls to disbelief. The works of such bear no fruit; they shall dwell in fire. The shrines of God shall be operated [or "visited"] by such as believe in God and the Last Day, establish ritual prayer, contribute the alms-tithe and fear God. It is they who are the truly guided . . .
> O believers, truly the pagans are unclean; so let them not approach the sacred shrine after this year (of grace) of theirs. And if you fear poverty (as a result), God will enrich, if He wills it, out of His own bounty. For God is all-knowing, all-wise. (Quran 9: 17–18, 28)

These Quranic announcements were made, according to the traditional chronological sequence, upon Muhammad's return from Tabuk, and they mark the final break with paganism. Previously the Prophet had conducted political relations with the pagans, or "associators" (mushrikun), as he invariably calls them. He had concluded treaties with non-Muslims and they had even taken part in his raids and shared the booty that came from them.[18] No longer. The pagans were to be granted a respite of four months; thereafter they would be killed wherever the Muslims encountered them.[19]

There was, of course, another option: they might convert and become part of the new, entirely Muslim, political order. The community (umma) had been redefined, as we have just seen, to include only Muslims, and the terms of membership mandated the institution of liturgical prayer (salat) and the payment into the community treasury of the *zakat,* an alms tithe to the Muslims and transparently a tax to those being threatened with conversion or extinction.

Later Muslims were somewhat uncertain about many elements of this tradition, as we shall see, including who precisely made the announcement.[20] Some traditionists said it was Abu Bakr or Abu Hurayra; others, as might be expected in a community where the division between Sunni and Shi'ite ran deep, maintained that it was Ali ibn Abi Talib: "Abu Bakr, during the pilgrimage which he conducted, before the Pilgrimage of Farewell, sent Abu Hurayra, among others, to announce on the day of the sacrifice that no polytheist would make the *Hajj* and that no naked person would perform the *tawaf*" (Bukhari, *The Sound,* vol. 5, p. 212).

The consequence is set out in another tradition: "Abu Bakr broke the treaties of the peoples in that year, and in the year of the Pilgrimage of Farewell during which the Prophet made his pilgrimage, no pagan performed the *Hajj*" (*ibid.,* vol. 4. p. 124).

And again, on the reputed testimony of Abu Hurayra, and in a manner calculated to save the Abu Bakr version and yet assert Ali's claim:

> Abu Bakr sent me among the heralds which he sent during that pilgrimage, on the day of sacrifice to announce at Mina that no pagan would perform the *Hajj* after that year and that no naked person would perform the circumambulation. Meanwhile the Prophet sent after us Ali ibn Abi Talib ordering him to announce the temporary immunity. Ali announced with us the immunity to the people at Mina on the day of sacrifice and that no pagan would perform the *Hajj* after that year and that no naked man would perform the circumambulation. (*Ibid.,* vol. 6, p. 81)

THE IDOLATORS SUBMIT

The tax apart, submission to the Prophet of Islam and his God was not always simple or easy, because the social, political, and psychological price of disavowing the customs of their own past was a large one. The Thaqif of Ta'if, for example, were willing to "submit" (*aslama*), but only on condition that they were exempted from paying the poor tax (*sadaqa*) or participating in what appeared might be the ongoing condition of "holy war" (*jihad*).[21] The Prophet seems to have yielded, at least temporarily—he turned down a request that the Thaqif not be required to prostrate themselves in prayer—but that was by no means the end of the matter. The text from the *Life* continues:

> Among the things they asked the Messenger was that they should be allowed to retain their idol al-Lat intact for three years. The Messenger refused and they continued to ask him for a year or two (grace), and he refused. Finally they asked for a month (dispensation) after their return home, but he refused to agree to any set time. All that they wanted, as they were trying to show, was to be safe from their fanatics and women and children by leaving al-Lat, and they did not want to frighten their people by destroying her until they had (all) accepted Islam. The Messenger refused this, but he sent Abu Sufyan and al-Mughira to destroy her (for them). They also asked him that he would excuse them from prayer and that they would not have to break the idol with their own hands. The Messenger said: "We excuse you from breaking your idols with your own hands, but as for prayer, there is no good in a religion which has no prayers." They said that they would perform them, though they were demeaning. (Ibn Ishaq 1955, pp. 615–616)

Whatever the concessions to the nearby and powerful Thaqif, they became moot with the eventual fall of Ta'if in December 630, when Muhammad sent a governor and, more pointedly, a tax collector to the city.[22] Nor did Ta'if itself play a very large role in the subsequent history of Islam. Though echoes of the cult of al-Lat lingered on for a spell, the city's chief renown was as a garden and summer resort for wealthy Meccans.

CHAPTER 11

The Pilgrimage of Farewell

> The months for the *Hajj* are well-known. If anyone undertakes that duty during them, let there be no obscenity, nor wickedness nor wrangling during the *Hajj*. And whatever good you do, God knows it.
>
> Take provision with you for the journey, but the best of provisions is righteous conduct. So fear Me, you who are wise. (Quran 2: 197)

The Quran had thus simply commanded that the *Hajj* be made, "during the well-known months"; that it was "a duty men owe to God," everyone, that is, "who is able to afford the journey" (3: 97). The command was, then, a plain and direct one, doubtless on the correct assumption that the parties addressed were well acquainted with this pre-Islamic ritual. But as we have seen, the rite was complex even at the beginning, and its complexities assured that a later generation of Muslims would have a host of questions on the subject. The Quran had already addressed some of them, the case of an interrupted pilgrimage, for example:

> Complete the *Hajj* or *'umra* in the service of God, but if you are prevented, send a sacrificial offering from what is available; do not, however, shave your heads [that is, signal the completion of the obligation] until the offering reaches the place of sacrifice. But if any of you becomes ill (after formally beginning the rites) or has a scalp ailment (requiring shaving), he should compensate by either fasting or feeding the poor. (Quran 2: 196)

As the citation itself reveals, the ritual complexities of the *Hajj* might be considerable—later they spawned an entire guild of guides to assist the pilgrim through them—and, as on other issues, the answers were sought among the *hadith*, the reported utterances of the Prophet himself, and more particularly those that clustered around the so-called farewell pilgrimage in 632 A.D. We know little of Muhammad's connection with Meccan rituals, including the *Hajj*, either before or after his call to prophet-

247

hood, though it seems safe to assume that he took part in the rituals of his native city.[1] Once removed to Medina, however, he was obviously in no position to participate in any of the cultic observances in Mecca and its vicinity, not, at any rate, until the month of Dhu al-Qaʻda (February) 629, when, as we have seen, he was permitted to perform the ʻumra as part of a general political settlement concluded at Hudaybiyya. Mecca fell in January 630, and though Muhammad performed the ʻumra in March of that year, he did not participate in the Hajj. In March 631 the Hajj was led by Abu Bakr, and Muhammad was once again absent. Thus it was not until Dhu al-Hijja (March) in 632 A.D., the year of his death, that Muhammad went on what was to be his first and final Hajj as a Muslim.[2]

All our sources agree that the Prophet delivered a discourse on the occasion of his final pilgrimage, and that it covered instruction on the performance of the pilgrimage as well as detailed prescriptions on a great variety of subjects. Ibn Ishaq has preserved one version, which he reproduced in his Life:

> In the beginning of Dhu al-Qaʻda the Messenger prepared to make the pilgrimage and ordered his men to get ready. Abd al-Rahman ibn al-Qasim from his father, from Aisha, the Prophet's wife, told me that the Messenger went on pilgrimage on the 25th of Dhu al-Qaʻda [20 February 632 A.D.]. . . . (In its course) the Messenger showed men the rites and taught them the customs of the Hajj . . . (Ibn Ishaq 1955, pp. 649–650)

The pilgrimage was, in fact, a pre-Islamic custom of long-standing with its own rituals and customs. The Prophet took what he found, discarded some elements of the cult, reshaped others, and integrated whatever was suitable into a new, specifically Muslim Hajj. At the end of Muhammad's sermon, for example, Ibn Ishaq records a tradition that shows the Prophet clarifying and redefining the sacred territory, the "stations," connected with the pilgrimage.

> Abdullah ibn Abi Najih told me that when the Apostle stood on Arafat he said: "This station goes with the mountain that is above it and all Arafat is a station." When he stood on Quza on the morning of Muzdalifa he said: "This is the station and all al-Muzdalifa is a station." Then when he had slaughtered in the slaughtering place in Mina he said, "This is the slaughtering place and all Mina is a slaughtering place."

Then Ibn Ishaq adds his own concluding summary, reprising what he had said at the outset:

> The Apostle completed the *Hajj* and showed men the rites and taught them what God had prescribed as to their *Hajj*, the "standing," the throwing of stones, the circumambulation of the temple and what He had permitted and forbidden. It was the pilgrimage of completion and the pilgrimage of farewell because the Apostle did not go on pilgrimage after that. (Ibn Ishaq 1955, p. 652)

AN ISLAMIC PILGRIMAGE

Though they cannot be dated with precision, the Quran includes verses that seem to be offering clarification on ritual points of the pilgrimage. Sura 22, for example, offers extensive and detailed instruction on the sacrifices performed during the *Hajj* and specifically addresses the question—which remains, as often, unasked in the body of the Quran but unmistakably underlies the answer—as to whether it permitted to eat the flesh of the animals offered for sacrifice:

> You are permitted (to eat) the sacrificial animals, except those specified (as prohibited), but shun the abomination of idols and shun the word that is false.
> In them [that is, the sacrificial animals] you have benefits for a term appointed; in the end their place of sacrifice is near the Ancient House.[3] To every community did We appoint a pious ritual, so that they might celebrate the name of God over the sustenance He gave them from animals . . . [4] (Quran 22: 33–34)

> For your benefit we have made the sacrificial camels one of the signs from God; there is good for you in them. So pronounce the name of God over them as they line up (for sacrifice), and afterwards as they lie slain, eat thereof and feed such as already have food and such as beg in humility; thus have We made animals subject to you, that you might be grateful.
> It is not their meat or their blood that reaches God; it is your piety that reaches Him. He has thus made them subject to you, that you may glorify God for the Guidance He has given you. (*Ibid.*, pp. 36–37)

Among the other things attempted by the Prophet during his Pilgrimage of Farewell was the combination of the two previously independent rituals of the 'umra and the *Hajj*, a topic already touched upon in the Quran. The verse in question seems to envision an interrupted 'umra being attached to a *Hajj*:

> And when you are in a state of security, if anyone wishes to resume (*tamatta*') the 'umra into the *Hajj*, he must make an offering such as he can afford; but if he cannot afford it, he should fast three days during the *Hajj* and seven days on his return, ten days in all. This is for those whose household is not in the Sacred Precinct. (Quran 2: 196)

The 'umra, we have seen, was primarily a Meccan feast, consisting chiefly in a ritual circumambulation of the Ka'ba and the sevenfold "running" between Safa and Marwa and brought to a formal end by the sacrificing of animals at Marwa, after which the pilgrim shaved his head and left the purified state.[5] It was a solemn and independent ritual, or rather, complex of rituals, because the rites of the Ka'ba and those of Marwa and Safa might themselves once have been distinct. Whatever the case, the rites of the 'umra and the *Hajj* were distinct rituals in the eyes of Muhammad and of the early Muslims and apparently celebrated by the Arabs at two different seasons of the year, the 'umra in the Fall and the *Hajj* in the Spring,[6] as they did in the year 632 A.D., when Muhammad made his "Farewell Pilgrimage."

The process of converting the 'umra and the Arafat festivals from a pagan into a Muslim ritual was not accomplished all of a sudden at the pilgrimage of 632. The Medinese *suras* of the Quran are filled with instruction and remarks linking Abraham and Ishmael not merely with the Ka'ba but with the rituals of the *Hajj* as well. Attention has already been drawn to the following verses of the twenty-second *sura*, which appear in the form of a command to Abraham after he had finished building the Ka'ba:

> Announce to the people the pilgrimage. They will come to you on foot and on every lean camel, coming from every deep and distant highway that they may witness the benefits and recollect the name of God in the well known days (*ayyam ma'lumat*) over the sacrificial animals he has provided for them. Eat thereof and feed the poor in want. Then let them complete their rituals[7] and perform their vows and circumambulate the Ancient House.
>
> Such is it [that is, the pilgrimage]. Whoever honors the sacred rites of God, for him is it good in the sight of his Lord . . . (Quran 22: 27–30)

The Quran merely suggests; the later Muslim tradition hastened, as we have already seen in Chapter I, to fill in the details explaining how Abraham, and indeed Adam before him, had initiated the *Hajj*,[8] and that whatever modifications Muhammad was undertaking represented a restoration of the original form of the *Hajj*.

THE BAN ON THE PAGANS

The third verse of Sura 9 of the Quran, which has already been cited in connection with the *Hajj* of the year 9 (630 A.D.) contains what it itself announces is a formal proclamation (*adhan*): "And a proclamation from God and His Apostle on the Day of the Great Pilgrimage—that God and His Apostle dissolve treaty obligations with the pagans. If you repent, it is better for you. But if you turn your backs, then know that you cannot frustrate God. Inform those who disbelieve of a painful punishment."

Although the surrounding verses might plausibly be assigned to the Abu Bakr-led pilgrimage of 631 A.D., this verse appears to be the fulfillment of that prior warning that *thereafter* the pagans would be excluded from the *Hajj*. Here they are themselves informed of the ban. The presence of pagans at a *Hajj* in which Muhammad himself led the Muslim contingent doubtless troubled many of the ancient authorities who preferred the keep the Prophet far from any taint of paganism. More disturbing for the traditional assignment of this verse to the pilgrimage of the previous year, there is no very convincing reason for calling the Abu Bakr pilgrimage the *Great Hajj*. The ancient commentators sensed the difficulty as well.

THE CALENDAR REFORMED

It was more certainly on the occasion of this pilgrimage that the Quran abolished the Arab practice of intercalation, the insertion of an interval into a time reckoning system in order to reconcile the solar year of 364¼ days and the lunar year of 360 days. The way the Arabs accomplished it was by periodically inserting an extra month (*nasi*) into the lunar year, and it was to that practice that the Quran averted:

In the sight of God the number of months is twelve, and so it was decreed on the day He created the heavens and the earth. Of them four are sacred: that is the correct religious practice, so do not wrong yourselves in them and fight the pagans altogether, as they fight you altogether. And know that God is with those who restrain themselves.

Know that intercalation (*nasi*) is an addition to disbelief. Those who disbelieve are led to error thereby, making it lawful in one year and forbidden in another in order to adjust the number of (the months) made sacred by God and make the sacred ones permissible. The evil of their course appears pleasing to them. But God gives no guidance to those who disbelieve. (Quran 9: 36–37)

The passage draws our attention to a confusion with the sacred months as the reason for the prescribed calendar reform: the "pagans" are accused of using the complex practice of intercalation to manipulate for their own advantage the sacred months in which shrines were visited, fighting was interdicted, and trade and commerce encouraged. Though we are not certain exactly how it was accomplished, it is easy to understand how the arbitrary juggling of the sacred months under the guise of intercalation might give an advantage to the Quraysh or any others who controlled a major shrine or market fair.[9]

It may not have been the only reason Muhammad had in mind.[10] The *Hajj* fell on March 10 in the intercalated year 632 A.D., the vernal equinox in the Julian calendar then in use, and if the traditionists were correct, in that year it coincided with the Passover and Easter tides. With intercalation, which annually tied the *Hajj* to the Spring season, that must not have been a rare occurrence, but Muhammad's abolition of the practice ensured that that coincidence would not soon happen again: henceforward the *Hajj* would occur according to the lunar cycle and thus annually retrogress, along with all other Muslim festivals, eleven days against the solar calendar. Both the ʿ*umra* and the *Hajj* forever lost their seasonal associations.

The abolition of intercalation, and so the cutting free of the Muslims from either the Christians' solar or the Jews' luni-solar calendar, had another effect that must have begun to be felt only somewhat later. It was not until 637 A.D., in the Caliphate of Umar (r. 634–644 A.D.), that a calendar commission proposed and Umar decreed that the Muslim era began with Muhammad's migration to Medina, an event that took place in September 622. The initial date of the new era was, however, pushed back for calendrical purposes to the first day of the first month of that year, 1 Muharram or July 16, 622 A.D. The intent was to introduce order and a degree of self-identity into the affairs of the new Islamic commonwealth, but one perhaps unanticipated side-effect was to introduce a degree of anarchy into the Muslims' recollection of the date of events during the intercalation era at Medina, with the result, as one modern Muslim author has remarked, that "there is more calendrical confusion connected with these ten years of Muhammad's mission in Medina than with any other decade of human history either before or after this period."[11]

CHAPTER 12

Illness and Death

The end, when it came, was sudden and unexpected.

> The Prophet began to suffer from the illness by which God took him to what honor and compassion He intended for him shortly before the end of (the month of) Saffar or the beginning of First Rabi'a. It began, so I have been told, when he went to the Ghar- qad cemetery in the middle of the night and prayed for the dead. Then he returned to his family and in the morning his sufferings began . . . (Ibn Ishaq 1955, p. 678)

When the illness reached its climax, Muhammad was in the apartment of his wife Aisha, the daughter of Abu Bakr, and this report goes back to her testimony:

> Ya'qub ibn Utba from al-Zuhri from Urwa from (Muhammad's wife) Aisha said: The Messenger came back to me from the mosque that day and lay on my lap. A man of Abu Bakr's family came in to me with a toothpick in his hand. The Messenger looked at it in such a way that I knew he wanted it, and when I asked him if he wanted me to give it to him, he said yes. So I took it and chewed it to soften it for him and gave it to him. He rubbed his teeth with it more energetically than I had ever seen him rub them before. Then he laid it down. I found him heavy on my breast, and as I looked into his face, lo his eyes were fixed and he was saying, "No, the most Exalted Companion is of Paradise." I said, "You were given the choice and you have chosen, by Him who sent you with the truth!" And so the Messenger was taken . . .
>
> Al-Zuhri said, and Sa'id ibn al-Musayyib from Abu Hurayra told me: When the Messenger was dead Umar got up (in the mosque) and said: "Some of the disaffected will allege that the Messenger is dead, but by God, he is not dead: he has gone to his Lord as Moses son of Imran went and was hidden [on Sinai] from his people for forty days. By God, the Messenger will return as Moses returned and will cut off the hands

feet of men who allege that the Messenger is dead." When Abu Bakr heard what had happened he came to the door of the mosque as Umar was speaking to the people. He paid not attention but went into Aisha's room to the Apostle, who way lying covered by a mantle of Yemeni cloth. He went and uncovered his face and kissed him saying, "You are dearer than my father and mother. You have tasted the death that God had decreed; a second death will never overtake you."

Then he replaced the mantle over the Apostle's face and went out. Umar was still speaking and Abu Bakr said, "Gently, Umar, be quiet." But Umar refused and went on talking, and when Abu Bakr saw that he would not be silent, he went forward himself to the people who, when they heard his words, came to him and left Umar. Giving thanks and praise to God, he said: "O men, if anyone worships Muhammad, Muhammad is dead; if anyone worships God, God is alive, immortal." Then he recited this verse "Muhammad is nothing but an Apostle. Apostles have passed away before him. Can it be that if he were to die or be killed you would turn back on your heels? He who turns back does no harm to God and God will reward the grateful." (Quran 3: 144) By God, it was as if the people did not know that this verse had not come down until Abu Bakr recited it that day. The people took it from him and it was constantly on their tongues. Umar said, "By God, when I heard Abu Bakr recite those words I was dumbfounded so that my legs would not bear me and I fell to the ground realizing that the Messenger was indeed dead." (Ibn Ishaq 1955, pp. 682–683)

When the preparations for his burial had been completed on the Tuesday, he was laid upon his bed in his house. Some were in favor of burying him in his mosque, while others wanted to bury him with his (already fallen) companions. Abu Bakr said, "I heard the Apostle say, 'No prophet dies but he is buried where he died.'" So the bed on which he had died (in Aisha's house) was taken up and they made a grave beneath it. Then the people came to visit the Prophet, praying over him by companies: first came the men, then the women, then the children. No man acted as prayer-leader in the prayers of the Apostle. The Apostle was buried in the middle of the night of the Wednesday. (Ibn Ishaq 1955, p. 688)

APPENDIX: THE QUEST OF THE HISTORICAL MUHAMMAD[1]

The history of Muhammad and the origins of Islam begins—and, some would say, ends—with the Quran. This is the sacred book of Islam, the collection of divinely-inspired utterances that issued from the mouth of the Prophet of Islam over the last twenty-two years of his life. What commends it so powerfully to the historian is its authenticity, not as the Word of God, of course, as the Muslims believe but as the secular historian cannot and should not, but rather as a document attesting to what Muhammad said at that time and place, early seventh century Mecca.

It is not a transcript, however; our present Quran is the result of an edition prepared under the orders of Uthman, Muhammad's third successor as head of the community of Muslims. This caliph, as he was called, appointed a committee to assemble all the available versions, most partial, some recollected and some written, and collect them into a single normative text.[2] That was in the late 640s or early 650s—Muhammad died in 632 A.D.—but the search for significant variants in the partial versions extant before Uthman's standard edition, what can be called the *sources* behind our text, has not yielded any differences of great significance.[3] Those pre-Uthmanic clues are fragmentary, however, and large "invented" portions might well have been added to our Quran or authentic material deleted. So it has been charged in fact by some Muslims who failed to find in the present Quran any explicit reference to the designation of a successor to the Prophet and so have alleged tampering with the original texts.[4] But the argument is so patently tendientious and the evidence adduced for the fact so exiguous that few have failed to be convinced that what is in our copy of the Quran is in fact what Muhammad taught, and is expressed in his own words.

Which is not to say that *no* hands have touched the Quranic material, as even the Muslim "collection" stories concede. An early investigator of the life of Jesus compared the Gospel stories about him to pearls whose string had been broken. The precious stones were reassembled in the sequel by the Evangelist, Mark, for example, who supplied both the narrative framework and within it connective links to "restring" them. The Quran gives somewhat the same impression of scattered pearls, though these have been reassembled in quite a different, and puzzling, manner. The Quran as we now possess it is arranged in 114 units called *suras* connected in no obvious fashion, each bearing a name and other introductory formulae, of greatly varying length and, more appositely to our present purpose, with little internal unity. There is no narrative framework, of course, and within the unconnected *suras* there are dislocations, interpolations, abrupt changes of rhyme and parallel versions, a condition that has led both Muslim and non-Muslims scholars alike to conclude that "it is not unlikely that some of the present *suras* or parts of them were once joined to others. . . . "[5] By whom? We do not know, nor can we explain the purpose.[6]

Nor do we know the aim or the person(s) who arranged the *suras* in their present order, roughly, the first *sura* apart, from the longest to the shortest. They are not, in any event, in the order of their revelation, as everyone agrees. But there the agreement ends. Early Muslim scholars settled on a gross division into "Meccan" and "Medinan" *suras*, which were labeled accordingly in copies of the Quran, and they even determined the relative sequence of the *suras*. But this system rested on a number of premises that were and remain unacceptable to modern Western scholars, to wit, that the present *suras* are the original units of revelation and, further, that the so-called prophetic traditions (*hadith*), the reports of deeds and sayings attributed to the Prophet, provide authentic evidence upon which to base such a sequence.[7]

Because there was no conviction that such premises would yield any certitude about the dates of the various parts of the Quran, Western scholars developed their own dating system, which, though it starts from other assumptions, is not radically different in its results from those arrived at by the early Muslim savants. As first expressed by Theodor Nöldeke in 1860 in his *Geschichte des Qorans*, then revised by Friedrich Schwally in 1909 and not basically altered since then, the current Western opinion takes as its point of departure the Quran's own references, few in number to be sure, to events that can be verified from other sources, the battle of Badr in Sura 3: 13, for example. Second, there is subject matter that can be very tentatively matched to circumstances, the halakhic passages, for instance, that would only make sense as legislation for an existing community at Medina. And finally, there is the stylistic criterion, admittedly somewhat subjective, that enables one to distinguish between the highly charged and emotive passages delivered to a pagan audience at Mecca and the more measured instruction given to the already converted at Medina.[8]

The Nöldeke-Schwally system, which, like that of the medieval Muslims, modestly distributes the *suras* into limited categories like "Early," "Middle," and "Late Meccan" or "Medinan," is of critical importance to the historian because it provides the ground for following the evolution of Muhammad's thought and at the same time for connecting passages in the Quran with events that the ancient Muslim authorities asserted had occurred in Muhammad's lifetime. And though the highly composite nature of many of the *suras* makes any such distribution enterprise highly problematic to begin with, an even more serious methodological flaw is that the standard Western system accepts as its framework the traditional Muslim substance, sequence, and dating of the events of the life of Muhammad, an acceptance made, as we shall see, "with much more confidence than is justified . . ."[9]

Even if we were far more certain of the size and sequence of the original revelations recorded in it, the Quran would still not be terribly *useful* for reconstructing the Meccan milieu nor the life of the man who uttered its words: it is a text without context. For Muhammad, unlike Jesus, there is no Josephus to provide a contemporary political context, no literary apocrypha for a spiritual context and no Qumran Scrolls to illuminate a Palestinian "sectarian milieu." From the era before Islam there is chiefly poetry, great masses of it, whose contemporary authenticity is somewhat suspect, but that was, nonetheless, "the main vehicle of Arab history in the pre-Islamic and early Islamic periods"[10] and that in any event testifies to a bedouin culture quite different from that of the sedentarized Arabs of urban Mecca.

The Quran therefore stands isolated like an immense composite rock jutting forth from a desolate sea, a stony eminence with few marks upon it to suggest how or why it appeared in this watery desert. The nearest landfalls for our bearings are the cultures of the Yemen to the south, Abyssinia across the Red Sea, and the distant Jewish and Christian settlements of Palestine-Syria to the north and of Christian Iraq to the northeast.[11] In the north we come the closest to the environment of Mecca because both Jewish and Islamic tradition agree that there were Jewish settlements in the northern Hijaz and, more important, the assertion is confirmed by epigraphical evidence.[12] But the fact remains that between the contemporary Greek, Roman, and Sasanian sources about Syria and Arabia and the later Islamic tradition about the same places there is a "total lack of continuity."[13] The result is that, despite a great deal of information supplied by later Muslim literary sources, we know pitifully little for sure about the political or economic history of Muhammad's native city of Mecca or of the religious culture from which he came.[14] And to the extent that we are ignorant of that history and culture, to that same extent we do not understand the man or the enormously effective religious movement that followed in his wake.

Muhammad's contemporaries thought they caught in the verses of the Quran echoes of a number of familiar charismatic types, seers or poets (Quran 52: 29–30; 69: 41–42)—which the Quran stoutly denies—or even a "rehasher of old stories" (25: 5). Some modern scholars think the first charge has some merit, though by no means for the entirety of the Quran.[15] But once again we are limited by an almost total lack of contextual background. We know little or nothing of the utterances of the "seer" (kahin); the preserved pre-Islamic poets are patently not the demonic (majnun) type to which Muhammad was being compared; and our only contemporary Arabian examples of "ancient tales" are precisely those told in the Quran.

There is something odd about those stories. As is clear from the Quran itself, whatever doubts Muhammad's audience may have had about the supernatural origin of what he was proclaiming, they had no problem in understanding it, and better in many cases than we ourselves do. The Quran is filled with biblical stories, for example, most of them told in an extremely elliptical or what has been called an *allusive* or *referential* style.[16] For someone who had not read or heard the Bible recited many of these Quranic narratives would make little sense. But they did, obviously, and we can only conclude that Muhammad's audiences were not hearing these stories for the first time, as the already cited remark about "rehashing old stories" itself suggests. Thus there were stories of Abraham and Ishmael (or Isaac), of Moses and Solomon, David and Enoch, current in early seventh century Mecca, though we have little idea how or for how long; and when Muhammad "retold" them in his allusive style in the Quran to make some other moral point, God's vengeance for the mistreatment of earlier prophets, to cite one common theme, his listeners might not agree with the point, but they apparently knew well enough what he was referring to.

We, however, cannot follow these narratives so easily, first, perhaps, because they have been broken up or pasted together in ways different from their original recitation, or, more pertinent to our present purpose, because these stories are "biblical" only in the sense that they take characters or incidents from the Bible as their point of departure. But their trajectory is haggadic, the residue, echo, recollection—we are at a loss precisely what to call it—of what is palpably Jewish *midrashim*, though which they were, or whence, we cannot even guess. We have only one biblical *midrash* current in seventh century Arabia, and that is the Quran itself.

The biblical stories apart, have we material in the Quran for a biography of Muhammad? It seems not because the form of the book is that of a disjointed discourse, a pastiche of divine monologues that can be assembled into a homily or perhaps a catechism but that reveals little or nothing about the life of Muhammad and his contemporaries.[17] On our assumption that the notions in the Quran are Muhammad's own—there is very little historical evidence that they are anyone else's—one can indeed approach them with much the same questions as the historian might bring to Jesus's reported teachings in the Gospels: are these words or sentiments likely to be authentic in the light of first, the context in which they were delivered, and second, the manner of their transmission? The Quran gives us no such assurance on the first question, nor indeed any instruction whatsoever on the context in which its contents were delivered, no clues as to when or where or why these particular words were being uttered; it is as little concerned with the events of the life of Muhammad and his contemporaries as Paul was with the narrative life of Jesus. The Quran, a prime document that has a very strong claim to being authentic, is of no use whatsoever as an *independent* source for reconstructing the life of Muhammad.

However, a somewhat less obvious facticity rests between the lines of Islam's Scripture. If the Quran is genuinely Muhammad's,

as it seems to be, and if, somewhat less certainly, the long traditional distinctions between "Early" and "Late Meccan" and
"Medinan" *suras* hold firm, then it is possible in the first instance
to retrieve a substantial understanding of the type of paganism
confronting Muhammad in his native city—the primary religious
Sitz im Leben of the Meccan *suras* of the Quran—and even to
reconstruct to some degree out of the progression of *suras* what
appears to be an evolution in Muhammad's own thinking about
God.[18]

This is genuine history, and it is more secure than anything else
we know about Muhammad. It is not very "occasional" perhaps—
we cannot firmly connect any of these religious changes with external events—and it tells us nothing about the social or economic life
of Mecca. Those aspects of his environment will not yield up their
secrets to the biographer unless additional context can be supplied
from some other source. There are, in fact, just such sources, later
literary lives of Muhammad by men who thought they had access
to actual witnesses to what had happened and even what had been
said in the Mecca and Medina of two generations earlier. These
siras or traditional biographies of the Prophet provide a richly
detailed narrative of the events of Muhammad's career into which
at least some Quranic material and other "teaching" has been
incorporated at the appropriate places.[19]

The "appropriate places" were the subject of a great deal of
speculative attention by Muslim scholars who studied them under
the rubric of "the occasions of revelations"; that is, the particular
set of historical circumstances at Mecca or Medina that elicited
the "revelation" or "sending down" of a given verse or verses of
the Quran. The results of this energetic quest are exceedingly
detailed, often ingenious, but not entirely convincing. There is
very little evidence, for example, that independent sources of
information were brought to bear on the enterprise, and the suspicion is strong that medieval Muslim scholars were recreating the
"occasion" backward out of the Quranic verses themselves, an
exercise at which a modern non-Muslim might thought to be
equally adept.[20]

If these "occasions of revelation" are strung together in
chronological order, a task accomplished by early Muslim scholars by arranging the *suras*, or parts of *suras*, of the Quran in *their*
chronological order—a procedure that rests, as has already been
suggested, upon somewhat problematic grounds—then a sem-

blance of a biography of the Prophet can be constructed, one that covers the events of his life at least from 610 to 632 A.D. This is in fact what was done, and the standard Muslim *sira* or traditional biography of the Prophet is built on that kind of framework, fleshed out by other material about his early life at Mecca and some considerably more elaborate descriptions of his later military expeditions at Medina.[21]

The earliest integral example we possess of such a *sira* is the quite expert *Life of the Apostle of God* composed out of earlier materials by the Muslim scholar Ibn Ishaq (d. 767). In some ways this by now standard Muslim *Life* looks like a Gospel, but the appearance is deceptive. Ibn Ishaq's original, before a certain Ibn Hisham (d. 833) removed the "extraneous material" from the work, was more in the nature of a "world history" than a biography. The story began with Creation, and Muhammad's prophetic career was preceded by accounts of all the prophets who had gone before the life of the man was the "seal" of their line.[22] This earlier, "discarded" section of Ishaq's work can to some extent be retrieved,[23] and although its remains are revealing of Ibn Ishaq's purpose and the milieu in which the work was finally composed,[24] they add nothing of substance to the portrait of the historical Muhammad.

To return to the extant "biographical" version of Ibn Ishaq's work by Ibn Hisham,[25] it begins, much the same way Mark's Gospel does, with a declaration that "This is the book of the biography of the Apostle of God,"[26] and provides, like Matthew and Luke, a brief "infancy narrative."[27] More, there is a consistent, though low-key, attempt to demonstrate the authenticity of the Prophet's calling by the introduction of miracles, a motif that was almost certainly a by-product of the eighth century biographer's contact with Jews and particularly Christians.[28] This is sometimes the result of an imitative or polemical piety and sometimes—and perhaps at an even earlier stage—of a simple desire to entertain,[29] and its manifestations are not difficult for the historian to discern and eliminate.

Though the biographical material in the *Life* is not generally used to mask any special doctrinal pleading on behalf of Islam, there are, in its frequent lists, genealogies, and honorifics, abundant reflections of the family and clan factionalism that troubled the first and second century Islamic community,[30] a sure sign that redactional concerns were shaping the material. And finally, there are chronological questions. The earliest "biographers" of the Prophet, whose work is preserved by Ibn Ishaq and others, were little more than collectors of the "raids" conducted by or under Muhammad; and they took the watershed battle of Badr as their starting point and anchor and dated major events in Muhammad's life from it. But for the years from Badr (624) back to the Migration to Medina (622) there is great uncertainty and, for the entire span of the Prophet's life at Mecca, hardly any chronological data at all.[31]

Despite these obvious and serious disabilities, Ibn Ishaq's *Life* is on the face of it a coherent and convincing account and certainly gives the historian something to work with, particularly if the latter closes his eyes to where the material came from. Muslim authorities like Ibn Ishaq cite their sources, by name, and generation by generation, back to the supposed eyewitnesses contemporary with Muhammad. There were early doubts about some of these alleged eyewitness reports, and it is not unnatural that historical criticism in Islam has concentrated on those chains of transmitting authorities rather than on the matter transmitted. In the nineteenth century, however, Western scholars looked more carefully at the accounts themselves and came to the generally accepted conclusion that a great many of the "prophetic traditions" (*hadith*) are forgeries fabricated to settle political scores or to underpin a legal or doctrinal ruling.[32]

This conclusion was drawn, however, from the analysis of material in reports chiefly legal in character, where both the motives and the signs of falsification are often quite obvious. What of the reports of purely historical events of the type that constitute much of the life of Muhammad? The obvious clues to forgery are by no means so obvious here, nor is the motive quite so pressing because it is not the events of Muhammad's life that constitute dogma for the Muslim but the teachings in the Quran. But so great has been the doubt cast on the bona fides of the alleged eyewitnesses and their transmitters in legal matters that there now prevails an almost universal Western skepticism on the reliability of *all* reports advertising themselves, often with quite elaborate testimonial protestations, as going back to Muhammad's day, or that of his immediate successors.[33]

Though most of the *hadith* critics concentrated chiefly on the legal *hadith*, early in this century the Italian aristocrat-scholar Leone Caetani and the Belgian Jesuit Henri Lammens argued in a number of works that the historical traditions are equally colored by the sensibilities of a later generation of Muslims and so largely unreliable for the reconstruction of the life of the historical Muhammad.[34] However objectionable his own motives and style,[35] Lammens' critical attack in particular has been decried but never refuted. Although some students of Muhammad and his times reject and some accept Lammens' criticism of the *hadith*, most adopt the main lines of the Jesuit's reconstruction, out of the same type material, of Meccan society and economy,[36] which in turn provides them with the foundation of their own interpretation of Muhammad's career. As Maxime Rodinson has observed, "Orientalists are tempted to do as the Orientals have tended to do without any great sense of shame, that is, to accept as authentic those traditions that suit their own interpretation of an event and to reject others."[37]

This is a gravely damaging charge for the historian because the early Muslim biographies of the Prophet, our only source outside the Quran, are little more than an assemblage of such reports. Most modern biographers of the Prophet have been willing to close their eyes to what must follow, and although conceding the general unreliability of the prophetic traditions or *hadith*, they have used these same collections as the basis of their own works, which differ from those of their medieval predecessors not so much in source material as in its interpretation.[38] This may be a calculated risk based on the plausibility and internal coherence of the material or it may simply be the counsel of despair: if the *hadith* are rejected, there is nothing notably better to put in their place.[39]

At every turn, then, the historian of Muhammad and early Islam appears betrayed by the sheer unreliability of the sources. One confronts a community whose interest in preserving revelation was deep and careful, but who came to history, even to the history of the recipient of that revelation, too long after the memory of the events had faded to dim recollections over many generations, had been embroidered rather than remembered, and was invoked only for what is for the historian the unholy purpose of polemic. Islam, unhappily for the modern historian, had no immediate need of a gospel and so chose carefully to preserve what it understood were the words of God rather than the deeds of the man who was His Messenger or of the history of the place in which he lived.

Is there anything valuable in this later Islamic tradition, what one scholar has pessimistically called the *debris of an obliterated past?* It seems that there must be.[40] It is inconceivable that the community should have entirely forgotten what Muhammad actually did or said at Mecca and Medina or that the tenaciously memoried Arabs should have allowed to perish all remembrance of their Meccan or West Arabian past, no matter how deeply it might now be overcast with myth and special pleading. Some historians think they can see where the gold lies;[41] what is lacking is a method of extracting that priceless ore from the redactional rubble in which it is presently embedded. Those redactional layers may be later and so thicker and less tractable than those over the figure of the historical Jesus, there is no reason why the enterprise within Islam should prompt either resignation or despair.

Faced with his or her own kind of unyielding tradition, the student of Islamic origins has at least two ways of proceeding, as Julius Wellhausen recognized a century ago in his classic *Prolegomenon* on biblical criticism: either to arrange the accounts, in this instance the *hadith*, in an internally coherent order that would then represent the growth of the tradition,[42] or else to deduce the evolution of matters at Mecca from a comparison with parallels in other religious cultures, a task that carried the biblical critic Wellhausen into his equally classic study of "the remains of Arab paganism."[43] This latter method, though terribly hypothetical, has the advantage of forming hypotheses about the religious phenomena themselves and not merely about the traditions regarding those phenomena.[44]

Both methods are painstakingly slow and yield results that are notably more successful in analyzing Jewish influences and cultic practices than in dealing with Christian ideas and more convincing when applied to pre-Islamic Mecca than to the Prophet's own life. And in dealing with Muhammad, where the Quran is the historian's chief "document," it seems most useful and productive simply to apply a combination of common sense and some modern heuristic devices to the traditional accounts. We must begin with traditional material and attempt to make some sense out of it.

Acccording to that traditional material, notably the Quran and the Muslim scholars who attempted to explain it, the religious history of Arabia began at Creation and unfolded, not without interruptions, down to the time when God revealed His Book to Muhammad. The interruptions were the long bouts of paganism—

"association of partners with God," as the Muslims expressed it—that engulfed the Arabs for long intervals even in God's favored place at Mecca. Viewed more generally, God's original promises and commands to Abraham were periodically renewed through later prophets, most notoriously, of course, by Moses and Jesus. The Quran says (10: 48) that there is to no people to whom a prophet was not sent and Muslim tradition generously set the number at 240,000. Twenty-five are mentioned by name in the Quran, most of them biblical, but three are distinctly non-biblical, Hud, Salih and Shu'ayb, and are said to have been sent specifically to the Arabs before Islam. By the Muslims' own accounts the paganism at Mecca went unchallenged and unrelieved, however, from the time Abraham's offspring began to drift away from the Holy City until the moment in the month Ramadan of 610 A.D. when Muhammad received his own prophetic call.

The Quran appears far more interested in the unfolding of Sacred History on the broader Near Eastern stage than in events either religious or political in Muhammad's Mecca and the surrounding Hijaz. The remembered pre-Islamic past of this region of Arabia lay only in local oral traditions that, even after the coming of Islam, still recollected and savored the old genealogies, the tribesmen's poetry of love and war, and even, it would appear, some dim memories of other gods worshipped in other times. The later biographers of the Prophet and historians of Mecca drew upon these memories to piece together the history of Arabia as Muhammad doubtless understood it but as the Quran never spells out: how the House and the town of the biblical patriarch and his son passed into the hands of this or that Arab tribe and finally into those of the Quraysh, Muhammad's own ancestors; how that passage of power was accompanied by a lapse into polytheism and idol worship. That was the gist of the great historical triptych of Ibn Ishaq already referred to, later pared down to a simple biography of the Prophet and available to us in the version of Ibn Hisham, though the unabridged original was used with profit by Tabari (d. 923) and other historians.[45] This is one strain of tradition. The other is the information collected and topically arranged by Hisham ibn al-Kalbi (d. 819) in his *Book of Idols,* the most substantial treatment we possess of the religious practices of pre-Islamic Arabia.

This was the material that formed the basis of the nineteenth century's favored approach to the subject, the reconstruction of the religious history of pre-Islamic Mecca and the Hijaz by what may be called the *comparative method*, extrapolating and expanding the scanty West Arabian evidence through parallel practices of other Arab or Semitic peoples or lands.[46] The comparative method was broadly and enthusiastically used in the nineteenth and early twentieth centuries, but is less often invoked by more contemporary scholars who prefer, like most of the great Muslim scholars of the past, to find their parallels in Jewish and Christian tradition. The Muslims were seeking *parallels*, however, on the not unreasonable assumption that the God of the three revelations was one, as indeed was His Truth, whereas the modern secular historian is seeking out *borrowings* on the equally plausible assumption that historical events have intelligible causes.[47] There was a great deal of reductionism in this latter approach, to be sure, particularly in the first half of this century when there was a far greater trust in what the later Muslim authorities had to say about pre-Islamic Arabia, and when there prevailed an innocent freedom to extrapolate from almost any Jewish or Christian source, whatever its date or provenance. As the Muslims feared, the formation of Muhammad was not infrequently reduced to the sum of the Christian, and particularly the Jewish, influences operating upon him.

The innocence has long since disappeared, however, and the contemporary student of the Meccan religious milieu is left, if not uniquely, then certainly principally, with whatever can be gleaned from the Quran. The Holy Book polemicizes against, and to some extent describes, the still flourishing paganism of Muhammad's day, and at the same time it sets forth the program called *Islam*, which, for all its radical tone, has little hesitation in incorporating some aspects of contemporary Meccan ritual—notably the *Hajj* or pilgrimage—into that program. It is with the Quran, then, that the inquiry into Muhammad and the origins of Islam must properly begin.

NOTES

PREFACE

1. Notably Buhl 1961; Watt 1953, 1956; Rodinson 1971; less critically, Lings 1983; and, more popularly, Glubb 1971 and Armstrong 1992.

1. THE FOUNDING FATHERS

1. Potts 1988, pp. 155–157, "Some Information on the Speed of Travel by Camel in Arabia," has conveniently collected the findings on camel travel observed by some more recent travelers in Arabia. Eph'al 1982, p. 140, cites the case of the Turkish army crossing the Sinai in 1915 with horse, camel and on foot: they marched for 8–9 hours a day and maintained the pace for eight days. This was, however, an army on the march (under German officers), and they were clearly pushing.

2. The ancient figures of from seventy to ninety days to cover the entire distance of 1710 miles from Shabwa in the Yemen to Gaza on the Mediterranean seems like a convincingly accurate estimate; so Sprenger 1875, #202, and Groom 1981, p. 211.

3. The Quran does refer to God's command to sacrifice his son (cf. Genesis 22), but in its version (Quran 37: 100–106) the son *appears* to be Ishmael, and the later Muslim tradition, which was uncertain whether Ishmael or Isaac was meant (cf. Firestone 1990, pp. 135–152), put the event in Mecca and connected it with the origin of the sacrificial ritual mandated by the *Hajj*; Gaudefroy-Demombynes 1923, p. 277 n. 2.

4. Firestone 1990, pp. 63–71, analyzes the three major versions, those of Ibn Abbas, Ali, and Mujahid, of the "transfer to Mecca." On Tabari's own account, see *ibid.*, p. 67.

5. The space between the northwest face of what would later be the Ka'ba and a low semicircular wall, the *hatim*, opposite it. See later.

6. Firestone 1990, p. 64, # 7.

7. So Tabari, *Annals*, vol. 1, pp. 281, 283. The events on the occasion of one of these later visits is used to explain something else. When Abraham calls Ishmael is off hunting and so he is greeted by Ishmael's wife, a woman of the Jurhum tribe. He asks for bread or wheat or barley

or dates. She has none and so offers him milk and meat, which he accepts and blesses. "Had she brought bread or wheat or dates or barley," the commentator explains, "Mecca would have been the most plentifully supplied with these things of any place on God's earth" (*ibid.*, p. 284).

8. Gaudefroy-Demombynes 1923, p. 234.

9. *Qa'imin* connects God's command with Abraham's action (cf. the *maqam Ibrahim*, the "standing place of Abraham"). *Rukka'* is a word redolent of Islamic practice—a Muslim's prayer is divided into so many *raka'at*, "bowings"—whereas *sujud* recalls the root meaning of *masjid*, the traditional word for both the shrine at Mecca and the later Islamic "mosque."

10. Abu Qubays is a mountain rising above the valley of Mecca on the east.

11. The rock under the "Dome of the Rock," the Muslim shrine that sits upon the Temple mount in Jerusalem; cf. Peters 1985, pp. 195–196.

12. Tabari, *Annals*, vol. 1, p. 1131 = Tabari 1988, p. 52.

13. Tabari, *Annals*, vol. 1, p. 1131; Azraqi 1858: 20–24, 25–29, 30–31.

14. Abraham is commonly referred to by Muslims as *Khalil*, "friend" (of God), on the basis of the biblical story of his generosity to (supernatural?) visitors at Hebron; cf. Peters 1985, pp. 4–5, 140–143, 240–241.

15. Though with a quite different intention, of course. Jesus' messianic credentials require his connection with David; Muhammad's, with Abraham.

16. Cf. Caetani 1905, p. 96.

17. Tabari, *Annals*, vol. 1, p. 215.

18. If the "Amalik" really were the Nabateans, whose political borders rested at Mada'in Salih and al-Ula in the northern Hijaz and who had a "market" named after them in Medina, it would provide some sort of chronological touchstone—the Nabateans flourished from the second century B.C. to the first century A.D.—in this otherwise free-floating narrative. Note later that Ishmael's son is called Nabat or Nabit.

19. But it is by no means the only one; the various possibilities are rehearsed by Gil 1984, p. 206.

20. Tabari, *Annals*, vol. 1, p. 352.

21. *Ibid.*, p. 215.

22. Ibn Ishaq 1955, pp. 35–36.

23. See M. J. Kister, "Khuza'a," *Encyclopaedia of Islam*, Leiden: E. J. Brill, 1961– (hereafter *EI*²).

24. It was not, of course, the stones that were being worshipped but an animated spirit within them (Dussaud 1955, p. 41 and n. 3).

25. Lammens 1928a.

26. There are in fact a number of hot springs in the Yarmuk valley on the border between Syria and Jordan.

27. The names themselves appear to mean stones; cf. Fahd 1968, p. 105.

28. Caetani 1905, vol. 1, pp. 99–100; Lammens 1924, p. 268.

29. Watt in Tabari 1988, p. xxix, notes: "Though the name of Quraysh is sometimes given to an ancestor, either Fihr or al-Nadr, in its origin it seems to have been a nick-name which was given to the supporters of Qusayy as a whole, perhaps meaning the 'little collection' . . . " On Tabari's own uncertainty about the name, see later.

30. Cf. Wellhausen 1897, pp. 1–4.

31. There is, as usual, more than one version of these events; cf. Caetani 1905, vol. 1, pp. 101–102.

32. Cf. Hawting 1990, pp. 70–71: "Regarding the function of the tradition about Qusayy and the offices in Muslim literature, it seems to me that it serves to bring together four entities which are essentially separate: the sanctuary (the Ka'ba), the town (Mecca), the 'priests' of the sanctuary (Qusayy and his descendants), and the people of the town (Quraysh). The effect of the stories about Qusayy and the control by his descendants of the 'sacred offices' is to blur the distinctions: control of the sanctuary is equated with control of the town, the 'founder' of the priesthood is virtually the founder of the Quraysh, and the Quraysh become both the people of the town and the people of the sanctuary. The Qusayy tradition is essentially a sanctuary tradition. Fundamentally it is the *wilayat al-bayt*, the control of the sanctuary, around which the story of Qusayy revolves. It is authority over the sanctuary to which he considers he is the legitimate claimant and which he either buys, or is given, or wins with the help of his allies. . . . " On earlier theories of Qusayy as a Mecca "saint," see Lammens 1926 and Hawting *ibid., p. 66;* and on the South Arabian parallel, Serjeant 1962, p. 53.

33. The meaning of *quraysh* in this context is unknown: Tabari 1988, p. 29, n. 41.

34. The only method of calculating dates here is to count "normal" generations back from the Prophet's birth—itself highly uncertain. The method led Caussin de Perceval (1847, vol. 1, p. 235) to put Qusayy's takeover of Mecca ca. 440 A.D. and Lammens (1924, p. 53) to date the event to sometime about 470.

35. Cf. Lammens 1924, p. 53.

36. Tabari, *Annals*, vol. 1, p. 1098.

37. Al-Azraqi 1858, p. 65. On the archetypical quality of age 40, see Chapter 4.

38. Lammens 1924, p. 53; on a similar sorting in pre-Islamic Medina, see Hasson 1989.

39. Qutb al-Din 1857, p. 34.

40. Al-Hayqatan, cited by Lammens 1924, p. 85, and cf. Lammens's own characterization the place in Lammens 1929, p. 16.

41. Ibn Ishaq 1955, p. 46.

42. *Kitab al-Aghani*, vol. 13, p. 108; al-Azraqi 1858, p. 47.

43. Bulliet 1975, p. 105, n. 40; Groom 1981, p. 193.

44. Crone 1987, p. 6–7.

45. Ibn Ishaq 1955, p. 132.

46. Muqaddasi 95; Lammens 1924, p. 89.

47. Al-Azraqi 1858, pp. 278, 289, 376; Ibn Ishaq 1955, p. 73; cf. Lammens 1924, p. 88.

48. The offices are reviewed and analyzed in Caetani 1905, vol. 1, pp. 104–105; Hamidullah 1938, pp. 261 ff.; Lammens 1924, pp. 65 ff.; Ibrahim 1982, p. 343; Hawting 1990, pp. 62–63, 70–71.

49. Tha'alibi, *Thimar al-qulub* 116, cited by Ibrahim 1982, p. 343.

50. Tabari, *Annals*, vol. 1, p. 1098.

51. This was one of the two offices—the other was the *siqaya* or the water distribution rights—that survived into the Islamic era and are, in fact mentioned in the Quran (9: 19). Muhammad granted the watering franchise to Abbas, who at some point lost them to the autonomous guild of the Zamzamis (cf. Gaudefroy-Demombynes 1923, p. 65), and that of the *hijaba* to Uthman ibn Talha of the Banu Abd al-Dar and it remained for many centuries under the control of the Banu Shayba, another branch of the Abd al-Dar, who will appear often in pilgrims' accounts; cf. Hawting 1990, pp. 63–65.

52. See Sourdel-Thomine 1971.

53. Serjeant 1962, p. 53.

54. Lammens 1924, p. 44: "The Meccan syndicate took care to compensate itself from foreign commerce; it subjected it to various charges: customs, residence and trading privileges, a whole series of taxes and also of arbitrary imposts which, under the Turkish regime and the Capitulations, came to be known as *avanies*. Customs had to be paid before entering Mecca. . . . Most of them [that is, the pilgrims], it is true, mixed commercial speculation in with their religious practices, a combination legitimized by the Quran (2: 198), which advises the faithful not to have scruples in this matter. . . . We see the Quraysh syndicate, so zealous of attracting clients to itself, showing no less energy in discouraging from its markets dangerous competitors. They wanted buyers and not rivals."

55. Fasi 1857, p. 142.

56. Ibn Sa'd, *Tabaqat*, vol. 1, p. 39; Tabari, *Annals*, vol. 1, pp. 1097–1096; al-Azraqi 1858, pp. 66–67; cf. Gaudefroy-Demombynes 1923, pp. 151–153.

57. Quran 23: 34 (the *mala'* of the people); 23: 48 ("the Pharaoh and his *mala'*; likewise 26: 33); 27: 29 (the Queen of Sheba and her

mala'); 27: 33 (Solomon and his *mala'*); cf. Lammens 1924, pp. 74–75: "The Quran cannot conceive of authority without a council of notables, the *Mala'*. It seems likely that the author saw it functioning with his own eyes. We think, then, that prior to the *hijra*, the Quraysh metropolis was governed by the oligarchic regime of the *Mala'*, *the urban equivalent of the tribal council, the majlis, among the nomads.* This assembly brought together the richest chiefs and those of the most influential families. Thus the Umayyads and the Makhzumis are the most often named members of the *Mala'*. Neither election nor birth necessarily conferred membership, but rather the éclat of services rendered, the prestige of intelligence, of fortune and great achievements."

58. Cf. Lammens 1924, p. 74: "The transformation of the *Dar al-Nadwa* into a senate seems to owe its origin to the megalomania of the editors of the *Sira* . . . "

59. Al-Azraqi 1858, pp. 464–465.

2. THE COLONIAL ERA IN ARABIA

1. Bulliet 1975.

2. The evidence for both the destructive and the positive effects of the encounters of Bedouin and sedentaries in Syria is reviewed in Peters 1977.

3. Bulliet 1975, pp. 87–110.

4. The entire process is described, obviously from eyewitness accounts, by two sources, the *Natural History* of Pliny (vol. 6, pp. 26, 101) and the anonymous *Periplus* or "Sailing around the Erythrean Sea" (Periplus 1989, p. 57).

5. The monsoons were blowing long before Hippalus, of course, and the existence of such useful winds must have been known to at least some of the Indian Ocean pilots and navigators. What Hippalus actually "discovered" has been discussed by Hourani 1951, pp. 25–26, and compare Casson's remarks in Periplus 1989, p. 224.

6. Peters 1977–1978.

7. Tabari was drawing on his Arab predecessors, chiefly Ibn al-Kalbi (d. 819), for his Iranian history, and they in turn had used early Arabic translations of the Iranian annals. For al-Hira Tabari could also invoke the Arab poets, and when Nöldeke translated and commented upon Tabari's pre-Islamic history (Tabari 1879), he exploited additional Arab testimonia, both poetry and prose. Twenty years after Nöldeke, and using the same range of materials, Gustav Rothstein wrote his history of the Lakhmids of al-Hira (Rothstein 1899), still the only consecutive account of those people and that place. Since Rothstein's work the most important additions to the portrait have been the details cast upon

the Mesopotamian and Euphrates Arabs by the Syriac chronicles and lives of saints (see, for example, their exploitation by Nau 1933 and Charles 1936), and, more recently, by Kister's perceptive reading of early Islamic sources, many of them still unpublished, unavailable to Nöldeke and Rothstein; cf. Kister 1968a.

8. For various unsuccessful attempts at determining its exact location, James 1969, pp. 36–57; Bibby 1970, pp. 307–328.

9. So Altheim and Stiehl 1964–1969, vol. 1, pp. 110–113; cf. Keall 1975.

10. Tabari 1879, p. 18; Widengren 1971, pp. 752–756.

11. Whitehouse and Williamson 1973, p. 32, and for the identification of Bushire as Rev Ardashir, ibid., pp. 35–41.

12. Tabari 1879, p. 20 and n. 3.; Altheim and Stiehl 1964–1969, vol. 5, pp. 163–169, compare Khatt with Kattenia in the territory of Gerrha where Antiochus III landed his fleet when he attempted to take Gerrha in 203 B.C.

13. Von Wissman and Ryckmans 1967; strenuous objections, however, from Altheim and Stiehl 1964–1969, vol. 4, pp. 279–283 and vol. 5, pp. 533–535.

14. Tabari 1879, pp. 23–24; Rothstein 1899, pp. 28–37.

15. For the etymology, see Kawar (Shahid) 1967.

16. Rothstein 1899, pp. 18–28.

17. Tabari 1879, p. 23.

18. Caskel 1969; on the Zenobia connection, Rothstein 1899, pp. 40, 44.

19. Bibby 1970, pp. 316, 320, 366, 373–374.

20. Tabari, Annals, vol. 1, p. 836.

21. Tabari, Annals, vol. 1, pp. 839, 1–14, and cf. Hamza al-Isfahani, Ar. 51–52/tr. 37–38; on this campaign see Tabari 1879, pp. 54–57; Altheim and Stiehl 1964–1969, vol. 5, p. 349, and Whitehouse and Williamson 1973, p. 32.

22. Christensen 1944, p. 235.

23. Res Gestae 22.6.11.

24. Bivar 1972.

25. Procopius, Wars I, pp. 18, 35–36.

26. Shapur too experimented in fixed fortifications near the edge of the steppe; see Altheim and Stiehl 1964–1969, vol. 5, pp. 349–351 and Frye 1977.

27. Malalas, p. 308.

28. Rothstein 1899, pp. 39–40; on the Tanukh in this era as the forerunners of the later foederati, see Graf 1978, p. 16.

29. See, most recently, MacAdam 1980 and Bellamy 1985.

30. Tabari, Annals, vol. 1, p. 833; on his son and successor Amr in the same role, ibid., p. 845.

31. Caskel 1954, p. 41.

32. Olinder 1927, pp. 21–25, 33; on the dating, Pirenne 1956, p. 176.

33. The earliest is Ry 535 (= Ryckmans 1956).

34. For Adulis's location somewhere in the vicinity of the modern port of Massawa, see Casson in Periplus 1989, pp. 102–106.

35. The chief opinions on the person of Zoskales and the extent of his kingdom are resumed by Casson, *ibid.,* pp. 109–110.

36. Desanges 1978, p. 347: "What we likely have in the middle of the third century is a commercial picture dominated by the coastal peoples of the Red Sea, those on both the African and the Arabian sides."

37. This latter possibility is argued by Kirwan 1972.

38. Ryckmans 1957, p. 84.

39. Dihle 1964; Thelamon 1981, pp. 49–60. Hourani 1951, p. 39 sees the confusion on *India* and *Indians* as a symptom of the decline of Roman trade, and contact, with the East.

40. Athanasius, *Apology to the Emperor Constantius* 30, which cites Constantius's letter; on "Aizanas and Sazanas," see Thelamon 1981, p. 77.

41. Anfray, Caquot, and Nautin, 1970.

42. Robin 1980, p. 86; Beeston 1984b, p. 271.

43. The body of these inscriptions—there are twenty-nine of them in all—are studied by Robin 1980, pp. 89–95.

44. As we shall see in more detail later, *al-Rahman*, "the Merciful," is one of the most common epithets applied to God in the Quran; indeed, it is almost a proper name (see 17:110: "Call upon God or call upon the Merciful; however you call upon Him, His are the beautiful names"), though it disappears completely from the later *suras*.

45. The word appears twelve times in the Quran; cf. 3:67 where Abraham is typically called a *hanif*. On *hanifs* at Mecca in the lifetime of Muhammad, see Chapter 5.

46. Beeston 1984a, p. 268.

47. Robin 1980, pp. 93–94.

48. Guillaume suggests (Ibn Ishaq 1955, p. 10, n. 2) that perhaps by books suspended from their necks phylacteries are meant.

49. *Ibid.,* p. 13.

50. The sources are thoroughly surveyed in Shahid 1971.

51. *Christian Topography* vol. 2, p. 101c.

52. Moberg 1924, pp. lxiv–lxvii.

53. *Book of the Himyarites* 7a = Moberg 1924, p. cv.

54. *Ibid.* 7b = Moberg 1924, p. cv.

55. *Ibid.,* 8a–13a = Moberg 1924, pp. cvi–cix; Ibn Ishaq 1955, pp. 17–18.

56. So, among others, Moberg 1924, pp. lv–lvi.

57. Kawar (Shahid) 1964.

58. So the headings of the unpreserved Chapters XXXIX and XL in Moberg 1924, p. civ.

59. Smith 1954, pp. 432–433.

60. One likely chronological formula would put the invasion of Ella Asbeha in 525 and the reign of the designated viceroy Aryat/Samu-yafaʿ in the interval between 525 and 533, when Abraha's revolt would have occurred; so Smith 1954, pp. 451–453.

3. THE ARABIAN *OIKOUMENE*

1. How thin is the ice beneath the ancient dates and how fragile are the attempts to build a chronology upon them may be illustrated by the remark of Hamidullah 1957, p. 303: "Baladhuri (*Ansab* 1: 36–37) has collected several accounts of the age of Abd al-Muttalib at his death: 82, 88, 110 . . . 140, which seems a little excessive to us. We hold to the median, 110, which is generally accepted, since it is mentioned by the sources that Abd al-Muttalib had become blind by reason of his age."

2. In most accounts these seasons and journeys are reversed.

3. Another possibility is that Hashim's benefaction could have been *free* food for pilgrims, as another version of the story suggests (cf. Caussin de Perceval 1847, pp. 256–257), a practice instituted as a result of the improved position of Mecca in the wake of Hashim's commercial treaties and Mecca's new mercantile prosperity, whereby its income did not solely rely on selling things to pilgrims. Thus the pilgrim trade could in effect be encouraged by a form of a food subsidy.

4. Cf. Kister 1965a, pp. 116–117.

5. Cf. the accounts cited in Hamidullah 1957, pp. 299–300, particularly that of the early ninth century historian Ibn Habib.

6. Tabari, *Annals*, vol. 1, p. 1089.

7. The report on Amorkesos/Imr al-Qays comes from the Byzantine historian Malchus, *Fragmenta Historiorum Graecorum*, vol. 4, p. 113.

8. See Kawar (Shahid) 1956, pp. 205–221.

9. Kawar (Shahid) 1957, pp. 376–378; Pigulevskaya 1969, pp. 261–262.

10. So Sozomen, a Christian historian of Gaza, writing ca. 440 A.D. in his *Church History*, vol. 6, pp. 38, 1–13. The history of these names in early Byzantine times is traced in Christides 1972.

11. On the unlikelihood that Ptolemy's "Makoraba" was Mecca, see now Crone 1987, pp. 134–137.

12. Menander fr. 11 in Müller, FHG, vol. 4, p. 212. The terms have been studied by Kawar (Shahid) 1956, pp. 192–213, and Pigulevskaya 1969, pp. 153–155.

13. Jones 1964, vol. 2, pp. 826–827.

14. *EI²*, *s.v.*, and, for the fluctuating use of the term in the sources, Kister 1965a, p. 117.

15. Tabari, *Annals*, vol. 1, p. 958; cf. Smith 1954, p. 442. On the career of Mundhir, see Nöldeke in Tabari 1879, p. 170, n. 1.

16. Described in the South Arabian inscription Ry 506 (= Ryckmans 1953, pp. 275–284); cf. Smith 1954, p. 435, and see Chapter 4.

17. Tabari 1879, pp. 314–316; Rothstein 1899, pp. 110–111, 128–129.

18. Rothstein 1899, pp. 22–24.

19. Nau 1933, pp. 39–40; Charles 1936, pp. 56–57.

20. Rothstein 1899, pp. 142–143; Charles 1936, pp. 160–161.

21. Rice 1932 and 1934; Monneret de Villard 1940, pp. 32–44.

22. The chief literary sources, notably al-Shabusti's *Book of Cloisters*, are noted in Fiey 1965–1968, vol. 3, pp. 212–230.

23. Tabari 1879, p. 315.

24. Chiefly thanks to the evidence brought forward in Kister 1968a.

25. Griffith 1985; to the contrary, see Shahid 1971, pp. 247–250.

26. The copious evidence is assembled in Jeffery 1938.

27. Rothstein 1899, pp. 119–120; Nau 1933, pp. 45–49.

28. Kister 1968a, p. 151.

29. Tabari 1879, pp. 332–335; Rothstein 1899, pp. 120–123.

30. Rothstein 1899, pp. 134–138; Kister 1968a, pp. 165–167.

31. Rothstein 1899, pp. 131–133.

32. Altheim and Stiehl 1957, pp. 149–151; Kister 1968a, pp. 145–147.

33. Kister 1965a, p. 117, citing Tha'alibi, *Thimar al-qulub*, pp. 89 ff.; cf. Shaban 1971, p. 6.

34. Kister 1965a, pp. 122–126 (and following him, Shaban 1971, p. 7) cites a number of traditions to the effect that Hashim's strategy included the poorer elements in Meccan society in the investment and the profit-sharing ends of his commercial enterprise. These may reflect a historical truth, but they may equally likely represent a retroactive explanation of Quran 106: 4; see later.

35. Watt 1953, pp. 72–73; Wolf 1951, pp. 334–336.

36. For some passing analogies between Mecca and Petra and Palmyra: Donner 1977, p. 250; and 1981, p. 15; and cf. Crone 1987, p. 8: "Why do Islamicists find it so easy to believe that the Meccans traded in incense, spices and the like? Presumably because Arabia is indelibly associated with this kind of goods. . . . The classical spice trade of Arabia is so famous, practically every account of Meccan trade tends to be cast in its image; or in other words, Meccan trade tends to be described on the basis of stereotypes."

37. The most influential statement of this thesis is undoubtedly that

made by Paret 1958, p. 438: "Epigraphy and archeology indicate that the cities which were strung out along the route (between Petra and Damascus) enjoyed, at the end of the sixth century, a considerable importance. Architectural activity became intense. . . . The multiplication of churches, even though in this matter one must exercise a special prudence, does not seem to be the result simply of an accumulation of wealth in the urban centers but was also a likely index to an increase in the population. This demographic evolution is not without a fundamental connection with a progressive modification of the ethnic composition of the population. In the second half of the sixth century the people of Arab origin becomes greater in the cities . . . " and (p. 441) "The development of the cities stretching along the caravan route from Arabia to Damascus seems, then, connected with the push of Arab elements toward the north; it likewise reveals a progressive growth of trade with Arabia." For a detailed analysis of the evidence and the plausibility of the conclusion, see Crone 1987 and Peters 1988, and for some earlier skepticism, Bulliet 1975, pp. 106–107.

38. There was a trade with the east in silk, but none of it came by way of Arabia.

39. Cf. Mayerson 1964, p. 190: "In Nessana, a small town on the border of the Tih desert, there is a burst of building activity between the years 601–605, which must attest not only to the prosperity but also to a high degree of stability and security in the region. . . . We can reasonably assume that the others towns in the Negeb were equally affluent and confident in the security of the region."

40. Lammens 1924, p. 47; Paret 1958, p. 441.

41. See Caskel 1954.

42. Schick 1987, p. 44 (Jews), 56 (bedouin), 129 ff. (Muslim conquest).

43. Cf. Crone 1987, p. 4: "The conventional account of Meccan trade begs one simple question: what commodity or commodities enabled the inhabitants of so unpromising a site to engage in commerce on so large a scale?"

44. Lammens 1924, pp. 210–236, has collected the Muslim reports on their millionaire ancestors.

45. Rodinson 1978, p. 28: "The society in which Islam was born, the society of Mecca, was already a center of capitalistic trade. The inhabitants of Mecca, belonging to the tribe of Quraysh, caused their capital to fructify through trade and loans at interest in a way that Weber would call rational. By buying and selling commodities they simply sought to increase their capital, which took the form of money. . . . When it was a matter of trading relations with the neighboring states, in connection with the transit trade that was their greatest source of profit, the Muslims had to some extent to submit to the system of fixed equiva-

lences laid down by those states. . . . To some extent Henri Lammens and Martin Hartmann are therefore justified in talking of capitalism. Nevertheless Mecca was only a small island in the huge peninsula of Arabia which was essentially still at the stage of subsistence economy, with only a very small share of its production directed towards the market. The spice trade that was carried on across Arabia brought income in money, especially to the organizers of the transport such as the Quraysh, and probably also to the leaders of the various tribes through whose territories the caravans passed. . . . " The profits on these enterprises allegedly ranged from 50 percent to 100 percent (Lammens 1924, p. 208), and according to Ibn Ishaq 1955, p. 82, Muhammad nearly doubled his wife's investment on his first trading venture in the north.

46. Lammens 1924, pp. 135 ff.; cf. Rodinson 1978, p. 254, n. 3.

47. Lammens 1924, pp. 127–128: "Money was rare in the Hijaz. It is scarcely mentioned in the Quran. The Greek coin called the drachma is mentioned only once, and then where one would least expect it, in the story of Joseph (12:20). The one mention of the dinar is in connection with the Jews (3:68). In Arabic all the names for money are of foreign origin. The principal transactions of the bedouin, the dowry of women, the ransoming of prisoners, compensation for homicide, blood money . . . are all calculated in camels, to which one may add, for the oases, quantities of wheat or dates."

48. Cf. Crone 1987, pp. 10–11: "The last allusion to the overland trade route dates from the first (or as some would have it, early second) century A.D., and the transit trade would appear to have been maritime from the start. Neither the incense nor the transit trade survived long enough for the Meccans to inherit them, and there was no such thing as a Meccan trade in incense, spices and foreign luxury goods. At least, the Islamic tradition is quite unaware that the Meccans are supposed to have handled this type of goods, and the Greeks to whom they are supposed to have sold them had never even heard of Mecca. Meccan trade there was, if we trust the Islamic tradition. But the trade described in this tradition bears little resemblance to that known from Lammens, Watt or their various followers."

49. Cf. Hawting 1984.

50. Cf. Crone 1987, pp. 6–7 and the material cited there, and the important remarks of Potts 1988, pp. 127–128 on what constitutes a trade route in Arabia.

51. Lammens 1924, p. 201: "Often the Meccan caravan is called *latima*, that is, a convoy charged with perfumes and rare essences. Among these products, the most valued came not from the Hijaz but from the Yemen or even from India and Africa. The summer caravan went to collect them at their ports of arrival in order to replenish the stocks accumulated at Mecca. . . . Once the winter came, the *latima* took

the road to the markets of Western Asia . . . " [p. 203] "We have just enumerated the principal articles exported by the Quraysh caravans: leather, precious metals, perfumes, resins and medicinal drugs. . . . All these were avidly sought after and bought dear by the luxury of the civilized countries. From the Yemen the skillful merchants of Mecca brought the products of Persia, of India and of the Far East, all stored in the warehouses of Arabia Felix. Let us likewise mention the silks of China, the stuffs called *adani* after Aden, the Yemenite port where disembarked the 'merchants' of the lands situated beyond Aden. In addition to gold dust, Africa supplied above all ivory and slaves. . . . " For a detailed refutation of most of the items on this list, see Crone 1987, pp. 51–78.

52. See Lammens 1924, pp. 190–191; cf. Crone 1987, pp. 98–101, 104–105, and 150–151: "Such information as we have leaves no doubt that their [that is, the Quraysh's] imports were the necessities and petty luxuries that the inhabitants of Arabia have always had to procure from the fringes of the Fertile Crescent. . . . The Meccans, in short, are presented as having exchanged pastoralist products with those settled agriculturalists within their reach. . . . Meccan trade was thus a trade generated by Arab needs, not by the commercial appetites of the surrounding empires . . . "

53. There remain serious problems with even this modest hypothesis; cf. Crone 1987, p. 157: "Exchanges of pastoralist products for those of settled agriculturalists usually takes place between communities located within reasonable distances of each other . . . or between settled communities and bedouin who, though sometimes very far away, regularly visit the communities in the course of their migratory cycle. But Mecca is separated from southern Syria by a distance of some 800 miles; the Meccan were not bedouin and the goods they sold, moreover, were readily available in Syria itself. The Meccans, in short, are described as having gone on regular journeys of an arduous nature in order to sell coal in Newcastle. . . . " Crone's own hypothesis (p. 162), to move the Quraysh trading center from Mecca to near the Syrian border, is not much more convincing.

4. THE FAMILY AND CITY OF MUHAMMAD

1. Ibn Habib, *Munammaq* 88–91, cited by Serjeant 1983, p. 129.
2. *Ibid.*
3. The not uncommon practice at Mecca of "sleeping in the *hijr*," the sanctified area next to the Ka'ba, which is here followed by a divine intervention, may have had far more to do with ritual incubation than with fatigue; cf. Fahd 1966, pp. 363–364; Rubin 1986, p. 112.
4. Guillaume's note on this oracular verse in Ibn Ishaq 1955, p. 59,

remarks: " . . . Most probably we should assume that the sacrificial victims were tethered at a certain spot [in the Haram] and that they would void ordure before they were led to the foot of the image at which they were slaughtered . . . "

5. That is, "The Citadel," a generic topographical name.

6. As Hawting 1990, p. 75, points out, there are obscure but unmistakable signs even during the Islamic era that the Zamzam and the *siqaya* were *not* identical.

7. Al-Azraqi 1858, p. 75.

8. Rubin 1986, pp. 115–117. The motif of buried and rediscovered shrine treasury is a common one in sanctuary traditions and has suggested (Hawting 1980, pp. 45–47) a borrowing from Jewish Temple lore.

9. This entire cleromantic incident has been analyzed in Fahd 1958.

10. Cf. Wellhausen 1897, pp. 115–116; Fahd 1968, p. 168.

11. For the ancient and somewhat more modern speculation, see the following and Muir 1861, vol. 1, p. 14 n.

12. See further Chapter 11.

13. As with most events connected with the era of Islam's emergence, there is here more than one version of events and more than one calculation of motives. For another, far more commercially minded account of what happened on this occasion and why, see Kister 1965c, pp. 429–430.

14. Al-Azraqi 1858, p. 91, adds here: "Deserters from the army, laborers and camp-followers remained in Mecca and became workers and shepherds for the population." If true, it is hard to imagine that these would have been any other than Christian Abyssinians, and thus the only known "People of the Book" present in Mecca in Muhammad's lifetime.

15. On the evidence for the identity of the two, Kister 1965c, pp. 425–428, and cf. Conrad 1987, pp. 227–228; for a different view, see Ryckmans 1953, p. 342; Smith 1954, pp. 436–437.

16. The anomalies are rehearsed in Birkeland 1956, pp. 102–121, Shahid 1981, p. 430; and Rubin 1984a, p. 177.

17. Shahid 1981, p. 432; Rubin 1984a, pp. 167–168.

18. Crone 1987; Peters 1988.

19. Rubin 1984a, p. 170.

20. Kister 1965c, pp. 431–434; Rubin 1984a, p. 176.

21. Cited by Rubin 1984a, p. 170.

22. Cited in *ibid.*, p. 174.

23. Cf. also Quran 9: 28: "O you who believe, truly the polytheists are unclean; so let them not, after this year of theirs, approach the Sacred Mosque. And if you fear poverty, soon will God enrich you, if He wills, out of His bounty . . . "

24. Rubin 1984a, p. 174, n. 59.

25. Cf. Crone 1987, p. 155: "The fairs in question are often described in a fashion which the innocent reader might take to suggest that the Meccans owned them. But this, at least, they did not. The fairs were cooperative ventures. The sites were located in the territories of various tribes (all non-Qurashi), but subject to no authority, being devoid of permanent inhabitants," citing al-Azraqi 1858, p. 131, to the effect that Ukaz was in the territory of Nasr of Qays Aylan, Majanna in that of Kinana, and Dhu al-Majaz, apparently, in that of Hudhayl.

26. Kister 1980, p. 36, defines the *Hums* as "a group closely connected by ties of loyalty and allegiance to the Ka'ba, observing distinctive ritual practices during the *Hajj* and enjoying special privileged position in Mecca." The word itself means "zealot" or "devotee," but one common derivation connected it with *al-hamsâ*, a name for the Ka'ba referring to the gray stones from which it was built (Kister 1965a, p. 139; Rubin 1986, p. 123), though it is just as likely the other way around, that the Ka'ba as *al-hamsâ* = the Ka'ba as "the *Hums'* thing."

27. Cf. Wellhausen 1897, pp. 79 ff.; Crone 1987, pp. 173–176.

28. This is the reverse of the usual siting of these two idols.

29. Cited by Rubin 1986, p. 123.

30. *Ibid.*, p. 126.

31. Wellhausen 1897, p. 87.

32. Here, as often, the text says *pillar* or *column* (*rukn*) when it is clearly the Black *Stone* being referred to; cf. Hawting 1982, p. 39.

33. Cf. Kister 1980, pp. 36–37, who remarks, "This may be a quite faithful exposition of their belief."

34. See later and Gibb 1962.

35. Ibn Ishaq 1955, p. 30; The chronological problem was already noted by Nöldeke (Tabari 1879, p. 204, n. 2). According to a minority tradition, the "expedition of the Elephant" took place twenty-three years before the birth of Muhammad, which would put it near or at the date of Abraha's expedition against the Ma'add described in Ry 506 (= Smith 1954, p. 435), a coincidence that has convinced at least one author that it was this latter raid that the Meccans later converted into an attack on Mecca; so Altheim and Stiehl 1957, p. 147.

36. Ibn Ishaq has Nu'man ibn Mundhir, but he did not succeed until 582.

37. Tabari 1879 has two versions of these events, one from Ibn Ishaq (pp. 219–227) and a second from Hisham (pp. 227–236), the latter of which appears somewhat sounder and is followed here.

38. Tabari 1879, p. 223, n. 2; Pigulevskaya 1969, p. 269.

39. Tabari 1879, pp. 226–227.

40. Tabari 1879, pp. 236–237; Pigulevskaya 1969, pp. 270–271.

41. Tabari 1879, pp. 237, 263–264, 349–351; Christensen 1944, p. 373, n. 5. On the *marzban*, see Pigulevskaya 1969, p. 271.

42. In the contemporary sources the Hadramawt, the heart of the southern spice lands, had lost its title of "the *libanos*-bearing land" and that honorific was now transferred to East Africa; Smith 1954, p. 426.

43. Caskel 1954, p. 40, who drew the inevitable conclusion: "As a result of the dropping out and the collapse of the border states, the caravan roads, and with them, the settlements in the interior began to be deserted. The impoverishment of the ancient world was a contributing factor. Let us not deceive ourselves. The trade which the Quraysh carried, somewhat later—one caravan a year to the north and one to the south and some maritime commerce with Abyssinia—cannot be called international trade." And particularly not if, as we have seen, that "summer and winter caravan" itself is called into question.

44. The memory of the house where Muhammad was born thus passes with all its links intact from the Prophet's day down to Ibn Ishaq's and beyond: Khayzuran was the wife of the Caliph al-Mahdi and probably got the property during her *Hajj* of 778 A.D. See Tabari, *Annals*, vol. 1, p. 986; al-Azraqi 1858, p. 422; and cf. Ibn Jubayr's account of his eleventh century visit: *Travels*, vol. 5, pp. 115, 167.

45. So the anonymous *Life* cited by Lammens 1911, p. 212: "The Prophet was born in this very year, fifty days or two months after the departure of the Elephant, or perhaps ten, fifteen or even twenty years afterward . . . "; cf. Conrad 1987, p. 234.

46. On the varying reports on the age of Muhammad at his death, see Tabari, *Annals*, vol. 1, pp. 1834–1837.

47. On how the calculation generally proceeded, see Lammens 1910, p. 32.

48. Cited by Kister 1965c, p. 427; cf. Conrad 1987, p. 238.

49. Conrad 1987, p. 234, and cf. Quran 46: 15.

50. Landau-Tasseron 1986, p. 45; and Conrad 1987, pp. 438–439.

51. Lammens 1911, p. 242: "The marriage to Khadija and its rich legend comes from the same workshop. This Quraysh woman could have been the grandmother of Muhammad in a land where there were 22-year-old grandmothers . . . (Ibn Ishaq's *Life*) very prudently hesitates when it is a question of determining the date of the marriage or the respective ages of the two spouses. The difference in the numbers supplied in this regard ranges from twenty to twenty-eight years."

52. Lammens 1911, pp. 218–219: "In the whole *Sira* only one datum seems acceptable, the ten years that passed between the Hijra and the death of Muhammad. . . . The Prophet would have died at Medina the 13th of First Rabi', year 11 of the Hijra = 8 June 632. That would put his arrival in the city about 622 of our era: 622 and 632, two dates that deserve to inspire our confidence, however relative. As for the prior period, that at Mecca, it remains wrapped in impenetrable darkness." And Conrad 1987, p. 239: "It is worth noting that well into the second

century A.H. scholarly opinion on the birth date of the Prophet displayed a range of variance of eighty-five years. On the assumption that chronology is crucial to the stabilization of any tradition of historical narrative, whether transmitted orally or in writing, one can see in this state of affairs a clear indication that (biographies of the Prophet) in the second century were still in a state of flux."

53. Cf. Lammens 1911, pp. 238–239.

54. *Ibid.*, p. 242; Fahd 1983, pp. 67, 71–72; cf. Wansbrough 1978, p. 4.

55. On this "opening of Mohammad's breast," see Chapter 6.

5. THE GODS AND THE SHRINE

1. Lammens 1926.

2. On the Quran's account, this was the form of paganism from which Abraham was converted to the worship of the One True God: Quran: 6: 74–79.

3. Wellhausen 1897, pp. 217–224.

4. Henninger 1959, p. 12.

5. Other sources say that it came from northern Jordan.

6. The most powerful of the Meccan opponents of Muhammad and an eventual convert to Islam.

7. Fahd 1968, p. 101: "Hubal, a divinized ancestor, would be one of the most ancient deities of the descendants of Ishmael. . . . His name appears in Nabatean and Thamudean inscriptions. . . . In passing from the camp of nomads into the sanctuary of sedentarized peoples, he was assimilated to the other figures of the Semitic pantheon. . . . When Amr ibn Luhayy brought his statue . . . , he brought only the (cornelian) statue of an anonymous archer, his right arm broken off. It was difficult for the Banu Ishmael to agree to represent the divinity in human form, but the Meccan caravaneers had seen, in the course of their travels, the production of statues in the Hellenistic cities and the ruins of ancient temples. To give to their sanctuary an appearance more or less conformed to what they had seen in nearby countries, whose progress must have dazzled them, they consented to the placement of imported statues and the production of paintings." On the paintings in the Ka'ba, see later.

8. See Ibn Ishaq 1955, pp. 66–67, and the same author's account of the "binding of Abdullah" recorded previously.

9. Al-Azraqi 1858, p. 111.

10. Cf. Fahd 1968, pp. 101–102.

11. So Ibn al-Kalbi, p. 11, and cf. Fahd 1968, p. 163, on the absence of the name from Semitic inscriptions.

12. Ibn al-Kalbi, p. 15.

13. Ibn al-Kalbi, p. 19; cf. Wellhausen 1897, p. 30.

14. On the equally problematic opening verse, see Chapter 6, note 7.

15. See Birkeland 1956, pp. 76–78, who remarks (pp. 85–86): "So it is a notorious fact that the Quran contains at least one *sura* from a time *before* Muhammad had abandoned the performance of religious rites customary in Mecca."

16. Henninger 1959, pp. 12–13; Watt 1988.

17. Wellhausen 1897, pp. 101 ff.; Goldziher 1889/1967, p. 211; Fahd 1968, p. 26.

18. Tabari, *Annals*, vol. 1, p. 1192; on this incident, see chapter 6.

19. Fahd 1968, p. 89.

20. Ibn al-Kalbi 12.

21. *Salat* is almost certainly a loan-word, borrowed from Aramaic-Syriac and so taken over from contemporary Jewish or Christian usage. Cf. Jeffery 1938, pp. 198–199 and Quran 22: 40 cited later, where the word *salawat* is used to denote synagogues.

22. Ryckmans 1951, pp. 20 ff.

23. *Ibid.*, p. 34.

24. See the evidence noted in Rubin 1987 and cf. Quran 20: 130 and 50: 39–40: "And praise your Lord *before* the rising of the sun and *before* its setting . . . " (emphasis added) and the prophetic traditions assembled in the canonical collections under the head "Do Not Get into the Habit of Prayer at the Time of the Rising of the Sun and Its Setting."

25. Wellhausen 1897, pp. 79–84; Crone 1987, p. 173.

26. Ibn Ishaq 1955, pp. 49–50; cf. Wellhausen 1897, p. 81, and the demur in Kister 1965a, p. 155.

27. Kister 1965a, p. 136, n. 1; 1980, pp. 37–38; Crone 1987, p. 176.

28. The commentators were not certain who raised the objection to mixing trade with the pilgrimage, whether the pre-Islamic Arabs or the early Muslims, but the preferred view was that it was the latter; see Crone 1987, p. 171 and n. 20.

29. The evidence is collected in Crone 1987, pp. 170–174.

30. And that eventually led to the desertion and disappearance of Ukaz, Dhu al-Majaz, and Majanna, which, whatever their earlier commercial (and religious?) importance, were assigned no *ritual* role in the Muslim version of the *Hajj*; cf. al-Azraqi 1858, p. 131, and Crone 1987, p. 157, n. 49.

31. On the rituals of Rajab, see Wellhausen 1897, pp. 74, 93; Gaudefroy-Demombynes 1923, pp. 192–194; Goitein 1966, pp. 92–93; Kister 1971.

32. Wellhausen 1897, pp. 94, 115–116.

33. Cf. Quran 2: 158: "So if you *Hajj* the House or '*umra* it . . . " (where both rituals are used as verbs), it is "no sin" to make a "turning" around Safa and Marwa, a ritual identified not with the pre-Islamic *Hajj* but with the '*umra*.

34. Al-Azraqi 1858, p. 134; cf. Kister 1980, pp. 33–34.

35. On the older, and now discredited, conviction that the "Abrahamic" aspects of Muhammad's preaching were only a consequence of his confrontation with the Jews at Medina, see Beck 1975 and Rubin 1990, p. 99, n. 68.

36. Beck 1975, pp. 116–122.

37. *Ibid.*, p. 119.

38. *Ibid.*, pp. 121–122; and cf. Dagorn 1981, pp 127–133.

39. *Ibid.*, pp. 124–126.

40. The consensus opinion was that Muhammad prayed facing Jerusalem before changing his prayer direction to the Ka'ba early in his stay in Medina (cf. Quran 2: 142–144), but there is a persistent strain of reports that he prayed toward the Ka'ba even before he prayed facing Jerusalem; see Rubin 1990, p. 102, and Chapter 8.

41. Ibn Ishaq 1955, p. 67; cf. Rubin 1990, pp. 103–104.

42. Cf. Rubin 1990, pp. 104–106; Firestone 1990, p. 143.

43. Josephus, *Ant.* 1, 12: 2; on pre-Islamic Arab circumcision, see Wellhausen 1897, pp. 174–176.

44. Jubilees 20: 11–13 (cf. Rubin 1990, p. 106); Babylonian Talmud *Sanhedrin* 91a.

45. It is clearly a loan-word in Arabic (Jeffery 1938, pp. 112–115), but its obvious antecedent, the Syriac plural *hanpe*, is used by pre-Islamic Christian writers to designate "pagans" or "idolators" and so in precisely the opposite sense from that invoked in the Quran.

46. Guillaume remarks (Ibn Ishaq 1955, p. 99, n. 2): "The influence of this Jewish formula, taken over by early Christianity (Acts 15:29) is clear."

47. Watt, *EI²*, art. "Hanif," thinks that many, if not all, such stories are retrospective Islamic projections for apologetic purposes, but among others, Fück 1981, p. 91, accepts some of them, as does Rubin 1990, pp. 85–86, particularly when they concern men who opposed Muhammad: "The reports concerning these persons must be taken as authentic, because as already noted by Fück, no Muslim could have any interest in characterizing those opponents of the Prophet as *hanifs* . . . "

48. Fück 1981, p. 91.

49. Studied by Gil 1987 and Rubin 1990, pp. 86–88, 90–94.

50. Ibn Ishaq 1955, p. 278; cf. Wellhausen 1897, p. 239.

51. Wellhausen 1897, p. 238, n. 1, doubted their authenticity, but Rubin 1990, p. 90, accepted them.

52. Rubin 1990, pp. 92–93.

53. *Ibid.*, pp. 94–97.

54. Kister 1970.

55. Cited by Kister 1970, p. 270.

56. Cf. Kister 1970, p. 275; Rubin 1990, p. 101.

57. Gibb 1962, p. 273.

58. *Ibid.*, pp. 274–275.

59. Gibb here remarks *(ibid.*, pp. 275–276) that "No evidence has yet been found either for the significance of Sirius in the ancient star-cults of Southern Arabia or for the existence of a contemporary star-worshipping community in Arabia. The early Islamic tradition is equally at a loss . . . " Not so. We have already noted the a liturgical chant of the *Hums* expressing the same sentiment (cf. Kister 1980, pp. 36, 37).

60. By Islamic times the verb *to sojourn* had taken on a technical meaning, to pass a shorter or longer period of time in pious prayer and practices at one of the preeminent mosques of Islam, notably, though by no means exclusively, at either of the "Twin Harams" of Mecca and Medina.

61. Guillaume in Ibn Ishaq 1955, p. 105 has: " . . . the Apostle would pray in seclusion and give food to the poor."

62. Cited by Kister 1968b, p. 224.

63. *Ibid.*, pp. 226–227.

64. *Ibid.*, pp. 228–230; cf. Watt 1953, p. 44.

65. Cited *by* Kister 1968b, p. 232.

66. Cited *ibid.*, p. 233.

67. See the analysis of the eight Quranic occurrences of the word *'akifa* in Wagtendonk 1968, pp. 72–74; and cf. Wellhausen 1897, p. 61. Quran 2: 187 underlines the fact that sexual abstention during the *'ukuf-*retreat was still in force even though the Muslims were freed of that restraint during the nights of Ramadan.

68. Wagtendonk 1968, p. 76. As Wagtendonk remarks, in its Islamic form, the "standing" at Arafat, the only one of the practices to survive into Islam, is an "empty rite," or at least a baffling one, because, with the replacement of all prayer by the Islamic liturgical variety (*salat*), it lost its supplicatory component.

69. See generally on this critical verse Birkeland 1956, pp. 28–33, and for the meaning of *dalla* and *hada, ibid.*, p. 28, and cf. 53: 2 where he defends himself against the charge of erring (*dalla*), of spreading nothing more than the old paganism, by citing his supernatural visions.

70. In a tradition preserved by the later exegete Razi, and cited by Birkeland 1956, p. 29, Kalbi paraphrased this Quranic verse as "He found you an unbeliever *(kafir)* in a people of error and guided you."

71. Birkeland 1956, pp. 29–30, and cf. *ibid.*: "The analysis made above of Muslim interpretation of the Quran has shown that this interpretation in the form it has been transmitted to us, viz. in its oldest stage as *hadith*, does not contain reliable information on the earliest period of Muhammad at Mecca."

72. *Ibid.*, p. 79.

73. Cf. *ibid.*, p. 85: " . . . it is a notorious fact that the Quran con-

tains at least one *sura* from a time before Muhammad had abandoned the performance of religious rites customary at Mecca."

6. A PROPHET AT MECCA

1. The same theme occurs after Muhammad begins his "public life"; cf. Wansbrough 1978, p. 4: "The passage *Sira* 1.204–232 [= Ibn Ishaq 1955, pp. 130–149] contains a fourfold account of the response, among various groups in the Arabian peninsula, to the earliest reports about the prophet Muhammad. The most easily observed feature of this account is the representative character of the four groups: soothsayers, Jews, Christians and men in search of God. The reactions of each to signs that a new prophetical age was imminent are determined to some extent by typical features (respectively: daemonism, messianic expectation, ascetic piety, dissatisfaction with traditional worship), but also by the order of the presentation: from the demonstrable inadequacy of the pagan oracle, the accurate though perversely rejected prognosis of the Jews, and the Christian stress upon the role of the saintly teacher, to the confident recognition by the *hanifs* of genuine and unadulterated faith with the figure of Abraham . . . "

2. Part of the celebrity of the Bahira story stems from the fact that early on the Christians expropriated it for their own purposes. In their versions, Bahira, now transformed into Sergius, is not so much the harbinger of the Prophet as his informant: it was the (apostate) monk Sergius who planted the idea of prophecy in Muhammad's head and then fleshed it out with half-baked Christian notions. The development of the story is traced in Khoury 1972, pp. 76–87.

3. Watt 1953, pp. 11, 14–15; Landau-Tasseron 1986; Crone 1987, pp. 145–148; see for the sources, Crone *ibid.*, p. 146, n. 62, and for the wider commercial implications of the wars, the differing viewpoints of Landau-Tasseron 1986, p. 51, and Crone 1987, pp. 147–148.

4. Landau-Tasseron 1986, p. 45; Conrad 1987, pp. 438–439; and more generally on the effect of the "impeccability" doctrine on Quranic interpretation, Birkeland 1956, pp. 29–30.

5. Cf. Lammens 1911, p. 242: "There is the same hesitation when it comes to indicating the birth year of the children of the Prophet and the order of their coming into this world. Let us leave Qasim to the side; his personality rests above all on the *kunya*, Abu'l-Qasim, of the Prophet. . . . As regards the daughters, we are better off. The most generally accepted opinion among the orthodox makes Zaynab the eldest and Fatima the youngest. On the subject of Ruqayya and Umm Kulthum there are widely divergent opinions. Why is Zaynab considered the eldest? Because she seems to have been the first to marry and Muham-

mad, reasons the Tradition, would have set up his eldest daughter first. A ✗
similar line of reasoning makes Fatima Muhammad's youngest daughter." Because Fatima did not marry Ali until after the battle of Uhud, she
would have been 20 at the time, rather too old, according to Lammens,
"in a society where girls were married at between 9 and 12." So they
pushed her birth forward to make her only 15, "with the result of giving
her a sexagenarian mother. Our authors debate between Khadija's 65 ✗
years and the 15 beyond which Ali's fiancee cannot go."

6. Birkeland 1956, p. 24.

7. The same dogma of an untroubled Muhammad both *before* and
during his prophetic career may likewise have affected the interpretation
of the first line of the early Sura 94, which we have already seen and
which reads: "Have We not given you abundance." The last word (*al-
kawthar*) was understood by the earliest traditionists as "abundant
worldly goods," and so must have also referred to Muhammad's change
in fortunes after his marriage. It was an interpretation the legend could
not support and so within a century and a half after Muhammad's death
it began to be understood as "a river in Paradise"; Birkeland 1956, p. 69.

8. The building history of the Ka'ba is given in summary in al-
Azraqi 1858, pp. 307 ff., and on a number of occasions by Qutb al-Din
1857, pp. 55 ff., 146 ff., 202, 207, 221 ff.

9. Rubin 1986, p. 99, cites reports that at the time of the Jurhum a
kind of "barrier" (*jidar*)—the builders were called *jadara*—or dam was
built near the Ka'ba.

10. One apparently historical allusion occurs in the opening verses
of Sura 30: "The Rum ["the Romans"; normally, the Byzantines] have
been defeated in the nearer land, and they, after their defeat, will be victorious within a few years." The Byzantines were in fact defeated by the
Persians throughout Syria-Palestine in the decade of Muhammad's first
revelations—Jerusalem fell to them in 614—and then began to reverse ⁄
the tide in 622 A.D., leading to the eventual defeat of the Persians in 628.
The complexities of this particular *sura*—where precisely is the "nearer
land"?—are meditated in Beck 1944–1945.

11. Cf. Goldfeld 1980, p. 58: "The concept of the Prophet Muhammad's literacy seems to have evolved in some circles of Muslim learning
not before the first half of the second century of the *Hijra*." There is a
brief sampling of the traditional Muslim Quranic commentary in Ayoub
1984, pp. 121–122; see also Chapter 8.

12. More revealing is 2: 78: "Among them are *ummis* who do not
know the Book except by hearsay . . . " which seems to define the *ummi*
as a pagan, someone who does not have, or know, Scripture, a meaning
that makes more sense in all the passages where the word occurs in the
Quran. Compare 29: 48: "You [that is, Muhammad] did not recite any ✗
Book before this, nor write one with your write hand," which the Mus-

lims commentators construe as a sign of absolute illiteracy—"you could not previously read or write"—whereas Western scholars understand it as attesting to "Scriptural illiteracy." The entire question is discussed in Zwemer 1921; Watt 1970, pp. 33–37. Denny 1977, pp. 39–40, reviews some of the translations-interpretations, which range from the Western hesitation between *laikos*, "one uninstructed in Scripture" and *ethnikos*, "a Gentile, a member of a community without Scripture," to the Muslims' *illiterate*. Denny's own preference is "unscriptured," whereas Watt 1970, p. 31, argues that either *Gentile* or *native* prophet does justice to the Quranic passages.

13. On the near-unanimity of scholars on the point, see Hurgronje 1894/1957; Bell 1926, pp. 110, 140; and on the unavailablity of Arabic translations until much later, Griffith 1985 and Lazarus-Yafeh 1992 *passim.*

14. The Quran is not "speaking" but a "recitation," usually a liturgical text, as its derivation from the Syriac *qeryana* indicates (Jeffery 1938, p. 234; Graham 1985, p.31), and so it is not clear from this passage whether Muhammad was already "reciting" the Quran or indeed whether its words had already been revealed or not; see, note 17.

15. *Dalla*, the same word used to describe Muhammad's pre-prophetic state in 93: 7.

16. So generally the Muslim tradition and Schrieke 1916 and Horovitz 1919 early on among the Westerners; *contra* Bell 1934a, pp. 98–99.

17. The word translated as "inspiration" in verse 10 (*wahy*) was generally understood as the "inspiration of (Scriptural) revelation" by later Muslims, but as Richard Bell has pointed out (Bell 1934b, pp. 94–96), the Quranic usage is more generally "to suggest" or "to prompt." As to "seeing the great signs (*ayat*) of the Lord," though *ayat* later comes to mean "verses of the Quran," it does not generally have that meaning in the Quran itself, though the recitation of "signs" is described in the Quran as the work of God's Messengers (39: 71); see Watt 1970, pp. 126–127.

18. The arguments were made early on in Schrieke 1916 and Horovitz 1919 and are still current in the new edition of the *Encyclopaedia of Islam*, s.v. *Mir'aj*.

19. So Wagtendonk 1968, p. 109.

20. Schrieke 1916, pp. 6–9.

21. On the original interpretation of Sura 94 and its evolving, dogma-driven exegesis, see Birkeland 1956, pp. 38–55; and for the connection of the purification ritual with the ascension in the typology, Schrieke 1916, p. 9.

22. Tabari, *Annals*, vol. 1, p. 1159.

23. See Bell 1934a and Watt 1953, pp. 39 ff., who analyzes the vari-

ous, and still not harmonized, accounts in Tabari, *Annals*, vol. 1, pp. 1147 ff. Sellheim 1987 has attempted to sort out the various versions and he appears to subscribe to Frantz Buhl's conclusion (Buhl 1955–1961, p. 136) that, in the light of the contradictory stories, Muhammad's very earliest revelations were in fact lost.

24. Cf. Watt 1953: "There is no effective objections to the almost universal view of Muslim scholars that this is the first part of the Quran to be revealed. No other passage can contest the claim of Sura 96 with any chance of success. A command to worship is just what we should expect to come first in view of the general tenor of the primary message of the Quran. The word 'recite' is addressed to Muhammad alone. and, although there is no difficulty in extending it to his followers in imitation of him, it is conceivable that the very thought of having followers had not occurred to him when it was revealed; that is, it may very well belong to a stage before he began to preach to others." Cf. Watt in Tabari 1988, p. xxxvii.

25. cf. Watt in Tabari 1988, p. xxxviii: "The receiving of passages of the Quran does not seem to have been accompanied by any visual experience, and so it is possible that Muhammad thought that it was 'his Lord' [as God is called in the earliest suras] himself who was putting the Quran in his heart. Interpreted in this way, the story may be essentially true, at least in those versions in which the words *ma aqra'u* are taken to mean 'what shall I recite?' At some point a Muslim scholar realized that these words could also mean 'I do not recite' or 'do not read.' By this time, in order to counter Christian claims that Muhammad had taken stories from the Bible, it had become a point of Muslim apologetic that Muhammad was unable to read; and so the story of the first revelation was sometimes modified to support this line of apologetic. Such modifications are certainly not original."

26. See Chapter 5.

27. Wansbrough 1977, p. 36.

28. See Chapter 8 for his choice at Medina of the "Night of Destiny" for the single and complete revelation of the Quran.

29. Muhammad is here referred to, as often, by his "name of paternity." Nothing more is known of al-Qasim, the Prophet's sole male child by Khadija.

30. See, on this entire incident, Watt 1953, pp. 51–52, and *idem.* in Tabari 1988, p. xxxviii.

31. On this so-called gap in the sequence of revelations, see Watt 1953, pp. 48–49, who would place it three years after the beginning of the revelations and so just before the beginning of Muhammad's "public ministry"; see later.

32. On the choice of Ramadan as the month in which the revelations began, see Wagtendonk 1968, pp. 82–122, and on 40 as the archetypical benchmark of maturity, see Conrad 1987, p. 234.

33. Cf. Watt 1953, p. 48.

34. Birkeland 1956, pp. 131–132; cf. Welch 1980, p. 734.

35. Cf. Birkeland, *ibid.*, p. 5: "I think I have demonstrated (from an analysis of these *suras*) that it was not the approaching day of Judgment . . . which formed the foundation of his [that is, Muhammad's] first preaching. The experience which became decisive for Muhammad's whole future activity must have the recognition of God's merciful guidance in the life of himself and his people, that means *in history.* . . . The *suras* treated in this paper reveal a stage in which Muhammad had not yet severed from Arab paganism, but had only experienced the divine power as a historic force, which meant a force active in the historic life of the Quraysh and the personal life of Muhammad himself. A divine activity of that kind was unknown in Arab paganism . . . "

36. *Ibid.*, pp. 132–133.

37. The sequence of these conversions is by no means certain; cf. the multiple variants in Tabari, *Annals*, vol. 1, pp. 1159–1168; and Watt 1953, p. 86.

38. A propos of this *sura*, Watt remarks (1953, p. 47): "There is a tradition from Jabir ibn Abdullah al-Ansari that the opening verses of Sura 74 were the first revelation. This is fitting in that it contains the words 'rise and warn,' which seem to be a command to enter upon the work of an apostle or messenger. This can only be the first revelation, however, if Muhammad entered abruptly on his public ministry without any period of preparation. If, however, there was such a preparatory period, and if there were revelations in that, then this would not be the first revelation; and . . . the 'recite' (of Sura 96) does not imply a public ministry. The persistence of this tradition, despite the general agreement at an early period that Sura 96 was the first revelation, suggests that there is a grain of truth in it; the most probable view is that it marks the beginning of the public ministry."

39. See Watt's (1953, pp. 61 ff.) summary of the earliest preaching. Though there is agreement *in sum* on the Quranic message at Mecca, the nuances of the *sequence* of the revelation, and hence of Muhammad's own spiritual evolution, are by no means so clear: cf. Hurgronje 1874/1957 and Paret 1983, pp. 186–193.

40. On the absence of the name *Allah* in the early suras, Jomier 1957, p. 371, n. 3; Watt in Tabari 1988, pp. xxxiii–xxxiv.

41. Welch 1980, p. 734.

42. Though this deity is called in Quran 106:3 the *Lord of this House,* that is, the Ka'ba, it might equally refer to Hubal; cf. Birkeland 1956, pp. 131–132; Ryckmans 1951, p. 14 and notes; on the possible Jewish or Christian influence, Birkeland 1956, p. 131; Watt in Tabari 1988, p. xxxiii.

43. So variously Welch 1980, p. 734 and *idem, EI²* s.v. *al-Kur'an.*

44. Jomier 1957, pp. 362–363.

45. Ryckmans 1951, pp. 47–48.

46. Like Muhammad, Musaylima used the rhymed prose manner of the seers (Tabari, *Annals*, vol. 1, p. 1738, and see later), but he too disclaimed any connection with a *jinn* or *a shaytan*: Musaylima also identified himself as a "messenger of God" (*ibid.*, p. 1749), and his revelations came from on high, from a source identified as either *al-Rahman* (*ibid.*, p. 1937) or simply "he who comes from heaven."

47. *Ibid.*, vol. 1, pp. 1932–1933; cf. Watt 1956, p. 135.

48. Tabari *Ibid.*, vol. 1, pp. 1932, 1941; cf. Eickelman 1967, p. 35.

49. Watt in Tabari 1988, pp. xxxiv–xxxv; verse 26 of the same *sura* accepts such a role on the part of the angels: "How many angels there are in heaven whose intercession is of no avail except when God gives leave to those whom He chooses and accepts."

50. Quran 53: 23.

51. Cf. Welch 1980, p. 740: "This (argument) does not mean that the Meccans believed that they were worshiping angels; on the contrary, the identification of the Arabian goddesses with angels seems to be a Quranic development. There is no evidence to show that the Meccans ever accepted this interpretation of the identity of their gods and goddesses."

52. Cf. Watt 1953, p. 108: "When the idolators are said to make *jinn* partners of God, this need not imply that the idolators regarded them as *jinn*; the Quran may express the matter thus because this was the view taken at the time by Muhammad and others who had abandoned idol-worship."

53. Welch 1980, p. 742.

54. *Ibid.*, p. 743.

55. *Ibid.*, p. 744.

56. *Ibid.*, p. 745: "The relationship between *jinn* and *shaytans* in the Quran is clear and unmistakable. In contexts where these demons are evil, mischievous or unbelieving, the two terms are synonymous or interchangeable. There are, however, significant differences in the Quranic usages of the two terms: *shaytan* has the connotation of evil or unbelieving, and in its latest usage, in early Medinan contexts, it clearly refers to Muhammad's human opponents, most likely the Jews; the *jinn*, on the other hand, are sometimes said to be believers and this term is never applied to human adversaries anywhere in the Quran."

57. Wensinck 1975, p. 74; Jeffery 1938, pp. 98–99.

58. Caetani has argued (1905, p. 434) that "the ritual and liturgical elements of Islam are for the most part a product of the Medina milieu, and there was little or nothing (of such) while the Prophet was debating alone with the Quraysh in Mecca."

59. *Ibid.*, p. 435.

60. Cited by Rubin 1987, p. 40.

61. This prayer did not survive as one of the canonical Muslim prayers. At some point very early on it was replaced by the *fajr* prayer performed shortly *before* sunrise; cf. Rubin 1987, pp. 56–57.

62. Rubin *ibid.*, pp. 54, 57, proposes that the Quraysh's objection to the *'asr* prayer, as well as the Prophet's substitution of a predawn for a postsunrise prayer (see the preceding note), is the result of Muhammad's deliberate adoption of Jewish models for these two prayers.

63. The Muslims generally explained the name as referring to a stone on which Abraham stood to build the Ka'ba (see Chapter 1), and such was later displayed in the Haram, but a far more likely explanation traces it back to Abraham's *place of prayer*: indeed, there is an explicit reference in Genesis 19: 17 to just such a place: "Abraham rose early and went to the place where he had stood (*maqom*) in the presence of the Lord," and that is the passage that the Talmud cites (Babylonian Talmud *Berakhot* 6b) when it recommends that each believer should have his own *maqom* for prayer.

64. Quran 57: 27; 5: 85; 9: 34.

65. Following Caetani, Welch 1983, pp. 21–22, has argued that not only the night vigils but the morning and evening *salat* were Muhammad's obligation alone at Mecca and that there is evidence to suggest that at Mecca "Muhammad performed the ritual publicly, while his followers participated mainly by their presence, listening in silence and possibly reciting (doxological) formulas . . . at various points. In any case, these passages [e.g., 11: 114–115; 40: 55] show that one of Muhammad's primary roles within the community during the Meccan period was as worship leader, and that he continued to perform the *salat* in spite of persecution and the temptation to discontinue it." Cf. Caetani 1905, vol. 1, p. 453: "What I conclude is that when in Medina he had the opportunity of praying repetitively in the course of a day, he had on each of those occasions a number of his followers ranged behind him in a composed and orderly manner and that they attempted to imitate the movements and prostrations that he used in prayer; and that he certainly had the custom of arranging his followers in the courtyard of his house, and that it is probably, in order to have a larger and more certain crowd of the faithful, he, in imitation of the Jews and Christians, took up the custom of preaching by preference on one day of the week (Friday). All of that is, however, a patriarchal, one might even say domestic, habit of the Prophet rather than a strict law for his followers. Muhammad himself, as is apparent from many traditions, (see for example the narrative of the pilgrimage of farewell) did not always pray in a regular fashion but rather as was convenient for him, that is, not at fixed hours, but at the individual stages of a journey, in whatever place or hour might have been the most convenient . . . "

66. Wensinck 1975, p. 77.
67. Jeffery 1938, pp. 233–234.
68. Graham 1985, p. 31.
69. Wansbrough 1978, pp. 68–69: "After Norden's meticulous analysis [*Agnostos Theos*, 1913] of basic prayer structure from the spheres of Hellenism, Judaism, and Christianity, it can be observed as a matter of course that the equivalent Muslim expressions conform to type. For eulogy, doxology, and basileia, Baumstark [1927] has noted phraseological correspondences. Such rhetorical devices as parallelism, alliteration, anaphora, and isokola are common to all four literatures, and certainly suggest a shared legacy. . . . What I have described (above) as Quranic formulae exhibit the same shared devices and appear to have filled the same liturgical functions. . . . " The clearest, and perhaps the most deliberate, example of a liturgical *sura* is undoubtedly Sura 1, the "Fatiha"; see Goitein 1966, pp. 82–84.

7. THE MIGRATION TO MEDINA

1. Cf. the passages examined by Watt 1953, pp. 60–85.
2. Watt in Tabari 1988, pp. xli–xlii.
3. Would a man who was then, on the traditional chronology, 43- or 44-years-old be referred to a "a youth of the clan of Abd al-Mut-talib"?
4. Cited by Watt 1953, p. 87.
5. Watt 1953, p. 101, regards the document cited by Tabari as likely genuine.
6. Zwettler 1990, pp. 77–88: " . . . the *Kahin* was a consultant on the occult, a soothsayer or oracle whose short, cryptic, rhymed, *jinn*-inspired pronouncements on such matters as lost camels, launching of raids, determination of paternity, and especially dream interpretation and other kinds of auguries were seldom volunteered but were besought and usually compensated. . . . Contrasted with the rhymed and cadenced *saj'*of the *kuhhan*, the utterances of the poets were far more regular and patterned in their formal structure. . . . Poets themselves seem to have participated to a much greater extent in the social life of the Jahiliyya, serving sometimes as respected spokesmen for their own tribes, feared hurlers of invective verse at enemies, welcome panegyricists before kings and chietains, and admired masters of verbal art in any assembly"; cf. Fahd 1966, pp. 91–104. But as Zwettler points out, there is no evidence that any Arabian seer or poet was ever given anything remotely resembling the kind of political power eventually granted to Muhammad at Medina.
7. Paret 1983, pp. 196–197; Zwettler 1990, p. 81. Considerable

attention has now been paid to the "poetic," or better, "prophetic" style of the earliest revelations (Crapon de Carpona 1981; Neuwirth 1981), though principally from the point of view of internal Quranic form criticism and not as a point of comparison with similar contemporary styles.

8. Not the least of the uncertainties is the identification and function of the group known as "the Abyssinians" (*ahabish*) who often show up in Mecca in pre-Islamic days. Lammens had suggested (1928b, pp. 238–294) that they were a band of African mercenaries who constituted the principal armed force of the Quraysh, and though the thesis has been attacked, the most recent inspection of the problem has supported Lammens' conclusions and gone a step further: "It is a fact that there was at Mecca an important colony of Abyssinians of a servile status who performed all sorts of tasks and occupied an important place in the Meccan economy. . . . It is likely that it was under the influence of this class that the Prophet chose Abyssinia as a refuge for his first followers when they were threatened by the Qurashite notables" (Fahd 1989, p. 542).

9. On the return, Ibn Ishaq 1955, pp. 526–528; and on the dubious religious standing of the emigrants, Caetani 1905, pp. 264–265, 279.

10. Watt 1953, pp. 114–115.

11. Mayerson 1964, pp. 190–195; Schick 1987.

12. Tabari 1897, p. 299, n. 4.

13. The pronounced Jewish quality of Abyssinian Christianity, noted by almost every later European visitor, is reviewed and analyzed by Ullendorff 1956.

14. The sources describe a formal three-year boycott; indeed, a document to that effect was reportedly affixed to the wall of the Ka'ba. Caetani has raised strenuous arguments against the traditional account, though he is certain that informal social and economic pressures were brought to bear: Caetani 1905, pp. 288–293.

15. Her own account is preserved in Tabari, *Annals*, vol. 1, pp. 1769–1770.

16. This, certainly the most controversial of his marriages, is referred to in the Quran (33: 37), wherein the Prophet is granted permission to marry his cousin Zaynab, who was also the recently divorced wife of his freedman and adopted son Zayd ibn Haritha. Zaynab, it is said, used to boast in consequence that it was God who had given her away in marriage and Gabriel who had served as the go-between; Tabari 1990, p. 134, n. 897.

17. The Muslim authorities, most of whom devoted considerable attention to Muhammad's wives (cf. Tabari, *Annals*, vol. 1, pp. 1766–1778), were highly uncertain about both the number and names of his spouses; cf. Tabari 1990, p. 127, n. 871.

18. Both the expression *pledge of the women (believers)* and the

conditions connected with it are taken verbatim from Quran 60: 12, whose context we do not know, though it was not very likely this occasion. The term used here (*bay'a*) is a political pledge of allegiance, the type given to a tribal leader or, later, to the ruler of the Muslim community.

19. Cf. Wensinck 1975, p. 80: "I give particular credence to this account. Tradition prefers not to acknowledge any dependence on Judaism or Christianity; rather, it would like to give the impression that the institutions of the cult are merely a continuation of the religion of Abraham. For this reason, a tradition such as this can be trusted since it cannot have been fabricated to serve dogmatic purposes."

20. Becker 1967, p. 495, and on the priority of the Friday prayer over the sermon (*khutba*) on that day, *ibid.*, p. 476.

21. Goitein 1968, pp. 112–113.

22. *Ibid.*, p. 116; Lecker 1985, pp. 53–55; and cf. Lecker 1986.

23. Goitein 1968, p. 117.

24. So Watt 1953, pp. 146–147.

25. Cf. Watt 1953, p. 148: "He cannot have intended them [that is, the Muslims who might have come with him] to remain permanently the idle guests of the Medinans, and he can hardly have expected them to settle down as farmers. . . . Muhammad must have realized that his migration to Medina would lead sooner or later to active hostility with the Quraysh and Muhammad would have foreseen that. How much of this did he communicate to the Medinans and in what form? And how much did they realize of themselves? . . . "

26. The imagery is probably biblical; the Jordan is a long way indeed from Mecca.

27. See Ali 1954, pp. 135, 137; and Watt in Tabari 1988, p. xlvi.

28. Cf. Ali 1954, p. 126: "There is more calendrical confusion connected with the ten years of Muhammad's mission in Medina than with any other decade of human history either before or after this period."

29. Cf. Lammens 1911, pp. 240–242.

8. THE CITY OF THE PROPHET

1. Lammens 1911, p. 245.

2. The settlement was still called *Yathrib* in the Quran (33: 13), but afterward the name was dropped and only *Medina* was used, now understood as *Madinat al-Nabi*, "The City of the Prophet"; cf. Hasson 1989, p. 3, n. 11.

3. Burton 1893, vol. 1, pp. 400–401.

4. Cited by Wensinck 1975, p. 10.

5. Hasson 1989, pp. 11–12.

6. *Ibid.*, pp. 7–8.

7. Wellhausen 1889, p. 17.

8. At Medina too the earliest settlers were supposed to be Amalekites, who blended with, or were replaced by, later arrivals from South Arabia.

9. Gil 1984, p. 208.

10. Cf. *ibid.*, pp. 209–210. Isfahani (d. 967) quotes a source in his *Kitab al-Aghani*, vol. 19, p. 94, that maintained that the Jews had come to Yathrib after they had been conquered by the Romans, and Gil's own view, which is based on an analysis of the traditions that trace some of the Jewish tribes back to the Banu Judham, a tribe of the region of the ancient Midian and probably reflecting the "sons of Jethro" of the Jewish sources, is that the Medinese Jewish tribes were originally proselytes of bedouin descent, converted by "Jewish refugees who fled from the Romans (most probably in A.D. 70, and perhaps also in 135) into Arabia. It is apparently these refugees who formed the first layer of the Jewish population of the northern Hijaz. During the centuries that followed, they increased in number through Arab tribes who converted, and adopted an agricultural life, taking over not only the Jews' religion and way of life, but their spoken language, Aramaic" (Gil 1984, pp. 218–219).

11. *Ibid.*, pp. 210–211.

12. Ahmad 1979, pp. 42–43.

13. Waqidi, *Maghazi*, vol. 1, p. 480.

14. Ibn Khurdadhbih, p. 128; cf. Kister 1968a, pp. 145–149; Gil 1984, p. 205, and Chapter 3.

15. Ibn Ishaq 1955, pp. 240–241; cf. Wellhausen 1889, p. 12, and Chapter 2 where Dhu Nuwas, the Jewish ruler of the Yemen, is said to have had in his service rabbis from the famous academic center of Tiberias.

16. So Waqidi, vol. 1, p. 184, where they are called *halif*, "allies," of the Aws and Khazraj.

17. Wellhausen 1889, p. 7; Caetani 1905, vol. 1, p. 384; Wensinck 1975, p. 24.

18. The picture is possibly overdrawn. There were thirteen Jewish tribes mentioned at Medina during this period, although Muhammad took action against only three. What of the others? They may have been minor affiliates of the three chief Jewish tribes and so suffered the same fate, or they may have been protected by special treaties with the Aws and Khazraj of the type mentioned in the latter clauses of the "Constitution of Medina" (Serjeant 1978, p. 3). There are, in fact, indications that a substantial part of the Jewish population retained its independence, if not its former sovereignty (cf. Wellhausen 1889, p. 11; Watt 1956, pp. 193–194), and continued to live in the most fertile and healthy parts of the oasis to the end of Muhammad's career (Wensinck 1975, pp. 25–26).

19. Hasson 1989, pp. 12–14. Hasson is aware, however, like others who have studied the place, that there was also a strong commercial tradition—four different pre-Islamic markets are mentioned—connected with Medina. The later Arab sources connect it (*ibid.*, p. 13, n. 80), like the one at Mecca, with a supposed international trade for which there is very little other evidence.

20. This may be literally true, but as we have already seen in Chapter 7, Mus'ab ibn Umayr had initiated a Friday service at Medina before the Prophet's arrival there.

21. Caetani 1905, p. 437: "The *dar* . . . at that time in Arabia consisted of a circle of small rooms collected in an irregular and concentric fashion around an open court, more of less roomy, according to one's means and the size of the family which lived in it. . . . The open space provided a meeting place for the whole family . . . "

22. Caetani 1905, pp. 439–440.

23. The history of this somewhat obscure remark is traced by Kister 1962.

24. *Ibid.*, p. 445: "The process of the transformation of the private residence of Muhammad into a public temple and into the sanctuary of Islam, was a long one, something that is not apparent if one accepts all the traditions without distinction. It was still going on after the death of the Prophet since Abu Bakr, Umar and Uthman used his house in exactly the way he had. . . . The great moral shift with respect to the home of the Prophet took place after Ali (r. 656–661 A.D.) moved the seat of government outside Arabia, and Medina declined to the rank of a provincial city and a place of memories. . . . People no longer came to Medina in search of careers, riches or honors, but merely to pursue to the great memories of the past."

25. The normal time for a caravan to traverse the same distance between Damascus and Medina was month or more. The imperial post could obviously do much better.

26. Al-Ali 1961, p. 86, and studied in Kister 1965b, cf. p. 276: "The scanty reports about the market established by the Prophet in Medina . . . are recorded by Umar ibn Shabba and Ibn Zubala, both competent authorities on the history of Medina. These reports were omitted in other sources because the event of the market was not of enough important in shaping the image of the Prophet and the early community by later authorities as the market itself did not survive and did not serve as a place of devotion."

27. Cited by Kister 1965b, p. 272, who sees a possible connection between these events and the assassination of the Jewish leader Ka'b al-Ashraf reported by Tabari (*Annals*, vol. 1, pp. 1368–1374) and others to have occurred on quite other grounds.

28. Though the argument for the composite nature of the text is

now generally accepted (Watt 1956, p. 226), Serjeant's reduction of it down to eight distinct documents (1964, 1978, the latter a detailed, clause by clause, philological and historical analysis of the text) is still conjectural, though obviously important for tracing the growth and evolving nature of Muhammad's power in Medina.

29. On the question of the authenticity of the so-called Constitution of Medina, see Watt 1956, pp. 225–226; Gil 1974, p. 45; Sergeant 1964, pp. 4–6.

30. There is a thorough analysis of Quranic usage of *umma* in Denny 1975. The word was known and used in pre-Islamic times, and even in the sense of a religious community. It appears most frequently in the Quran in the years just prior to and following Muhammad's departure for Medina; Denny 1975, pp. 37, 44. As Denny, pp. 35–36, points out, this earliest Medina community will eventually develop into the community of Muslims, but only after the unbelievers, "hypocrites," and Jews of the original covenant were either converted or expelled.

31. Serjeant remarks, 1978, p. 5: "It would indeed be surprising if the Quran made no reference to, at least, documents A and B, that are fundamental as establishing the confederation at Yathrib and conceding Muhammad political supremacy," and sees a "clear and unmistakable reference to the pact(s)" in Quran 3: 101–104, but to find it he must resort to a somewhat tortured reediting of the verses (*ibid.*, 5–6).

32. Serjeant 1962, p. 48, points out that Muhammad had already been rejected as a candidate for a similar position by the Banu Hanifa and the Thaqif of Ta'if. On the documents' understanding of the "community," see the not entirely congruant views of Wellhausen 1975, pp. 129–132; Watt 1956, pp. 240–241; Serjeant 1964; Denny 1977.

33. According to Serjeant 1978, p. 9, the eight documents that constitute Ibn Ishaq's "Constitution of Medina" were somewhat shuffled out of their original order: "A credible explanation for this disorder is that they were written on small separate sheets (*sahifah*) which became confused, or on the back of earlier documents of the series." Bell had earlier used the same explanation for the "disorder" within some of the *suras* of the Quran; see Watt 1970, pp. 101–107.

34. Cf. Wellhausen 1975, p. 134; Watt 1956, pp. 221 ff.; Serjeant 1978, p. 26.

35. Serjeant 1978, p. 26, has argued that the detailed clauses pertaining to the Jews were an attempt made shortly after the original agreement to settle uncertainties over the specific Arab affiliation of each Jewish group.

36. Denny 1975, p. 60, remarks: " ... *din* in the Quran, like *umma*, comes increasingly, and by Medina, definitively, to mean reified religion, and Islam as this reified religion par excellence"; cf Quran 5: 4: "This day I have perfected your religion (*din*) for you, and completed my favor unto you; and have chosen for you a religion (*din*) Islam."

37. The terms of the debate are traced in Denny 1977, p. 44.
38. *Wafa' al-wafa'*, vol. 1, pp. 76–77; cf. Serjeant 1978, p. 34.
39. Serjeant 1978, p. 34.
40. Serjeant 1962, p. 50; Shaban 1971, p. 12.
41. Shaban 1971, p. 237; Ahmad 1979, pp. 40–42. According to Ahmad, whose estimate of the Jewish population at 36,000–42,000 has already been cited, the departure of the Banu al-Nadir and the decimation of the Banu Qurayza would still have left between 24,000–28,000 Jews at Medina.

42. This is Ibn Ishaq's, and very much the standard Muslim, understanding, "disaffected nominal Muslims in Medina," of the term *munafiqun* that appears often in the Quran (e.g. Sura 63, entitled *al-Munafiqun*). Serjeant 1978, pp. 11–12, connects it with the *nafaqa*, a kind of special war tax mentioned in the "Constitition of Medina" and understands the *munafiq* as "a reluctant payer of *nafaqa* alongside others readily accepting this obligation," citing, in addition, Quran 63: 7: "They [the *munafiqun*] are the ones who say, 'Spend nothing on those who are with God's Apostle'." Only later, Serjeant argues, did the term take on its more generalized meaning of "hypocrite."

43. The evidence must be used with care. In addition to the frequent apostrophes to "People of the Book!," the many dialectical "They say . . ." passages in the Medina *suras* are equally suggestive that there are also Christians present ("They say, become Jews or Christians . . . " 2: 135, etc.); there is, however, no evidence whatsoever that there were any such at Medina.

44. Cf. Wensinck 1975, p. 88: "The widely disseminated tradition informing us of the institution of the Islamic *ashura* is colored by posterity. . . . The obvious intention of Ibn Abbas, who transmitted the account, was to dispel any notion that Muhammad might have followed Medinan Judaism. It hardly needs saying that this was most certainly the case. Since in the first year of the *Hijra* he had not made any distinction yet between 'modern' and 'pure' Judaism as he did later on because of the dogma of the religion of Abraham, he must have been inspired by Judaism."

45. So called in Hebrew, *ashor*, in Leviticus 16: 29.
46. On the prohibition of intercalation, see Chapter 11.
47. Goitein 1966, p. 97, who cites the evidence, all rabbinic: Babylonian Talmud *Ta'anith* 30b; *Baba Bathra* 129a; *Seder Olam* Chap. 6; *Pirqe de Rabbi Eliezer* Chap. 46.
48. Cf. Wagtendonk 1968, p. 95: "The judgment scene of *sura* 97, determined by a traditional, cyclical way of thinking, is difficult to reconcile with the strongly eschatological preaching of the judgment in the Meccan *suras*. For this reason alone, the *sura* cannot stem from the Meccan period."

49. Goitein 1966, p. 102, and compare Wagtendonk 1968, pp. 84–85, who translates *laylat al-qadr* as "the night of the measuring-out" or "night of the decree," a "typical New Year's night." The Jewish parallel is important: the Heavenly Book is opened on New Year's day, the first of Tishri, but it is not closed until the tenth, the *ashor/ashura* of Tishri, and the intervening ten days, the "Ten Days of Penitence" of the Jewish tradition, are a potent occasion for prayer and penitence, a view that found, as we shall see, a notable, if temporary, echo in Islam.

50. Cf. Wagtendonk 1968, p. 95: " . . . Elsewhere in the Quran, whenever the descending of the angels and the Spirit is mentioned, it is in connection with the Judgment. So Quran 78: 38, 89: 22, 70: 4."

51. On the basis of that verse a later generation of Muslims thought that the Night of Destiny must have fallen in the month of Ramadan, though they were highly uncertain on what day. The guess does not seem correct because Ramadan has no pre-Islamic significance as a holy month and no date in it was ever celebrated as a New Year's day. A far more likely candidate is Rajab, the annual Spring holy month when the pre-Islamic *'umra* festival was held. See Wellhausen 1897, pp. 97–99; Kister 1971, p. 191; and Wagtendonk 1968, pp. 106–108, 112, who thinks it was the 27th of Rajab, a date often associated with Muhammad's Night Journey.

52. As we shall see later, Muhammad's other significant move away from Jewish practice, his change in his direction of prayer, took place in the month of Rajab, seventeen months after his arrival in Medina; presumably the switch from *Ashura* to the "Night of Destiny" would have occurred about the same time.

53. It was left to the later Muslim commentators to harmonize the two apparently contradictory versions of how the Quran had been "sent down." One way was to explain that the "Night of Destiny" referred to God's sending down the entire Quran from the highest to the lowest of the seven heavens, whence it was despatched piecemeal by Gabriel to Muhammad as occasion and God's will determined. This is Tabari's explanation in his *Commentary* on Quran 2: 185, whose contents will be reviewed later, but for many others (Zamakhshari, Razi, Baidawi), the sending down of the Quran on the Night of Destiny referred only to Muhammad's *first* revelation: the Quran *began to be revealed* on the Night of Destiny. Cf. Wagtendonk 1968, p. 86: "The exegesis that 97: 1 refers to the sending down of the whole revelation at once has, on the basis of 44: 2 ff. and 2: 185, more claim to authenticity than the exegesis that 97: 1 refers to Muhammad's first revelation. Nowhere in the Quran is the moment of the first revelation mentioned." Cf. Gätje 1976, p. 49; Ayoub 1984, pp. 191–192.

54. Bell 1934b.

55. See Watt 1970, pp. 61–65.

56. Wagtendonk 1968, p. 50; Watt 1970, pp. 142–143, building on Richard Bell and citing Bell's notion that Sura 12: 1 was an opening for the Book ("Alif, Lam, Ra. These are verses of the Book that makes manifest"), whereas verses 2–3 ("Truly, We have revealed it, a recitation (*qur'an*) in Arabic. We narrate it to you, the best of narratives that we have inspired in you this Quran, though before you were among the heedless") were intended for the Quran.

57. Tabari, *Tafsir*, vol. 2, pp. 4, 13; cf. Wensinck 1975, pp. 78–79; and Rubin 1986, p. 103, n. 29.

58. The difficulties inherent in these verses is discussed by Watt 1956, p. 202.

59. Though it is generally regarded as the outcome of the Prophet's polemic response to the Jews of Medina, Edmund Beck at least has argued that notion of Islam as the "religion of Abraham" was born at Mecca: "Die Bildung des Terminus *millatu Ibrahima* geht nicht ausschliesslich auf die frümedinische Polemik mit Juden (und Christen) zurück. Begriff und Ausdruck entstammen einer Entwicklung, die tief in die mekkanische Periode zurüchreicht. Die Entwicklung selber ist organisch vor sich gegangen, begünstigt und beschleunigt durch die jüdisch-christlicher Gegner, deren Argumente Muhammad geschicht für sich selber zu verwerten wusste" (Beck 1975, p. 133).

60. The "binding of Isaac," is described only once in the Quran, though at some length, in 3: 102–113.

61. Abraham is called a *muslim* a number of times in the Quran.

9. FIGHTING IN GOD'S CAUSE

1. They are so called in Quran 9: 100, 117. The "Migrants" are rather straightforwardly "those who had made the Hijra"; "Helpers" seems to be an echo of Quran 62: 14, citing Jesus's instructions to his disciples to be "God's helpers" (*ansar Allah*). Though the Quran groups all the Medinese converts together as "the Helpers," it is noteworthy that the original "constitution" drawn up between Muhammad and the Medinese cited the latter as separate tribal units of the Aws and Khazraj. Unity was not easily achieved at Medina; cf. Hasson 1989, p. 23.

2. Cf. Watt 1956, p. 4.

3. Watt 1956, p. 7, has argued that this statement of intent was a later revision of the account to free Muhammad of any responsibility for what eventually happened.

4. Ibn Ishaq 1955, p. 289.

5. Welch 1980, pp. 745–746.

6. *Ayah* (pl. *ayat*) means both a sign and a verse of the Quran.

7. Cf. Welch 1980, p. 748: "The heightened significance of angels in

post-Badr revelations involves their roles, their nature, and their relationship to Allah and man. In pre-Badr contexts the major roles of angels
involve their services to Allah in a variety of celestial, Last Judgment and
infernal scenes; in post-Badr contexts the major roles of the angels
involve their relationship or assistance to man in current, historical
events. Angels are thus brought closer to people. Significantly, this development occurs at the same time that *jinn*, demons, and Iblis and his
'hosts' ceased to be mentioned in further revelations, which happens also
to be the time when emphasis on the Oneness of Allah and the nonexis-
tence of other deities reaches its zenith in the development of major
themes in the revelation . . . "

8. In the Quran's developed usage the word used is *sawm*, but it
occurs only once in the Meccan *suras*, and then in connection with
Mary, the mother of Jesus, who in 19: 26 is made to say, in an incident
not recorded in the Gospels, that she has "vowed a *sawm* to al-Rahman"
and then seems to gloss the word by adding "I will not speak to anyone
today." The word, then, appears originally to have meant something like
"to be at rest"; so Wensinck 1975, p. 87, with substantiation from the
Arab lexicographers.

9. On the translation of this last clause, Wagtendonk 1968, pp.
54–55.

10. Eventually some Jews did further extend "Ten Days of Peni-
tence" (1–10 Tishri) backward to cover the entire previous month of
Elul, but this seems to have occurred well after the establishment of
Ramadan; cf. Wagtendonk 1968, p. 26.

11. Wagtendonk 1968, pp. 76, 117. Though we know the "standing" at Arafat took place on the 9th of the month of Dhu al-Hijja
because Muhammad left the pre-Islamic practice untouched, the original
chronology of both the *ihram* and the *'umra* in Rajab is far less certain.

12. Goitein 1966, pp. 103–104; Wagtendonk 1968, pp. 72–73,
117, and passim.

13. Wagtendonk 1968, pp. 70–71 has argued that Sura 2: 186,
which answers a question whether or not God hears prayer (*du'a*), also
refers to the *'ukuf*-retreat: "Since 2: 186 appears in a context which concerns fasting, and since the *du'a* must have been part of the *'ukuf* which
is mentioned in 2: 187, it is very probably that 2: 186 is indirectly also
about the *'ukuf*. The original position of 2: 186 in the pericope can best
be imagined to be after 183 because immediately after the establishment
of the fast of the *counted days*, that presumably had a partially pagan
background, the question must have arisen as to the meaning of the *du'a*,
which also comes from paganism and must have belonged to the *'ukuf*
that . . . was also connected with the fast of the counted days."

14. Jeffery 1938, pp. 225–229; cf. Goitein 1966, p. 101.

15. The argument identifying the victory of Badr with the *Furqan*

has been made in great detail by Wagtendonk 1968, pp. 62–63, 92–93 and passim, and somewhat reluctantly accepted by Watt 1970, pp. 145–146. From a chronological point of view, Sura 8: 41, referring back to Badr, and 2: 185 and 187 prescribing and regulating the Ramadan fast would all have been revealed after Badr, possibly in the following year before the fast of the "counted days" in Rajab, which this fast replaced, was scheduled to begin (*ibid.*, pp. 118–119).

16. Cf. Donner 1979, pp. 231–232: "The reasons for the expulsion of the Banu Qaynuqaʿ are never really clarified in the sources." Donner's own inclination is toward the Qaynuqaʿ's connection with artisanry and trade which "put them in close contact with the Meccan merchants against whose commerce Muhammad was beginning to take hostile measures."

17. Even more plausible is a connection with the Meccans at Uhud; see Donner 1979, p. 233.

18. Ibn Khurdadhbih, *Masalik* 129.

19. Yaʿqubi 1: 313.

20. That is, August 626 A.D. if the Muslim intercalation is taken into account. Otherwise, *rabiʿa* was the Arabs' Spring, a far more likely time for such a raid, illustrating once again the problem of sorting out early memories from later methods of calculation.

21. Cf. Ibn Ishaq's interesting remark a propos of the raid on the equally distant Tabuk: "The Apostle nearly always referred allusively to the destination of a raid and announced that he was making for a place other than that which he actually intended. This was the sole exception . . . because journey was long, the season difficult and the enemy in great strength . . . " (Ibn Ishaq 1955, p. 602). The Muslims did eventually capture the oasis in November of 630 A.D., but with forces under Khalid ibn al-Walid sent from Tabuk and not Medina. This time Ukaydir was caught unawares, captured and forced to capitulate: in addition to providing immediate booty—2000 camels, 800 slaves, 400 suits of armor and 400 lances—he and his people were bound to the Muslims by a treaty specifying the payment of an annual poll tax (*jizya*): Ibn Ishaq 1955, pp. 607–608; cf. Musil 1927, pp. 539–542.

22. Cf. Watt 1956, pp. 37–39, and Donner 1979, pp. 235–236, for different judgments on the outcome.

23. On the medieval Muslim juridical defense of the slaughter of the Banu Qurayza, see Kister 1986, pp. 66–70.

24. The whole affair is, of course, far less surprising if Muhammad had something other than pilgrimage in mind, as at least some of the Muslim sources seem to suggest; see Watt 1956, p. 46.

25. For the degree to which this matter continued to bother later generations of Muslims, see the passage from al-Sarakhsi (d. 1090) cited by Lecker 1984, p. 4, on the permissibility of accepting "critical" terms

in a truce if the results are "beneficial" to the Muslim community, with specific reference to the truce of Hudaybiyya.

26. This aspect of the armistice is analyzed by Lecker 1984; cf. Donner 1979, p. 242: "The Quraysh, by failing to insist on some clause extending the truce to include their allies at Khaybar, made the fatal miscalculation upon which Muhammad was, perhaps, depending."

27. Both medieval and modern travelers frequently commented on the continued presence of Jews in Muslim Khaybar; see, for example, Burton 1893, vol. 1, p. 346, n. 1.

28. Ibn Ishaq 1955, pp. 526–530. Thirty-four others were unaccounted for (ibid., p. 529). On this occasion, Watt 1953, pp. 111–112, thinks the migration to Abyssinia began to be regarded as the equivalent of a hijra (so Ibn Ishaq 1955, p. 146), like that of Muhammad and his other companions to Medina, so that the Abyssinian migrants might also be regarded, and so honored, as "Migrants."

29. Wellhausen 1897, p. 77; and cf. Rubin 1986, p. 126: "In fact, some reports state that the Muslims performed the tawaf between Safa and Marwa during this 'umra, while the pre-Islamic idols were still situated upon these hills: the pre-Islamic idols were not demolished until the conquest of Mecca in 630 A.D." (al-Azraqi 1858, pp. 75, 77; Waqidi, vol. 2, pp. 841–842).

30. Cf. Schacht 1950, p. 153.

31. Though not quite so "outside" as might first appear. It now seems fairly certain that Theophanes had access to an Arab Muslim course, probably through a Syriac intermediary, which he used for the life of the Prophet and the events in the early Arab conquests; see Proudfoot 1974 and Conrad 1990.

32. An obvious confusion on Theophanes's part.

33. Conrad 1990, pp. 24–24, cites this as a clear indication of a Muslim source. Neither Theophanes nor any other Christian historian would refer to this Christian ritual as "idolatry."

10. "THE TRUTH HAS COME AND FALSEHOOD HAS PASSED AWAY"

1. Hawting 1986, pp. 14–15, and cf. p. 23: "These (accounts of the purification of the sanctuary) may have been subject to some (later) development aimed at giving the sanctuary a more prominent place in them." Hawting raises doubts that the conquest of Mecca and the purification of the sanctuary, both called in Arabic al-fath, "the opening," and both treated as one in the sources, were actually one and the same event.

2. There is more on the pictures in al-Azraqi 1858, pp. 104–106, already cited in Chapter 2.

3. Ibn Sa'd 2/1, p. 106; Tabari, *Annals*, vol. 1, p. 1649.

4. Tabari, vol. 1, pp. 1691–1692. The memory lingered, however; cf. Wellhausen 1897, p. 31, and Fahd 1968, p. 120: "The site of the ancient pagan sanctuary was marked, in the time of Ibn al-Kalbi, as the same place as that occupied by the left minaret of the mosque of Ta'if. But in the middle of the last century travelers to Ta'if were being shown a square white rock as if it were the stone of al-Lat."

5. The battle and its political ramifications are analyzed by Watt 1956, pp. 70–73, 99–101.

6. Ibn Ishaq 1955, pp. 587–589, and cf. Tabari 1990, p. 20.

7. There has been a great deal of debate, and even as much uncertainty, about the Prophet's motives in attempting such a long-distance project: see Watt 1956, pp. 105–117; Shoufani 1972, pp. 38 ff.; cf. Shaban 1971, p. 14 ("to impress the Byzantine authorities and the Arab tribes on the Syrian border with his strength"); Donner 1981, pp. 108–109: "We may summarize our findings as follows. Muhammad's political consolidation, which among other things aimed at the subjection of nomadic tribal groups by the Islamic state's ruling elite of settled folk from the Hijaz, involved sustained and partly successful efforts to bring the tribes of the northern Hijaz and of southern Syria into Muhammad's sphere of influence, or, better yet, under his form of control. Though the campaigns of Dhat al-Atlah and Mu'ta were disastrous defeats for the Muslims, the raid on Dhat al-Salasil appears to have bolstered Medina's influence in the Wadi al-Qura and northern Hijaz, and the Tabuk campaign brought several towns of the northern Hijaz and southern Syria under Muhammad's control, as well as establishing his influence over local nomadic tribes."

8. Waqidi, *Maghazi*, vol. 3, pp. 989–992; Ibn Sa'd 2/1, p. 119.

9. Cf. Shoufani 1972, pp. 40–42.

10. Jarba' was a fortress on the road between Busra and the Red Sea. One mile south of Jarba' was the former Roman legionary camp of Adhruh.

11. Mayerson 1964, pp. 169–171.

12. *Ibid.*, pp. 175–176.

13. According to Watt 1956, p. 247, the Quran ceases using the term *umma* after the Battle of Uhud in 625, nor does it show up in any of the documents or treaties cited in the sources, where it is replaced by other expressions; see Denny 1977, p. 44.

14. The reference is to Quran 110: "When comes the help of God, and victory, and you see the people enter God's religion in batches, then celebrate the praises of your Lord . . . "

15. Cf. *ibid.* 9: 5.

16. Ibn Sa'd 2/1, p. 115; cf. Shoufani 1972, p. 44: "The most plausible explanation for this matter is that, although the revelation for the

imposition of the tax came in the year 9, it was not announced to the tribes until the end of the year, during the pilgrimage period, when they congregated in the sanctuary of Mecca. If so, then the collectors were sent each to his destination during the year 10. And before those agents of Muhammad had returned with the tax to Medina, he had died, at the beginning of year 11. . . . "

17. Which verses precisely and in what order is a highly complex and difficult question. Bell 1937 is one not very convincing attempt at unpacking the enigma by cutting and pasting, and cf. Rubin 1982 and 1984b, which investigate the traditional interpretations.

18. Rubin 1984b, p. 17.

19. As Rubin 1984b, pp. 18–20 points out, the announcement was necessarily an abrogation of earlier verses of the Quran prescribing a quite different treatment of the pagans, 190, 8: 61 and 2: 191, for example, which prescribes war only against attackers; 60: 8: "God does not forbid that you should be loyal and righteous toward those who did not fight you in religion and did not drive you out of your abode."

20. Bell 1937, pp. 233–234; Rubin 1982, p. 258.

21. Kister 1979, pp. 1–3.

22. Ibid., p. 11.

11. THE PILGRIMAGE OF FAREWELL

1. Cf. Tabari, Annals, vol. 1, p. 1765: "The Prophet made three hajjs, two before the Migration and one after, (the latter also) with the 'umra."

2. There was even some dispute on these matters; cf. Tabari, Annals, vol. 1, p. 1765: "(A report from Ibn Umar had it that) the Messenger of God performed two 'umras before performing the Hajj. When this report reached Aisha, she said, 'The Messenger of God performed four 'umras. Abdullah ibn Umar knew that. One (of the 'umras) was with the Hajj (of Farewell).'"

3. At the time of this verse the place of sacrifice was apparently still near the Ka'ba, as it had been throughout Islamic times; as we have already seen, during the Farewell Pilgrimage the Prophet limited sacrifice to the "slaughtering place" at Mina.

4. As has been seen, ritual (mansak/manasik) is connected in the Quran with the notion of a religious community, and here it appears to refer, as often, to the ritual sacrifice associated with the Hajj, though now spiritualized by the practice of "commemorating the name of God" over the sacrifices. The spiritualization of the sacrificial ritual continues through the following verses.

5. Wellhausen 1897, pp. 74, 93; Gaudefroy-Demombynes 1923, pp. 192–198; Goitein 1966, pp. 92–93.

6. Cf. Rubin 1982, pp. 244, and the literature cited there. On the likelihood that the Arabs' pilgrimage festivals of the seventh and twelfth months—the ordinal numbers are unimportant in this context—like the Israelites' Tabernacles and Passover *haggim*, were both originally equinoctial feasts, see Segal 1961, pp. 80–82 and Ali 1954, p. 128.

7. The literal reference is to the removal of the growth of hair, fingernails, etc., which could not be done while in the state of ritual pilgrimage purity.

8. Cf. Lazarus-Yafeh 1981, p. 44, on the not entirely successful attempts to connect various parts of the ritual with Abraham's sacrifice of Isaac/Ishmael.

9. Generally we are told that in pre-Islamic times there were four sacred months, but at one point Ibn Ishaq (66 = 1955, p. 44) remarks that *basl* was the name given to the "eight months of the year which the Arabs unreservedly regard as sacred," an anomaly that may have arisen out of just such calendrical juggling.

10. On the various motives modern scholars have attributed to the Prophet for the abolition of the *nasi*, see Rubin 1982, p. 251.

11. Ali 1954, p. 126; Ali has argued (p. 136) that Umar also introduced a standard lunar calendar for the events of 622–632 A.D., a chronology that "ousted to some extent the older chronology involving intercalation and . . . naturally found its way into the chronicles of many historians of the period."

APPENDIX: THE QUEST OF THE HISTORICAL MUHAMMAD

1. This appendix follows the same lines of development as an article of mine that appeared, under the same title, in *The International Journal of Middle East Studies* 23 (1991), 291–315.

2. This is the standard Muslim account, and most, though not all modern researchers—Burton 1977 and Wansbrough 1977 are the two chief recusants—are inclined to agree.

3. Cf. Jeffery 1937; Paret 1975, pp. 141–142.

4. See Eliash 1969; Kohlberg 1973.

5. Welch 1981, pp. 409, 415; cf. Watt 1970, pp. 89–101.

6. For Richard Bell's ingenious but unconvincing hypothesis, see his own translation of the Quran (= Bell 1937–1939), and now, after a very long interval, his notes on the text (= Bell 1990).

7. Welch 1981, p. 415.

8. *Ibid.*, p. 416.

9. Watt 1970, p. 114: "Like all those who have dated the Quran, Bell accepted the general chronological framework of Muhammad's life

as this is found in the *Sira* . . . and other works." The value judgment is that of Welch 1981, p. 417.

10. Abbott 1957, p. 18, and Buhl 1955, pp. 21 ff. The pre-Islamic poetry makes its inevitable appearance in modern surveys on the "background sources" on Muhammad (see Rodinson 1981, p. 37), but, except for Henri Lammens's work (see notes 34 and 36), it is far less in evidence when it comes to actually describing that background.

11. All likewise dutifully reported in surveys of the "sources for the life of Muhammad"; cf. Rodinson 1981, pp. 29–39.

12. Gil 1984.

13. Crone 1980, p. 11.

14. Compare Lammens 1924 where the Arab literary evidence is collected (and perhaps distorted; see later), Crone 1987, passim, and Peters 1988. A more sober approach than Lammens's to the same pre-Islamic milieu has been taken over the last quarter century by M. J. Kister of the Hebrew University; see, note 42.

15. Watt 1970, pp. 77–79; cf. Serjeant 1983, pp. 126–127.

16. Wansbrough 1977, pp. 40–43, 47–48, 51–52, etc.; and 1978, pp. 24–25. Rippin 1985, p. 159, commenting on Wansbrough's delineation of this style, notes: "The audience of the Quran is presumed able to fill in the missing details of the narrative, much as is true of work such as the Talmud, where knowledge of the appropriate biblical citations is assumed or supplied by only a few words . . . "

17. Cf. Buhl 1955, p. 366. Michael Cook succinctly sums up the contemporary historical data provided by the Quran: "Taken on its own, the Qur'an tells us very little about the events of Muhammad's career. It does not narrate these events, but merely refers to them; and in doing so, it has a tendency not to name names. Some do occur in contemporary contexts: four religious communities are named (Jews, Christians, Magians, and the mysterious Sabians), as are three Arabian deities (all female), three humans (of whom Muhammad is one), two ethnic groups (Quraysh and the Romans), and nine places. Of the places, four are mentioned in military connections (Badr, Mecca, Hunayn, Yathrib), and four are connected with the sanctuary (Safa, Marwa, Arafat, while the fourth is 'Bakka,' said to be an alternative name to Mecca). The final place is Mount Sinai, which seems to be associated with the growing of olives. Leaving aside the ubiquitous Christians and Jews, none of these names occurs very often: Muhammad is named four or five times (once as 'Ahmad'), the Sabians twice, Mount Sinai twice, and the rest once each" (Cook 1983, pp. 69–70).

18. Much of Watt's work since the publication of Muhammad's biography has been along these lines: see Watt 1971, 1976, 1979 and, particularly, 1988. Alford Welch too (1979, 1980) has been mining the same vein.

19. Summarily on the *sira* genre, Kister 1983.

20. The consensus opinion—and reservations—are rendered in Welch 1981, p. 414. Similar, and stronger, reservations on the "occasions of revelation" are expressed by Wansbrough 1977, p. 141; Cook 1983, p. 70; and Rippin 1985, p. 153: " . . . their [the "occasions of revelation" narratives] actual significance in individual cases of trying to interpret the Qur'an is limited: the anecdotes are adduced, and thus recorded and transmitted, in order to provide a narrative situation in which the interpretation of the Qur'an can be embodied. The material has been recorded within exegesis not for its historical value but for its exegetical value. Yet such basic literary facts about the material are frequently ignored within the study of Islam in the desire to find positive historical results . . . "

21. On Quranic exegesis posing as biography, see Watt 1962, and on the "raids of the Prophet," which Watt regards as the "essential foundation for the biography of the Prophet and the history of his times," *ibid.*, pp. 27–28, and Jones 1983.

22. Abbott 1957, pp. 87–89.

23. The most substantial attempt is Newby 1989.

24. Abbott 1957, p. 89.

25. Available in an English version by Alfred Guillaume as Ibn Ishaq 1955. What happened to Ibn Ishaq's material between the completion of his work and the appearance of the extant Ibn Hisham version is highly complex; see Sellheim 1987, pp. 12–13.

26. Ibn Ishaq 1955, p. 3.

27. *Ibid.*, pp. 69–73, cf. what Ibn Ishaq calls "Reports of Arab Soothsayers, Jewish Rabbis and Christian Monks" about the birth of the Prophet (*ibid.*, pp. 90 ff.).

28. Sellheim 1965–1966, pp. 38–39, 59–67; Kister 1983, pp. 356–357; and, for a more general consideration of "polemic as a history-builder," Wansbrough 1978, pp. 40–45.

29. Kister 1983, pp. 356–357, on the early *sira* of Wahb ibn Munabbih (d. 728 or 732) and the "popular and entertaining character of the early *sira* stories, a blend of miraculous narratives, edifying anecdotes and records of battles in which sometimes ideological and political tendencies can be discerned." Cf. Cook 1983, p. 66.

30. Sellheim 1965–1966, pp. 49–53; Kister 1983, pp. 362–363.

31. Wansbrough 1978, p. 35; cf. Noth 1973, pp.40–45, 155–158. The reason for the vague "distributional chronology," as Wansbrough calls the pre-Hijra system, was certainly not, as Watt has suggested (in Tabari 1988, p. xxi), that "there were fewer outstanding events." The call of the Prophet, the earliest revelation of the Quran, and the making of the first converts would all appear to be supremely important, though the Muslim tradition had little certainty, chronological or otherwise,

about them (*ibid.*, pp. xxii, xxv–xli), likely because there was either no way or no reason to remember the date. See further later.

32. Cf. the classic treatment in Goldziher 1971 and, following him, Schacht 1950.

33. On these latter see the trenchant form-criticism analysis in Noth 1973.

34. Caetani 1905, pp. 28–58, 121–143, 192–215, etc.; and on Lammens's approach: Lammens 1910, 1912, and cf. Becker 1967 and Salibi 1962.

35. Maxime Rodinson, a contemporary biographer of Muhammad, characterized Lammens as "filled with a holy contempt for Islam, for its 'delusive glory,' for its 'dissembling' and 'lascivious' Prophet . . . " (Rodinson 1981, p. 26), and compare Buhl 1955, p. 372: "H. Lammens . . . dessen Belesenheit und Scharfsinn man bewundern muss, der aber doch oft die Objectivität des unparteischen Historikers vermissen lässt."

36. Principally in Lammens 1924.

37. Rodinson 1981, p. 42. Rodinson, who, as we shall see shortly, had even less faith than Watt in the source material, may have himself done precisely the same thing in his own biography of the Prophet.

38. Crone 1980, p. 13: "The inertia of the source material comes across very strongly in modern scholarship on the first two centuries of Islam. The bulk of it has an alarming tendency to degenerate into mere arrangements of the same old canon—Muslim chronicles in modern languages and graced with modern titles. Most of the rest consists of reinterpretation in which the order derives less from the sources than from our own ideas of what life ought to be about—modern preoccupations graced with Muslim facts and footnotes."

39. One attempt to substitute "genuine" eyewitness testimony, if not to Muhammad himself, then to the first appearance of the Islamic movement on the early seventh century Near East, has been Crone and Cook 1977, and although it was a brave and provocative book, it has tempted few others to follow its suggestion (3): "The historicity of the Islamic tradition is . . . to some degree problematic: while there are no cogent internal grounds for rejecting it, there are equally no cogent external grounds for accepting it. . . . The only way out of the dilemma is thus to step outside the Islamic tradition altogether and start again." What the external testimony to early Islam amounts to, and it is not a great deal, is summarized in Cook 1983, pp. 73–76, and the limitations of this approach are underscored in Wansbrough 1978, pp. 116–117.

40. Cf. Sellheim 1987, p. 3: "Über keinen der grossen orientalischen Religionsstifter sind biographische Nachrichten in so reichem Masse auf uns gekommen, wie über Muhammed. Nicht wenige von ihnen dürften in ihrem Kern, in ihrer Tendenz tatsächlichem Geschehen entsprechen oder doch diesem nahe kommen."

41. Paret 1975; Watt 1962, p. 28, and in Tabari 1988, pp. xxi–xxv; Sellheim 1965–1966, pp. 73–77; Kister 1983, pp. 352–353.

42. So for pre-Islamic Mecca, M. J. Kister and, after him, Uri Rubin, Michael Lecker, and others often cited in the pages that follow. Kister and his students have painstakingly compared variants in early, and largely unpublished, Muslim traditions on various topics and attempted to construct the original understanding behind them, on the assumption that the "original" tradition is to some degree a historical "fact." They do not, however, directly address the critical question of the authenticity of any of the *hadith* materials with which they are so scrupulously dealing, though Kister for one is, as we have seen (note 29), is well aware of the historiographical problems posed by the inauthenticity of the *hadith*.

43. Wellhausen 1897.

44. It is instructive of the two methods to compare Hawting 1982 with Rubin 1986, both of which deal with the pre-Islamic sanctuary at Mecca.

45. Ibn Ishaq composed his work out of a great many discrete reports, and he did not use or even know of all such reports, of course, and so a good deal of independent material is to be found in bits and snippets in other historians like Ibn Sa'd (d. 844), Ya'qubi (d. 891), Mas'udi (d. 956), and even later authors like Yaqut (d. 1229); cf. Sellheim 1987, pp. 11–13.

46. The skillful exploitation of comparative material produced the last century's classic and still useful presentations of the subject, Julius Wellhausen's 1887 *Reste arabischen Heidentums* ("Survivals of Arab Paganism"), already cited, W. R. Smith's *Lectures on the Religion of the Semites* (first edition 1889), Ignaz Goldziher's 1889 essay "Muruwwa und Din," and Theodore Nöldeke's article "Arabs (Ancient)" in the 1908 edition of *Hasting's Encyclopedia of Religion and Ethics*. The chief additions to the evidence since the publication of these nineteenth century classics has been the publication of a great many inscriptions from South Arabia and the less formal graffiti of northern tribes like the Thamudeans and Lihyanites presented by Winnett 1938, 1940. The new epigraphical material was substantially incorporated into later syntheses like Ryckmans 1951, Henninger 1959, and Fahd 1968.

47. The latter search was begun as early as Abraham Geiger's *Judaism and Islam* (originally published in Latin in 1832 (rpt. New York, 1970 from the translation published in 1898), and then later notably renewed by Charles Cutler Torrey in his *The Jewish Foundations of Islam* (New York, 1933; rpt. New York, 1967). An almost equally convincing case was also made for a "Christian Muhammad," by Richard Bell, for example, in *The Origin of Islam in Its Christian Environment* (London, 1926; rpt. London, 1968).

REFERENCES

Except where specifically noted, ancient and medieval texts are cited according to their standard editions.

Abbott, Nabia. 1957. Abbott, *Studies in Arabic Literary Papyri*, vol. 1, *Historical Texts*. Chicago: University of Chicago Press.

ᵗ Ahmad. Barakat. 1979. *Muhammad and the Jews. A Re-Examination.* New Delhi: Vikas Publishing House.

ᶜ Ali, Hashim Amir. 1954. "The First Decade in Islam. A Fresh Approach to the Calendrical Study of Early Islam." *Muslim World* 44: 126–138.

Ali, S. 1961. "Studies in the Topography of Medina." *Islamic Culture* 35: 65–92.

Ali Bey 1816. Domingo (Ali Bey) Badia y Leyblich, *Travels of Ali Bey in Morocco. Tripoli, Cyprus, Egypt, Arabia and Syria...*; rpt. London: Gregg, 1970.

Altheim, F., and R. Stiehl. 1957. *Finanzgeschichte der Spätantike*. Frankfort: Klostermann.

———. 1964–1969. *Die Araber in der alten Welt*, 5 vols. Berlin: de Gruyter.

Anfray, F., A. Caquot, and P. Nautin. 1970. "Une nouvelle inscription grecque d'Ezana, roi d'Axoum." *Journal des Savants*.

˜ Armstrong, Karen. 1992. *Muhammad. A Biography of the Prophet.* San Francisco: HarperSanFrancisco.

Ayoub, Mahmoud. 1984. *The Qur'an and Its Interpreters*, vol. 1. Albany: State University of New York Press.

al-Azraqi, Abu al-Walid Muhammad. 1858. *Akhbar Makka*, ed. F. Wüstenfeld, *Die Chroniken der Stadt Mekka*, vol. 1. Leipzig, 1858; rp. Khayats, 1964.

ᵃ Baumstarck, Anton. 1927. "Jüdischer und christlicher Gebetstypus im Koran." *Der Islam* 16: 229–248.

Beck, E. 1944–1945. "Die Sure al-Rum (30)." *Orientalia* n.s. 13: 334–355; 14: 118–142.

———. 1952/1975. "Die Gestalt des Abraham am Wendepunkte der Entwicklung Muhammeds." Originally in *Le Muséon* 65: 73–84. Cited from its reprint in Rudi Paret (ed.), *Der Koran*. Darmstadt: Wissensehaftliche Buchgesellschaft.

Becker, C. H. 1924/1967. *Islamstudien*, vol. 1. Leipzig, 1924; rpt.

Hildesheim; Georg Olms, 1967.

Beeston, Alfred F. L. 1984a. "The Religions of Pre-Islamic Yemen." In Joseph Chelhod (ed.), *L'Arabie du Sud. Histoire et Civilisation*, vol. 1, *Le Peuple Yemenite et Ses Racines*, pp. 259–270. Paris: G.-P. Maisonneuve et Larose.

———. 1984b. "Judaism and Christianity in Pre-Islamic Yemen." In Joseph Chelhod (ed.), *L'Arabie du Sud. Histoire et Civilisation*, vol. 1, *Le Peuple Yemenite et Ses Racines*, p. 271–278. Paris: G.-P. Maisonneuve et Larose.

Bell, Richard. 1926. *The Origins of Islam in Its Christian Environment*. London: Macmillan.

———. 1934a. "Mohammed's Call." *Muslim World* 24: 13–19.

———. 1934b. "Muhammad's Visions." *Muslim World* 24: 145–154.

———. 1937. "Muhammad's Pilgrimage Proclamation." *Journal of the Roysal Asiatic Society*: 233–244.

———. 1937–1939. *The Qur'an, Translated, with a Critical Re-Arrangement of the Surahs*, 2 vols. Edinburgh: T & T. Clark.

———. 1990. *A Commentary on the Qur'an*, C. Edmund Bosworth and M. E. J. Richardson, 2 vols. Manchester: University of Manchester Press.

Bellamy, J. A. 1985. "A New Reading of the Namarah Inscription." *Journal of the American Oriental Society* 105: 31–52.

Bibby, Geoffrey. 1970. *Looking for Dilmun*. New York: Knopf.

Birkeland, H. 1956. *The Lord Guideth. Studies on Primitive Islam*. Oslo: H. Aschehaug.

Bivar, A. D. H. 1972. "Cavalry Equipment and Tactics on the Euphrates." *Dumbarton Oaks Papers* 26: 273–291.

Braudel, F. 1972. *The Mediterranean and the Mediterranean World in the Age of Phillip II*. New York: Harper and Row.

Buhl, Frants. 1955. *Das Leben Muhammeds*, trans. Hans Heinrich Schaeder (1955) from the second Danish edition of 1953; rpt. Heidelberg: Quelle and Meyer, 1961.

Bulliet, R. W. 1975. *The Camel and the Wheel*. Cambridge, Mass.: Harvard University Press.

Burton, John. 1977. *The Collection of the Qur'an*. New York: Cambridge University Press.

Burton, Richard F. 1893. *A Personal Narrative of a Pilgrimage to al-Madina and Meccah*. Originally published 1855; rpt. of third, memorial edition of 1893, New York: Dover Books, 1964.

Caetani, Leone. 1905. *Annali dell'Islam*, vol. 1. Milan: Hoepli.

Caskel, Werner. 1954. "The Bedouinization of Arabia." *American Anthropologist, Memoir* 76: 36–46.

———. 1969. "Die Inschrift von en-Nemara neugesehen." *Mélanges de l'Université Saint Joseph* 45: 367–379.

Caussin de Perceval, A. P. 1847. *Essai sur l'Histoire des Arabes avant l'Islamisme*, 3 vols. Paris.

Charles, Henri. 1936. *Le Christianisme des arabes nomades sur le limes et dans le désert syro-mesopotamien aux alentours de l'Hégire*. Paris: Bibliotheque de l'Ecole des Hautes-Etudes.

Christensen, A. 1944. *L'Iran sous les Sasanides*. Copenhagen: Munksgaard.

Christides, V. 1972. "The Name "Arabes" etc. and Their False Eytmologies." *Byzantinische Zeitschrift* 65: 329–339.

Conrad, Lawrence J. 1987. "Abraha and Muhammad: Some Observations a propos of Chronology and Literary Topoi in the Early Arabic Historical Tradition." *BSOAS* 50: 225–240.

———. 1990. "Theophanes and the Arabic Historical Tradition: Some Indications of Intercultural Transmission." *Byzantinische Forschungen* 15: 1–44.

Cook, Michael. 1983. *Muhammad*, New York: Oxford University Press.

Crapon de Caprona, Pierre. 1981. *Le Coran: Aux Sources de la Parole Oraculaire. Structures rhythmiques des sourates mecquoises*. Paris: Publications orientalistes de France.

Crone Patricia. 1980. *Slaves on Horses: The Evolution of the Islamic Polity*, Cambridge University Press.

———. 1987. *Meccan Trade and the Rise of Islam*, Princeton University Press.

———, and Michael Cook. 1977. *Hagarism. The Making of the Islamic World*. Cambridge: Cambridge University Press.

Dagorn, René. 1981. *La Geste d'Ismael d'après l'onomastique et la tradition arabes*. Paris: Champion.

Denny, Frederich Mathewson. 1975. "The Meaning of *Ummah* in the Qur'an." *History of Religions* 15: 34–70.

———. 1977. "*Ummah* in the Constitution of Medina." *Journal of Near Eastern Studies* 36: 39–47.

Desanges, J. 1978. *Recherches sur l'activité des mediterranéens aux confines de l'Afrique*. Rome and Paris: École français de Rome.

Dihle, A. 1964. "The Conception of India in the Hellenistic and Roman Literarure." *Proceedings of the Cambridge Philological Society* 190: 15–23.

Donner, Fred M. 1977. "Mecca's Food Supply and Muhammad's Boycott." *Journal of the Economic and Social History of the Orient* 20: 249–266.

———. 1979. "Muhammad's Political Consolidation in Arabia up to the Conquest of Mecca." *Muslim World* 69: 229–247.

———. 1981. *The Early Islamic Conquests*, Princeton, N.J.: Princeton University Press.

Dussaud, R. 1955. *La pénétration des Arabes en Syrie avant l'Islam*, Paris: P. Geuthner.

Eickelman, Dale. 1967. "Musailama." *Journal of the Economic and Social History of the Orient* 10: 17–52.

Eliash, J. 1969. "The Shi'ite Qur'an: A Reconsideration of Goldziher's Interpretation." *Arabica* 16: 15–24.

Eph'al, Israel. 1982. *The Ancient Arabs: Nomads on the Borders of the Fertile Crescent, 9th–5th Centuries B.C.* Jerusalem: The Magnes Press, and Leiden: E. J. Brill.

Fahd, Toufic. 1958. "Une pratique cléromantique à la Ka'ba pre-Islamique." *Semitica* 8: 55–79.

———. 1966. *La divination arabe*. Leiden: E. J. Brill.

———. 1968. *Le panthéon d'Arabie centrale à la veille de l'hégire*, Paris: Paul Geuthner.

———. 1983. "Problèmes de typologie dans la 'Sira' d'Ibn Ishaq." In *La vie du prophète Mahomet (Colloque de Strasbourg 1980)*, pp. 67–75. Leiden: E. J. Brill.

———. 1989. "Rapports de la Mekke préislamique avec l'Abyssinie: le Cas des *Ahabish*." In Toufic Fahd (ed.), *L'Arabie préislamique et son environnement historique et culturel. Actes du Colloque de Strasbourg, 24–27 Juin 1987*, pp. 539–548. Leiden: E.J. Brill.

al-Fasi, Muhammad ibn Ahmad. 1857. *Shafa' al-gharam bi akhbar al-balad al-haram*, ed. F. Wüstenfeld, *Chroniken II*. Leipzig, 1857; rpt. Hildesheim: G. Olms, 1981.

Fièy, J. M. 1964. "Balad et le Beth Arabiye irakien." *Orient Syrien* 10: 189–232.

———. 1965–1968. *Assyrie Chrétiene*, 3 vols. Beirut: Dar al-Mashriq.

Firestone, Reuven . 1990. *Journeys into Holy Lands: The Evolution of the Abraham-Ishmael Legends in Islamic Exegesis*. Albany: State University of New York Press.

Frye, Richard. 1977. "The Sasanian System of Walls for Defense,." In Myriam Rosen-Ayalon (ed.), *Studies in Memory of Gaston Wiet*, pp. 7–15. Jerusalem: The Hebrew University.

Fück, J. 1936/1981. "The Originality of the Arabian Prophet." Translated from German in Merlin L. Swartz (ed.), *Studies on Islam*, pp. 86–98. New York: Oxford Univeristy. First published in ZDMG 90 (1936): 509–525;

Gätje, Helmut. 1976. *The Quran and Its Exegesis*, trans. and ed. Alford T. Welch. Berkeley and Los Angeles: University of California Press.

Gaudefroy-Demombynes, M. 1923. *Le pelerinage à la Mekke*. Paris: P. Geuthner.

Gibb, H. A. R. 1962. "Pre-Islamic Monotheism in Arabia." *Harvard Theological Review* 55: 269–280.

Gil, Moshe. 1974. "The Constitution of Medina: A Reconsideration." *Israel Oriental Studies* 4: 44–66.

———. 1984. "The Origin of the Jews of Yathrib." *Jerusalem Studies in Arabic and Islam* 4: 203–224.

———. 1987. "The Medinan Opposition to the Prophet." *Jerusalem Studies in Arabic and Islam* 10: 65–96.

Glubb, John Bagot. 1971. *The Life and Times of Muhammad*. New York: Stein and Day.

Goitein, S. D. 1966. *Studies in Islamic History and Institutions*. Leiden: E. J. Brill; rpt. 1968.

Goldfeld, Isaiah. 1980. "The Illiterate Prophet (*Nabi Ummi*): An Inquiry into the Development of a Dogma in Islamic Tradition." *Der Islam* 57: 58–67.

Goldziher, Ignaz. 1889/1967. "On the Veneration of the Dead in Paganism and Islam." In *Muslim Studies* ed. S. M. Stern, vol. 1, pp. 209–238. London: George Allen and Unwin, 1967. Originally published in 1889.

———. 1890/1971. "On the Development of the Hadith." In *Muslim Studies*, edited by S. M. Stern, vol. 2, pp. 17–254. London. Originally published in 1890.

Graf, David. 1978. "The Saracens and the Defenses of the Arabian Frontier." *Bulletin of the Schools of Oriental Research* 229: 1–26.

Graham, William A. 1983. "Islam in the Mirror of Ritual." In Richard G. Hovannisian and Speros Vryonis (eds.), *Islam's Understanding of Itself*, pp. 53–73. Malibu, Calif.: Undena Publications.

———. 1985. "Qur'an as Spoken Word: An Islamic Contribution to the Understanding of Scripture." In R. M. Martin (ed.), *Approaches to Islam in Religious Studies*, pp. 19–40. Tucson: University of Arizona Press.

Griffith, Sidney. 1985. "The Gospel in Arabic: An Inquiry into Its Appearance in the First Abbasid Century," *Oriens Christianus* 69: 126–167.

Groom, N. 1981. *Frankincense and Myrhh. A Study of the Arabian Incense Trade*. London and New York: Longmans.

Hamidullah, M. 1938. "The City-State of Mecca." *Islamic Culture* 12: 253–266.

———. 1957. "*Al-Ilaf*, ou les rapports économico-diplomatiques de la Mecque pré-islamique." *Mélanges Massignon* (Damascus) 2: 293–311.

Hasson, Isaac. 1989. "Contributions à l'étude des Aws et des Khazraj." *Arabica* 36: 1–35.

Hawting, G. R. 1980. "The Disappearance and Rediscovery of Zamazam and the 'Well of the Ka'ba'." *Bulletin of the School of Oriental and African Studies* 43: 44–54.

✦ ——. 1982. "The Origins of the Islamic Sanctuary at Mecca." In G. H. A. Juynboll, *Studies on the First Century of Islam,* pp. 25–47. Carbondale: University of Southern Illinois Press.

——. 1984. "The Origin of Jedda and the Problem of Suʿayba." *Arabica* 31: 318–326.

——. 1986. "Al-Hudaybiyya and the Conquest of Mecca: A Reconsideration of the Tradition about the Muslim Takeover of the Sanctuary." *Jerusalem Studies in Arabic and Islam* 8: 1–23.

——. 1990. "The 'Sacred Offices' of Mecca from Jahiliyya to Islam." *Jerusalem Studies in Arabic and Islam* 13: 62–84.

Henninger, J. 1959/1981. "Pre-Islamic Bedouin Religion." Trans. from French. Rome. In Merlin L. Swartz (ed.), *Studies on Islam,* pp. 3–22. New York: Oxford University Press, 1981. Originally in F. Gabrieli (ed.), *L'antica societa beduina* (1959).

Horovitz, Josef. 1919. "Muhammeds Himmelfahrt." *Der Islam* 9: 159–183.

Hourani, George. 1951. *Arab Seafaring in the Indian Ocean in Ancient and Early Medieval Times.* Princeton, N.J.: Princeton University Press.

Hurgronje, C. Snouck. 1894/1957. "Une nouvelle biographie de Mohammed." Revue de l'histoire des religions" 30: 49–70, 149–178; rpt. in G. H. Buosquet and J. Schacht (eds.), *Selected Works of C. Snouck Hurgronje.* Leiden: E. J. Brill, 1957, 109–149.

✦ Ibn Ishaq. 1955. *The Life of Muhammad. A Translation of Ishaq's "Sirat Rasul Allah,"* with Introduction and Notes by Alfred Guillaume. Oxford: Oxford University Press.

Ibn al-Kalbi. 1952. Nabih Faris, *Ibn al-Kalbi's Book of Idols.* Princeton, N.J.: Princeton University Press.

╰ Ibrahim, M. 1982. "Social and Economic Conditions in pre-Islamic Mecca." *International Journal of Middle Eastern Studies* 14: 343–358.

James, W. E. 1969. "On the Location of Gerrha." In Franz Altheim and Ruth Stiehl, *Die Araber in der alten Welt,* vol. 5, pp. 36–57.

Jeffery, Arthur. 1930. "Was Muhammad a Prophet from His Infancy?" *Muslim World* 20: 226–234.

——. 1937. *Materials for the History of the Text of the Qur'an.* Leiden: E. J. Brill.

——. 1938. *Foreign Vocabulary in the Qur'an.* Baroda: Oriental Institute.

Jomier, Jaqcues. 1957. "Le nom divin al-Rahman dans le Coran." *Mélanges Massignon* (Damascus) 2: 361–381.

Jones, A. H. M. 1964. *The Later Roman Empire,* 3 vols. Oxford: Oxford University Press.

Jones, J. M. B. 1983. "The *Maghâzi* Literature." In A. F. L. Beeston et al. (eds.), *Arabic Literature to the End of the Umayyad Period,* pp. 344–351. Cambridge: Cambridge University Press.

Kawar, Irfan (Shahid). 1956. "The Arabs and the Peace Treaty of A.D. 561." *Arabica* 3: 181–213.

———. 1957. "Procopius and Arethas." *BZ* 50: 39–67, 362–382.

———. 1964. "Byzantino-Arabica: The Conference of Ramla, A.D. 524." *Journal of Near Eastern Studies* 23: 115–131.

———. 1967. "The Etymology of Hira." *Linguistic Studies in Honor of R. S. Harrell*, pp. 163–173. Washington, D.C.: Georgetown University Press.

Keall, E. J. 1975. "Parthian Nippur and Vologesias' Southern Strategy: An Hypothesis." *Journal of the American Oriental Society* 95: 620–632.

Khoury, Adel-Théodore. 1972. *Polémique byzantine contre l'Islam (VIII–XIII S.)*. Leiden: E. J. Brill.

Kirwan, Lawrence P. 1972. "The *Christian Topography* and the Kingdom of Axum." *Geographical Journal* 138: 166–177.

Kister, M. J. 1962. "'A Booth Like the Booth of Moses . . . ': A Study of an Early Hadith." *Bulletin of the School of Oriental and African Studies* 25: 150–155.

———. 1965a. "Mecca and Tamim." *Journal of the Economic and Social History of the Orient* 8: 113–163.

———. 1965b. "The Market of the Prophet." *Journal of the Economic and Social History of the Orient* 8: 272–276.

———. 1965c. "The Campaign of Huluban. A New Light on the Expedition of Abraha." *Le Muséon* 78: 425–436.

———. 1968a. "Al-Hira. Some Notes on Its Relations with Arabia." *Arabica* 15: 143–169.

———. 1968b. "Al-Tahhanuth: An Inquiry into the Meaning of a Term." *Bulletin of the School of Oriental and African Studies* 31: 223–236.

———. 1970. "'A Bag of Meat': A Study of an Early *Hadith*." *Bulletin of the School of Oriental and African Studies* 33: 267–275.

———. 1971. "'Rajab is the Month of God . . . ': A Study in the Persistence of an Early Tradition." *Israel Oriental Studies* 1: 191–223.

———. 1979. "Some Reports Concerning Taif." *Jerusalem Studies in Arabic and Islam* 1: 1–18.

———. 1980. "*Labbayka, Allahumma, Labbayka.* . . . On a Monotheist Aspect of a Jahiliyya Practice." *Jerusalem Studies in Arabic and Islam* 2: 33–57.

———. 1983. "The *Sira* Literature." In A. F. L. Beeston et al. (eds.), *Arabic Literature to the End of the Umayyad Period*, pp. 352–367. Cambridge: Cambridge University Press.

———. 1986. "The Massacre of the Banu Qurayza: A Re-examination of a Tradition." *Jerusalem Studies in Arabic and Islam* 8: 61–96.

Kohlberg, E. 1973. "Some Notes on the Imamite Attitudes Toward the

Qur'an." *Islamic Philosophy and the Classical Tradition. Essays . . . Richard Walzer*, pp. 209–224. Columbia: University of South Carolina Press.

Lammens, Henri. 1910. "Qoran et tradition. Comment fut composée la vie de Mahomet?" *Recherches de Science Religieuse* 1: 25–61.

———. 1911. "L'Age de Mahomet et la chronologie de la *sira.*" *Journal Asiatique*, 10th series, 17: 209–250.

———. 1912. *Fatima et les filles de Mahomet*. Rome.

———. 1924. *La Mecque à la Veille de l'Hégire*. Beirut.

———. 1926. "Les Sanctuaires pré-Islamiques dans l'Arabic occidentale." *Mélanges de l'Université Saint-Joseph* 11: 39–173.

———. 1928a. "Le culte des bétyles et les processions religieuses chez les Arabes préislamites." In Henri Lammens, *L'Arabie occidentale avant l'Hégire*, pp. 100–180. Beirut: Imprimerie Catholique.

———. 1928b. "Les 'Ahabish' et l'organisation militaire de la Mecque au siècle de l'Hégire." In Henri Lammens, *L'Arabie occidentale avant l'Hégire*, pp. 237–294. Beirut: Imprimerie Catholique.

———. 1929. *Islam. Beliefs and Institutions*. London: Frank Cass; rpt. London, 1968.

Landau-Tasseron, E. 1986. "The Sinful Wars: Religious, Social and Historical Aspects of the *hurub al-fijar.*" *Jerusalem Studies in Arabic and Islam* 8: 37–59.

- Lazarus-Yafeh, H. 1981. "Muslim Festivals." In her *Some Religious Aspects of Islam*. Leiden: E. J. Brill.

———. 1993. *Intertwined Worlds. Medieval Islam and Bible Criticism*. Princeton, N.J.: Princeton University Press.

Lecker, Michael. 1984. "The Hudaybiyya-Treaty and the Expedition against Khaybar." *Jerusalem Studies in Arabic and Islam* 5: 1–11.

———. 1985. "Muhammad at Medina: A Geographical Approach." *Jerusalem Studies in Arabic and Islam* 6: 29–62.

———. 1986. "On the Markets of Medina (Yathrib) in Pre-Islamic and Early Islamic Times." *Jerusalem Studies in Arabic and Islam* 8: 133–147.

Lings, Martin. 1983. *Muhammad, His Life Based on the Earliest Sources*. Rochester, Vt.: Inner Traditions International.

MacAdam, Henry I. 1980. "The Nemara Inscription: Some Historical Considerations." *Al-Abhath* 28: 3–16.

Mayerson, Philip. 1964. "The First Muslim Attacks on Southern Palestine (A.D. 633–634)." *Transactions and Proceedings of the American Philological Association* 95: 155–199.

Moberg, Axel. 1924. *The Book of the Himyarites. Fragments of a Hitherto Unknown Syriac Work*. Lund: C. W. K. Gleerup.

Monneret de Villard, Ugo. 1940. *Le Chiese della Mesopotamia*. Rome.

Muir, William. 1861. *The Life of Mahomet. With Introductory Chap-*

ters on the Original Sources for the Biography of Mahomet, and on the Pre-Islamite History of Arabia, 2d ed. London, 1861; rpt. Osnabrück.

Musil, Alois. 1927. *Arabia Deserta*. New York: The American Geographical Society.

Nau, François. 1933. *Les arabes chrétiens de Mesopotamie et de Syrie du VIIe au VIIIe siècle*, Paris: Imprimerie Nationale.

Neuwirth, Angelica. 1981. *Studien zur Komposition der Mekkanischen Suren*. Berlin: Walter de Gruyter.

Newby, Gordon. 1989. *The Making of the Last Prophet: A Reconstruction of the Earliest Biography of Muhammad*. Columbia: University of South Carolina Press.

Noth, Albrecht. 1973. *Quellenkritische Studien zu Themen, Formen und Tendenzen frühislamischer Geschichtsüberlieferung I Themen und Formen*. Bonn: Selbstverlag des Orientalischen Seminars der Universität.

Olinder, Gunnar. 1927. *The Kings of Kinda*, Lund and Leipzig.

Paret, Roger. 1958. "Les villes de Syrie du Sud et les routes commerciales d'Arabie a la fin du VIe siecle." *Akten des XI Internationalen Byzantinisten Kongresses* (Munich): 438–444.

Paret, Rudi. 1975. "Der Koran als Geschichtsquelle." In Rudi Paret (ed.), *Der Koran*. Darmstadt: Wissenschaftliche Buchgesellschaft. Originally in *Der Islam* 37 (1961): 24–42.

———. 1983. "The Qur'ân-I." In A. F. L. Beeston et al. (eds.), *Arabic Literature to the End of the Umyyad Period*, pp. 186–227. Cambridge: Cambridge University Press.

Periplus. 1989. *The Periplus Maris Erythraei*, text with Introduction, trans. and commentary by Lionel Casson. Princeton, N.J.: Princeton University Press.

Peters, F. E. 1977. "The Nabateans in the Hawran." *Journal of the American Oriental Society* 97: 263–277.

———. 1977–1978. "Byzantium and the Arabs of Syria." *Annales archéologiques arabes syriennes* 27–28: 97–113.

———. 1985. *Jerusalem: The Holy City in the Eyes of Chroniclers, Visitors, Pilgrims and Prophets from the Days of Abraham to the Beginning of Modern Times*. Princeton, N.J.: Princeton University Press.

———. 1988. "The Commerce of Mecca Before Islam." In Farhad Kazemi and R. D. McChesney (eds.), *A Way Prepared. Essays . . . Richard Bayly Winder*, pp. 3–26. New York: New York University Press.

Pigulevskaya, N. 1969. *Byzanz auf den Wegen nach Indien*. Berlin: Akademie-Verlag.

Pirenne, Jacqueline. 1956. *Paléographie des inscriptions sud-arabes. Contribution à la chronologie et à l'histoire de l'Arabie du Sud antique*, vol. 1. Brussels: Institute Orientaliste.

Potts, Daniel. 1988. "Trans-Arabian Routes of the Pre-Islamic Period."
In Jean-Francois Salles (ed.), *L'Arabie et ses Mers Bordières* I *Itin-
eraires et Voisinages*, pp. 126–162. Paris: GS-Maison de l'Orient.

Proudfoot, A. S. 1974. "The Sources of Theophanes for the Heraclian
Dynasty." *Byzantion* 44: 367–439.

Qutb al-Din. 1857. *Kitab al-iʻlam bi aʻlam bayt allah al-haram*, ed. F.
Wüstenfeld, *Chroniken der Stadt Mekka*, vol. 3, Leipzig; rpt.
Hildesheim: G. Olms, 1981.

Rice, David Talbot. 1932. "The Oxford Excavations at al-Hira." *Antiq-
uity* 6: 276–291.

———. 1934. "The Oxford Excavations at Hira." *Ars Islamica* 1: 51–73.

Rippin, Andrew. 1985. "Literary Analysis of Qur'an, Tafsir, and Sira:
The Methodologies of John Wansbrough." In Richard Martin (ed.),
Approaches to Islam in Religious Studies, pp. 151–163. Tucson: Uni-
versity of Arizona Press.

Robin, C. 1980. "Judaisme et Christianisme en Arabie du Sud." *Arabian
Studies* 10: 85–96.

Rodinson, Maxime. 1957. "The Life of Muhammad and the Sociologi-
cal Problem of the Beginnings of Islam." *Diogenes* 20: 28–51.

———. 1971. *Mohammed*, trans. Anne Carter. New York: Pantheon
Books.

———. 1978. *Islam and Capitalism*. Austin: University of Texas Press.

———. 1981. "A Critical Survey of Modern Studies of Muhammad." Trans.
in Merlin Swartz, *Studies on Islam*, pp. 23–85. New York: Oxford University Press. First published in *Revue historique* 229 (1963): 169–220.

Rothstein, G. 1899. *Die Dynastie der Lakhmiden in al-Hira*. Berlin:
Reuther and Richard.

Rubin, Uri. 1982. "The Great Pilgrimage of Muhammad: Some Notes
on Sura IX." *Journal of Semitic Studies* 27: 241–260.

———. 1984a. "The *ilaf* of Quraysh. A Study of sura CVI." *Arabica* 31:
165–188.

———. 1984b. "Bara'a: A Study of Some Quranic Passages." *Jerusalem
Studies in Arabic and Islam*: 13–32.

———. 1986. "The Kaʻba, Aspects of Its Ritual, Functions, and Position
in Pre-Islamic and Early Islamic Times." *Jerusalem Studies in Arabic
and Islam* 8: 97–131.

———. 1987. "Morning and Evening Prayers in Early Islam." *Jerusalem
Studies in Arabic and Islam* 10: 40–64.

———. 1990. "Hanifiyya and Kaʻba. An Inquiry into the Arabian Pre-
Islamic Background of the *din Ibrahim*." *Jerusalem Studies in Arabic
and Islam* 13: 85–112.

Ryckmans, G. 1951. *Les religions arabes préislamiques*, Louvain.

———. 1953. "Inscriptions sud-arabes, dixième série." *Le Muséon* 66:
267–317.

————. 1956. "Aspects nouveaux du problème thamoudéen." *Studia Islamica* 5: 5–17.

————. 1957a. "Petites royaumes sud-arabes d'après les auteurs classiques." *Le Museon* 70: 75–96.

Salibi, K. S. 1962. "Islam and Syria in the Writings of Henri Lammens." In Bernard Lewis and P. M. Holt, *Historians of the Middle East*, pp. 330–342. London: London University, School of Oriental and African Studies.

Schacht, Joseph. 1950. *The Origins of Muhammadan Jurisprudence.* Oxford: Clarendon Press.

Schick, Robert. 1987. "The Fate of Christians in Palestine During the Byzantine-Umayyad Transition." Unpublished Ph.D. dissertation, University of Chicago.

Schrieke, B. 1916. "Die Himmelreise Muhammeds." *Der Islam* 6: 1–30.

Schumacher, G. 1886. *Across the Jordan.* London.

Segal, J. B. 1961. "The Hebrew Festivals and the Calendar." *Journal of Semitic Studies* 6: 74–94.

Sellheim, Rudolf. 1965–1966. "Prophet, Calif und Geschichte. Die Muhammad Biographie des Ibn Ishaq." *Oriens* 18–19: 33–91.

————. 1987. "Muhammadeds erstes Offenbarungserlebnis. Zum Problem mündlicher und schriftlicher Überlieferung im 1./7. und 2./8. Jahrhundert." *Jerusalem Studies in Arabic and Islam* 10: 1–16.

Serjeant, R. B. 1962. "Haram and Hawtah, the Sacred Enclosures in Arabia." In A. Badawi (ed.), *Mélanges Taha Husain*, pp. 41–58. Cairo: al-Ma'arif.

————. 1964. "The Constituition of Medina." *Islamic Quarterly* 8: 3–16.

————. 1978. "The *Sunnah Jami'ah*, Pacts with the Yathrib Jews, and the *Tahrim* of Yathrib: Analysis and Translation of the Documents of the Documents Comprised in the So-Called 'Constitution of Medina'." *Bulletin of the School of Oriental and African Studies* 41: 1–42.

————. 1983. "Early Arabic Prose." In A. F. L. Beeston et al. (eds.), *Arabic Literature to the End of the Umayyad Period*, pp. 114–153. Cambridge: Cambridge University Press.

Shaban, M. A. 1971. *Islamic History* A.D. 600–750 (A.H. 132). A New Interpretation, Cambridge: Cambridge University Press.

Shahid, Irfan. 1971. *The Martyrs of Najran.* Brussels: Societé des Bollandistes.

————. 1981. "Two Qur'anic Suras: al-Fil and Quraysh." In W. al-Qadi (ed.), *Studia Arabica et Islamica, Festschrift for Ihsan Abbas*, pp. 429–436. Beirut: American University of Beirut.

Shoufani, E. 1972. *Al-Riddah and the Muslim Conquest.* Toronto: University of Toronto Press.

Smith, Sidney. 1954. "Events in Arabia in the Sixth Century A.D.." *Bulletin of the School of Oriental and African Studies* 16: 425–468.

Sourdel-Thomine, J. 1971. "Clefs et serrures de la Ka'ba. Notes d'epigraphie arabe." *Revue des Etudes Islamiques* 39: 29–86.

Sprenger, A. 1875. *Die alte Geographie Arabiens*. Bern.

Tabari, Theodor Nöldeke. 1879. *Geschichte der Perser und Araber zur Zeit der Sasaniden aus der arabischen Chronik des Tabari übersetzt.* . . . Leipzig.

———. 1987. The History of al-Tabari, vol. 7, *The Foundations of the Community*, trans. M. V. McDonald, annotated by W. Montgomery Watt. Albany: State University of New York Press.

———. 1988. *The History of al-Tabari*, vol. 6, *Muhammad at Mecca*, trans. and annotated by W. Montgomery Watt and M. V. McDonald. Albany: State University of New York Press.

———. 1990. *The History of al-Tabari*, vol. 9, *The Last Years of the Prophet*, trans. and annotated by Ismail Poonawala. Albany: State University of New York Press.

Thelamon, Françoise. 1981. *Paiens et Chrétiens au IVe Siècle. L'apport de l'"Histoire ecclésiastique" de Rufin d'Aquilée*. Paris: Etudes Augustiniennes.

Ullendorff, E. 1956. "Hebraic-Jewish Elements in Abyssinian (Monophysite) Christianity." *Journal of Semitic Studies* 1: 216–256.

Von Wissman, H., and J. Ryckmans 1967. "Zur Kenntnis von Ostarabien, besonders al-Qatif, in Altertum." *Le Muséon* 80: 489–512, with an appendix by J. Ryckmans.

Wagtendonk, K. 1968. *Fasting in the Koran*. Leiden: E. J. Brill.

Wansbrough, John. 1977. *Qur'anic Studies: Sources and Methods of Scriptural Interpretation*. Cambridge: Cambridge University Press.

———. 1978. *The Sectarian Milieu: Content and Composition in Islamic Salvation History*. Oxford: Oxford University Press.

Watt, W. M. 1953. *Muhammad at Mecca*. Oxford: Clarendon Press.

———. 1956. *Muhammad at Medina*, Oxford: Clarendon Press.

———. 1962. "The Materials Used by Ibn Ishaq." In Bernard Lewis and P. M. Holt, *Historians of the Middle East*, pp. 23–34. London: London University, School of Oriental and African Studies.

———. 1970. *Bell's Introduction to the Qur'an*, completely revised and enlarged by W. Montgomery Watt. Edinburgh: Edinburgh University Press.

———. 1971. "Belief in a 'High God' in Pre-Islamic Mecca." *Journal of Semitic Studies* 16: 35–40.

———. 1976. "Pre-Islamic Arabian Religion in the Qur'ân." *Islamic Studies* 15: 73–79.

———. 1979. "The Qur'an and Belief in a 'High God'." *Der Islam* 56: 205–211.

———. 1988. *Muhammad's Mecca. History in the Qur'ân*, Edinburgh: Edinburgh University Press.

Welch, A. T. 1979. "Allah and Other Supernatural Beings: The Emergence of the Qur'anic Doctrine of *Tawhid.*" *Journal of the American Academy of Religion* 47: 733–758.

———. 1980. "Allah and Other Supernatural Beings: The Emergence of the Qur'anic Doctrine of Tawhid." In Welch (ed.), *Studies in Qur'an and Tafsir*, pp. 733–758. *JAAR* Thematic Issue 47, 1979. Chico, Calif.: American Academy of Religion.

———. 1981. "Kur'an." In *The Encyclopaedia of Islam*, 2d ed., pp. 400–432. Leiden: E. J. Brill.

Y ———. 1983. "Muhammad's Understanding of Himself: The Koranic Data." In Richard G. Hovannisian and Speros Vryonis (eds.), *Islam's Understanding of Itself*, pp. 15–52. Malibu, Calif: Undena Publications.

Wellhausen, Julius. 1897. *Reste Arabischen Heidentums*, 2d ed., Berlin: Reimer.

———. 1899. "Medina vor Islam." In *Skizzen und Vorarbeiten* IV, pp. 3–64. Berlin, 1889; rpt. Berlin and New York: Walter de Gruyter, 1985.

———. 1975. "Muhammad's Constitution of Medina." An excursus in A. J. Wensinck, *Muhammad and the Jews of Medina.*

Wensinck, Arent Jan. 1975. *Muhammad and the Jews of Medina*, with the excursus "Muhammad's Constitution of Medina" by Julius Wellhausen, trans. and ed. Wolfgang Behn. Freiburg: Klaus Schwarz Verlag.

Whitehouse, David, and Andrew Williamson. 1973. "Sasanian Maritime Trade." *Iran* 11: 29–49.

Widengén, Georg. 1971. "The Establishment of the Sassanian Dynasty in the Light of New Evidence." In *La Persia nel Medioevo*, pp. 711–782. Rome: Accademia Nazionale dei Lincei.

Winnett, F. V. 1938. "Allah Before Islam." *Muslim World* 28: 239–248. Y

———. 1940. "The Daughters of Allah." *Muslim World* 30: 113–140.

Wirth, Eugen. 1971. *Syrien. Eine geographische Landeskunde.* Darmstadt: Wissenschaftliche Buchgesellschaft.

Wolf, E. 1951. "The Social Organization of Mecca and the Origins of Islam." *Southwestern Journal of Anthropology*: 329–356.

Zwemer, S. M. 1921. "The 'Illiterate' Prophet: Could Muhammad Read and Write?" *Muslim World* 11: 344–363.

Zwettler, Michael. 1990. "A Mantic Manifesto: The Sura of 'the Poets' and the Quranic Foundations of Prophetic Authority." In James L. Kugel (ed.), *Poetry and Prophecy: The Beginnings of a Literary Tradition.* Ithaca: Cornell University Press.

INDEX